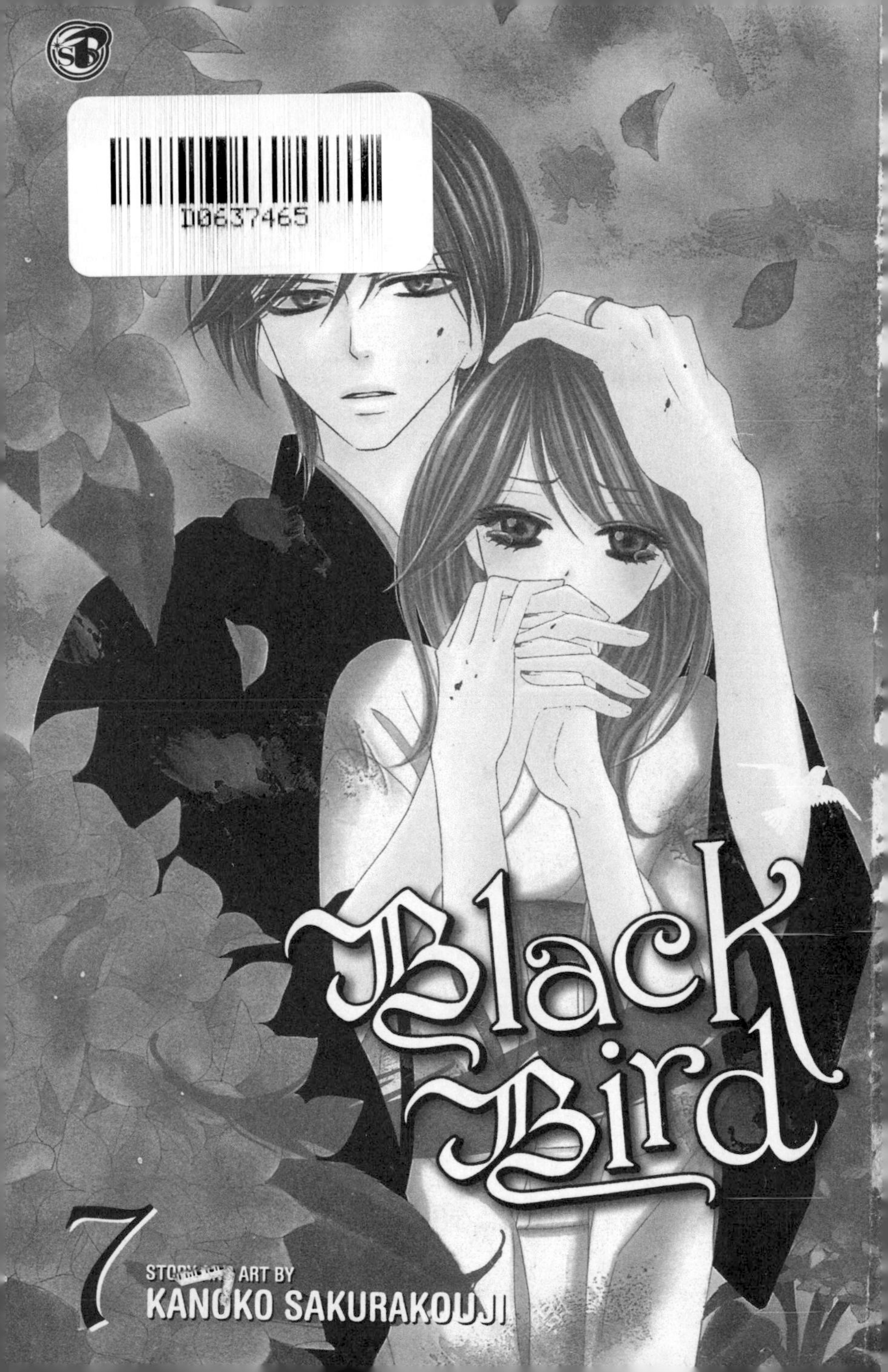
Black Bird
7
ART BY
KANOKO SAKURAKOUJI

Black Bird

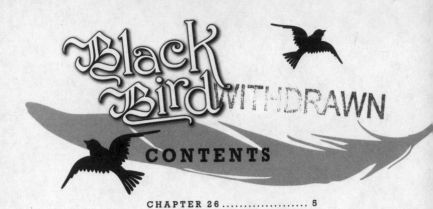

CONTENTS

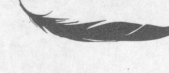

CHARACTERS

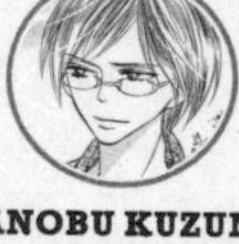

TADANOBU KUZUNOHA
Kyo's close friend since childhood. Current leader of the Kitsune clan.

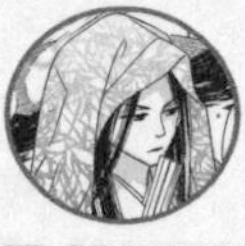

PRINCE OF KENGAMINE
Incarnation of a dragon. He wants Kyo to bed his sister in order to cure her.

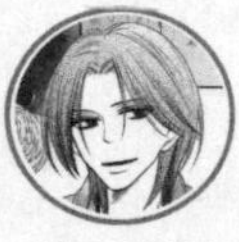

SHO USUI
Kyo's older brother and a member of the Eight Daitengu. He is also known as Sojo. He is currently incarcerated after injuring Misao in an attempt to gain leadership of the clan.

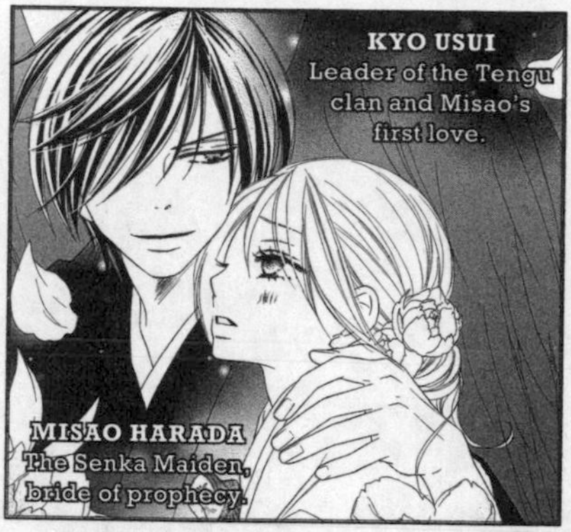
KYO USUI
Leader of the Tengu clan and Misao's first love.
MISAO HARADA
The Senka Maiden, bride of prophecy.

THE EIGHT DAITENGU
Kyo's bodyguards. Their names designate their official posts.

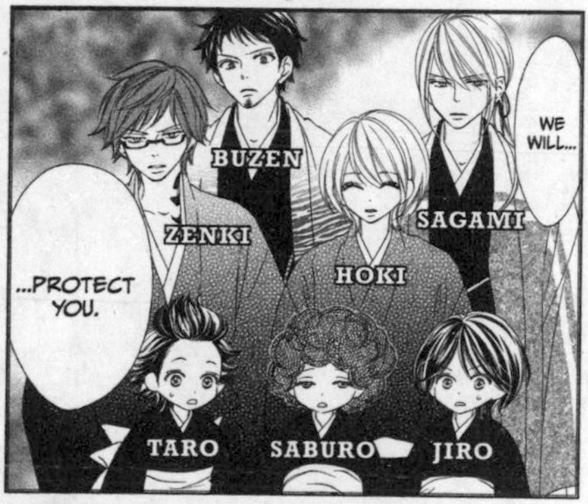
WE WILL...
...PROTECT YOU.
BUZEN
SAGAMI
ZENKI
HOKI
TARO
SABURO
JIRO

STORY THUS FAR

Misao can see spirits and demons, and her childhood sweetheart Kyo has been protecting her since she was little.

"Someday, I'll come for you, I promise." Kyo reappears the day before Misao's 16th birthday to tell her, "Your 16th birthday marks 'open season' on you." She is the Senka Maiden, and if a demon drinks her blood, he is granted a long life. If he eats her flesh, he gains eternal youth. And if he makes her his bride, his clan will prosper...And Kyo is a *tengu*, a crow demon, with his sights firmly set on her.

But no one knows if Misao, a human, will survive being bedded by a demon. The answer can only be found in the *Senka Roku*, the record of the previous Senka Maiden kept by the Kuzunoha Clan. During a battle between Kyo and Tadanobu, the head of the Kuzunoha Clan, the *Senka Roku* is stolen by unidentified demons!

Kyo is under a lot of pressure to bed Misao and solidify his position as leader of the Usui Clan. But Kyo decides he will destroy his brother Sho instead. With no rival to his claim, it won't matter if he doesn't sleep with Misao.

Kyo returns to his home village Tengu no Sato with Misao. She is gravely injured when she uses herself as bait in a trap for Sho, but the plan works and Kyo's leadership is now unchallenged.

But before Misao and Kyo can celebrate their victory, the dragon Prince of Kengamine appears before Kyo and orders him to bed his sister in exchange for the *Senka Roku*!

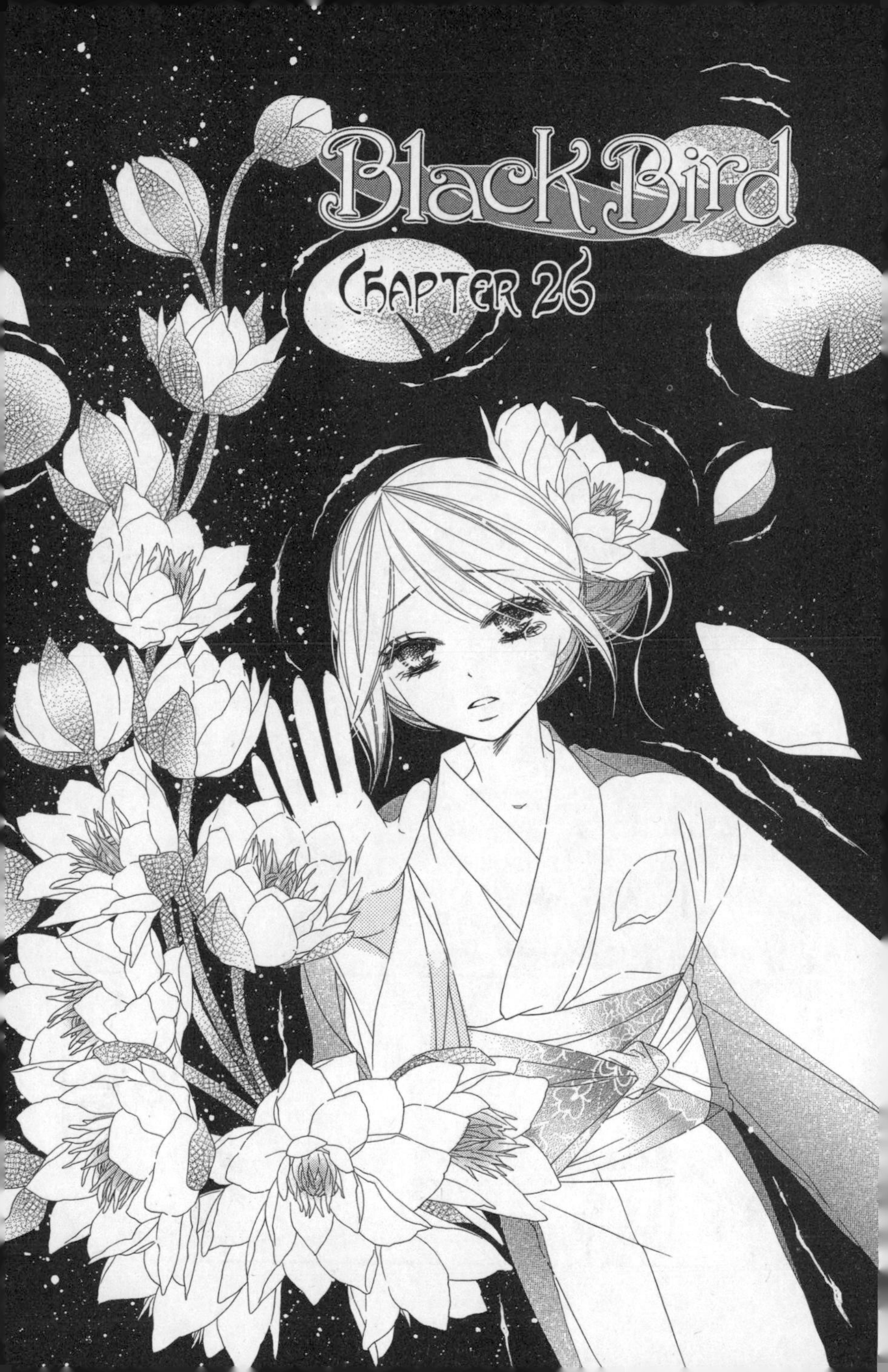
Black Bird
Chapter 26

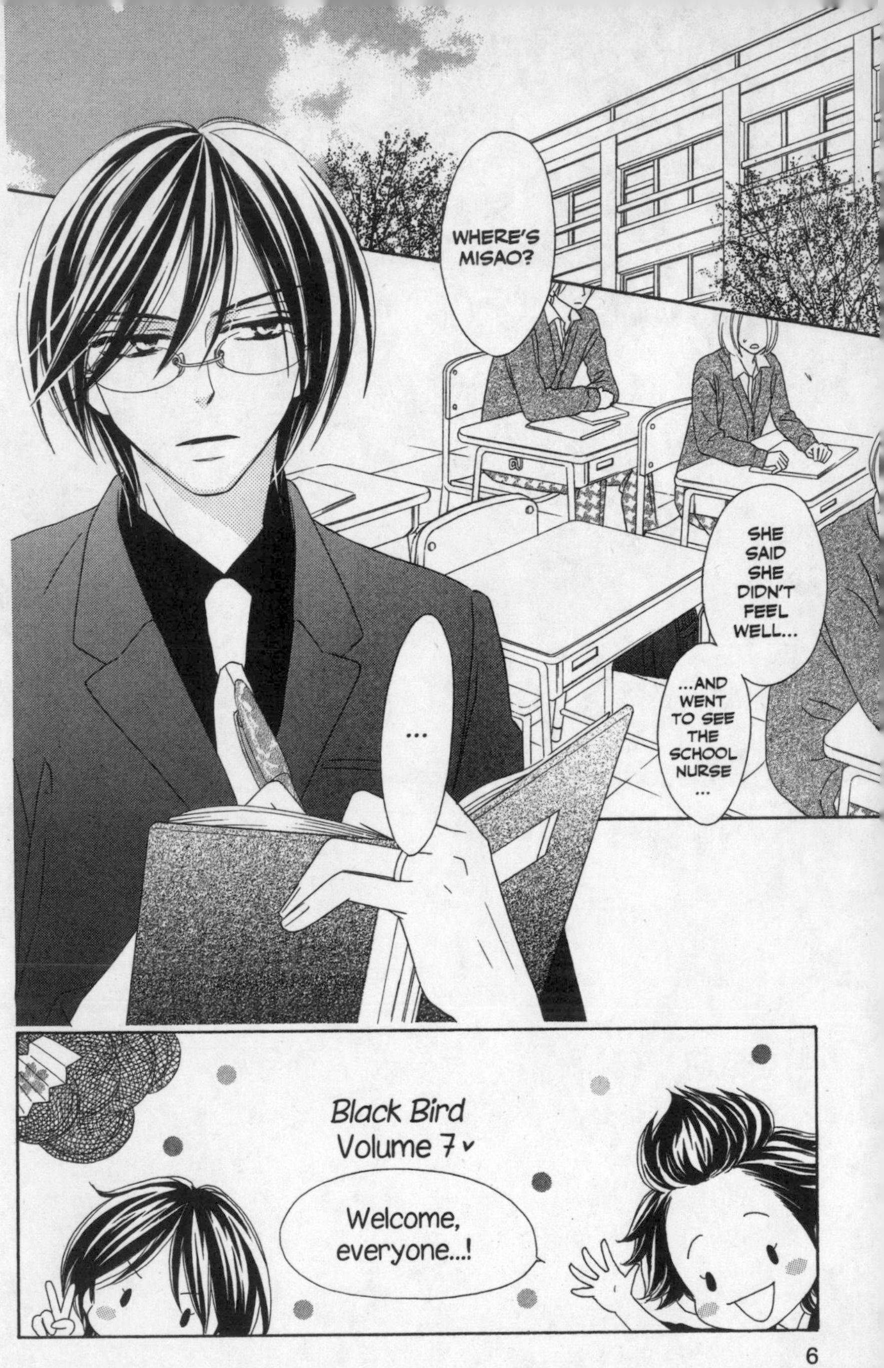
WHERE'S MISAO?
SHE SAID SHE DIDN'T FEEL WELL...
...AND WENT TO SEE THE SCHOOL NURSE...
...
Black Bird Volume 7
Welcome, everyone...!

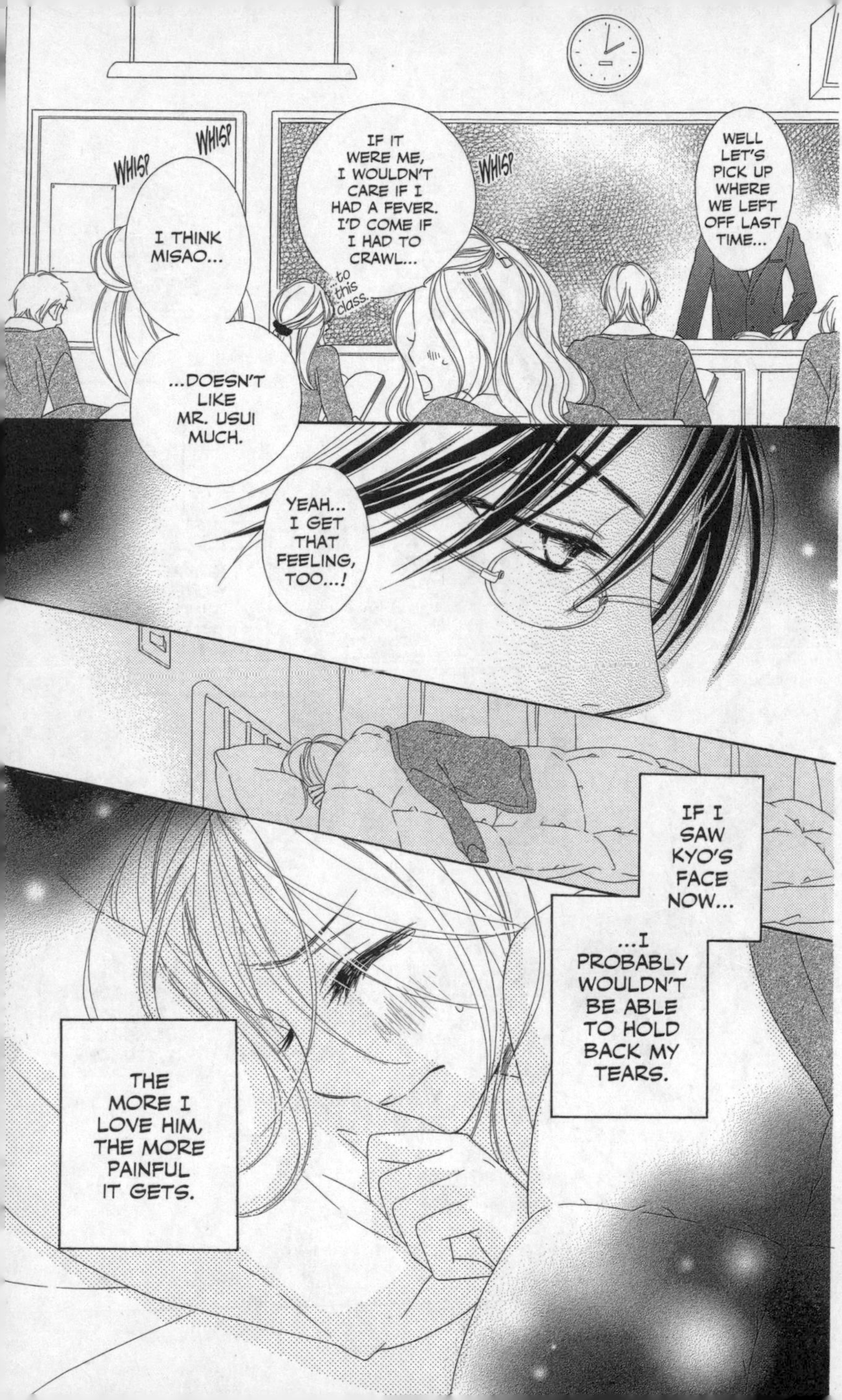
WELL LET'S PICK UP WHERE WE LEFT OFF LAST TIME...
WHISP
IF IT WERE ME, I WOULDN'T CARE IF I HAD A FEVER. I'D COME IF I HAD TO CRAWL...
...to this class.
WHISP
WHISP
I THINK MISAO...
...DOESN'T LIKE MR. USUI MUCH.
YEAH... I GET THAT FEELING, TOO...!
IF I SAW KYO'S FACE NOW...
...I PROBABLY WOULDN'T BE ABLE TO HOLD BACK MY TEARS.
THE MORE I LOVE HIM, THE MORE PAINFUL IT GETS.

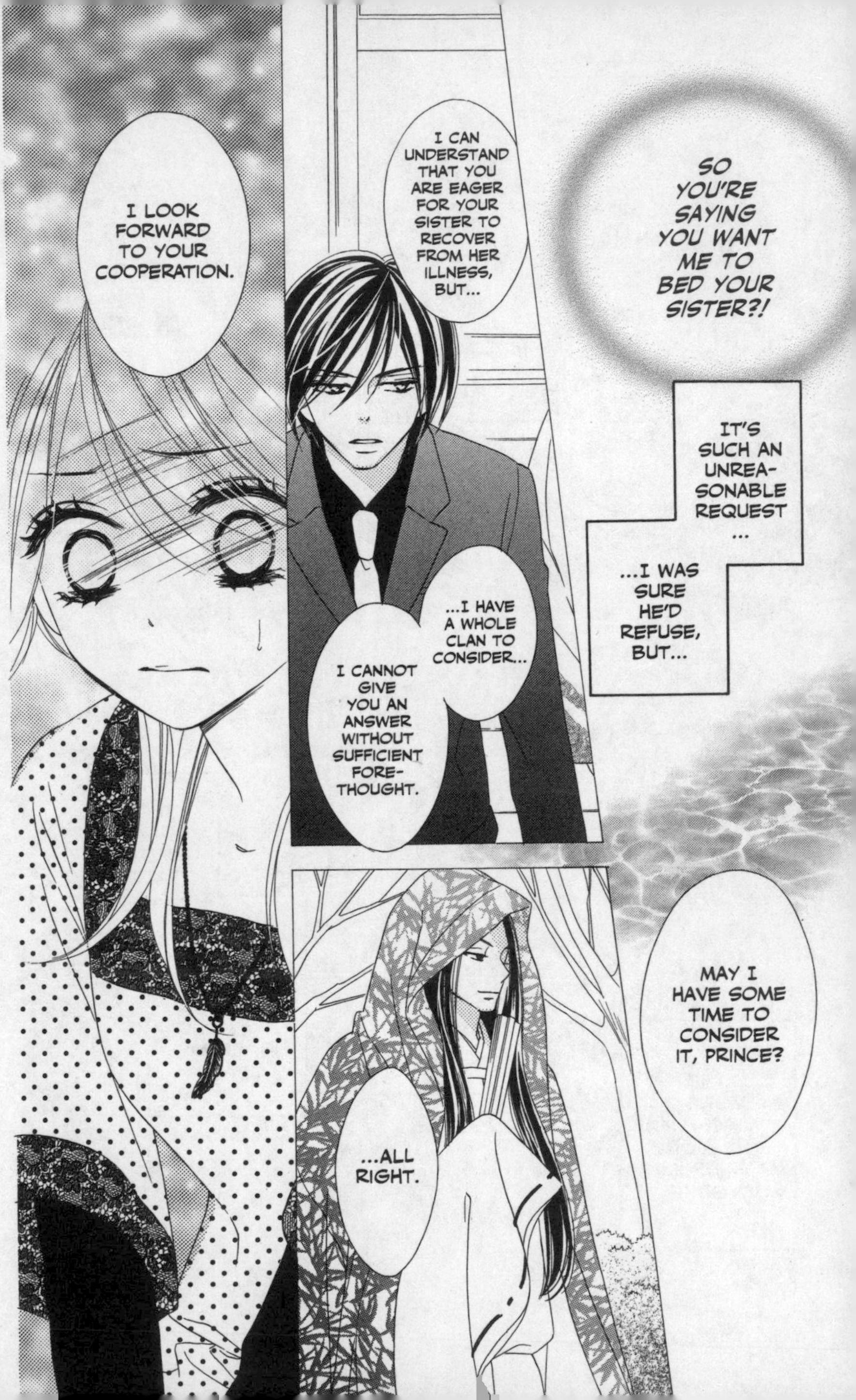
SO YOU'RE SAYING YOU WANT ME TO BED YOUR SISTER?!
IT'S SUCH AN UNREA-SONABLE REQUEST ...
...I WAS SURE HE'D REFUSE, BUT...
I CAN UNDERSTAND THAT YOU ARE EAGER FOR YOUR SISTER TO RECOVER FROM HER ILLNESS, BUT...
...I HAVE A WHOLE CLAN TO CONSIDER...
I CANNOT GIVE YOU AN ANSWER WITHOUT SUFFICIENT FORE-THOUGHT.
MAY I HAVE SOME TIME TO CONSIDER IT, PRINCE?
...ALL RIGHT.
I LOOK FORWARD TO YOUR COOPERATION.

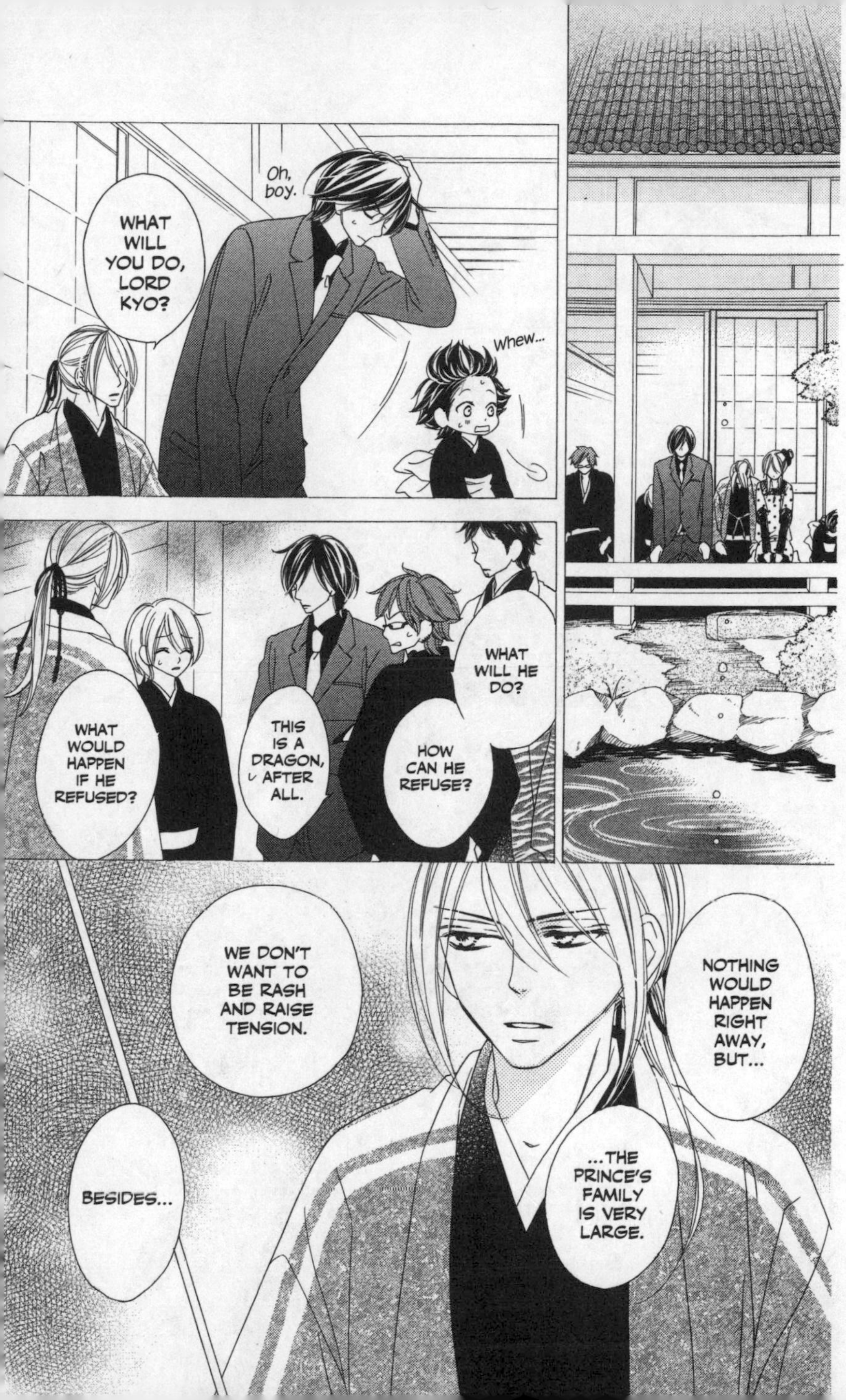
Oh, boy.
WHAT WILL YOU DO, LORD KYO?
Whew...
WHAT WILL HE DO?
HOW CAN HE REFUSE?
THIS IS A DRAGON, AFTER ALL.
WHAT WOULD HAPPEN IF HE REFUSED?
NOTHING WOULD HAPPEN RIGHT AWAY, BUT...
...THE PRINCE'S FAMILY IS VERY LARGE.
WE DON'T WANT TO BE RASH AND RAISE TENSION.
BESIDES...

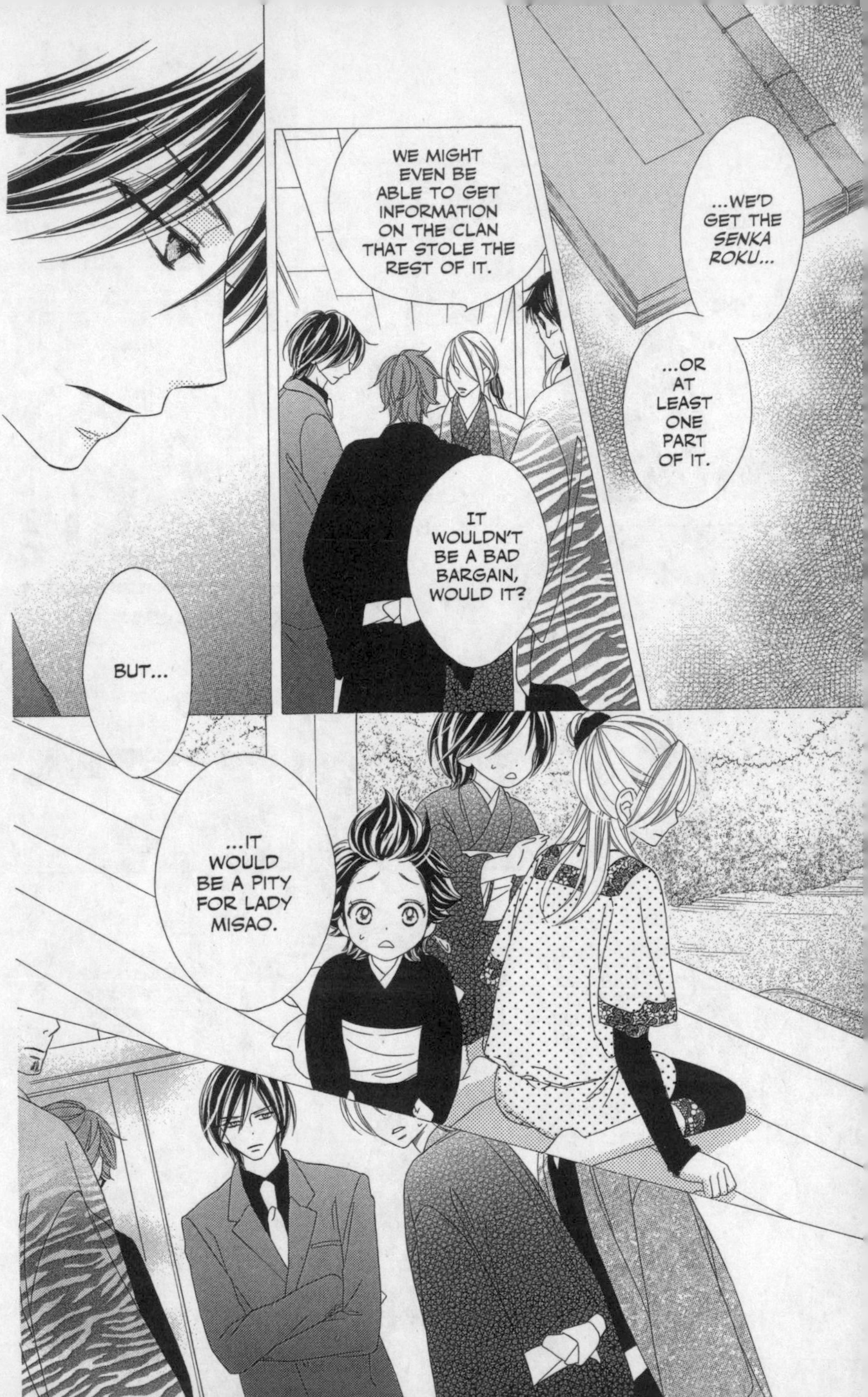
...WE'D GET THE SENKA ROKU...
...OR AT LEAST ONE PART OF IT.
WE MIGHT EVEN BE ABLE TO GET INFORMATION ON THE CLAN THAT STOLE THE REST OF IT.
IT WOULDN'T BE A BAD BARGAIN, WOULD IT?
BUT...
...IT WOULD BE A PITY FOR LADY MISAO.

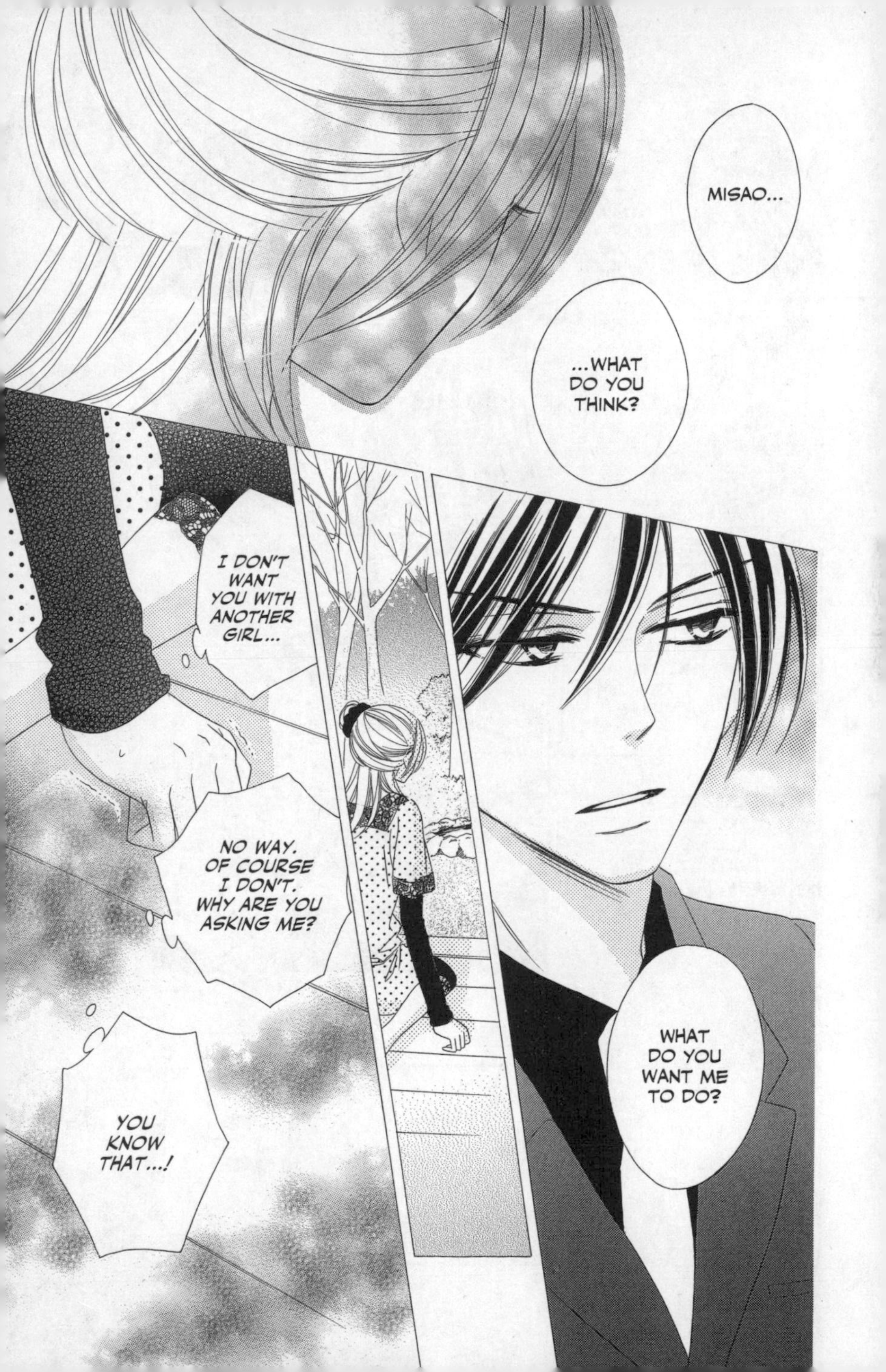
MISAO...
...WHAT DO YOU THINK?
WHAT DO YOU WANT ME TO DO?
I DON'T WANT YOU WITH ANOTHER GIRL...
NO WAY. OF COURSE I DON'T. WHY ARE YOU ASKING ME?
YOU KNOW THAT...!

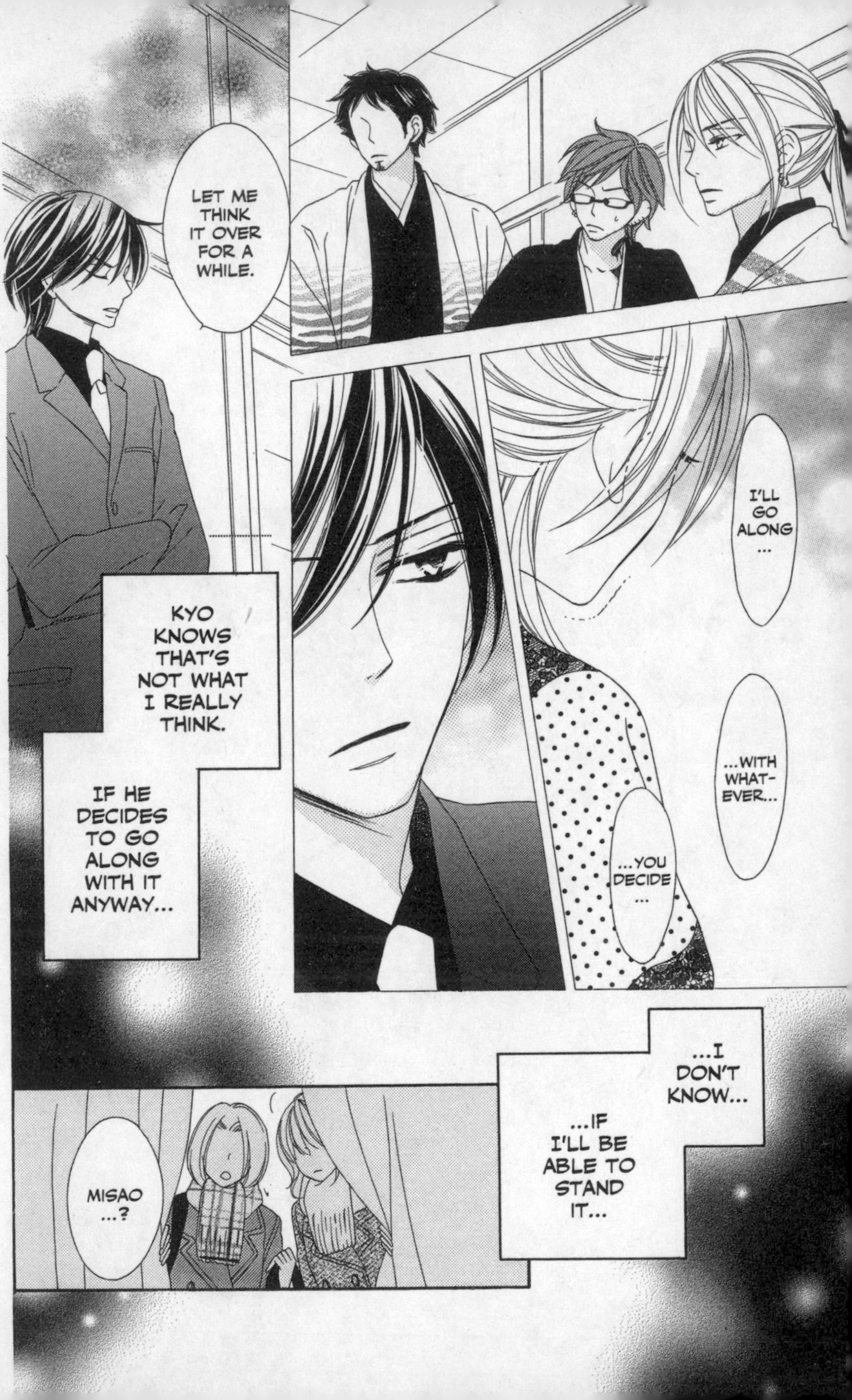
I'LL GO ALONG...
...WITH WHAT-EVER...
...YOU DECIDE...
LET ME THINK IT OVER FOR A WHILE.
KYO KNOWS THAT'S NOT WHAT I REALLY THINK.
IF HE DECIDES TO GO ALONG WITH IT ANYWAY...
...I DON'T KNOW...
...IF I'LL BE ABLE TO STAND IT...
MISAO ...?

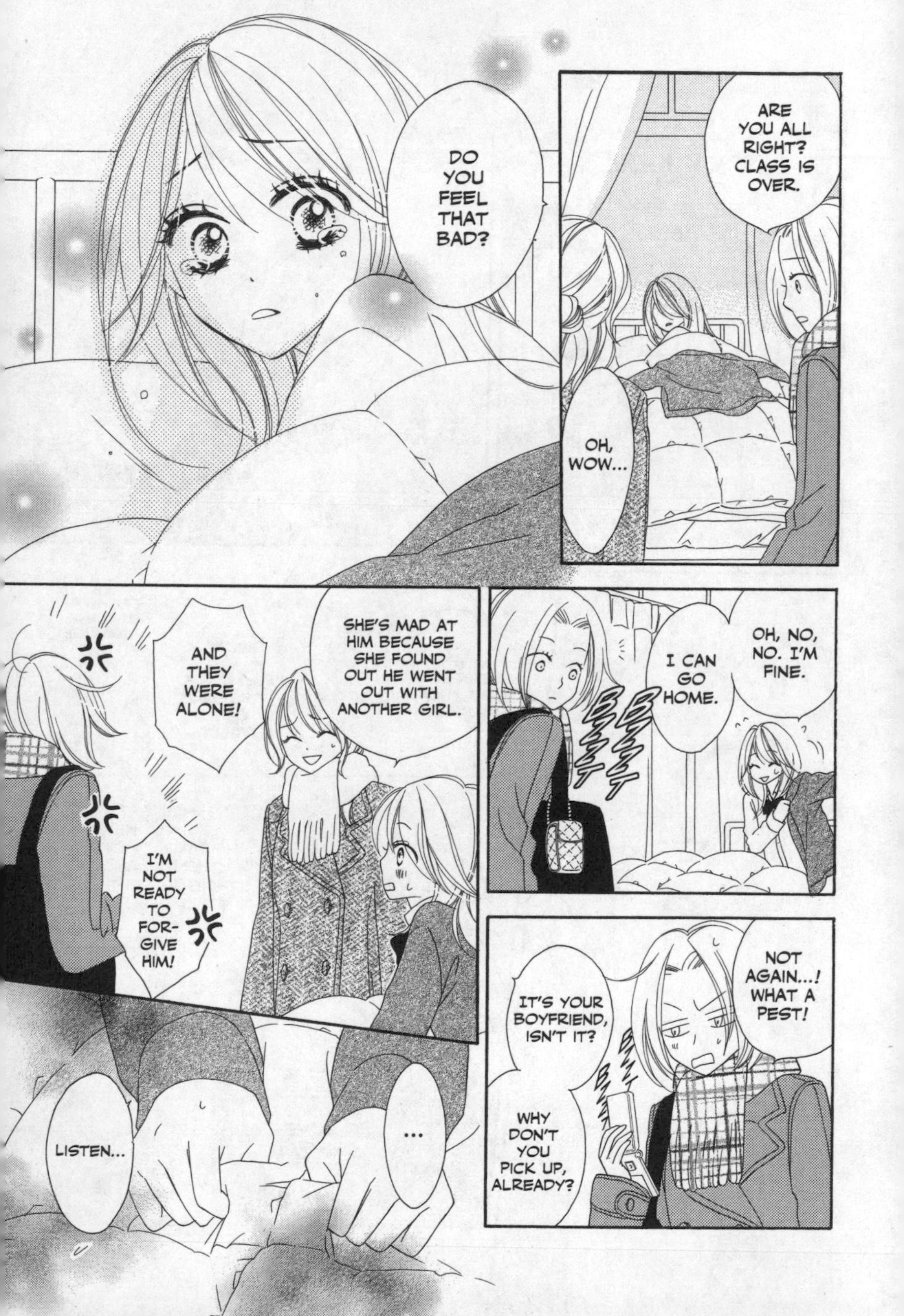
ARE YOU ALL RIGHT? CLASS IS OVER.
OH, WOW...
DO YOU FEEL THAT BAD?
OH, NO, NO. I'M FINE.
I CAN GO HOME.
NOT AGAIN...! WHAT A PEST!
IT'S YOUR BOYFRIEND, ISN'T IT?
WHY DON'T YOU PICK UP, ALREADY?
SHE'S MAD AT HIM BECAUSE SHE FOUND OUT HE WENT OUT WITH ANOTHER GIRL.
AND THEY WERE ALONE!
I'M NOT READY TO FOR-GIVE HIM!
...
LISTEN...

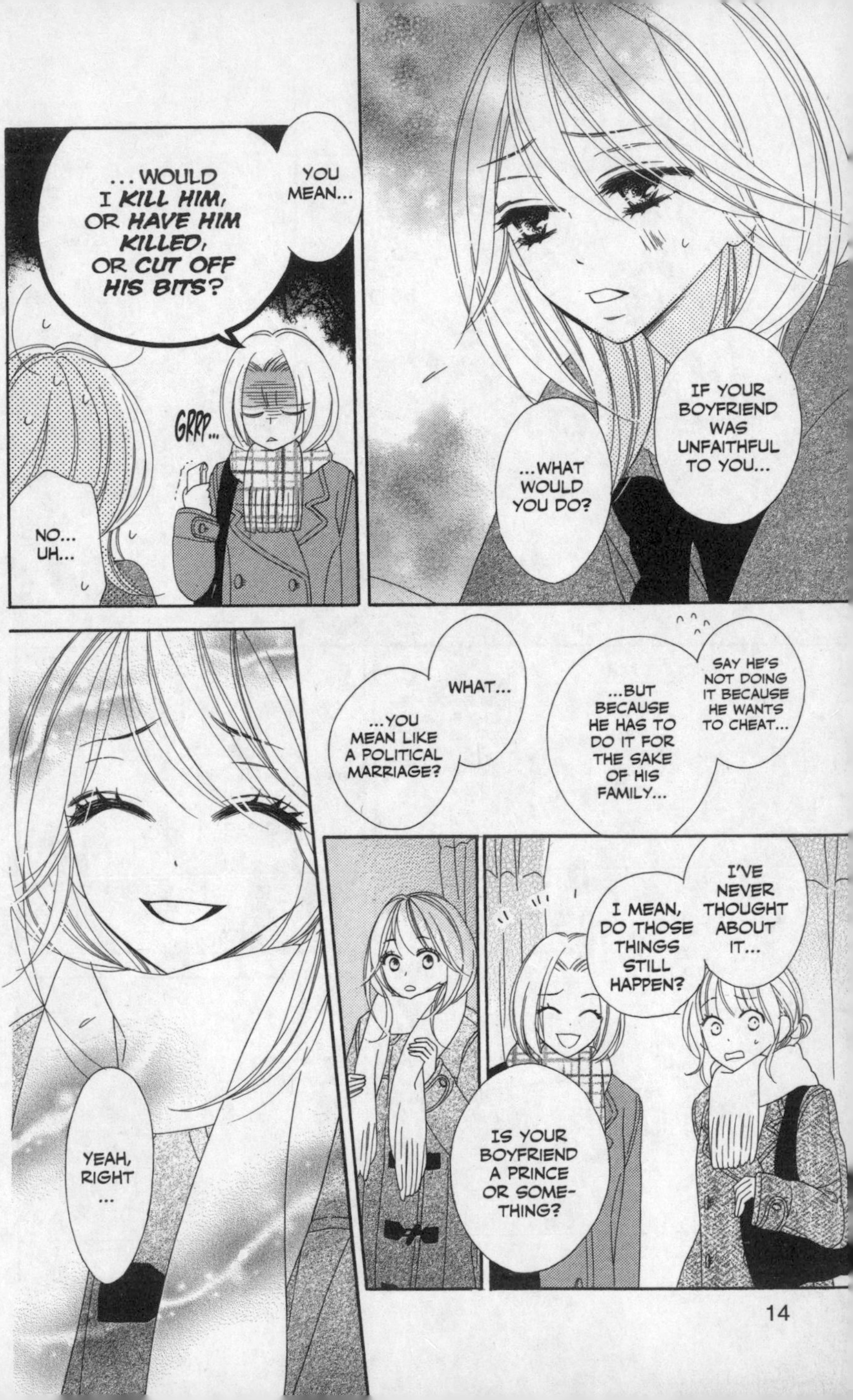
IF YOUR BOYFRIEND WAS UNFAITHFUL TO YOU...
...WHAT WOULD YOU DO?
YOU MEAN...
...WOULD I **KILL HIM**, OR **HAVE HIM KILLED**, OR **CUT OFF HIS BITS**?
GRRP...
NO... UH...
SAY HE'S NOT DOING IT BECAUSE HE WANTS TO CHEAT...
...BUT BECAUSE HE HAS TO DO IT FOR THE SAKE OF HIS FAMILY...
WHAT...
...YOU MEAN LIKE A POLITICAL MARRIAGE?
I'VE NEVER THOUGHT ABOUT IT...
I MEAN, DO THOSE THINGS STILL HAPPEN?
IS YOUR BOYFRIEND A PRINCE OR SOME-THING?
YEAH, RIGHT...

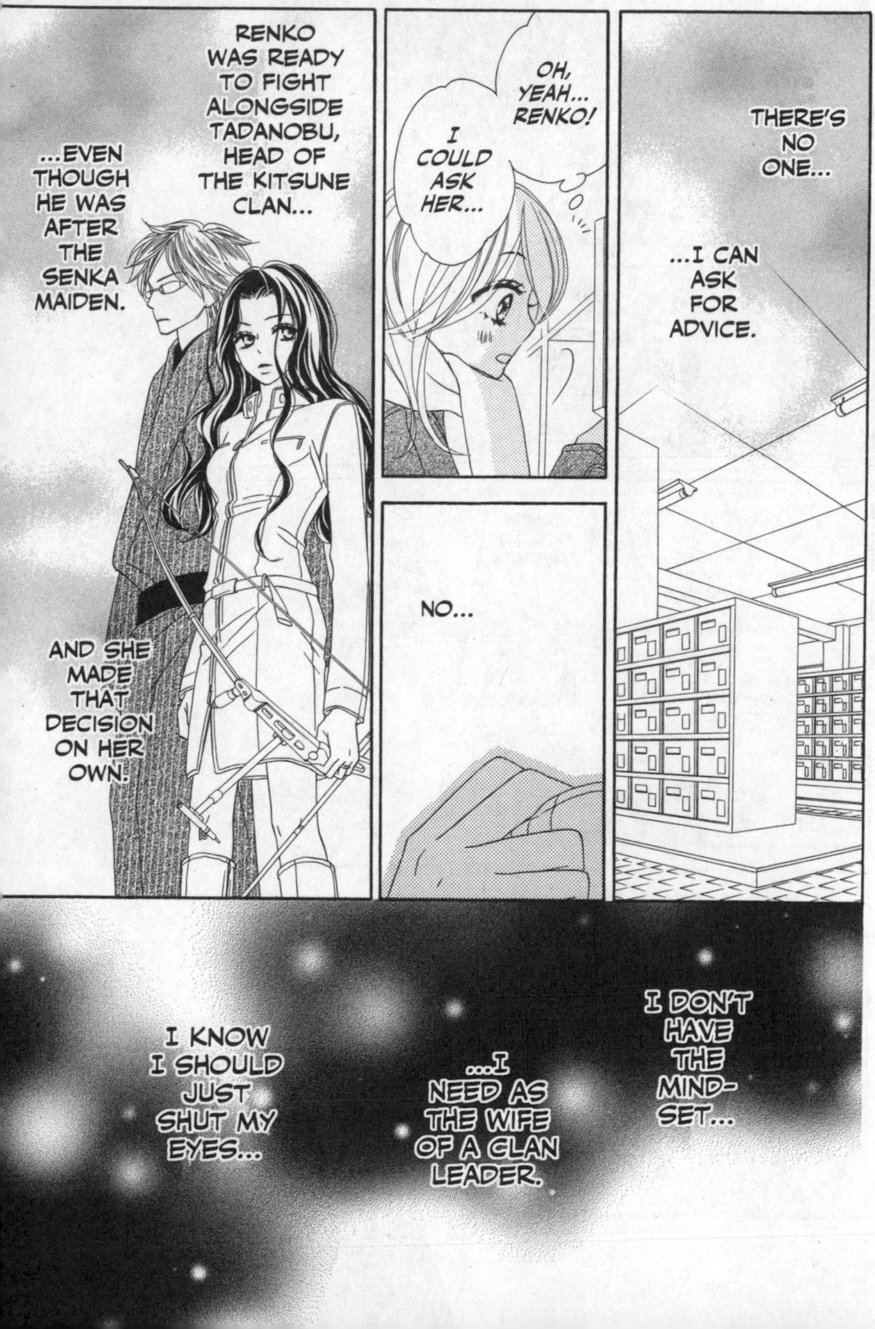
THERE'S NO ONE...
...I CAN ASK FOR ADVICE.
OH, YEAH... RENKO!
I COULD ASK HER...
NO...
RENKO WAS READY TO FIGHT ALONGSIDE TADANOBU, HEAD OF THE KITSUNE CLAN...
...EVEN THOUGH HE WAS AFTER THE SENKA MAIDEN.
AND SHE MADE THAT DECISION ON HER OWN.
I DON'T HAVE THE MIND-SET...
...I NEED AS THE WIFE OF A CLAN LEADER.
I KNOW I SHOULD JUST SHUT MY EYES...

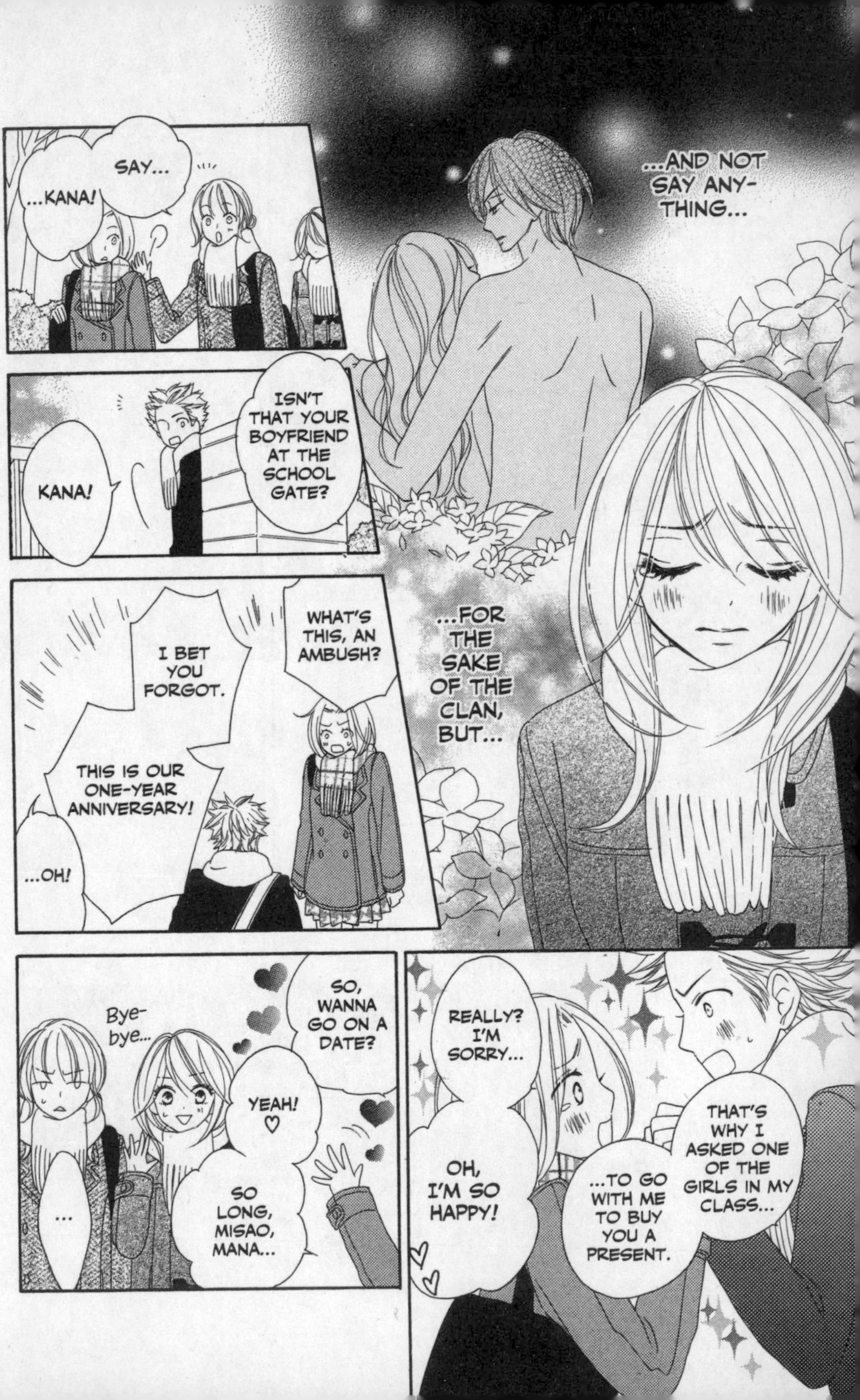
...AND NOT SAY ANY-THING...
...FOR THE SAKE OF THE CLAN, BUT...
SAY...
...KANA!
ISN'T THAT YOUR BOYFRIEND AT THE SCHOOL GATE?
KANA!
WHAT'S THIS, AN AMBUSH?
I BET YOU FORGOT.
THIS IS OUR ONE-YEAR ANNIVERSARY!
...OH!
REALLY? I'M SORRY...
THAT'S WHY I ASKED ONE OF THE GIRLS IN MY CLASS...
...TO GO WITH ME TO BUY YOU A PRESENT.
OH, I'M SO HAPPY!
SO, WANNA GO ON A DATE?
YEAH! ♡
SO LONG, MISAO, MANA...
Bye-bye...
...

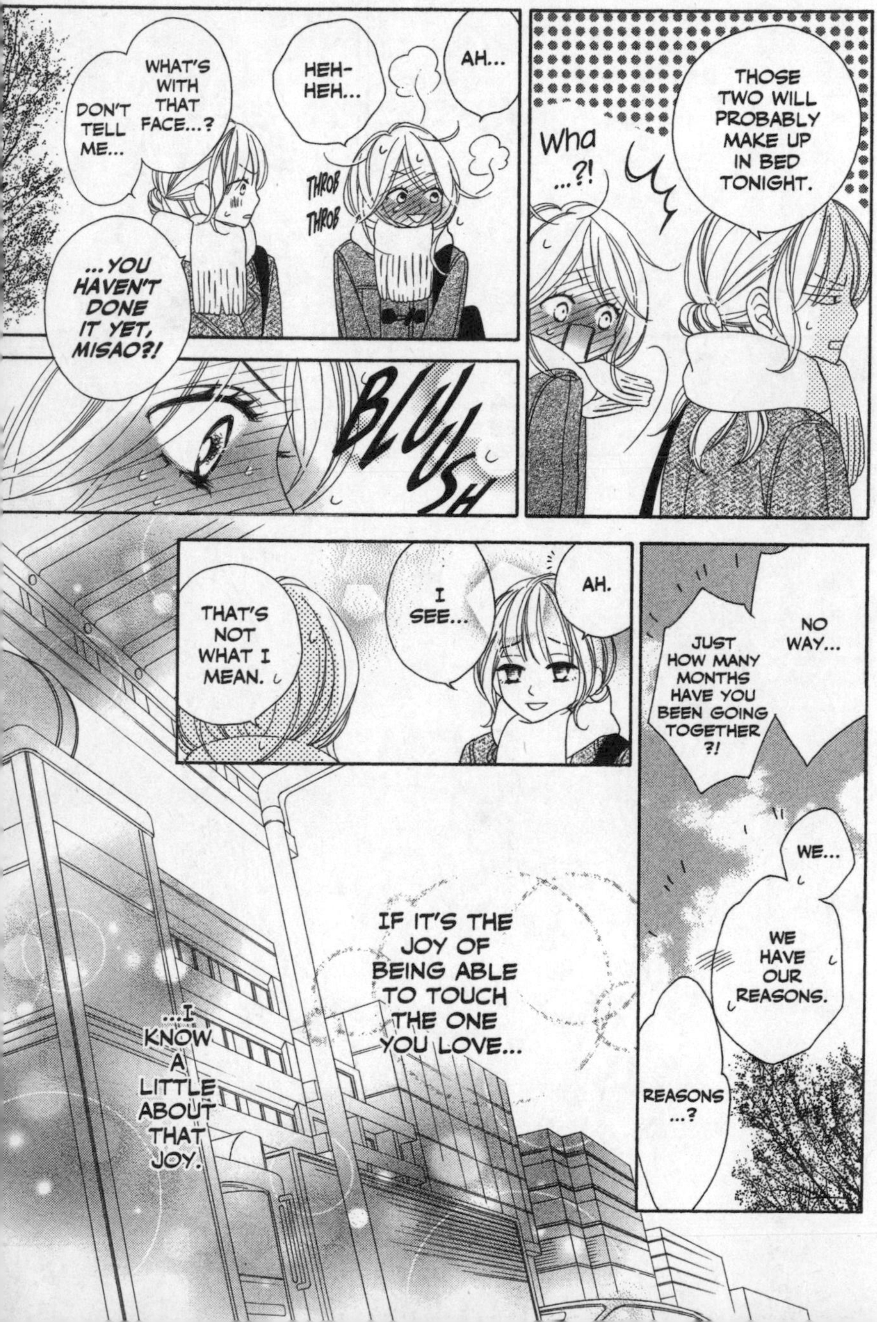
THOSE TWO WILL PROBABLY MAKE UP IN BED TONIGHT.
Wha ...?!
AH...
HEH-HEH...
THROB THROB
WHAT'S WITH THAT FACE...?
DON'T TELL ME...
...YOU HAVEN'T DONE IT YET, MISAO?!
BLUUSH
NO WAY...
JUST HOW MANY MONTHS HAVE YOU BEEN GOING TOGETHER ?!
WE...
WE HAVE OUR REASONS.
REASONS ...?
AH.
I SEE...
THAT'S NOT WHAT I MEAN.
IF IT'S THE JOY OF BEING ABLE TO TOUCH THE ONE YOU LOVE...
...I KNOW A LITTLE ABOUT THAT JOY.

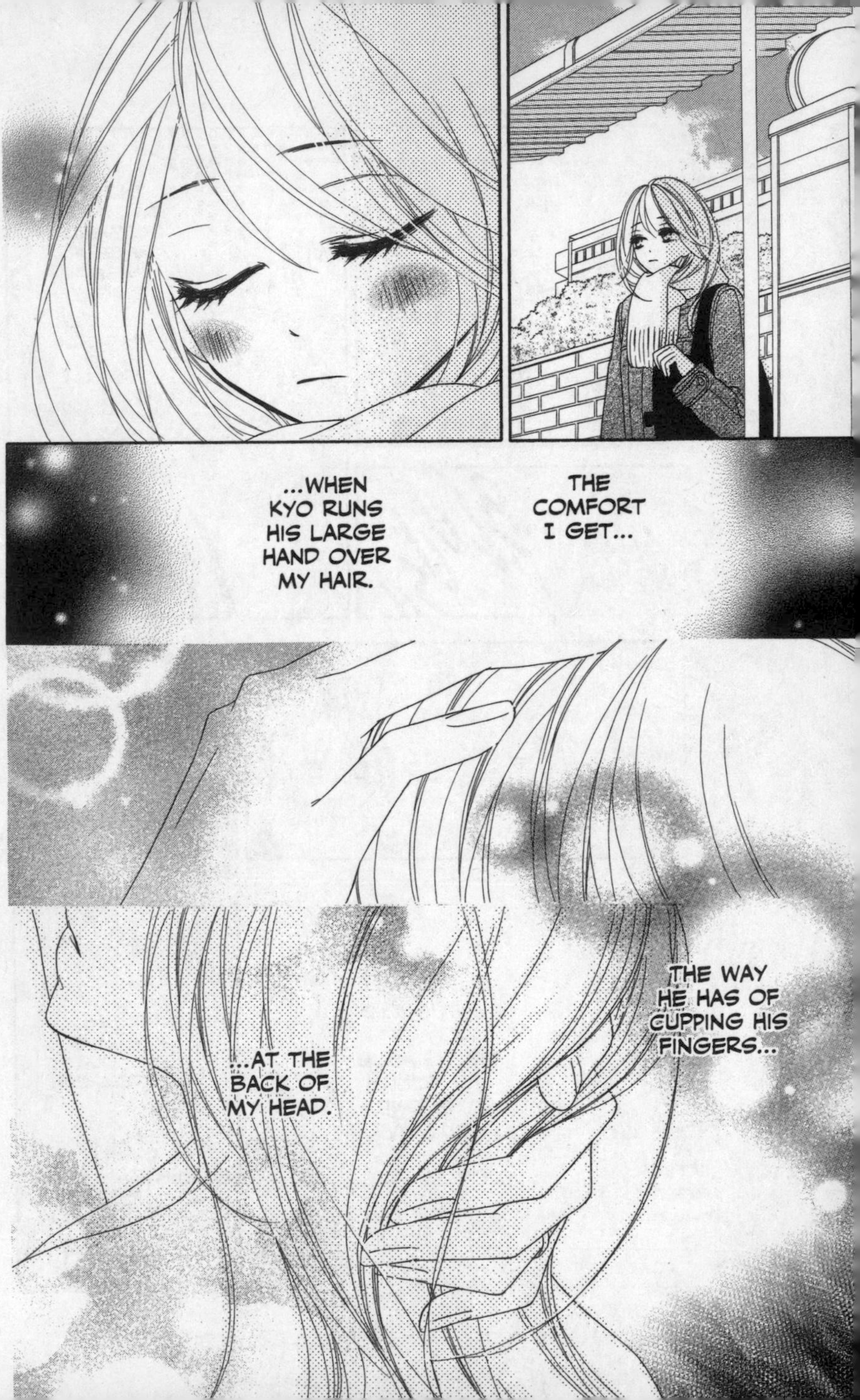
THE COMFORT I GET...
...WHEN KYO RUNS HIS LARGE HAND OVER MY HAIR.
THE WAY HE HAS OF CUPPING HIS FINGERS...
...AT THE BACK OF MY HEAD.

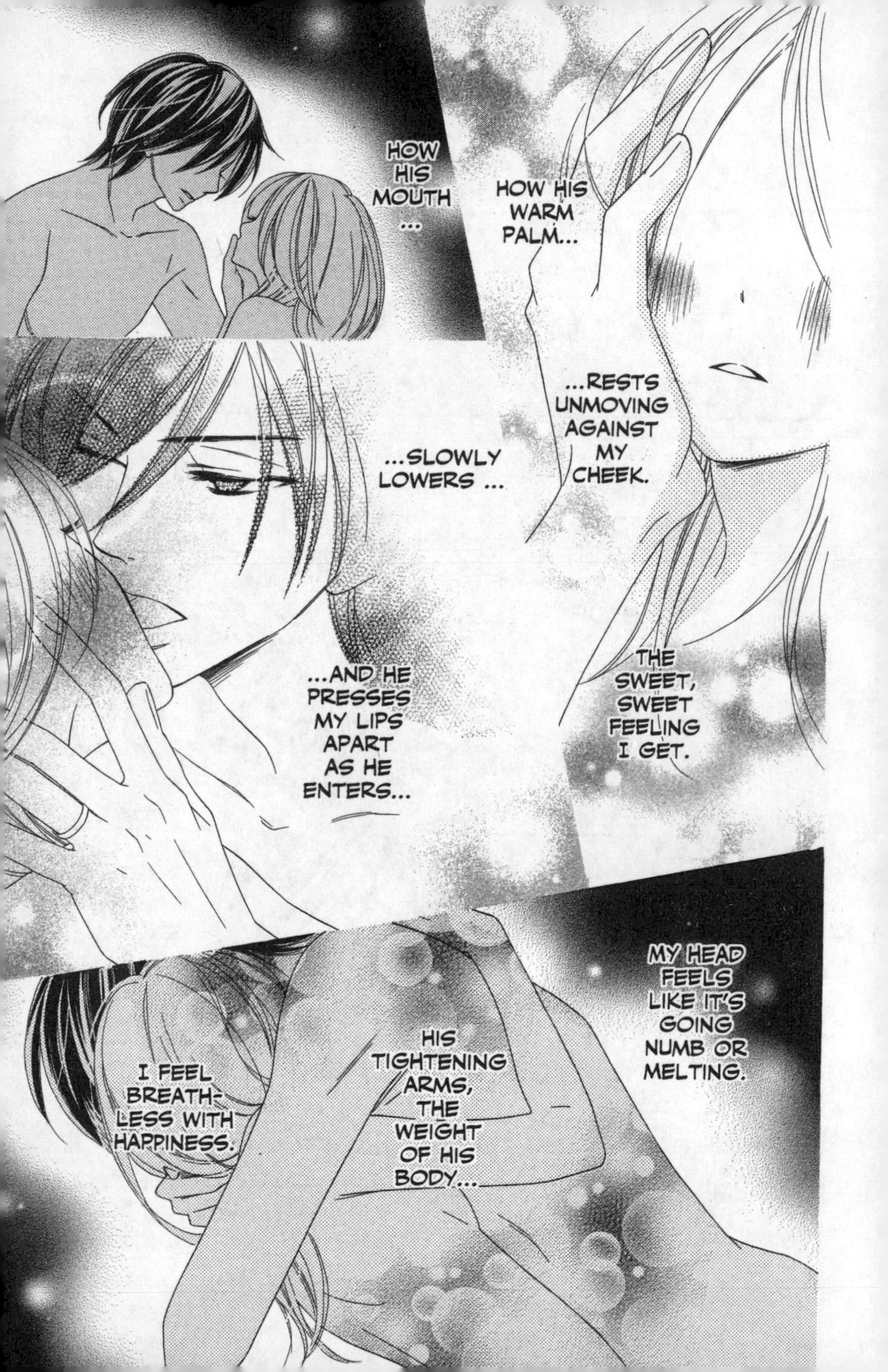
HOW HIS WARM PALM...
...RESTS UNMOVING AGAINST MY CHEEK.
HOW HIS MOUTH ...
...SLOWLY LOWERS ...
...AND HE PRESSES MY LIPS APART AS HE ENTERS...
THE SWEET, SWEET FEELING I GET.
MY HEAD FEELS LIKE IT'S GOING NUMB OR MELTING.
HIS TIGHTENING ARMS, THE WEIGHT OF HIS BODY...
I FEEL BREATH-LESS WITH HAPPINESS.

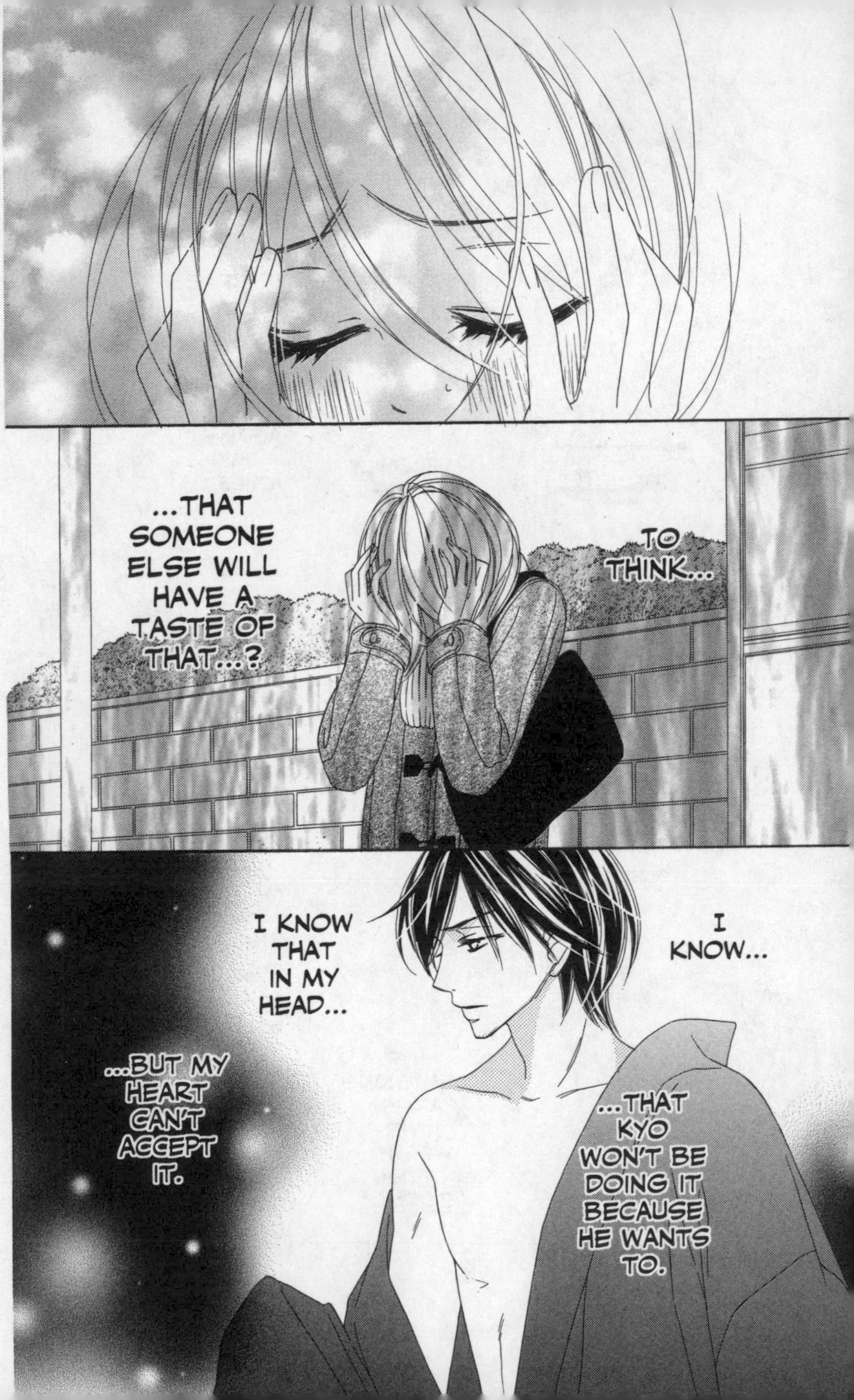
TO THINK...
...THAT SOMEONE ELSE WILL HAVE A TASTE OF THAT...?
I KNOW...
...THAT KYO WON'T BE DOING IT BECAUSE HE WANTS TO.
I KNOW THAT IN MY HEAD...
...BUT MY HEART CAN'T ACCEPT IT.

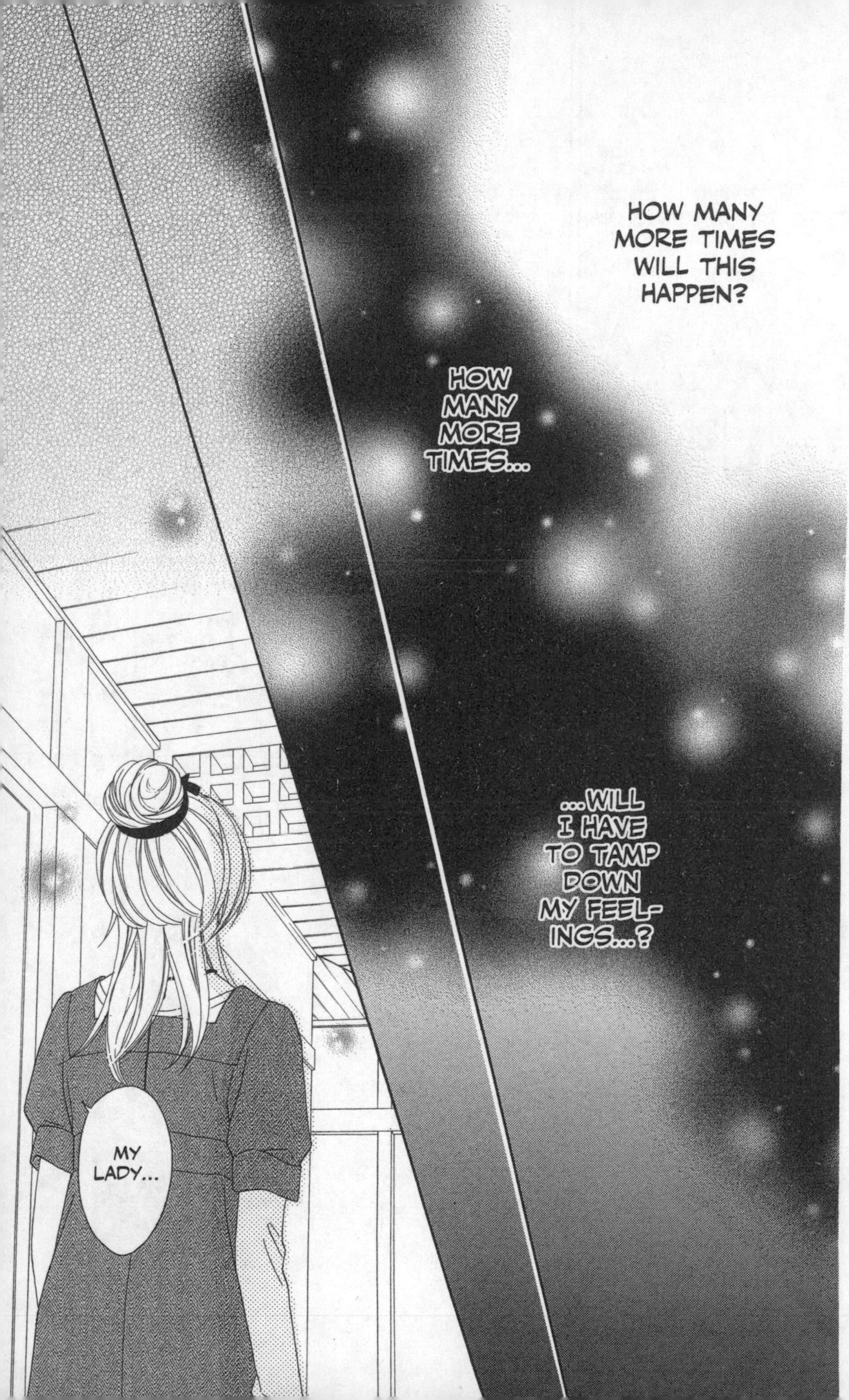
HOW MANY MORE TIMES WILL THIS HAPPEN?
HOW MANY MORE TIMES...
...WILL I HAVE TO TAMP DOWN MY FEEL-INGS...?
MY LADY...

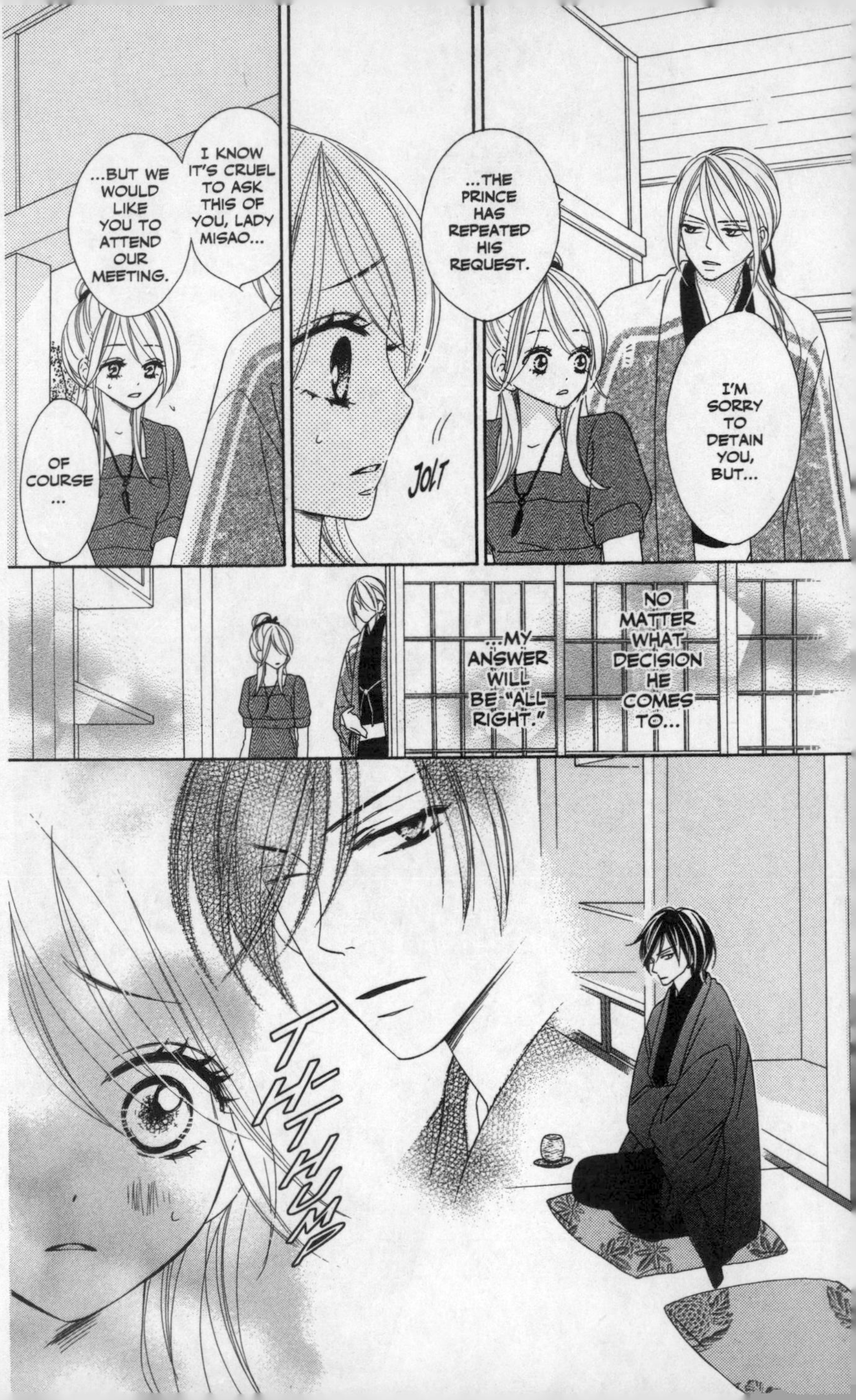
I'M SORRY TO DETAIN YOU, BUT...
...THE PRINCE HAS REPEATED HIS REQUEST.
JOLT
I KNOW IT'S CRUEL TO ASK THIS OF YOU, LADY MISAO...
...BUT WE WOULD LIKE YOU TO ATTEND OUR MEETING.
OF COURSE...
NO MATTER WHAT DECISION HE COMES TO...
...MY ANSWER WILL BE "ALL RIGHT."
TH-THUMP

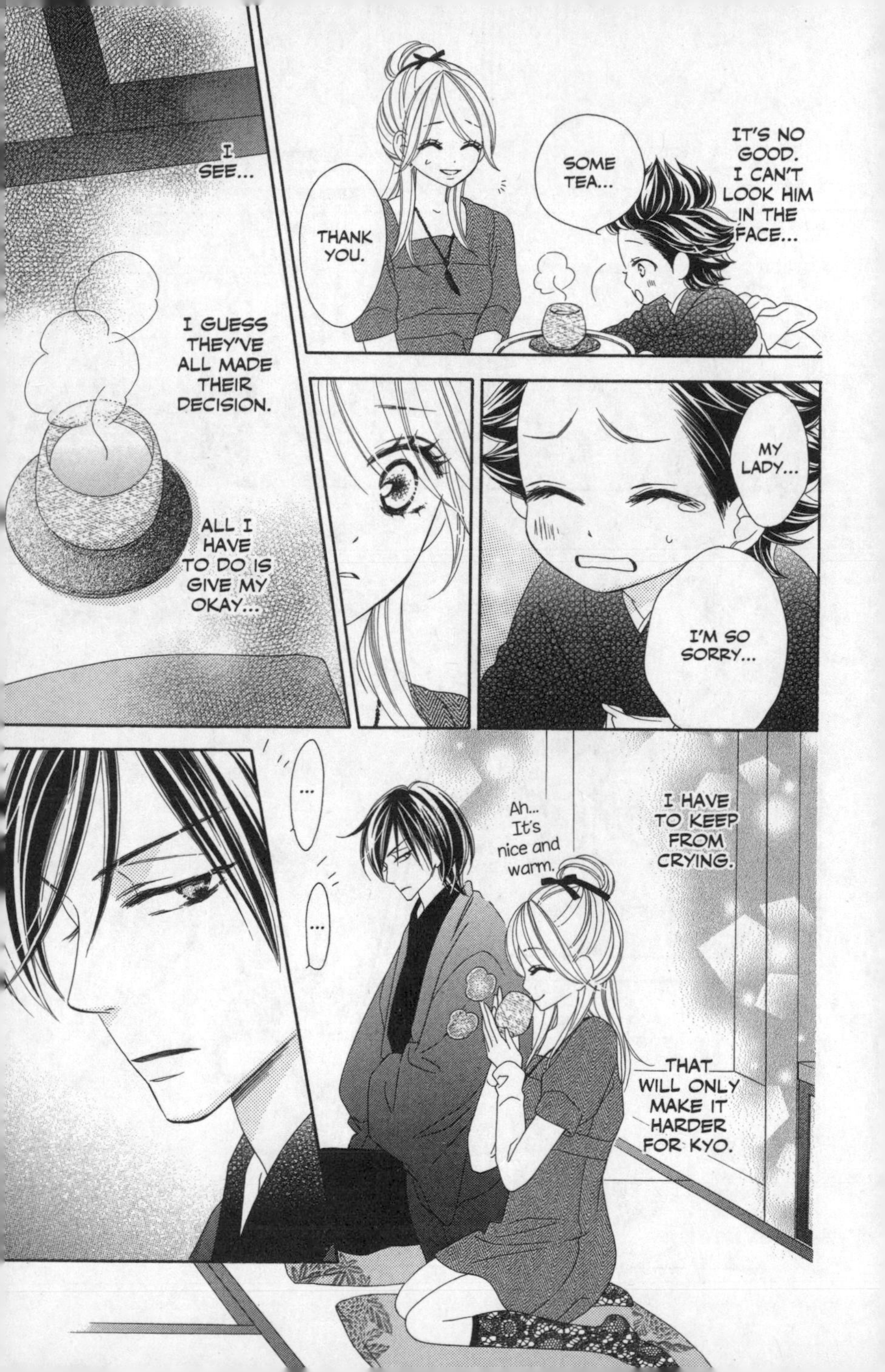
IT'S NO GOOD. I CAN'T LOOK HIM IN THE FACE...
SOME TEA...
THANK YOU.
MY LADY...
I'M SO SORRY...
I SEE...
I GUESS THEY'VE ALL MADE THEIR DECISION.
ALL I HAVE TO DO IS GIVE MY OKAY...
I HAVE TO KEEP FROM CRYING.
Ah... It's nice and warm.
...
...
THAT WILL ONLY MAKE IT HARDER FOR KYO.

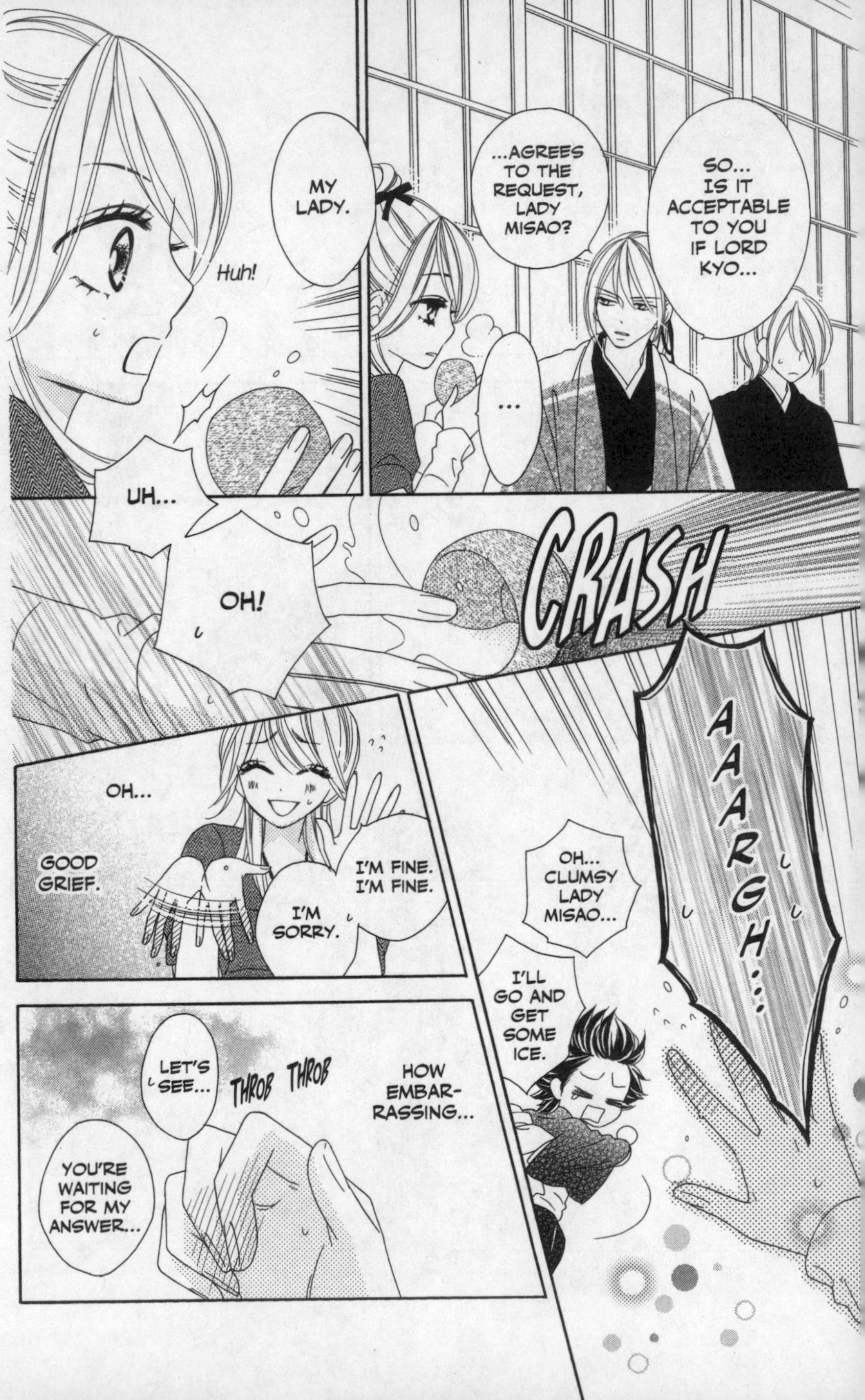
SO... IS IT ACCEPTABLE TO YOU IF LORD KYO...
...AGREES TO THE REQUEST, LADY MISAO?
...
MY LADY.
Huh!
UH...
OH!
CRASH
AAAARGH...
OH... CLUMSY LADY MISAO...
I'LL GO AND GET SOME ICE.
I'M FINE. I'M FINE.
I'M SORRY.
OH...
GOOD GRIEF.
HOW EMBAR-RASSING...
THROB THROB
LET'S SEE...
YOU'RE WAITING FOR MY ANSWER...

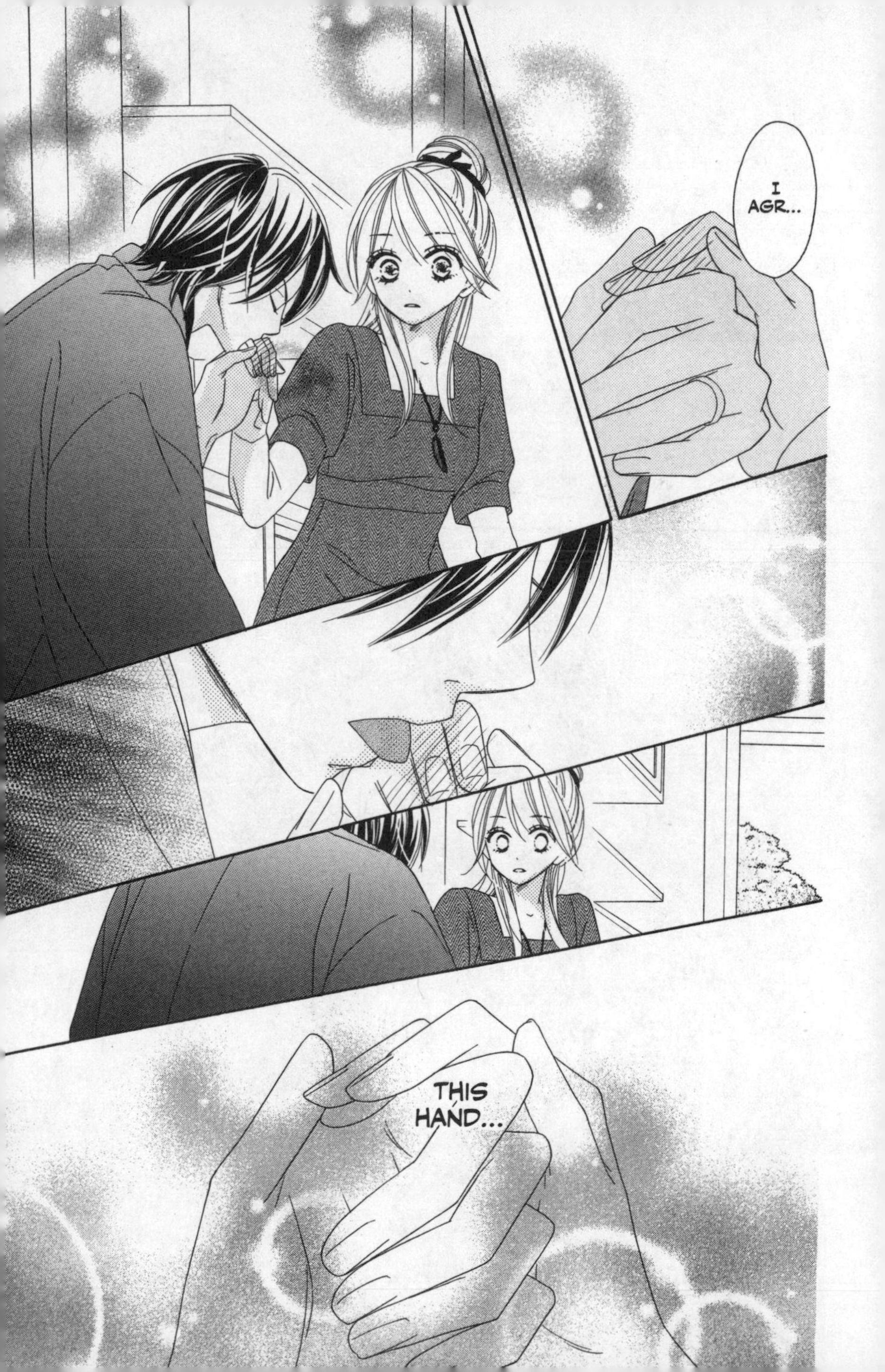
I AGR...
THIS HAND...

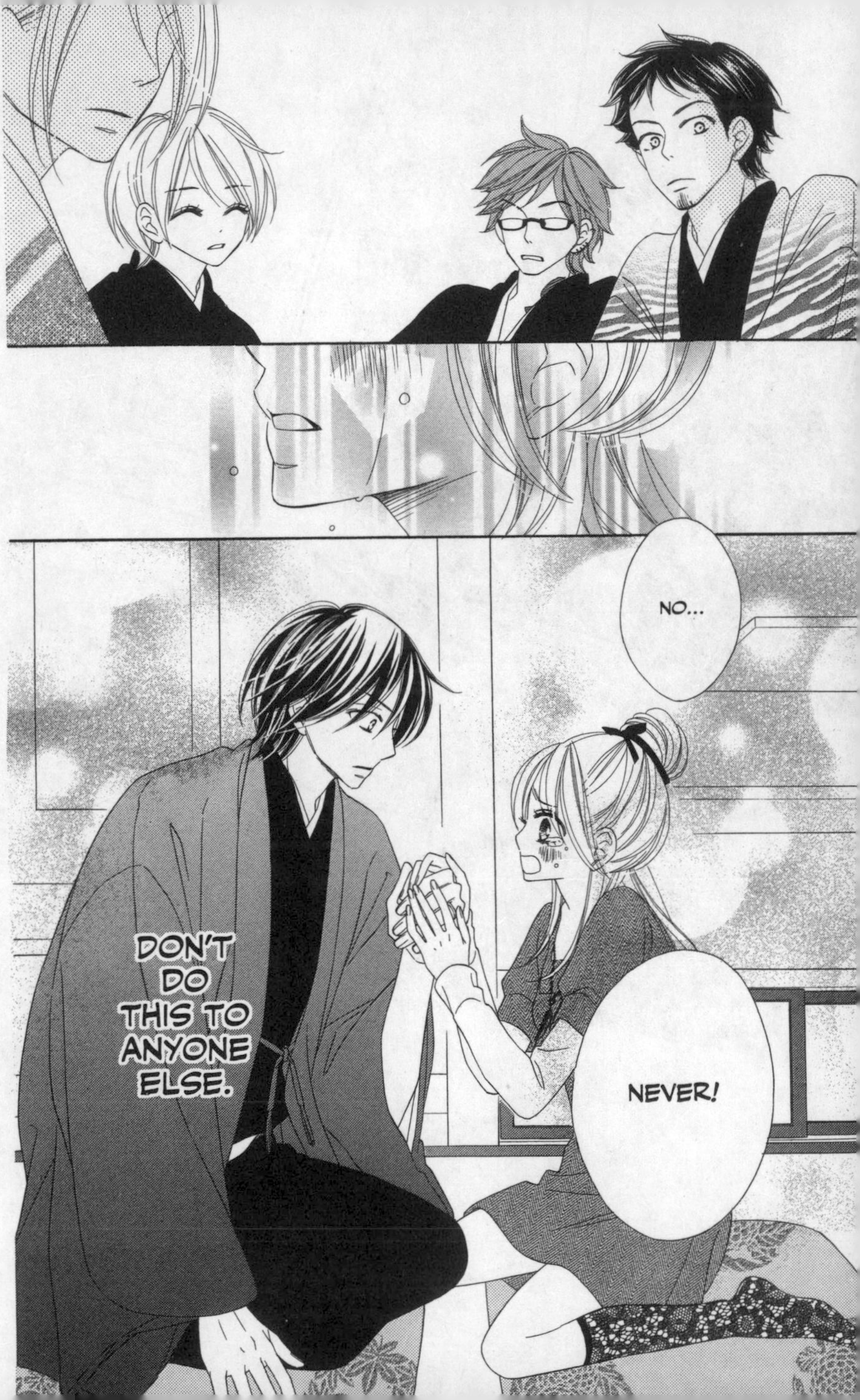
NO...
DON'T DO THIS TO ANYONE ELSE.
NEVER!

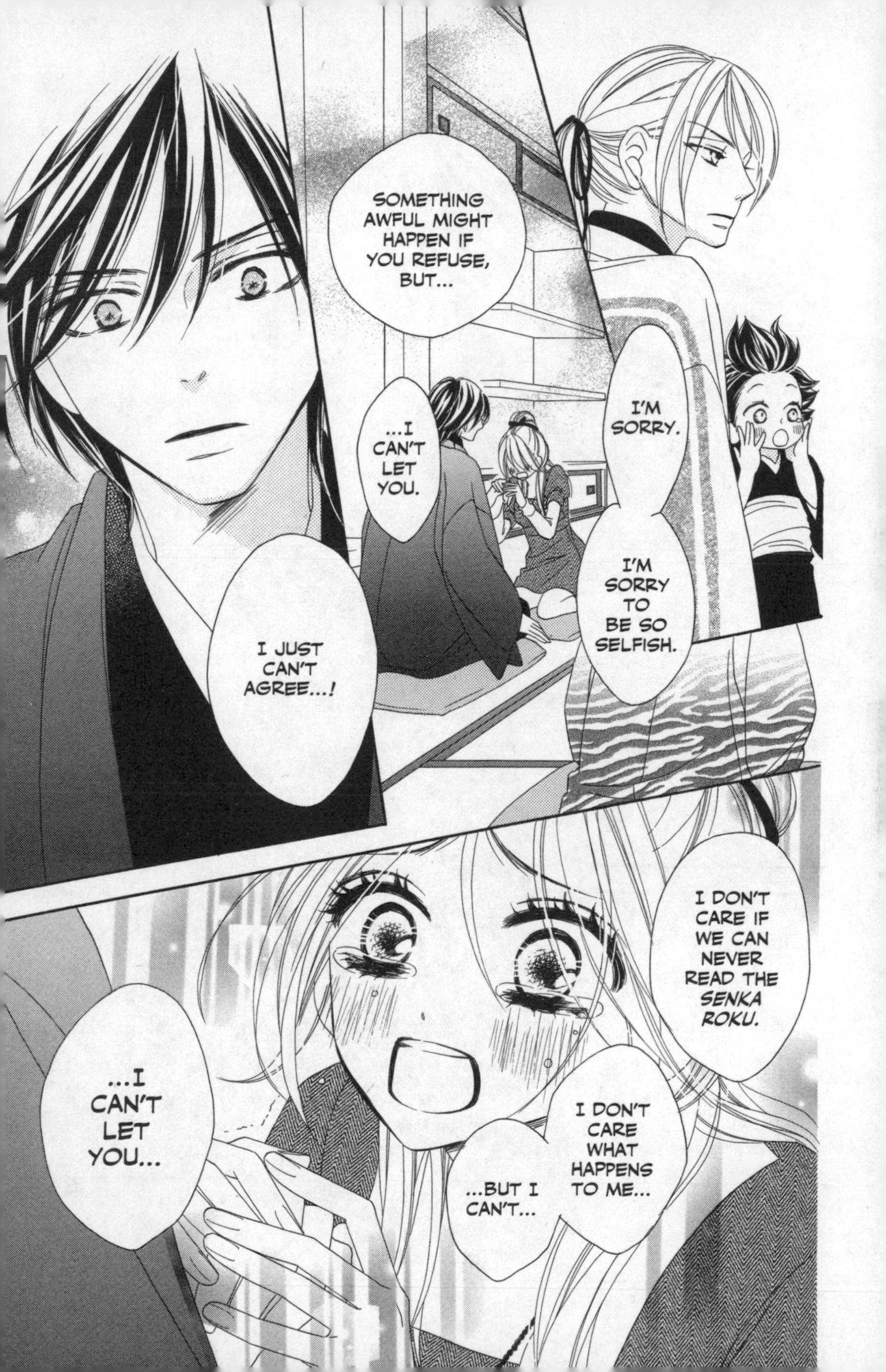
I'M SORRY.
I'M SORRY TO BE SO SELFISH.
SOMETHING AWFUL MIGHT HAPPEN IF YOU REFUSE, BUT...
...I CAN'T LET YOU.
I JUST CAN'T AGREE...!
I DON'T CARE IF WE CAN NEVER READ THE *SENKA ROKU.*
I DON'T CARE WHAT HAPPENS TO ME...
...BUT I CAN'T...
...I CAN'T LET YOU...

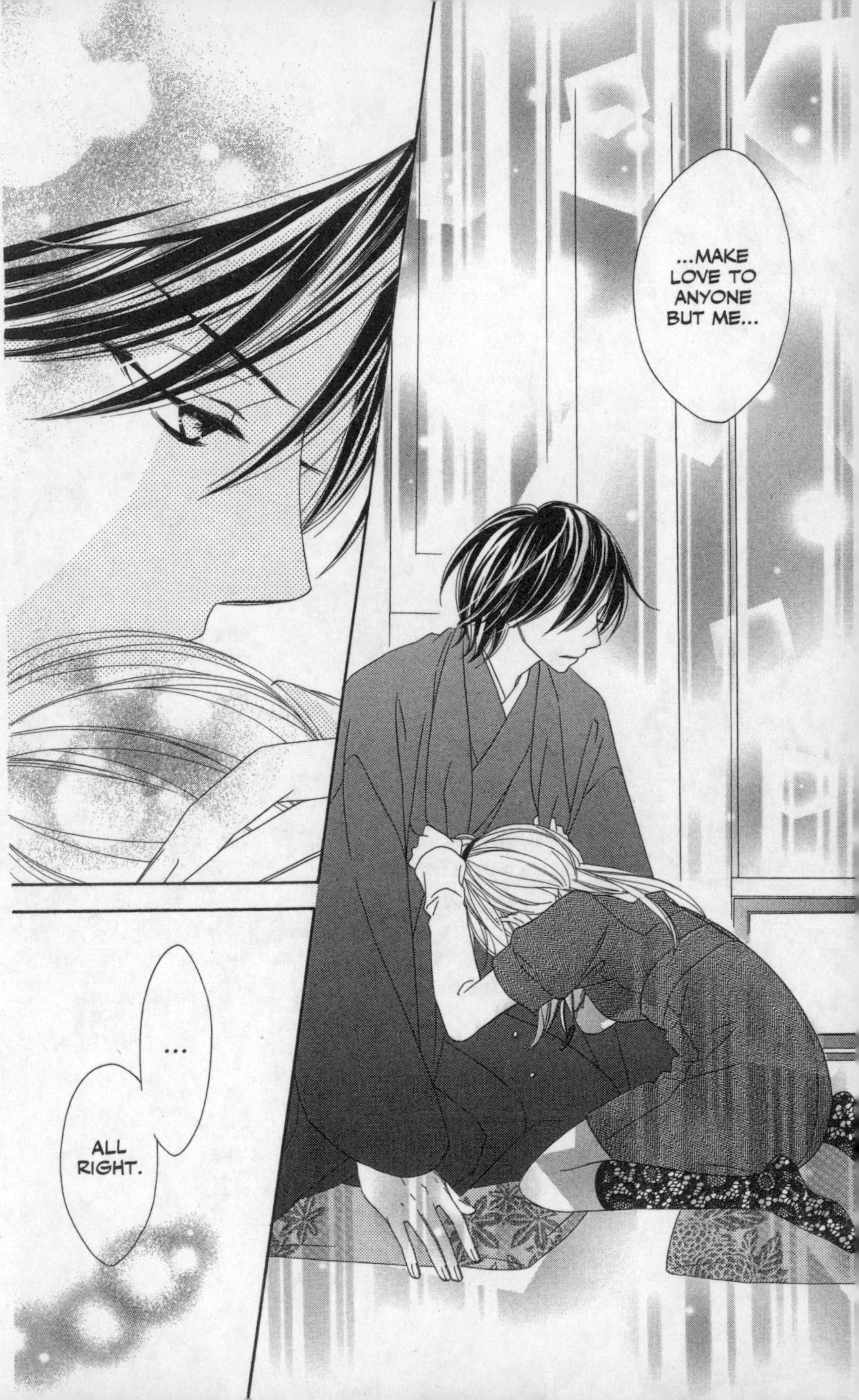
...MAKE LOVE TO ANYONE BUT ME...
...
ALL RIGHT.

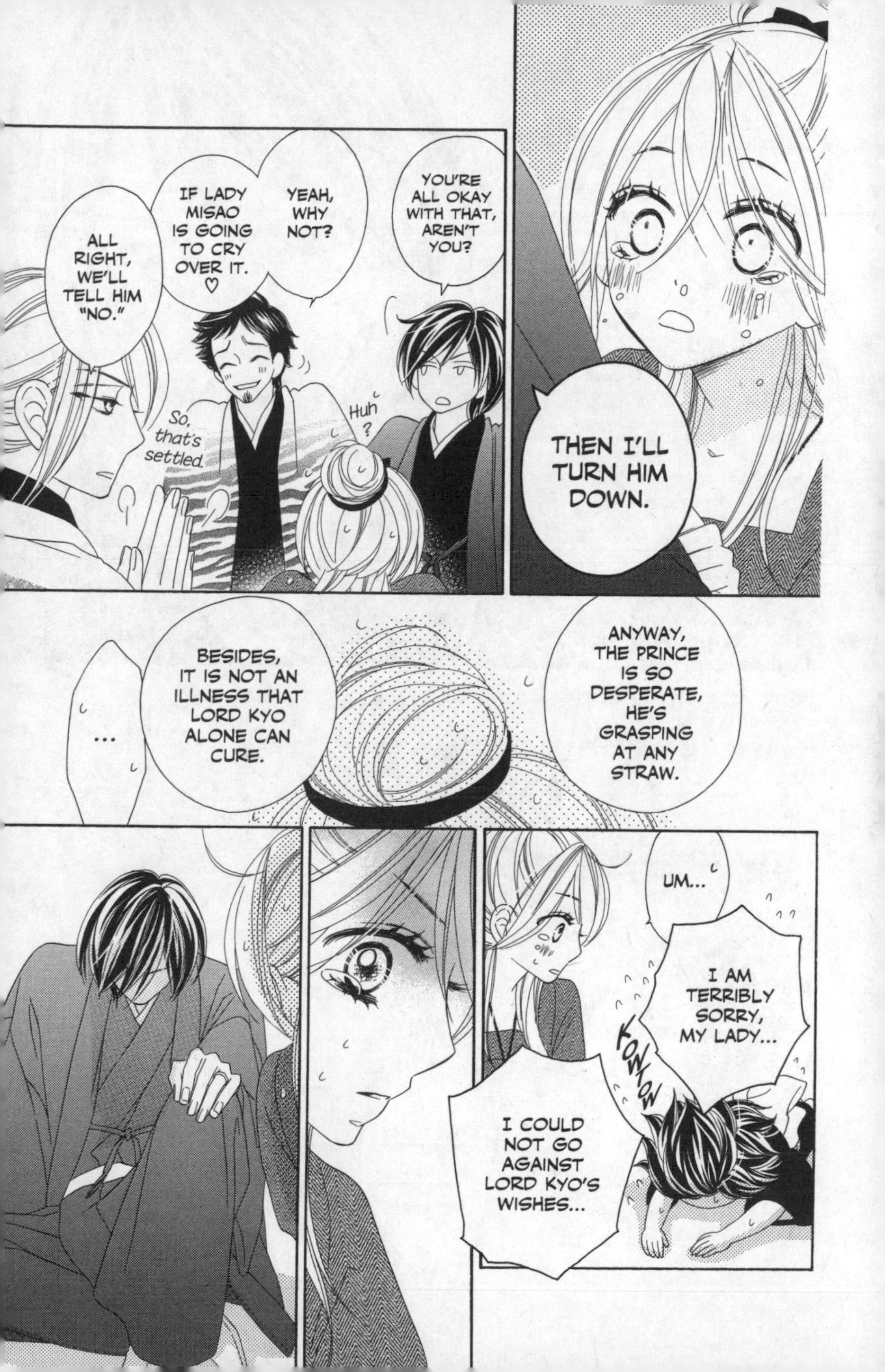
THEN I'LL TURN HIM DOWN.
YOU'RE ALL OKAY WITH THAT, AREN'T YOU?
YEAH, WHY NOT?
IF LADY MISAO IS GOING TO CRY OVER IT. ♡
ALL RIGHT, WE'LL TELL HIM "NO."
Huh?
So, that's settled.
ANYWAY, THE PRINCE IS SO DESPERATE, HE'S GRASPING AT ANY STRAW.
BESIDES, IT IS NOT AN ILLNESS THAT LORD KYO ALONE CAN CURE.
...
UM...
I AM TERRIBLY SORRY, MY LADY...
KOWTOW
I COULD NOT GO AGAINST LORD KYO'S WISHES...

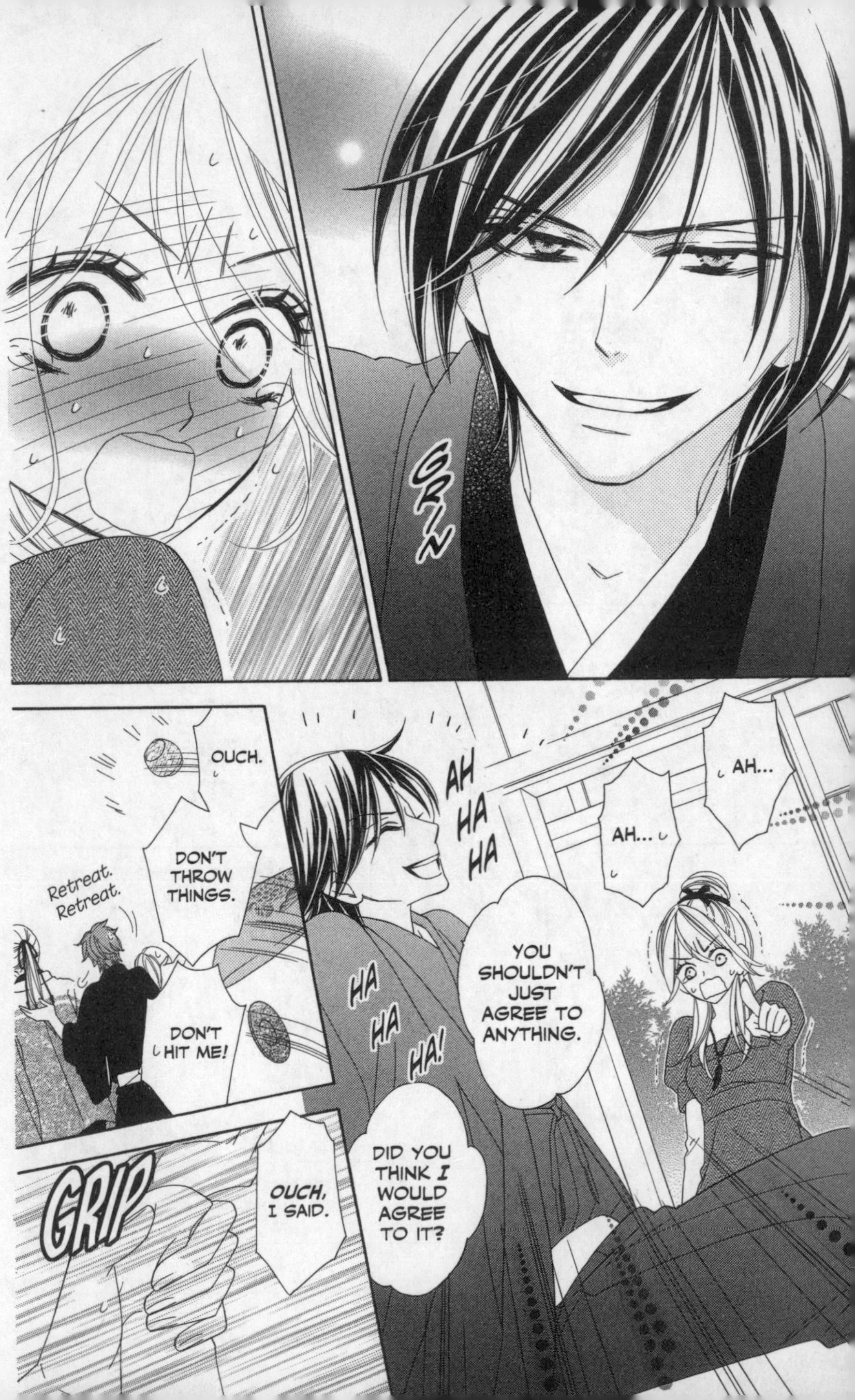
GRIN
AH...
AH...
AH HA HA HA
YOU SHOULDN'T JUST AGREE TO ANYTHING.
HA HA HA!
DID YOU THINK *I* WOULD AGREE TO IT?
OUCH.
DON'T THROW THINGS.
Retreat. Retreat.
DON'T HIT ME!
OUCH, I SAID.
GRIP

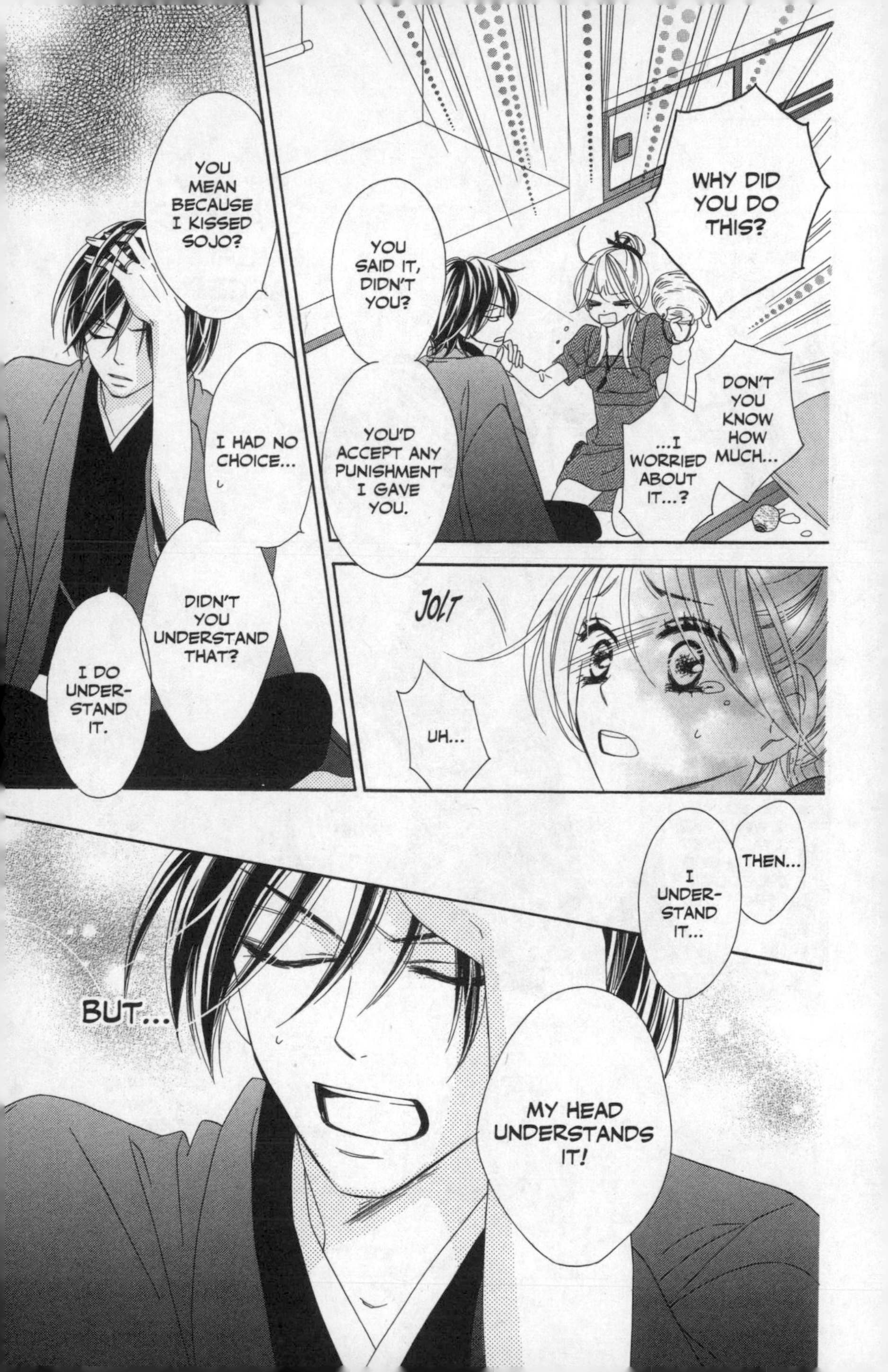
WHY DID YOU DO THIS?
DON'T YOU KNOW HOW MUCH...
...I WORRIED ABOUT IT...?
YOU SAID IT, DIDN'T YOU?
YOU'D ACCEPT ANY PUNISHMENT I GAVE YOU.
JOLT
UH...
YOU MEAN BECAUSE I KISSED SOJO?
I HAD NO CHOICE...
DIDN'T YOU UNDERSTAND THAT?
I DO UNDER-STAND IT.
THEN...
I UNDER-STAND IT...
BUT...
MY HEAD UNDERSTANDS IT!

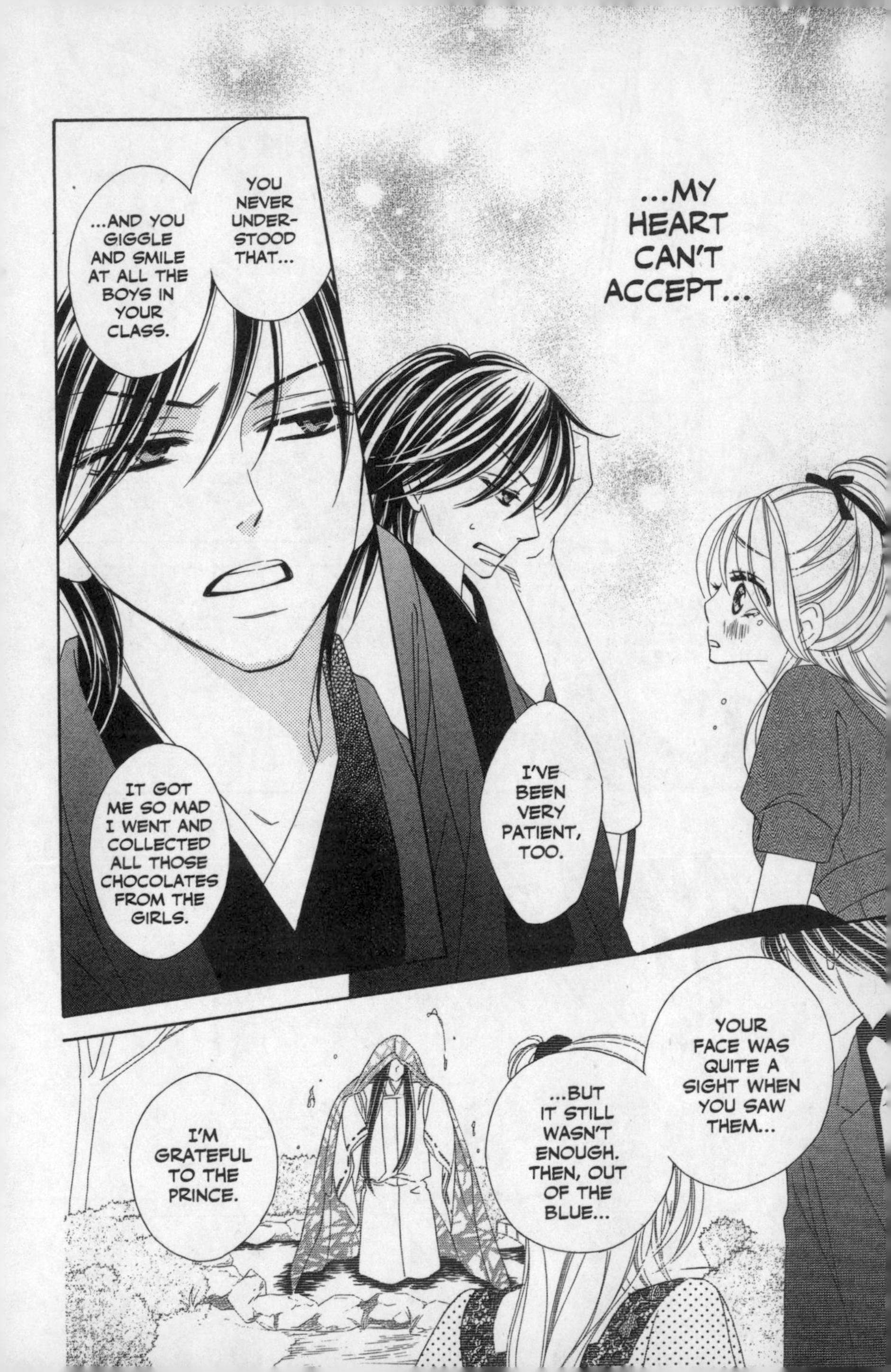
...MY HEART CAN'T ACCEPT...
YOU NEVER UNDER-STOOD THAT...
...AND YOU GIGGLE AND SMILE AT ALL THE BOYS IN YOUR CLASS.
I'VE BEEN VERY PATIENT, TOO.
IT GOT ME SO MAD I WENT AND COLLECTED ALL THOSE CHOCOLATES FROM THE GIRLS.
YOUR FACE WAS QUITE A SIGHT WHEN YOU SAW THEM...
...BUT IT STILL WASN'T ENOUGH. THEN, OUT OF THE BLUE...
I'M GRATEFUL TO THE PRINCE.

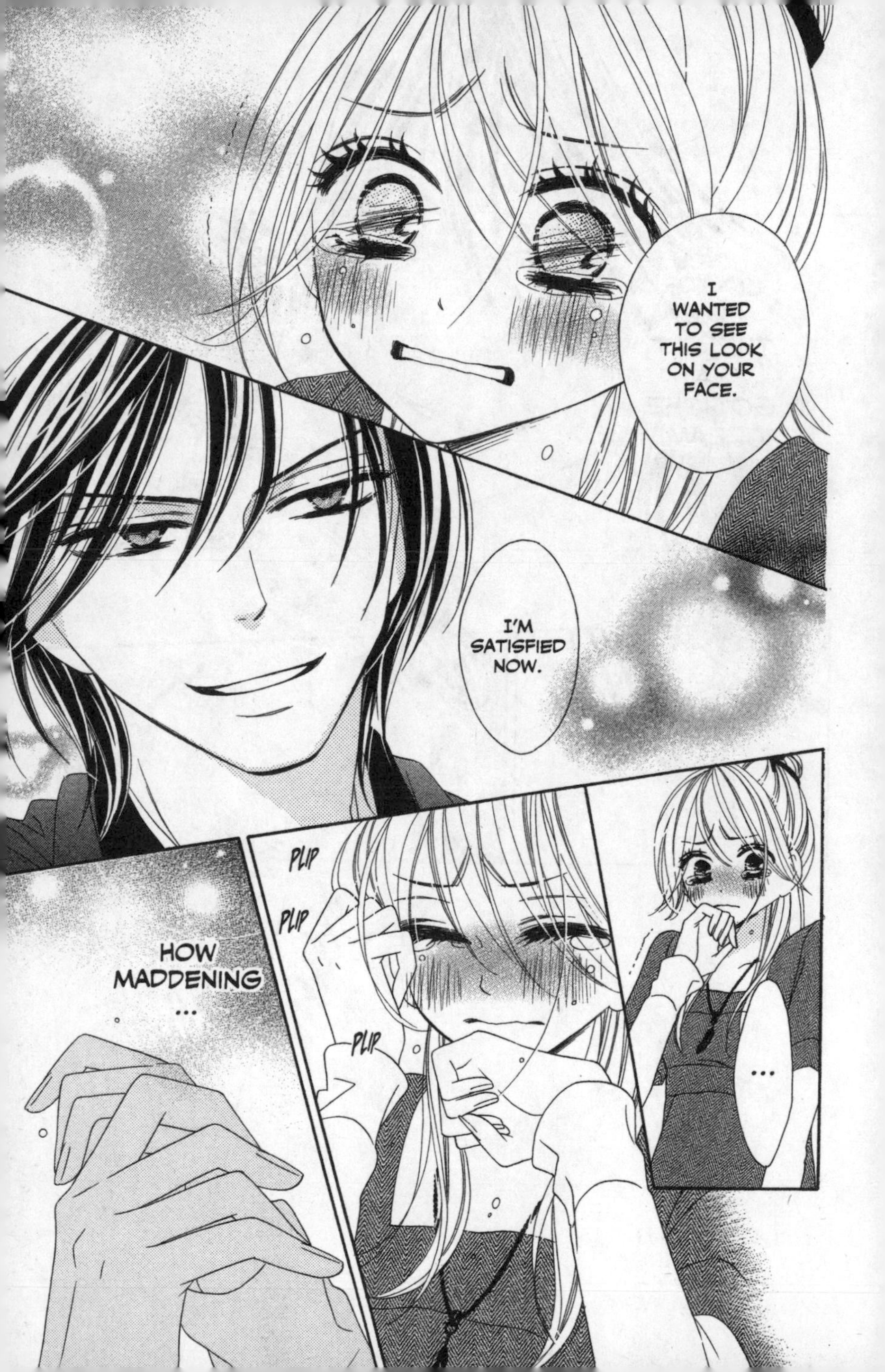
I WANTED TO SEE THIS LOOK ON YOUR FACE.
I'M SATISFIED NOW.
...
PLIP
PLIP
PLIP
HOW MADDENING ...

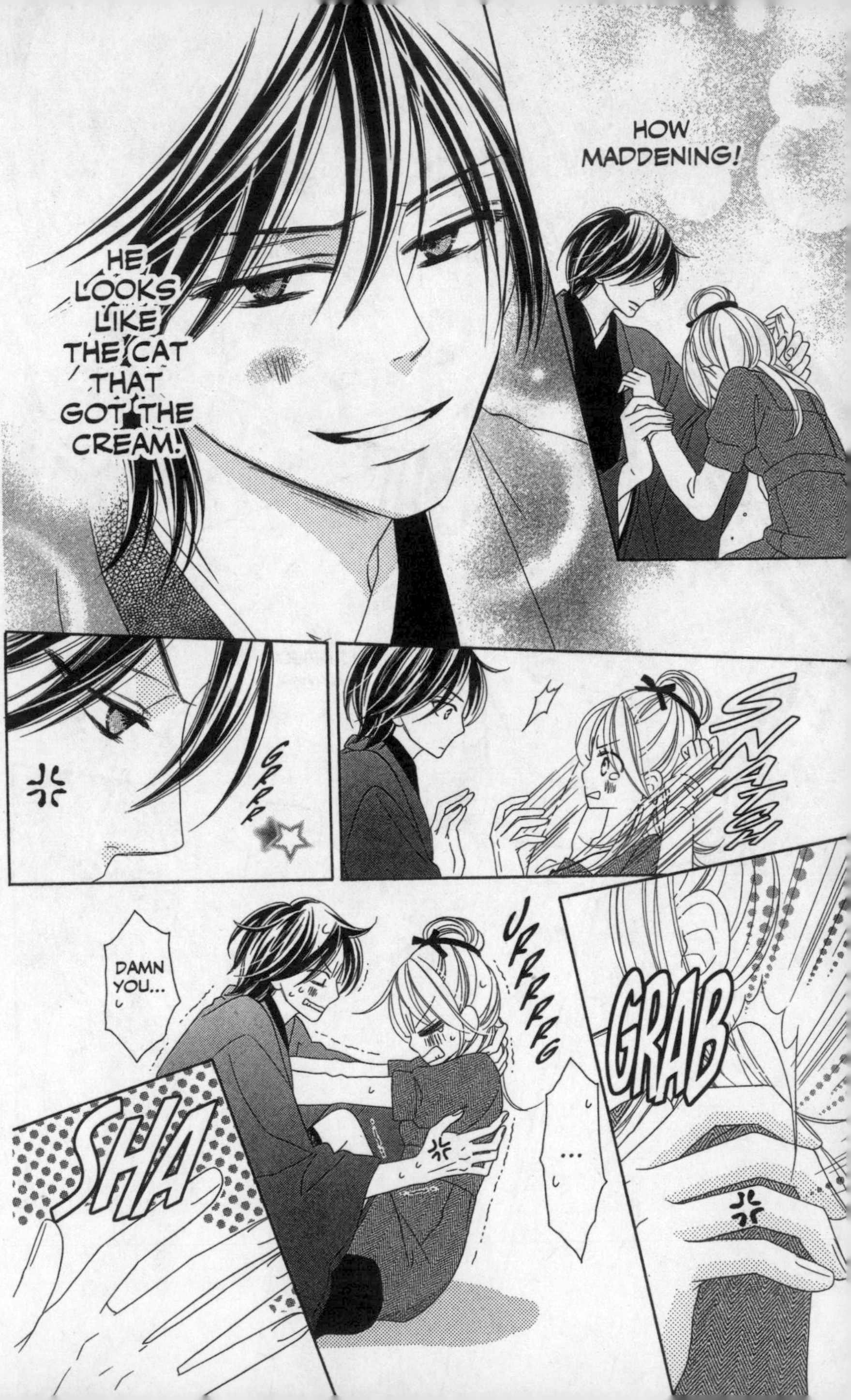
HOW MADDENING!
HE LOOKS LIKE THE CAT THAT GOT THE CREAM!
SNATCH
GRRR
GRAB
...
URRRRRG
DAMN YOU...
SHA

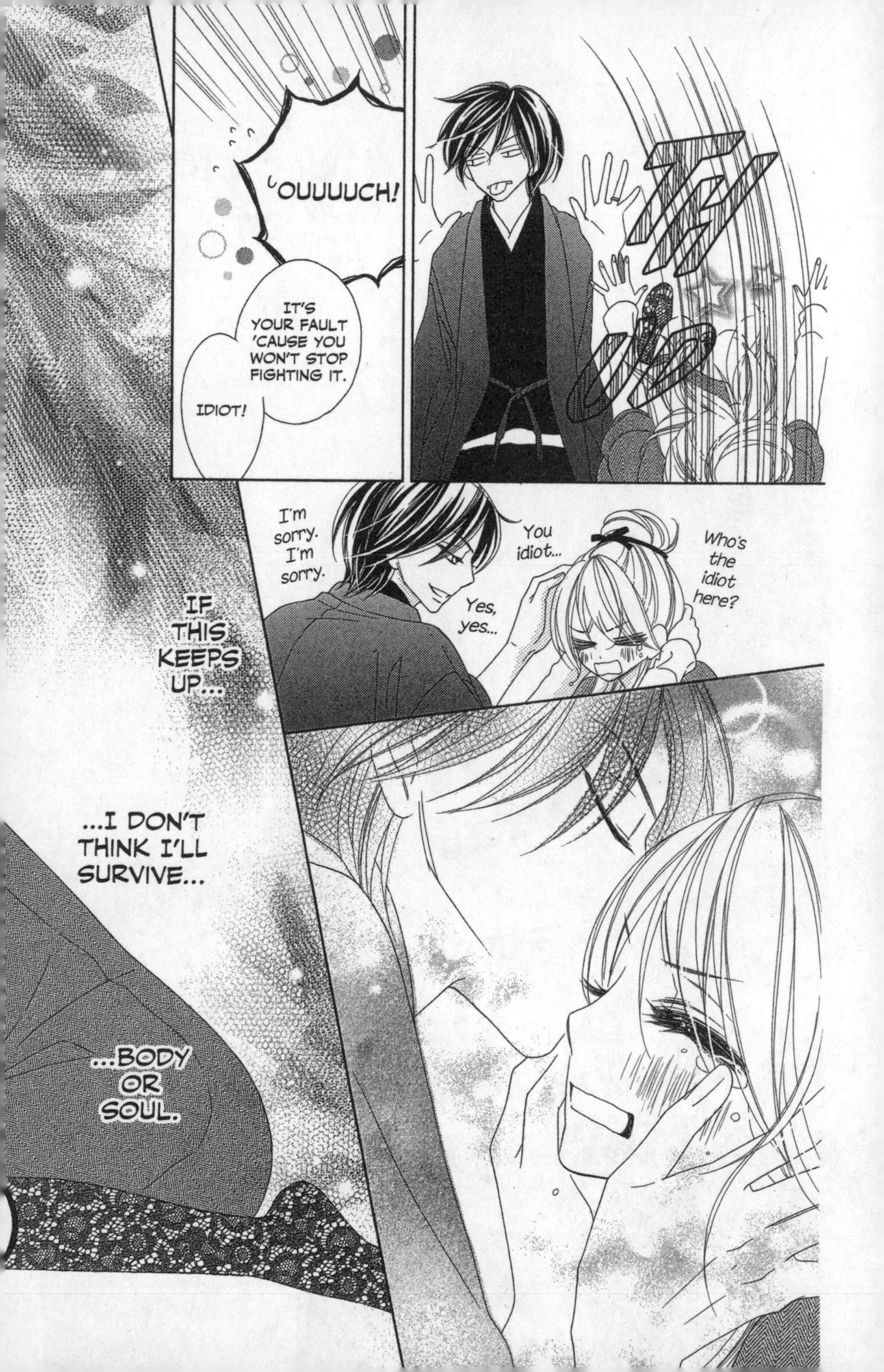
OUUUUCH!
IT'S YOUR FAULT 'CAUSE YOU WON'T STOP FIGHTING IT.
IDIOT!
Who's the idiot here?
You idiot...
I'm sorry. I'm sorry.
Yes, yes...
IF THIS KEEPS UP...
...I DON'T THINK I'LL SURVIVE...
...BODY OR SOUL.

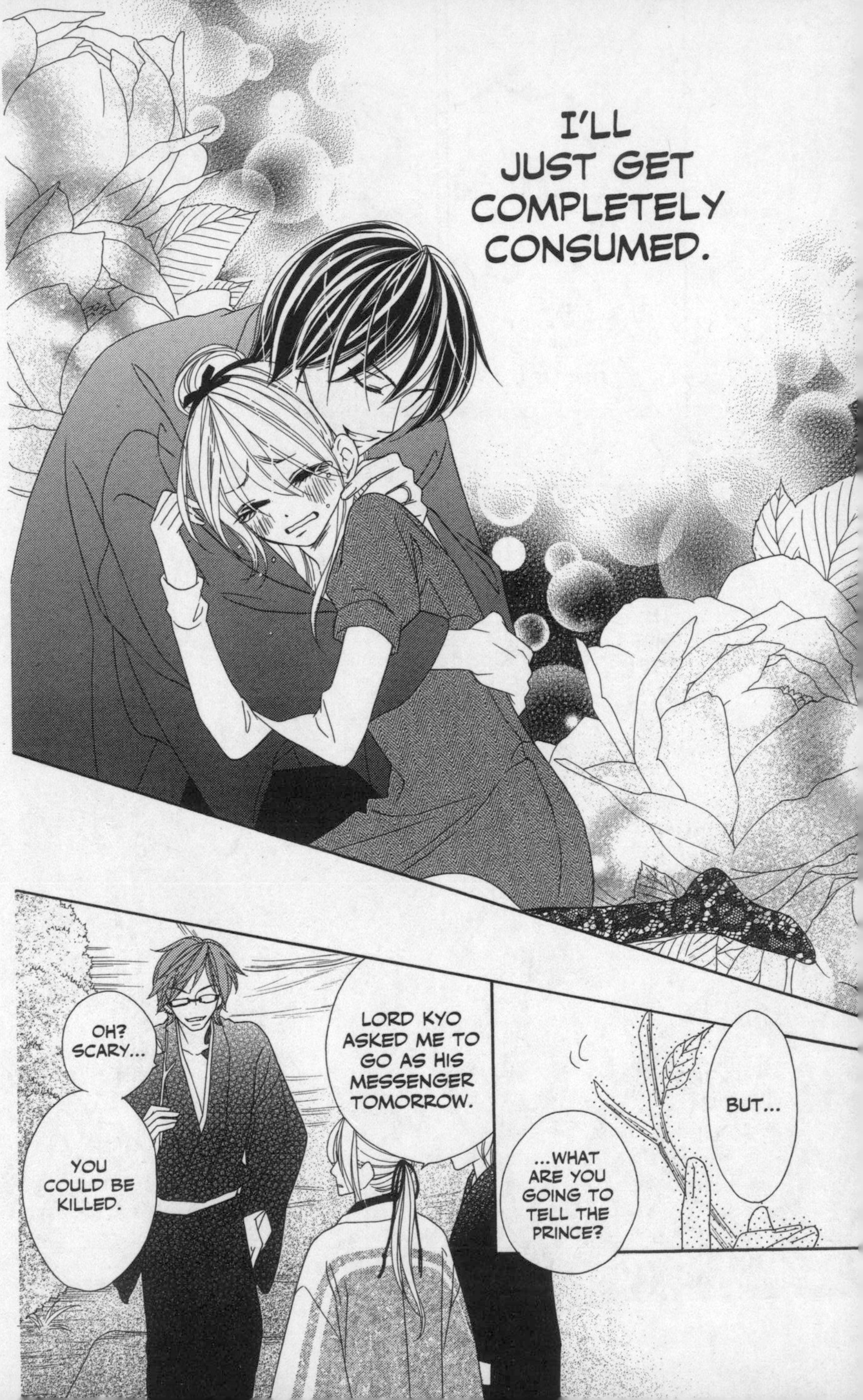
I'LL JUST GET COMPLETELY CONSUMED.
BUT...
...WHAT ARE YOU GOING TO TELL THE PRINCE?
LORD KYO ASKED ME TO GO AS HIS MESSENGER TOMORROW.
OH? SCARY...
YOU COULD BE KILLED.

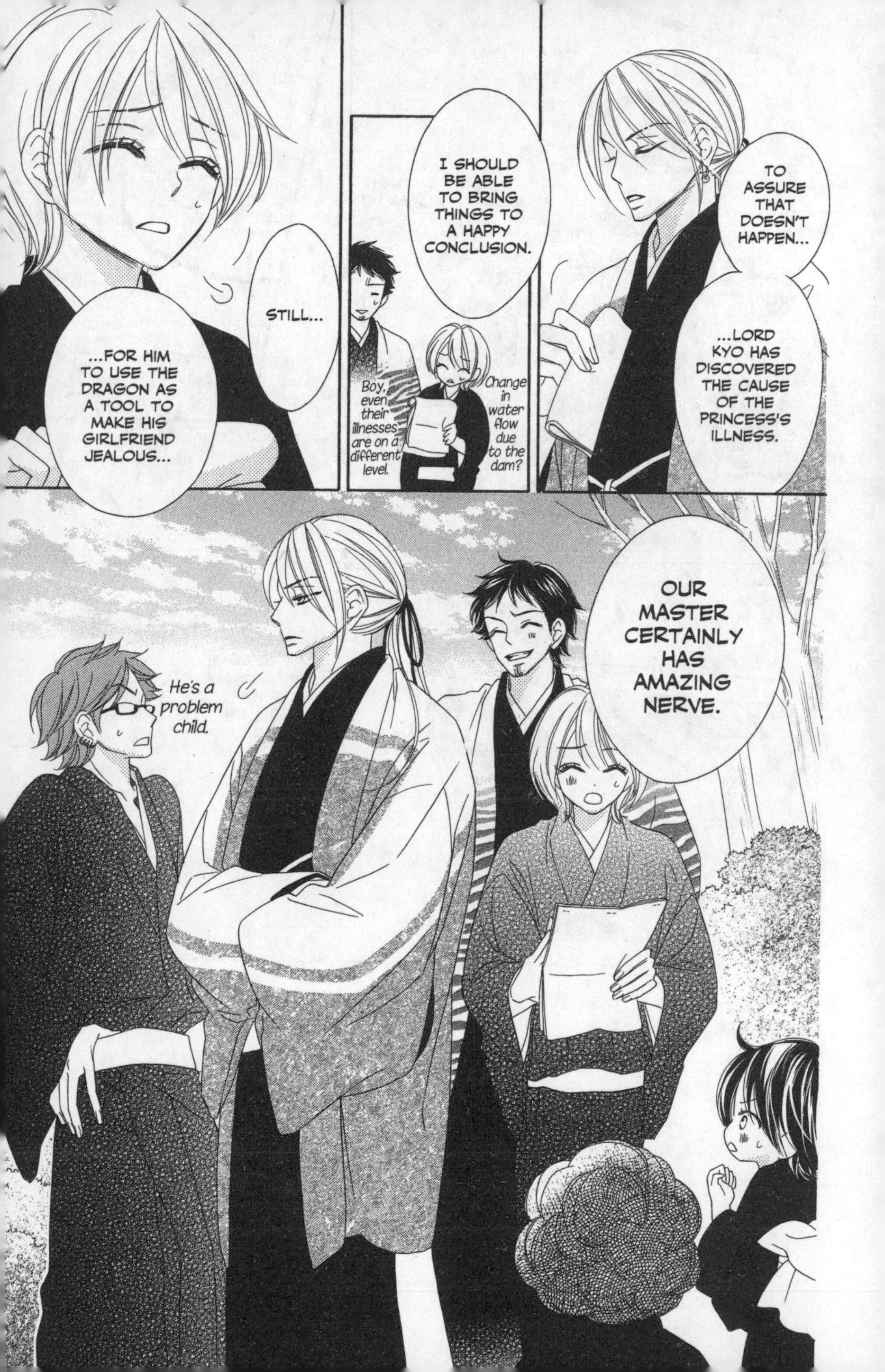
TO ASSURE THAT DOESN'T HAPPEN...
...LORD KYO HAS DISCOVERED THE CAUSE OF THE PRINCESS'S ILLNESS.
I SHOULD BE ABLE TO BRING THINGS TO A HAPPY CONCLUSION.
Change in water flow due to the dam?
Boy, even their illnesses are on a different level.
STILL...
...FOR HIM TO USE THE DRAGON AS A TOOL TO MAKE HIS GIRLFRIEND JEALOUS...
OUR MASTER CERTAINLY HAS AMAZING NERVE.
He's a problem child.

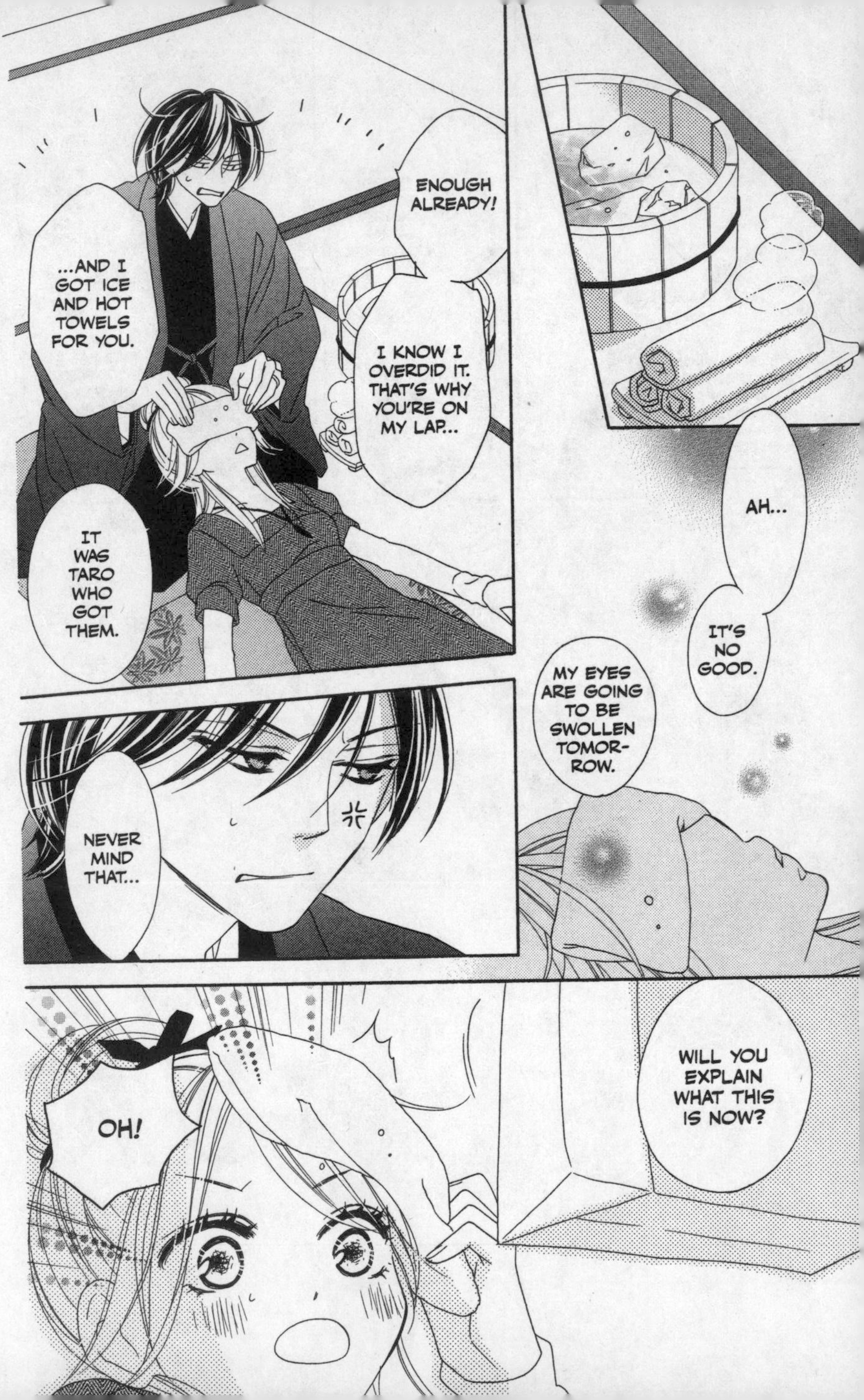
ENOUGH ALREADY!
I KNOW I OVERDID IT. THAT'S WHY YOU'RE ON MY LAP...
...AND I GOT ICE AND HOT TOWELS FOR YOU.
IT WAS TARO WHO GOT THEM.
AH...
IT'S NO GOOD.
MY EYES ARE GOING TO BE SWOLLEN TOMOR-ROW.
NEVER MIND THAT...
WILL YOU EXPLAIN WHAT THIS IS NOW?
OH!

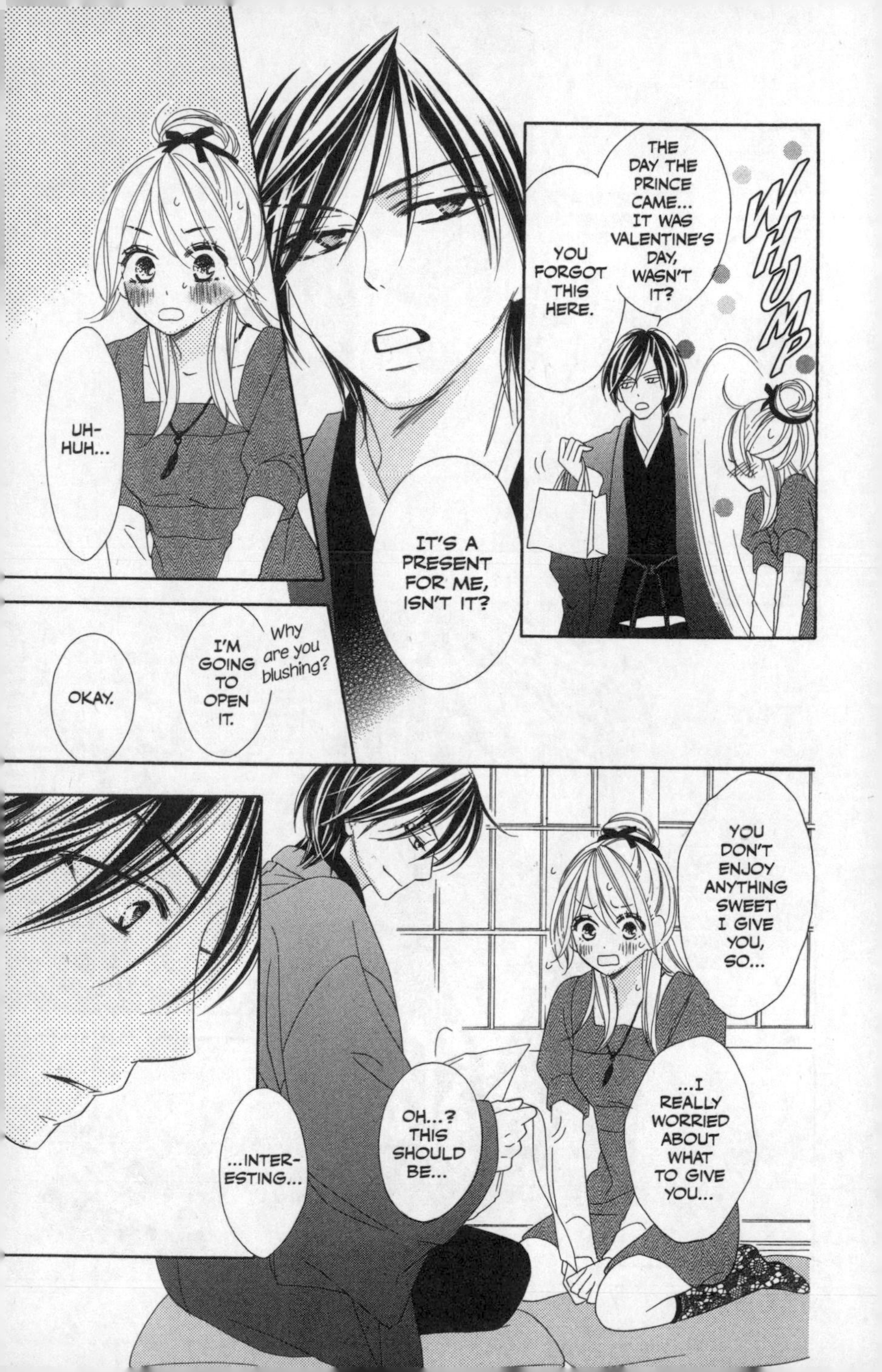
WHUMP
THE DAY THE PRINCE CAME... IT WAS VALENTINE'S DAY, WASN'T IT?
YOU FORGOT THIS HERE.
IT'S A PRESENT FOR ME, ISN'T IT?
UH-HUH...
Why are you blushing?
I'M GOING TO OPEN IT.
OKAY.
YOU DON'T ENJOY ANYTHING SWEET I GIVE YOU, SO...
...I REALLY WORRIED ABOUT WHAT TO GIVE YOU...
OH...? THIS SHOULD BE...
...INTER-ESTING...

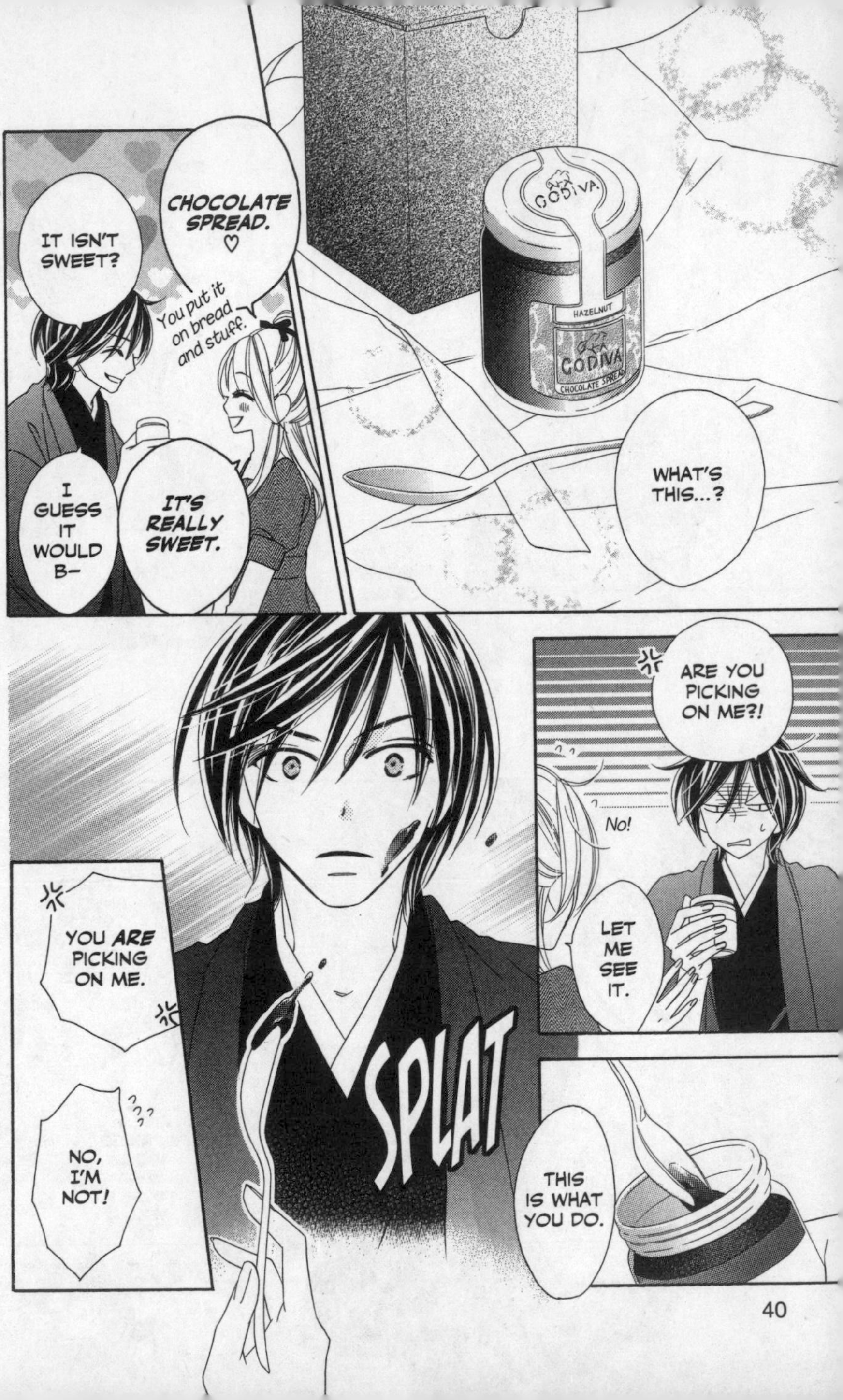
WHAT'S THIS...?
CHOCOLATE SPREAD. ♡
You put it on bread and stuff.
IT ISN'T SWEET?
IT'S REALLY SWEET.
I GUESS IT WOULD B–
GODIVA
HAZELNUT
GODIVA CHOCOLATE SPREAD
ARE YOU PICKING ON ME?!
No!
LET ME SEE IT.
THIS IS WHAT YOU DO.
SPLAT
YOU ARE PICKING ON ME.
NO, I'M NOT!

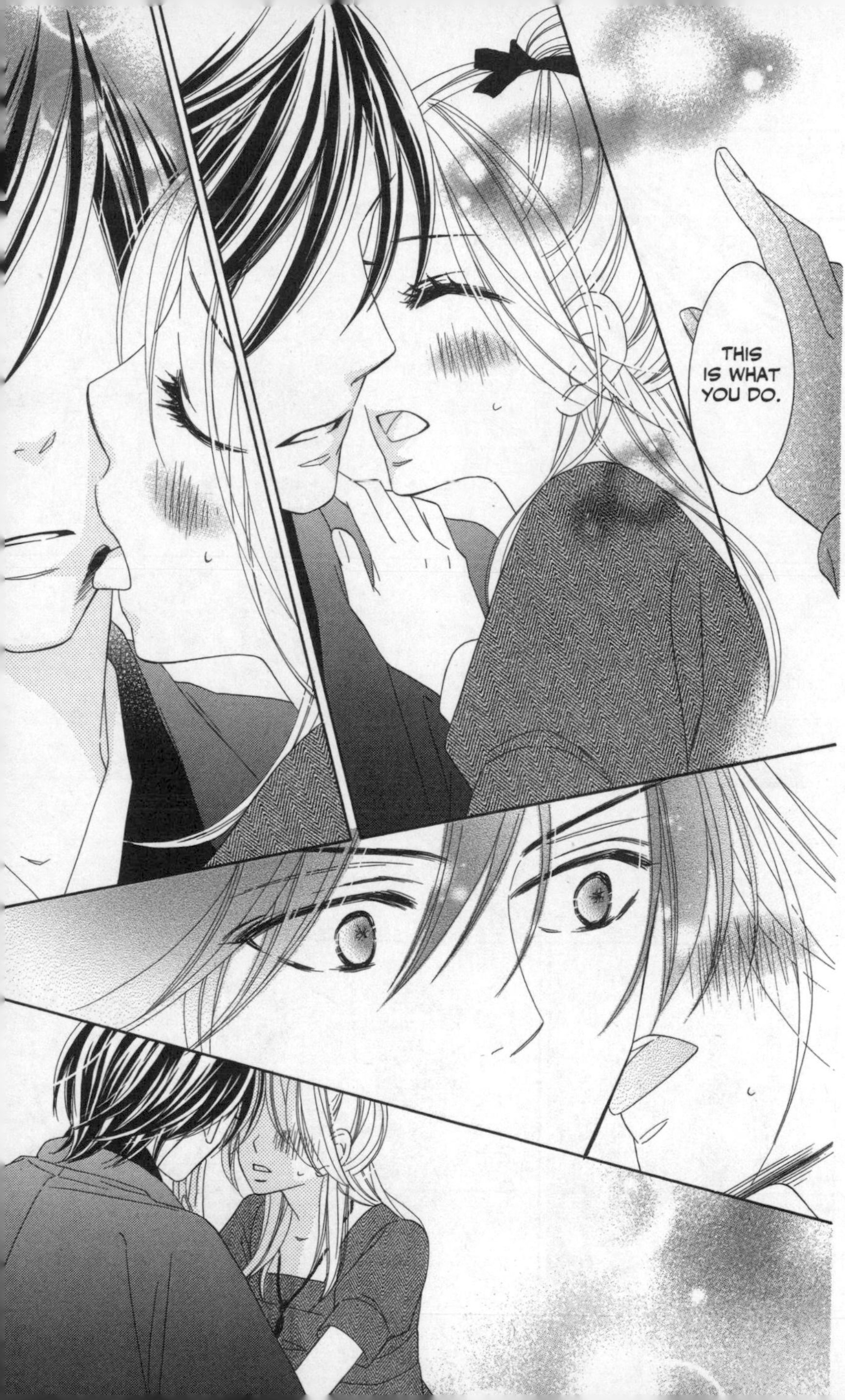
THIS IS WHAT YOU DO.

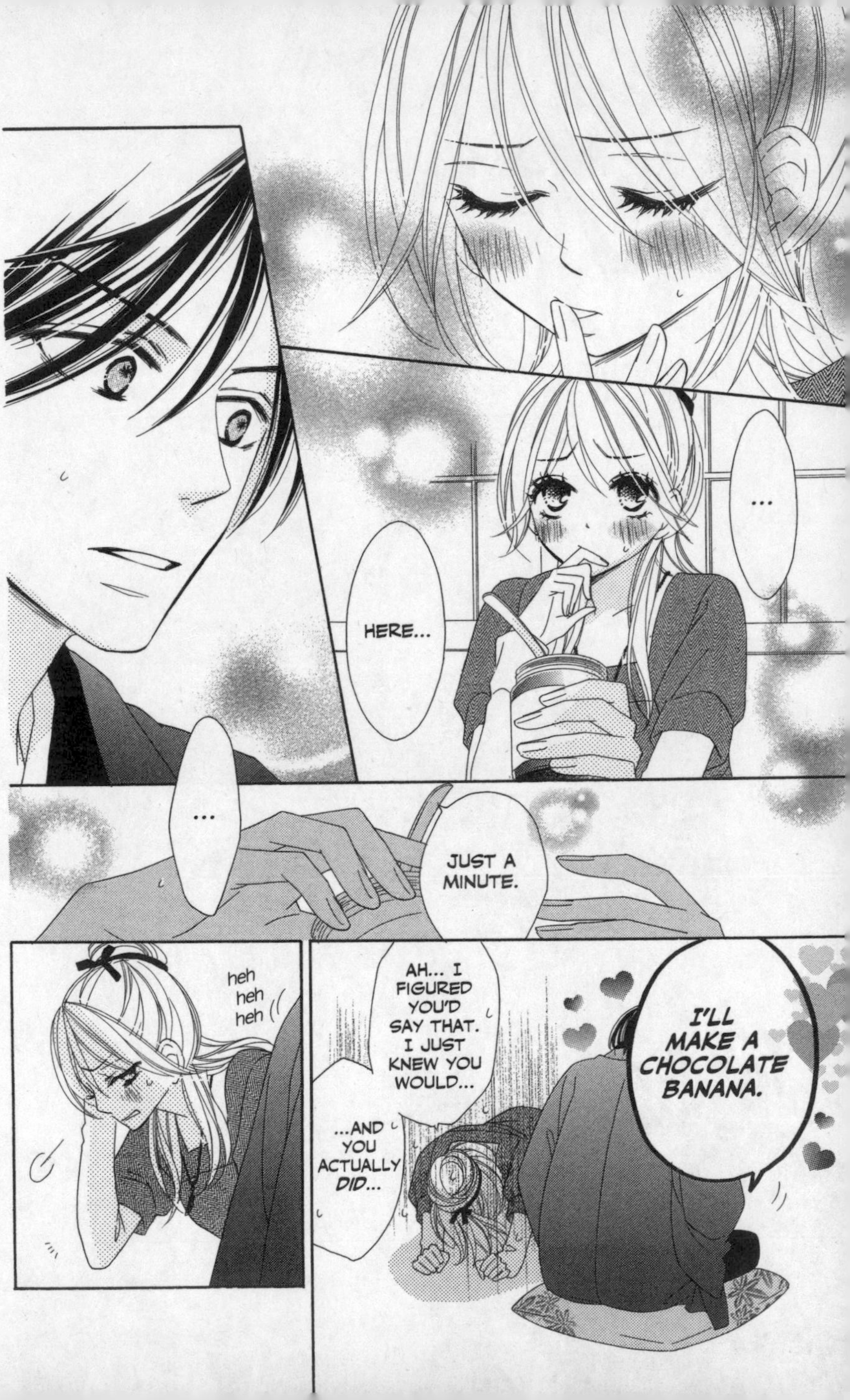
...
HERE...
JUST A MINUTE.
...
I'LL MAKE A CHOCOLATE BANANA.
AH... I FIGURED YOU'D SAY THAT. I JUST KNEW YOU WOULD...
...AND YOU ACTUALLY DID...
heh heh heh

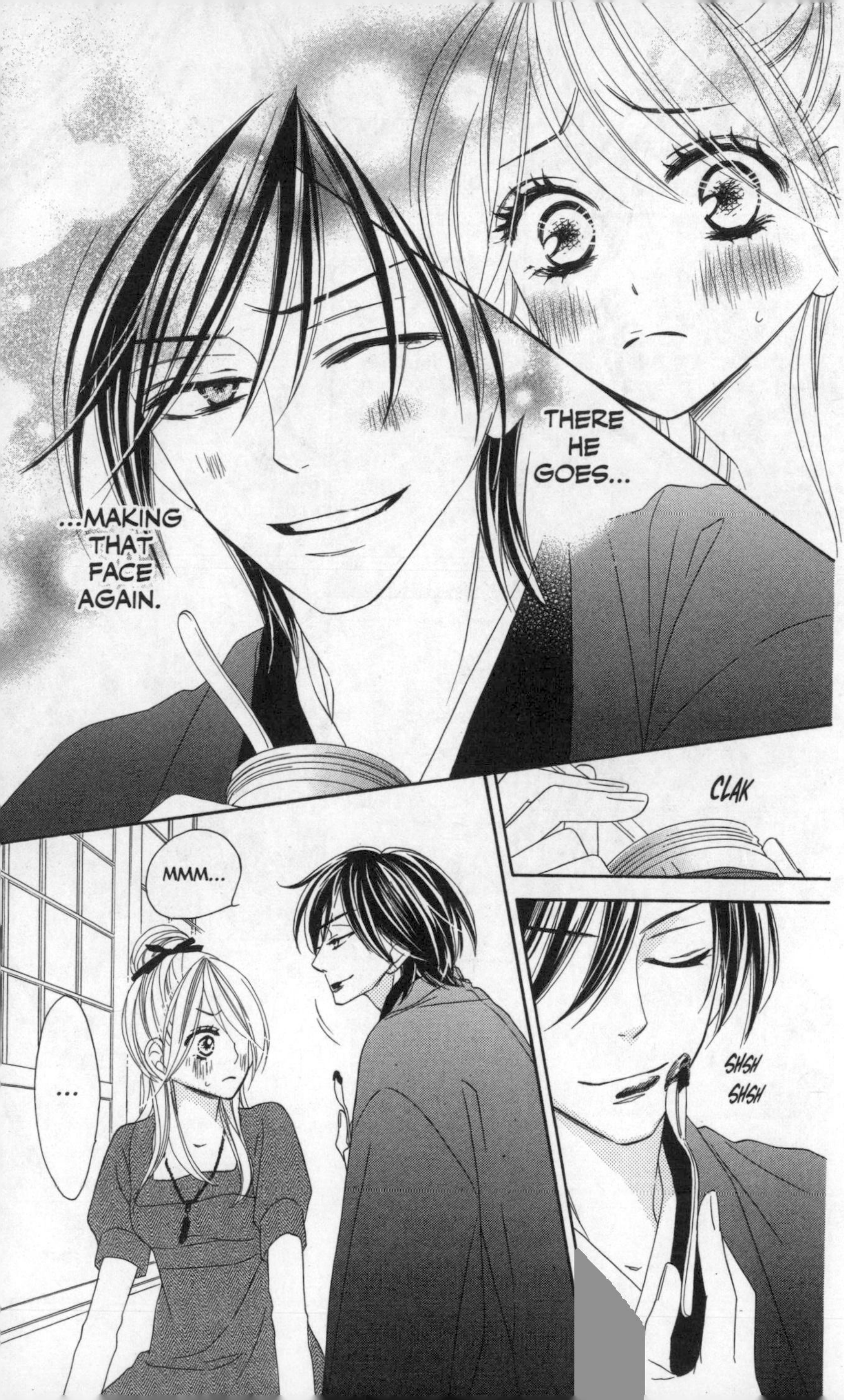
THERE HE GOES...
...MAKING THAT FACE AGAIN.
CLAK
SHSH SHSH
MMM...
...

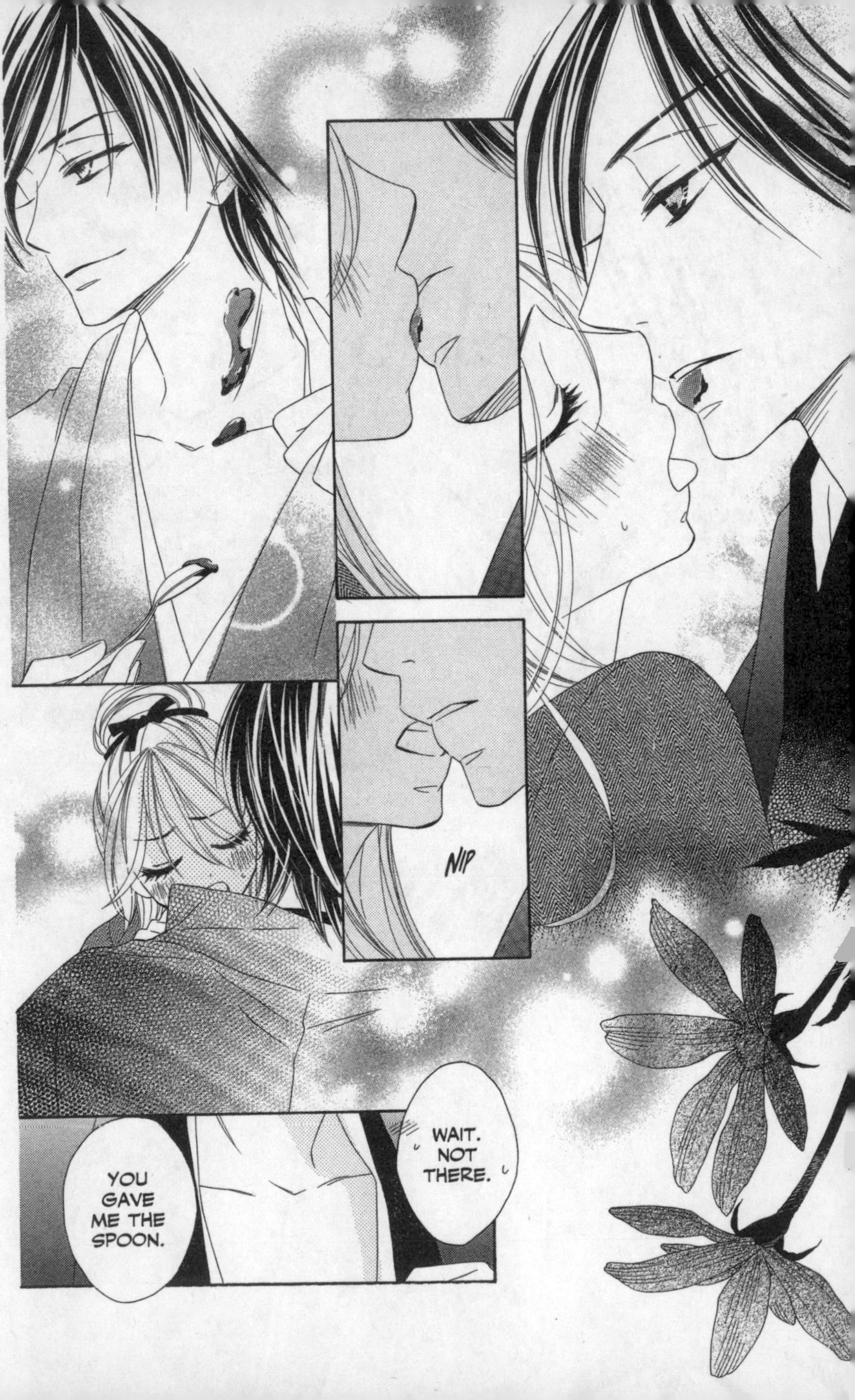
NIP
WAIT. NOT THERE.
YOU GAVE ME THE SPOON.

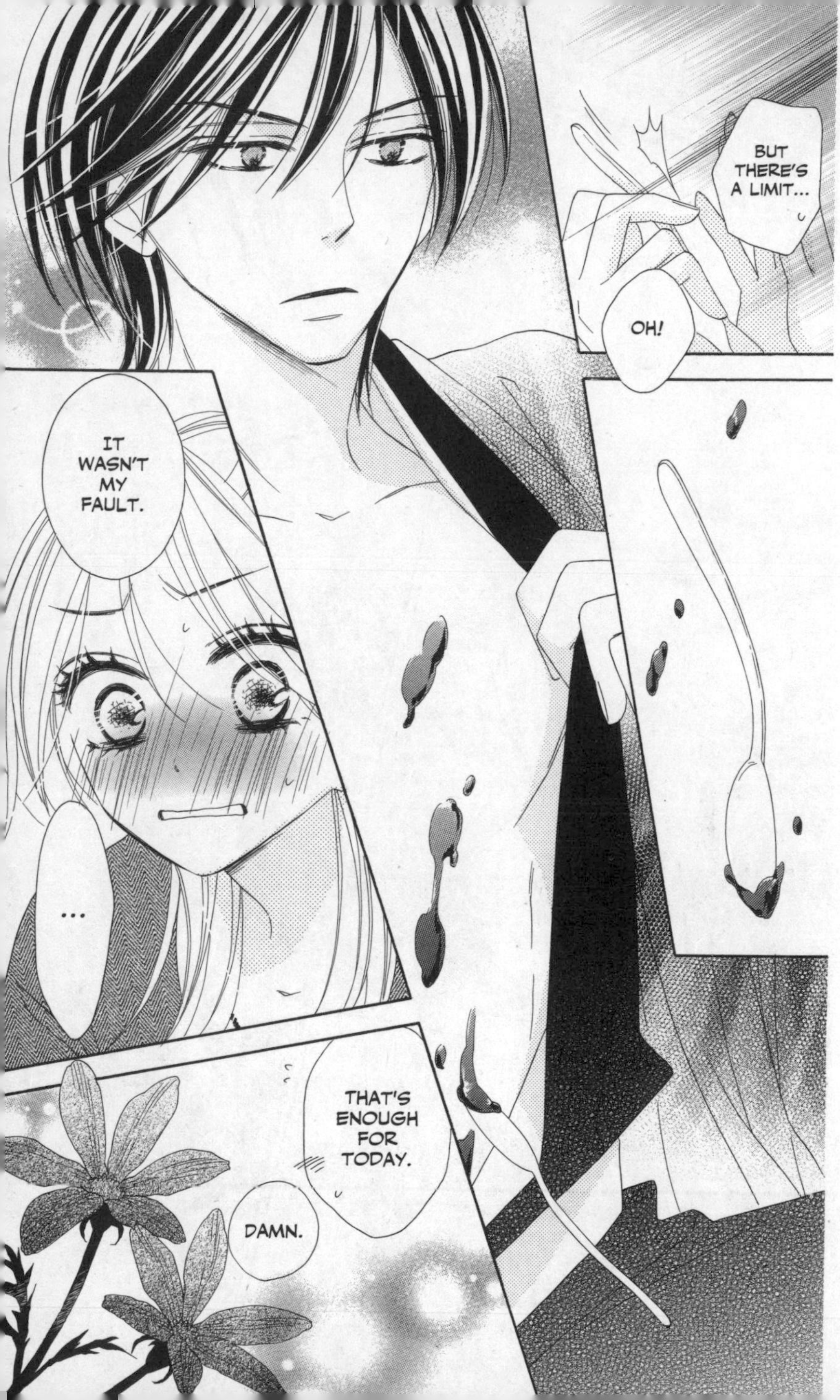
BUT THERE'S A LIMIT...
OH!
IT WASN'T MY FAULT.
...
THAT'S ENOUGH FOR TODAY.
DAMN.

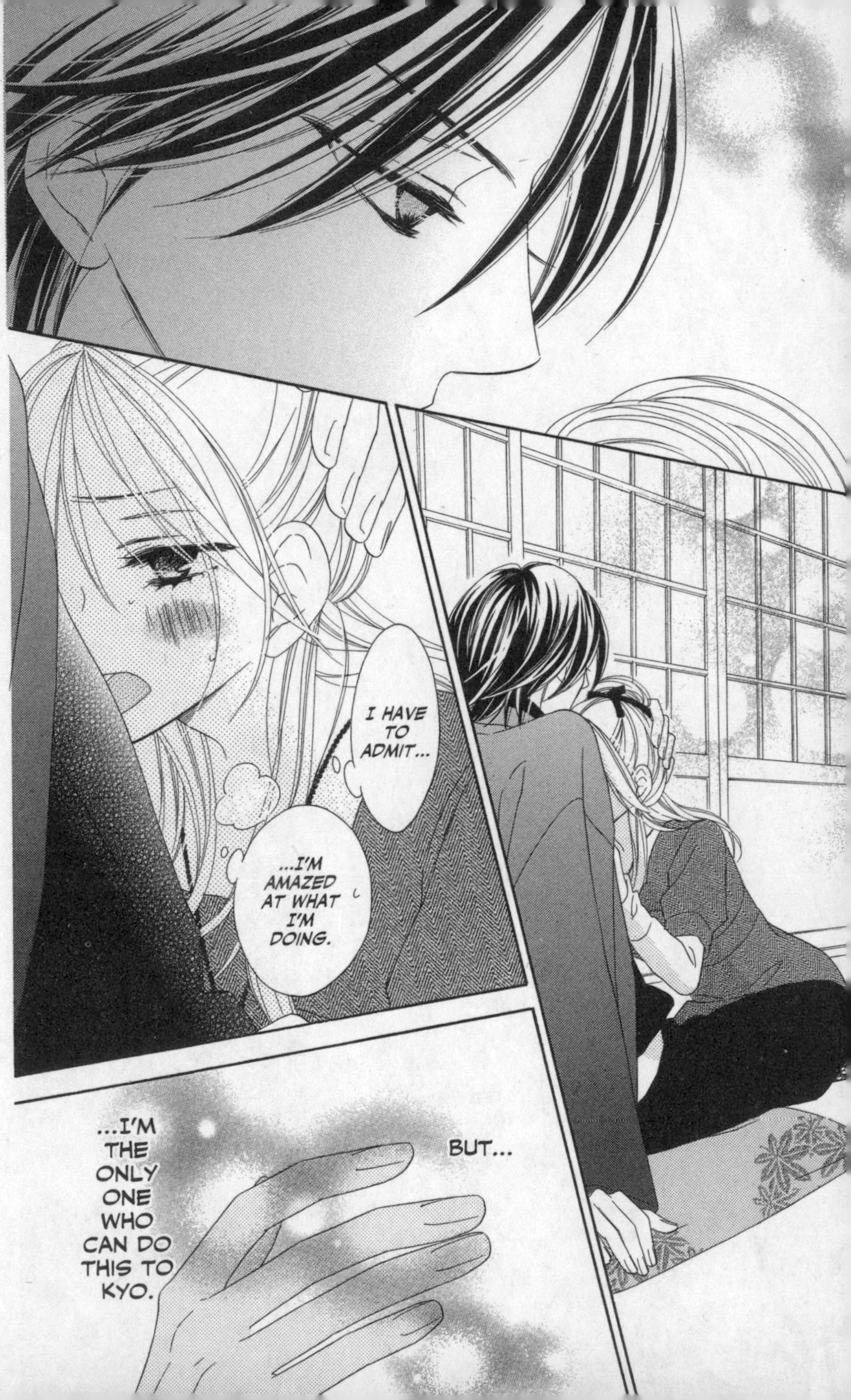
I HAVE TO ADMIT...
...I'M AMAZED AT WHAT I'M DOING.
BUT...
...I'M THE ONLY ONE WHO CAN DO THIS TO KYO.

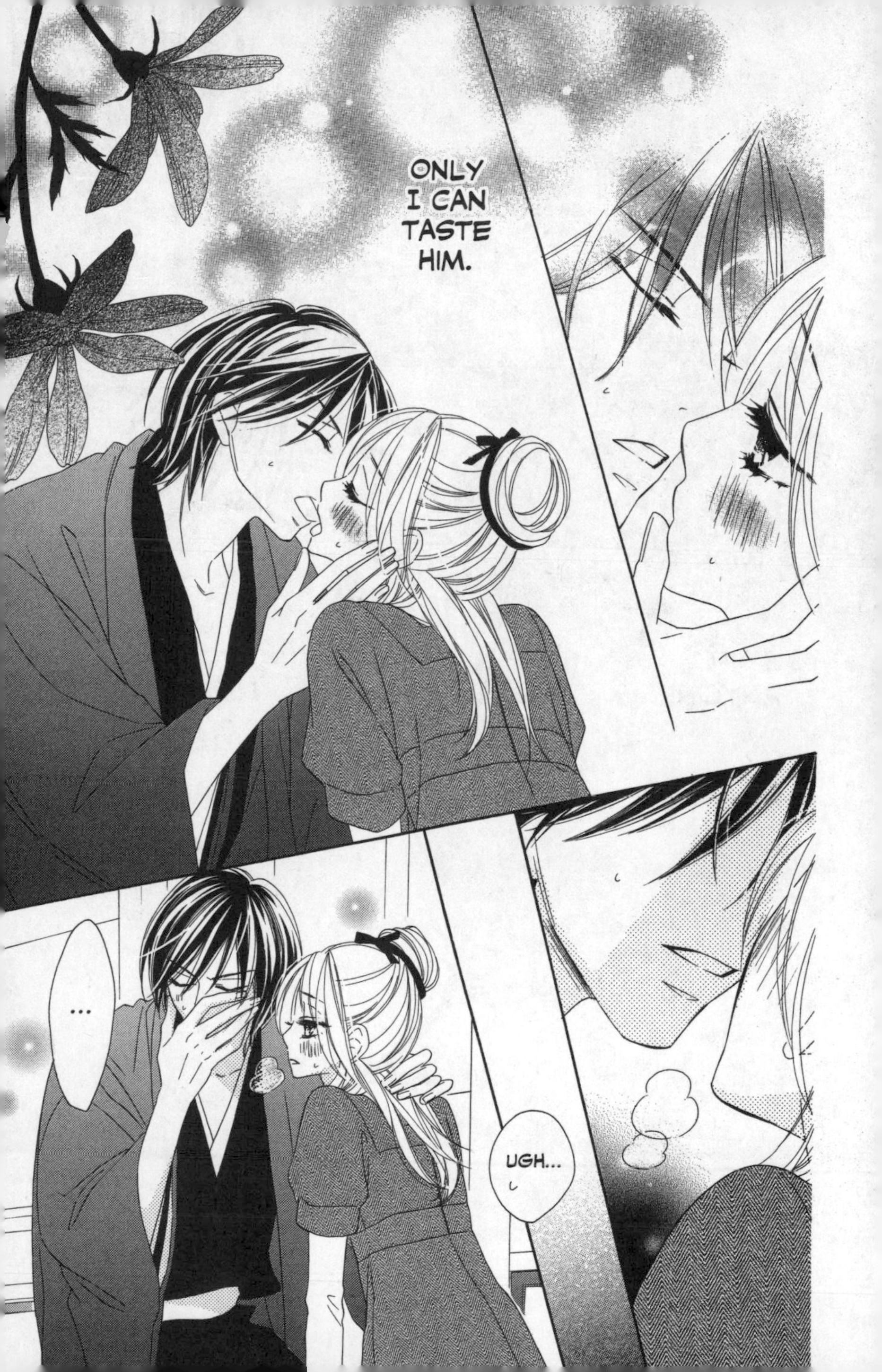
ONLY I CAN TASTE HIM.
UGH...
...

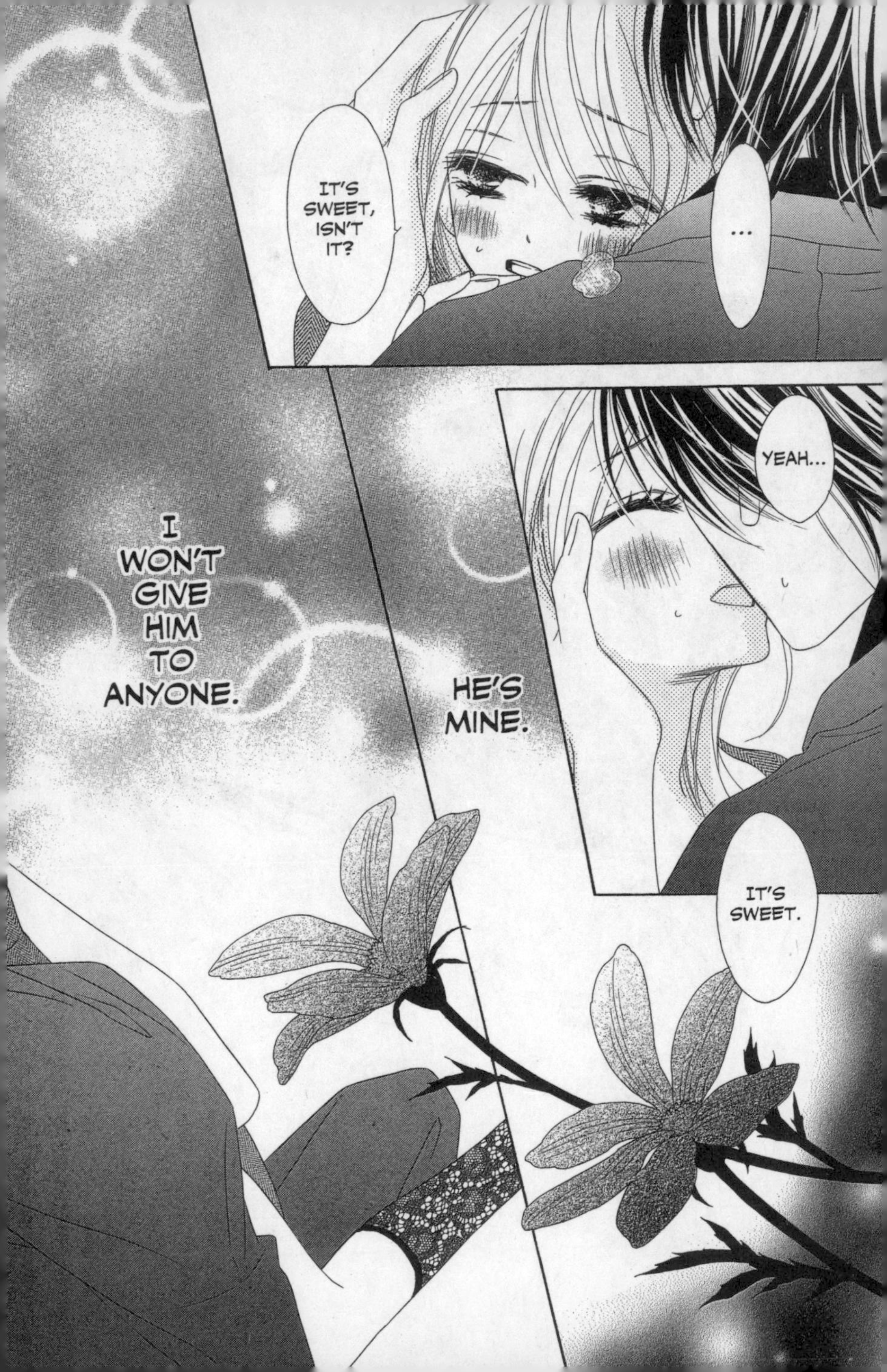
...
IT'S SWEET, ISN'T IT?
YEAH...
IT'S SWEET.
HE'S MINE.
I WON'T GIVE HIM TO ANYONE.

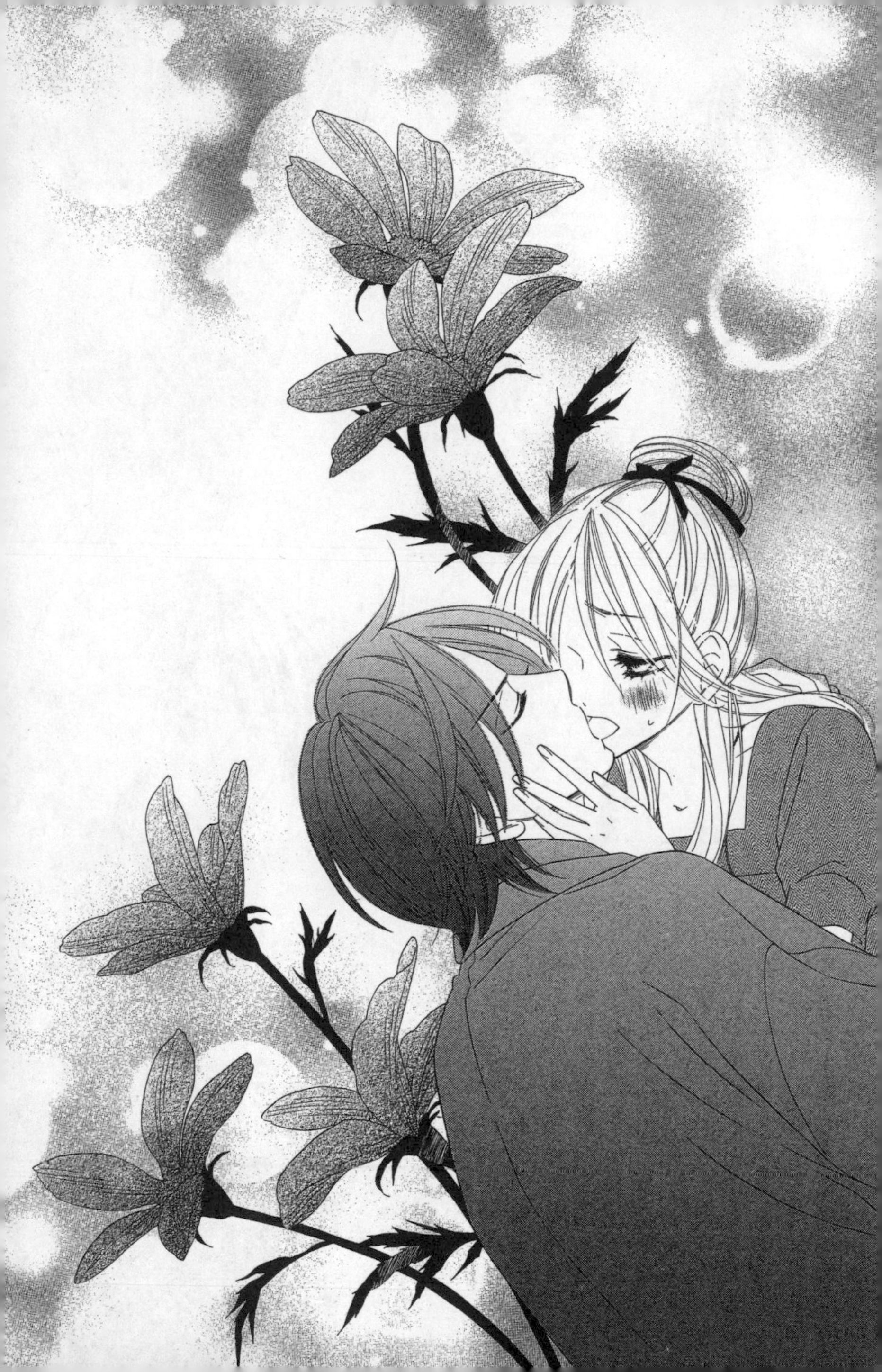

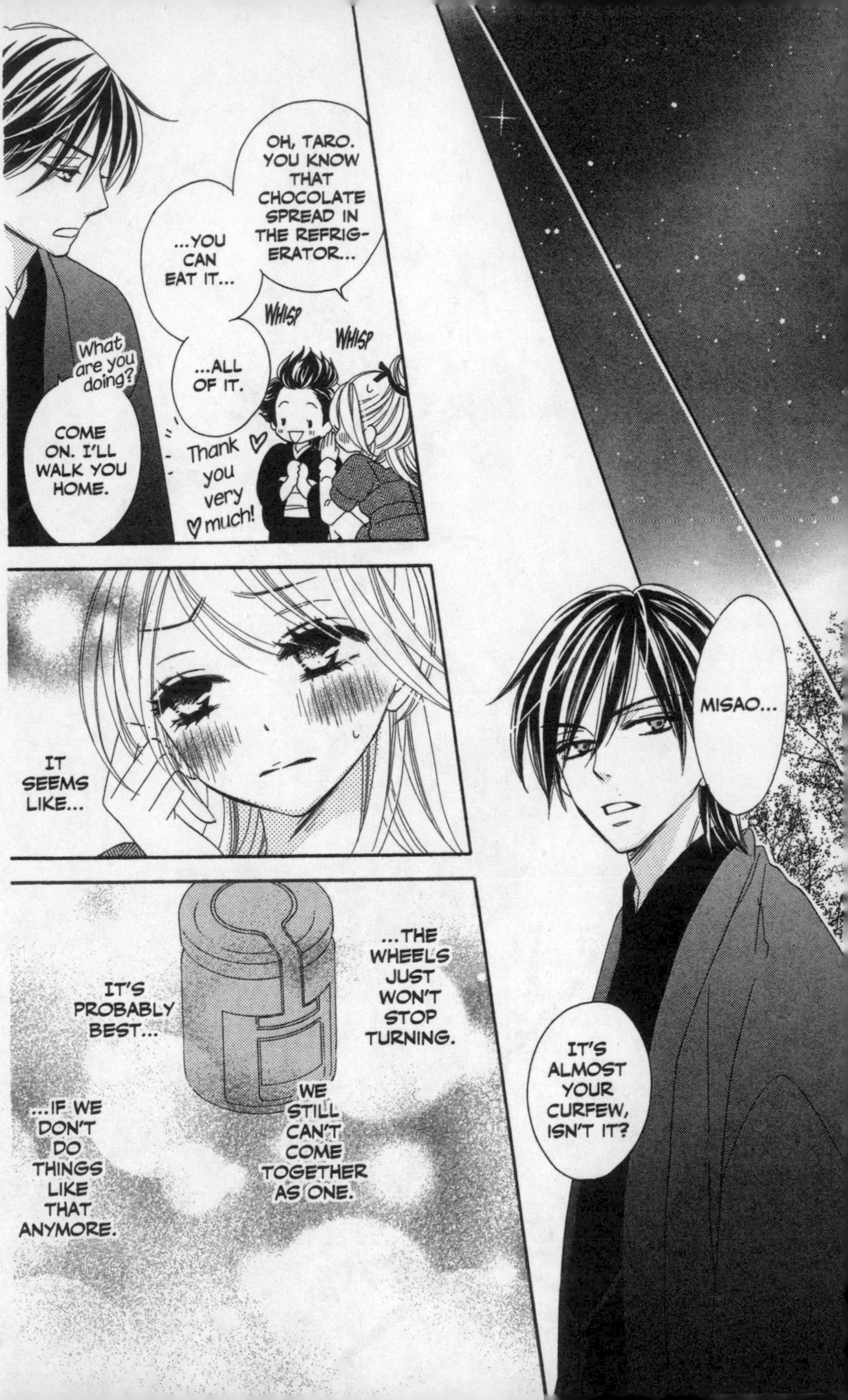
MISAO...
IT'S ALMOST YOUR CURFEW, ISN'T IT?
OH, TARO. YOU KNOW THAT CHOCOLATE SPREAD IN THE REFRIG-ERATOR...
...YOU CAN EAT IT...
WHISP
WHISP
...ALL OF IT.
Thank you very ♡ much!
What are you doing?
COME ON. I'LL WALK YOU HOME.
IT SEEMS LIKE...
...THE WHEELS JUST WON'T STOP TURNING.
IT'S PROBABLY BEST...
WE STILL CAN'T COME TOGETHER AS ONE.
...IF WE DON'T DO THINGS LIKE THAT ANYMORE.

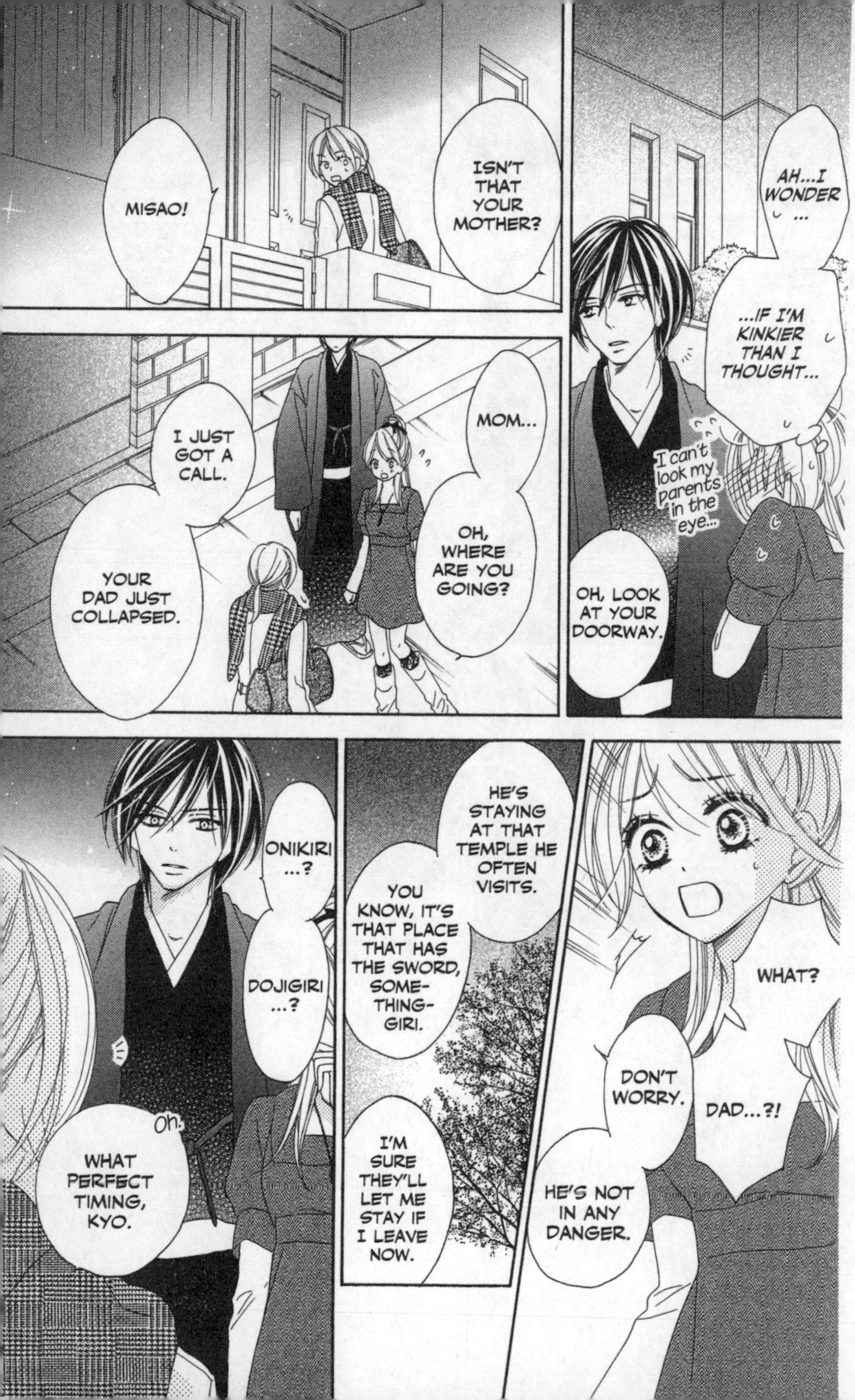
AH...I WONDER...
...IF I'M KINKIER THAN I THOUGHT...
I can't look my parents in the eye...
OH, LOOK AT YOUR DOORWAY.
ISN'T THAT YOUR MOTHER?
MISAO!
MOM...
OH, WHERE ARE YOU GOING?
I JUST GOT A CALL.
YOUR DAD JUST COLLAPSED.
WHAT?
DAD...?!
DON'T WORRY.
HE'S NOT IN ANY DANGER.
HE'S STAYING AT THAT TEMPLE HE OFTEN VISITS.
YOU KNOW, IT'S THAT PLACE THAT HAS THE SWORD, SOME-THING-GIRI.
I'M SURE THEY'LL LET ME STAY IF I LEAVE NOW.
ONIKIRI...?
DOJIGIRI...?
Oh.
WHAT PERFECT TIMING, KYO.

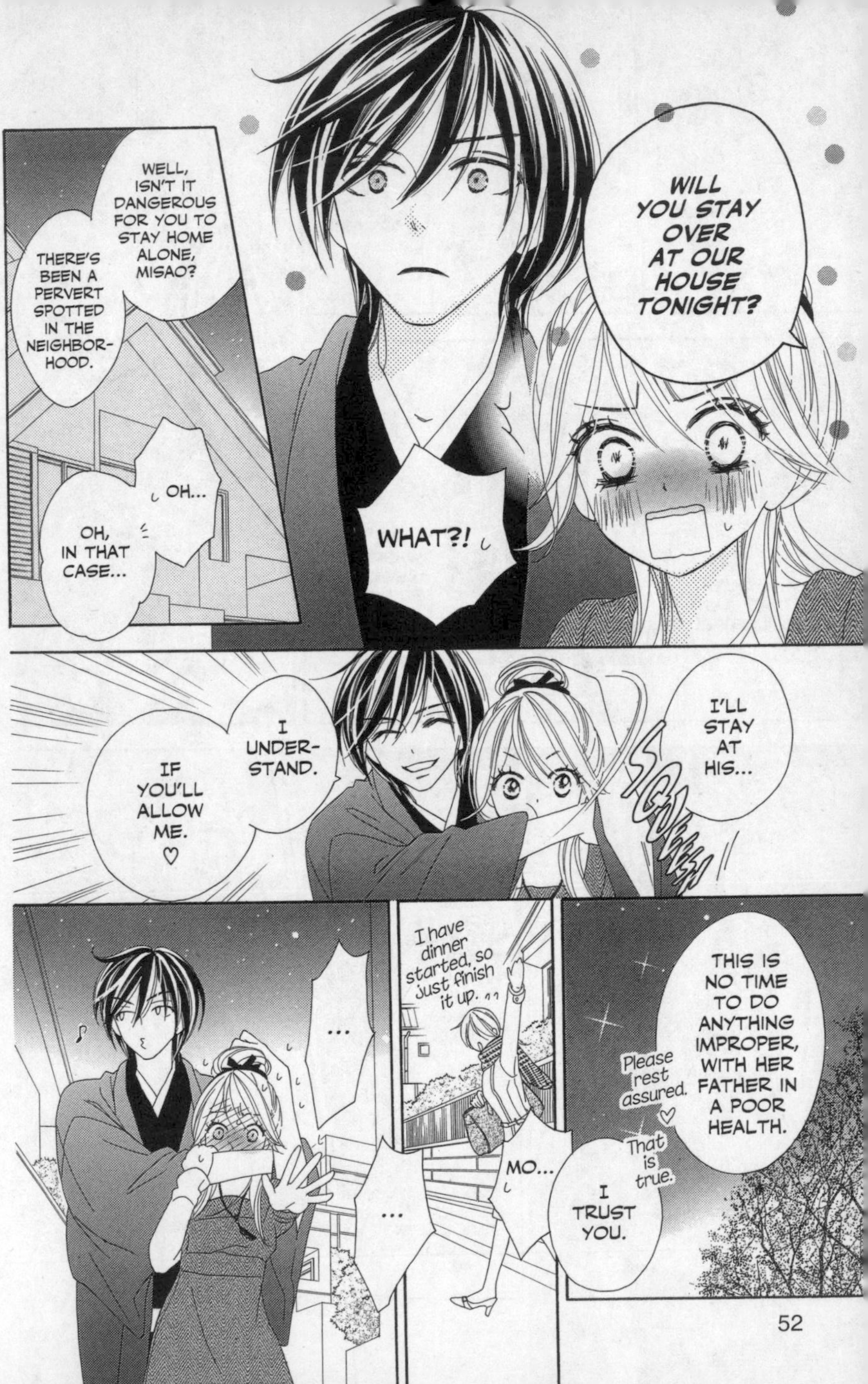
WILL YOU STAY OVER AT OUR HOUSE TONIGHT?
WHAT?!
WELL, ISN'T IT DANGEROUS FOR YOU TO STAY HOME ALONE, MISAO?
THERE'S BEEN A PERVERT SPOTTED IN THE NEIGHBOR-HOOD.
OH...
OH, IN THAT CASE...
I'LL STAY AT HIS...
I UNDER-STAND.
IF YOU'LL ALLOW ME. ♡
THIS IS NO TIME TO DO ANYTHING IMPROPER, WITH HER FATHER IN A POOR HEALTH.
Please rest assured. ♡
That is true.
I TRUST YOU.
I have dinner started, so just finish it up.
MO...
...
...

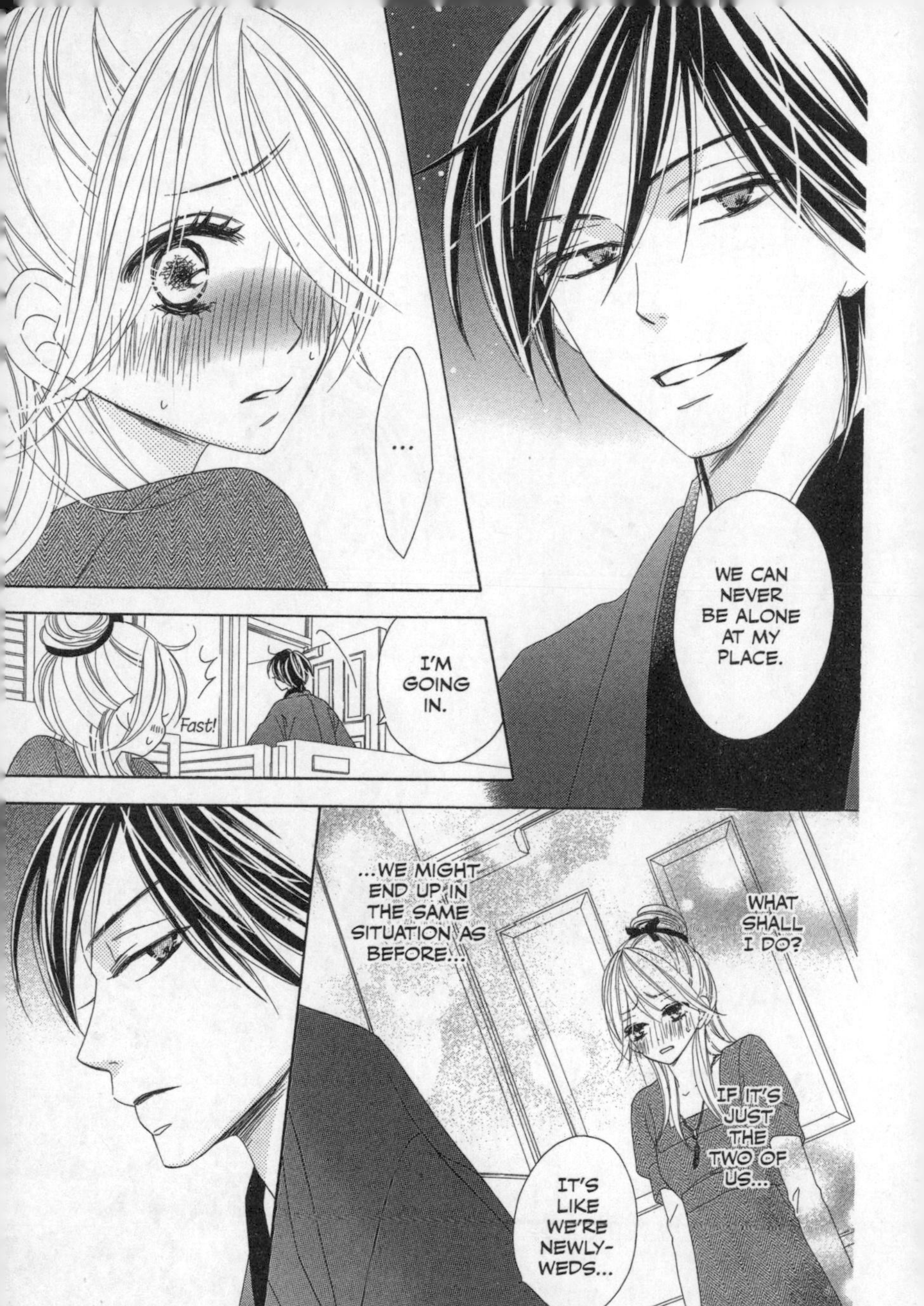
WE CAN NEVER BE ALONE AT MY PLACE.
...
I'M GOING IN.
Fast!
WHAT SHALL I DO?
IF IT'S JUST THE TWO OF US...
IT'S LIKE WE'RE NEWLY-WEDS...
...WE MIGHT END UP IN THE SAME SITUATION AS BEFORE...

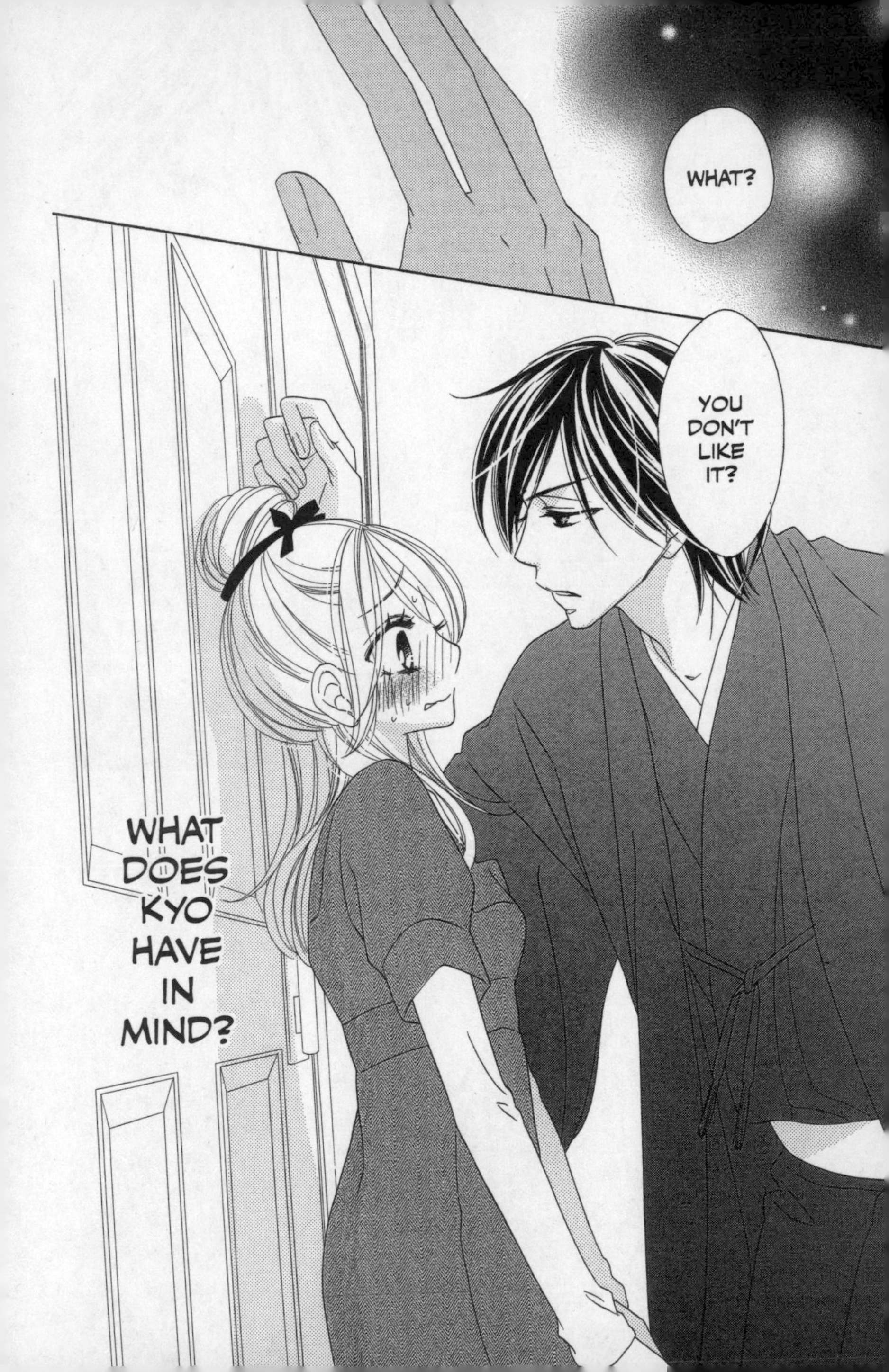
WHAT?
YOU DON'T LIKE IT?
WHAT DOES KYO HAVE IN MIND?

Illustration Request NumberTen

"Western"

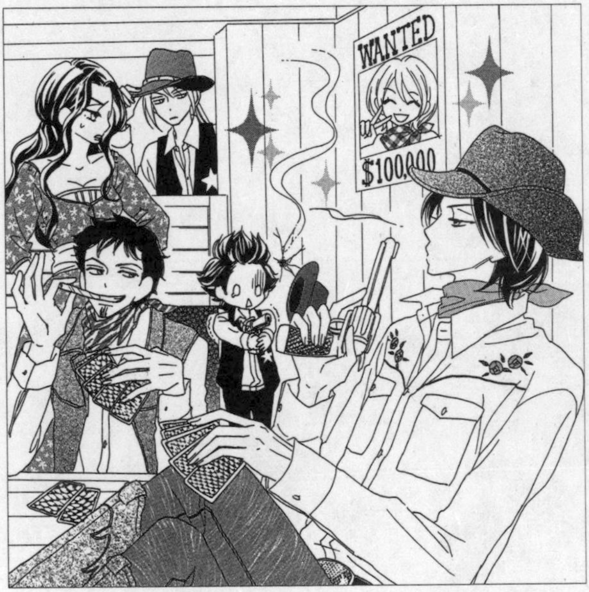
WANTED
$100,000

Taro and Sagami are supposed to be sheriffs.
I had so much fun with this that
I finished it in no time.

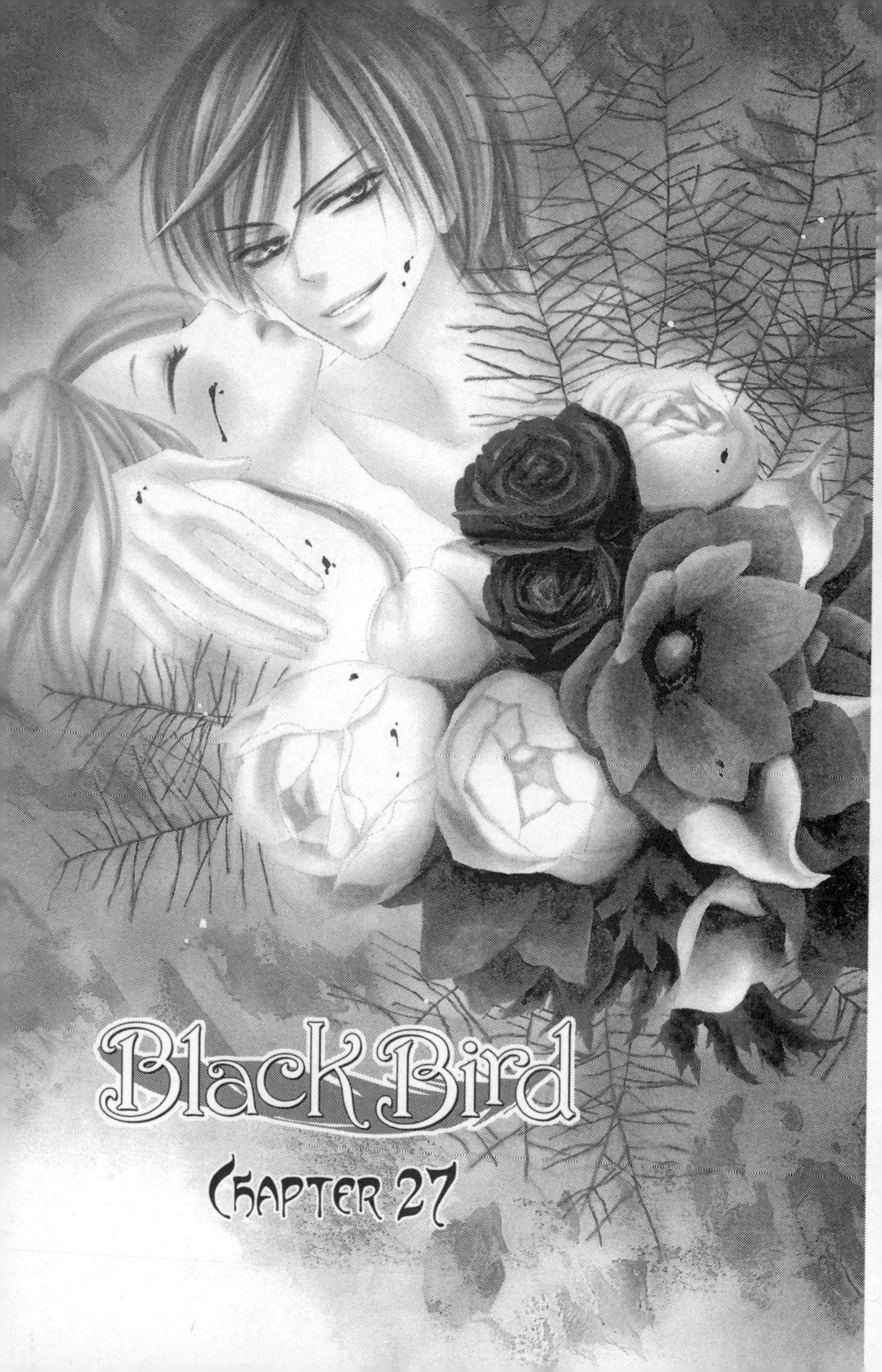
Black Bird
Chapter 27

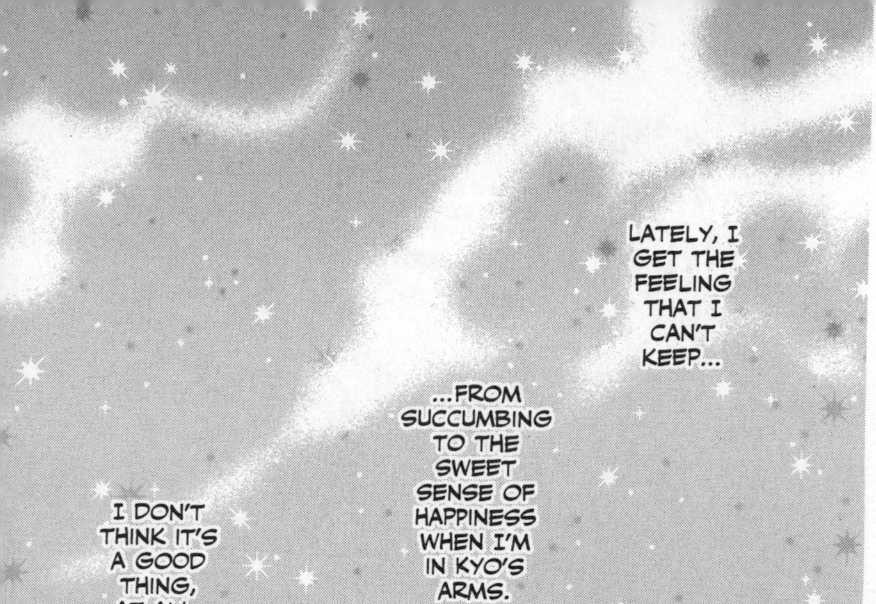
LATELY, I GET THE FEELING THAT I CAN'T KEEP...
...FROM SUCCUMBING TO THE SWEET SENSE OF HAPPINESS WHEN I'M IN KYO'S ARMS.
I DON'T THINK IT'S A GOOD THING, AT ALL.

• Character Introduction • Prince of Kengamine

Actually, I do have a model—or source—for this character. It's a character named "Young Prince of Hakuja ga Ike, Kengamine" who appears in name only in the play called *Yasha ga Ike* by Izumi Kyoka. It doesn't say that he is a dragon, but his lover is a descendant of a dragon, so I just changed things a little. I just love that play.♥ I'd been hoping to use that character one day...just a cameo. Forgive me, Mr. Izumi...

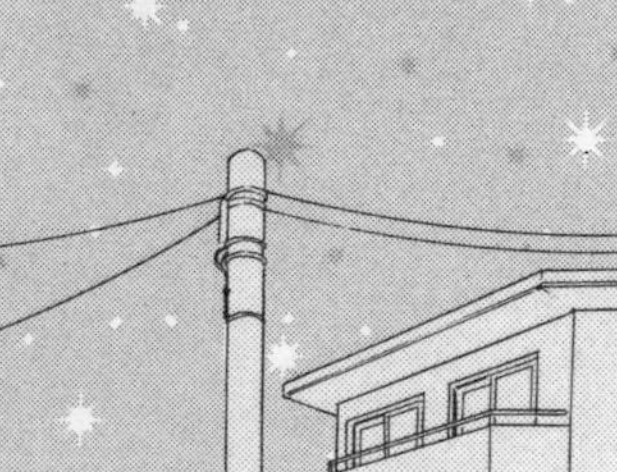
Cameo...

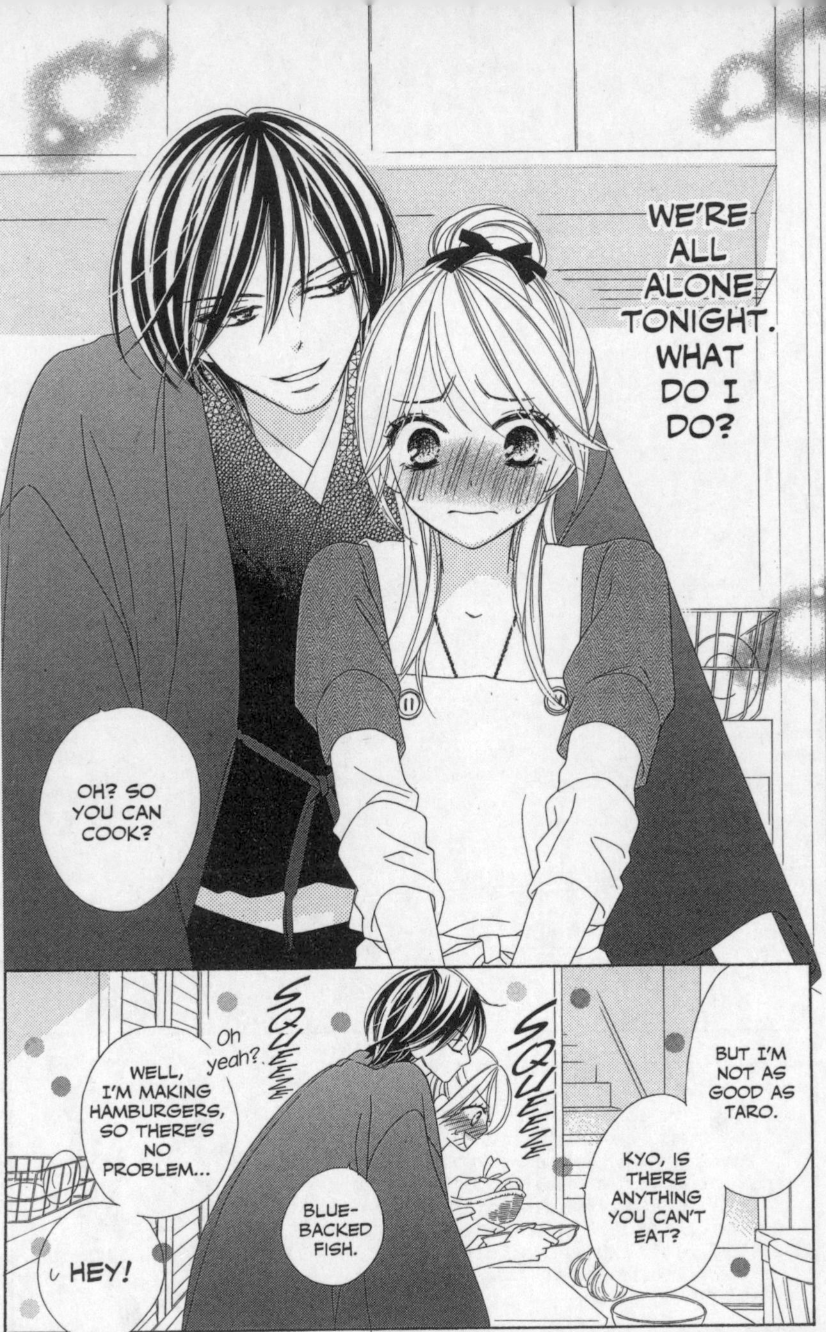

WE'RE ALL ALONE TONIGHT. WHAT DO I DO?
OH? SO YOU CAN COOK?
BUT I'M NOT AS GOOD AS TARO.
KYO, IS THERE ANYTHING YOU CAN'T EAT?
SQUEEEEZE
BLUE-BACKED FISH.
SQUEEEEZE
Oh yeah?
WELL, I'M MAKING HAMBURGERS, SO THERE'S NO PROBLEM...
HEY!

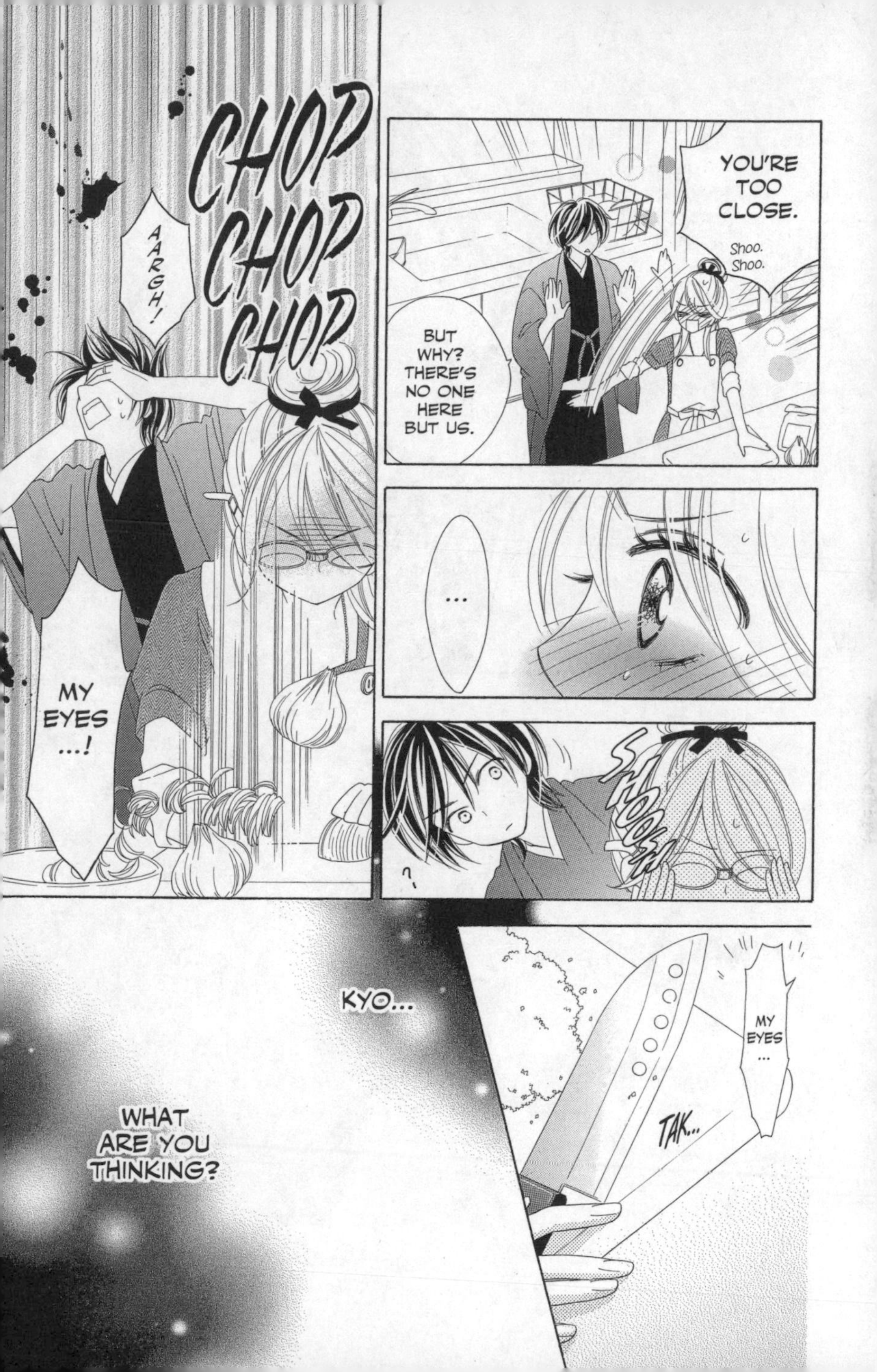
YOU'RE TOO CLOSE.
Shoo. Shoo.
BUT WHY? THERE'S NO ONE HERE BUT US.
...
SHOOM
?
CHOP CHOP CHOP
AARGH!
MY EYES ...!
MY EYES ...
TAK...
KYO...
WHAT ARE YOU THINKING?

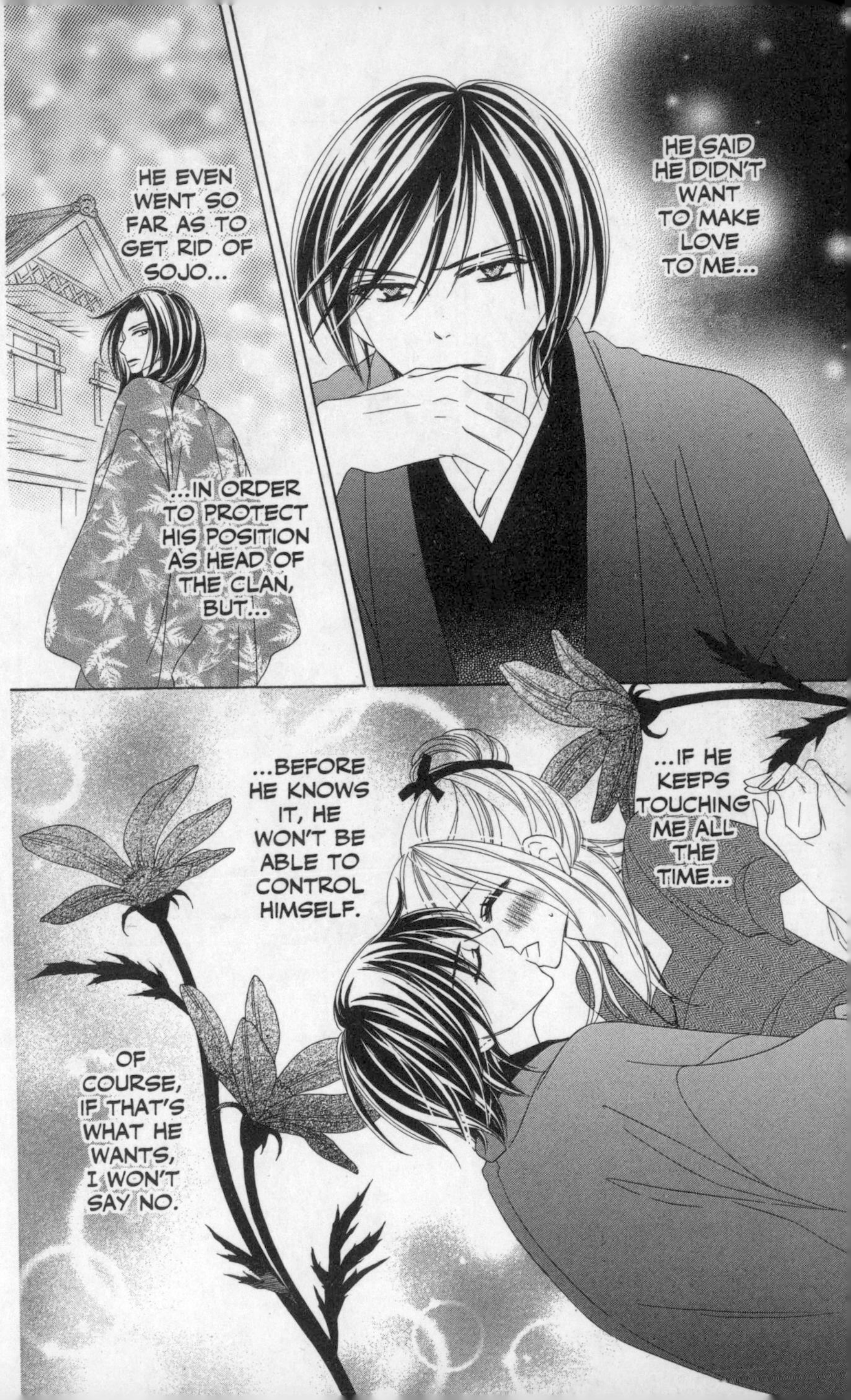
HE SAID HE DIDN'T WANT TO MAKE LOVE TO ME...
HE EVEN WENT SO FAR AS TO GET RID OF SOJO...
...IN ORDER TO PROTECT HIS POSITION AS HEAD OF THE CLAN, BUT...
...IF HE KEEPS TOUCHING ME ALL THE TIME...
...BEFORE HE KNOWS IT, HE WON'T BE ABLE TO CONTROL HIMSELF.
OF COURSE, IF THAT'S WHAT HE WANTS, I WON'T SAY NO.

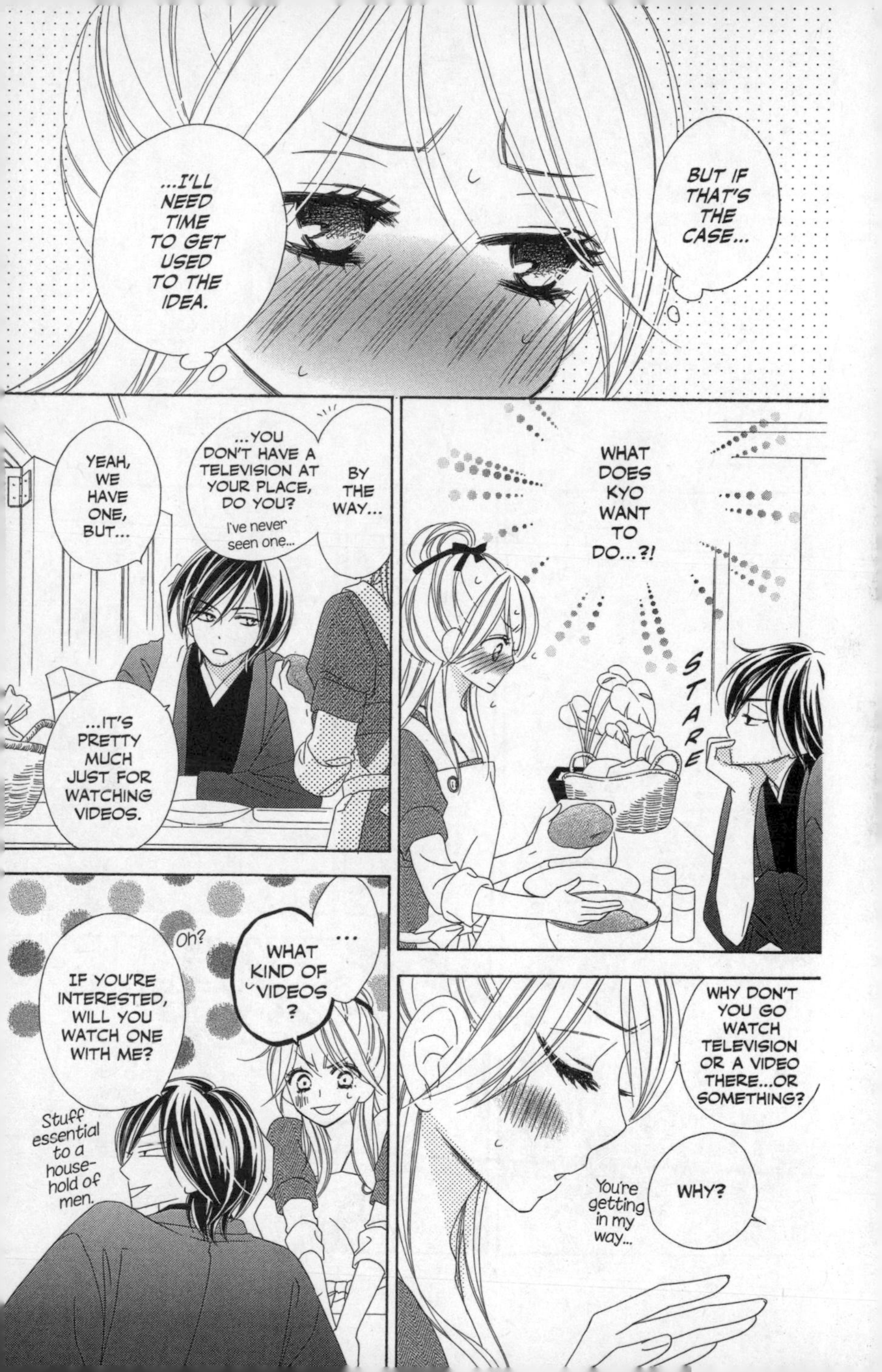
BUT IF THAT'S THE CASE...
...I'LL NEED TIME TO GET USED TO THE IDEA.
WHAT DOES KYO WANT TO DO...?!
STARE
WHY DON'T YOU GO WATCH TELEVISION OR A VIDEO THERE...OR SOMETHING?
WHY?
You're getting in my way...
BY THE WAY...
...YOU DON'T HAVE A TELEVISION AT YOUR PLACE, DO YOU?
I've never seen one...
YEAH, WE HAVE ONE, BUT...
...IT'S PRETTY MUCH JUST FOR WATCHING VIDEOS.
...
WHAT KIND OF VIDEOS?
Oh?
IF YOU'RE INTERESTED, WILL YOU WATCH ONE WITH ME?
Stuff essential to a house-hold of men.

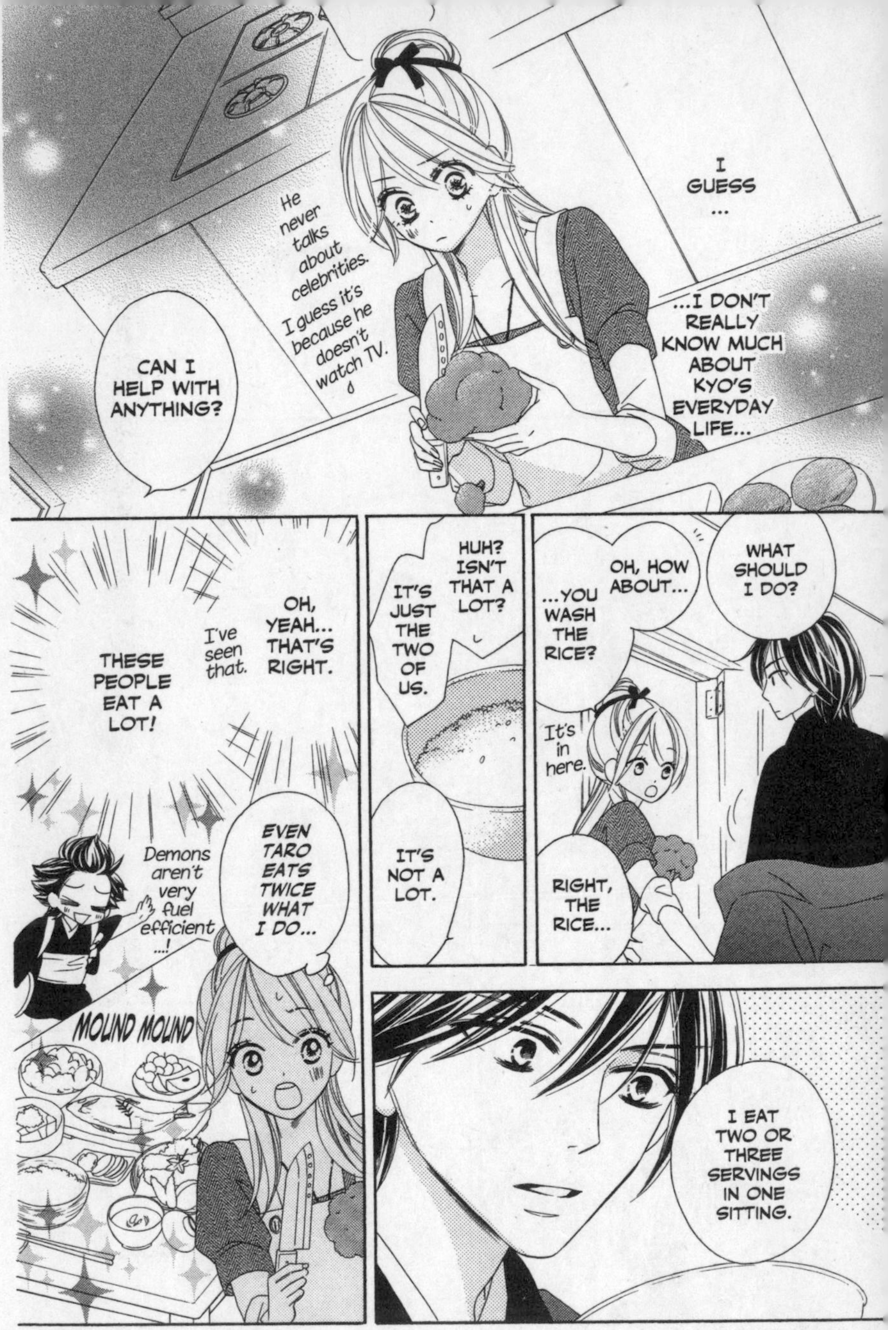
I GUESS...
...I DON'T REALLY KNOW MUCH ABOUT KYO'S EVERYDAY LIFE...
He never talks about celebrities. I guess it's because he doesn't watch TV.
CAN I HELP WITH ANYTHING?
WHAT SHOULD I DO?
OH, HOW ABOUT...
...YOU WASH THE RICE?
It's in here.
RIGHT, THE RICE...
HUH? ISN'T THAT A LOT?
IT'S JUST THE TWO OF US.
IT'S NOT A LOT.
I EAT TWO OR THREE SERVINGS IN ONE SITTING.
OH, YEAH... THAT'S RIGHT.
I've seen that.
THESE PEOPLE EAT A LOT!
EVEN TARO EATS TWICE WHAT I DO...
Demons aren't very fuel efficient...!
MOUND MOUND

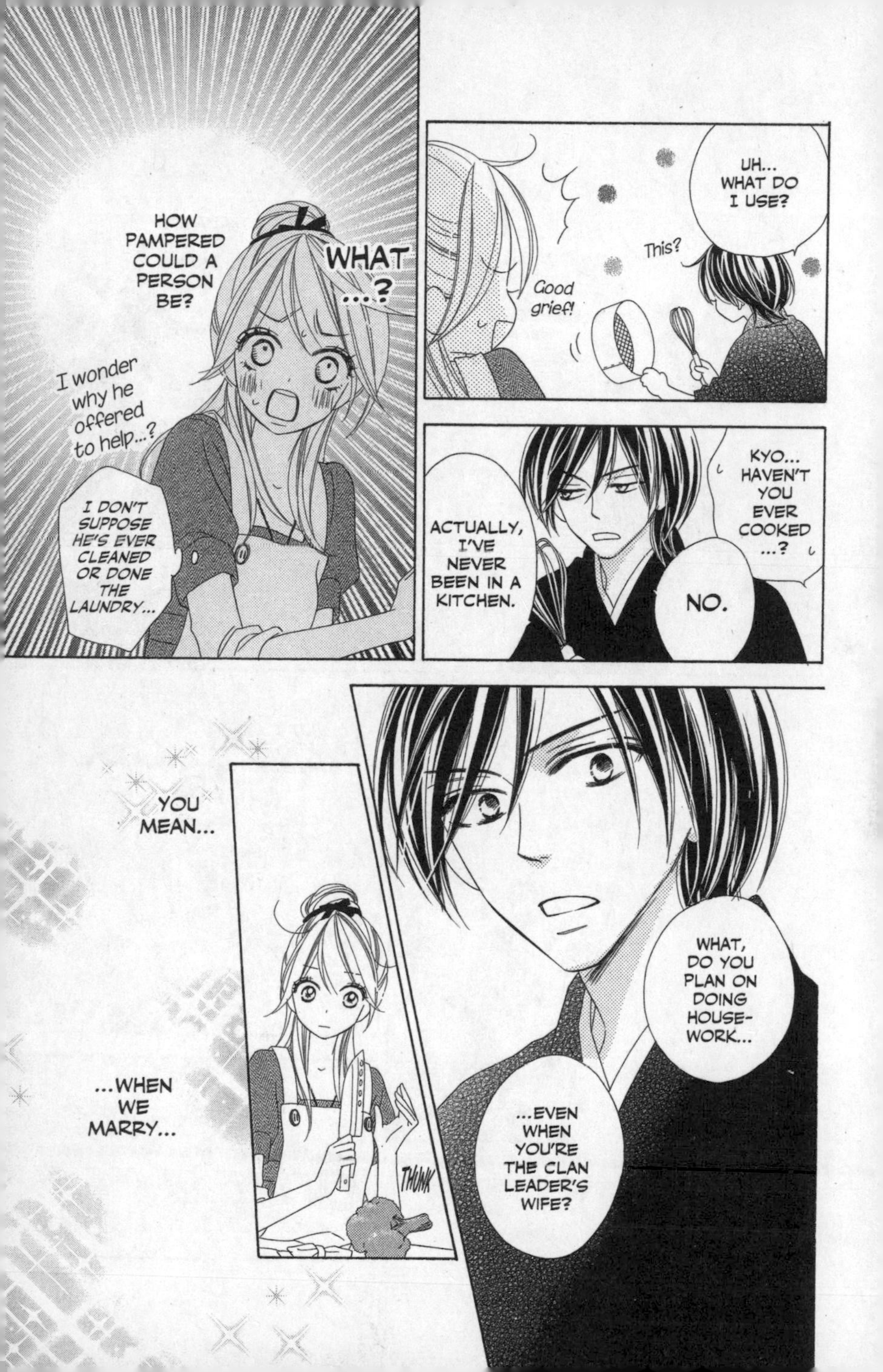
UH... WHAT DO I USE?
This?
Good grief!
KYO... HAVEN'T YOU EVER COOKED ...?
NO.
ACTUALLY, I'VE NEVER BEEN IN A KITCHEN.
WHAT ...?
HOW PAMPERED COULD A PERSON BE?
I wonder why he offered to help...?
I DON'T SUPPOSE HE'S EVER CLEANED OR DONE THE LAUNDRY...
WHAT, DO YOU PLAN ON DOING HOUSE-WORK...
...EVEN WHEN YOU'RE THE CLAN LEADER'S WIFE?
THUNK
YOU MEAN...
...WHEN WE MARRY...

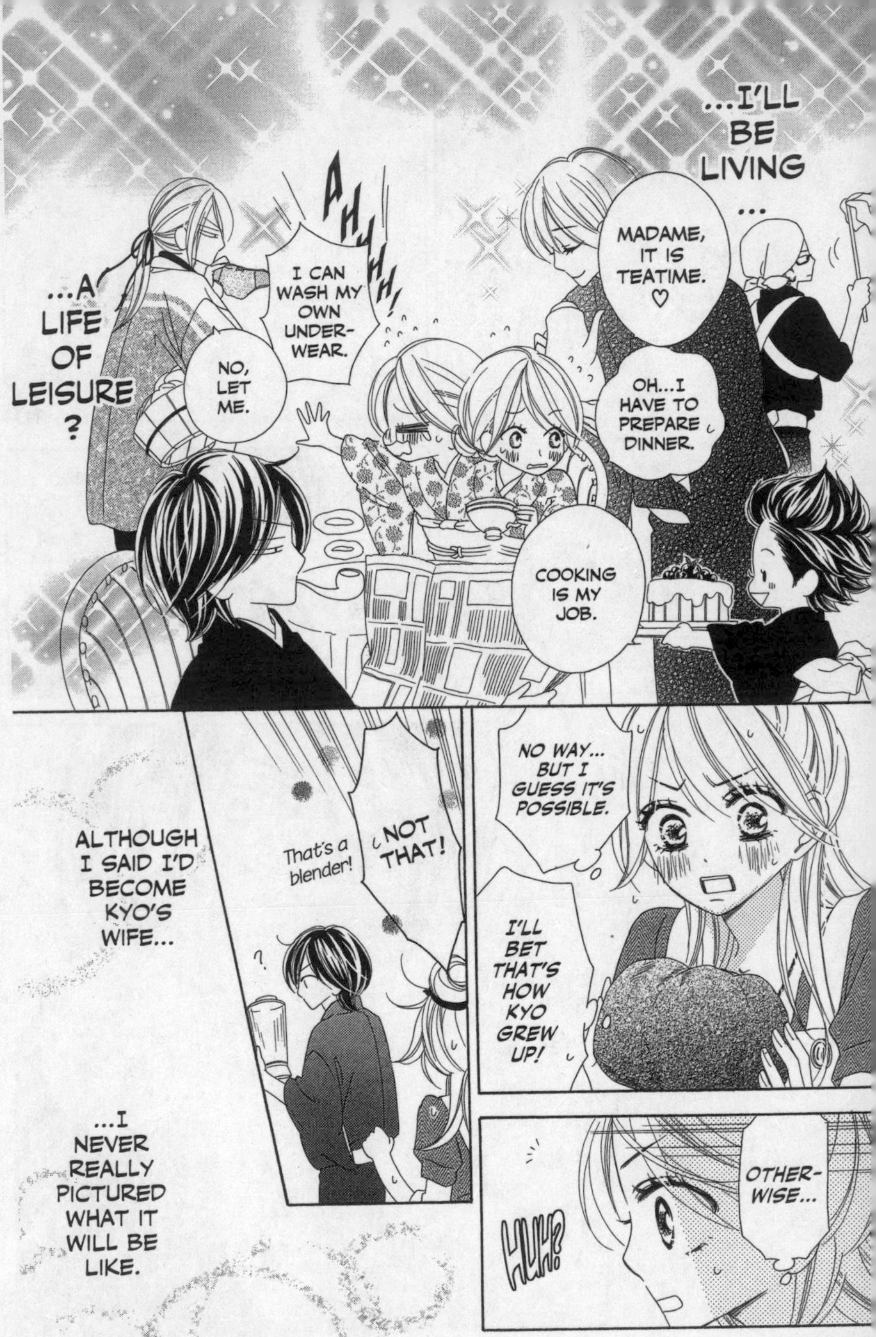
...I'LL BE LIVING...
MADAME, IT IS TEATIME. ♡
OH...I HAVE TO PREPARE DINNER.
COOKING IS MY JOB.
I CAN WASH MY OWN UNDER-WEAR.
AHHHH!
NO, LET ME.
...A LIFE OF LEISURE?
NO WAY... BUT I GUESS IT'S POSSIBLE.
I'LL BET THAT'S HOW KYO GREW UP!
OTHER-WISE...
HUH?
NOT THAT!
That's a blender!
ALTHOUGH I SAID I'D BECOME KYO'S WIFE...
...I NEVER REALLY PICTURED WHAT IT WILL BE LIKE.

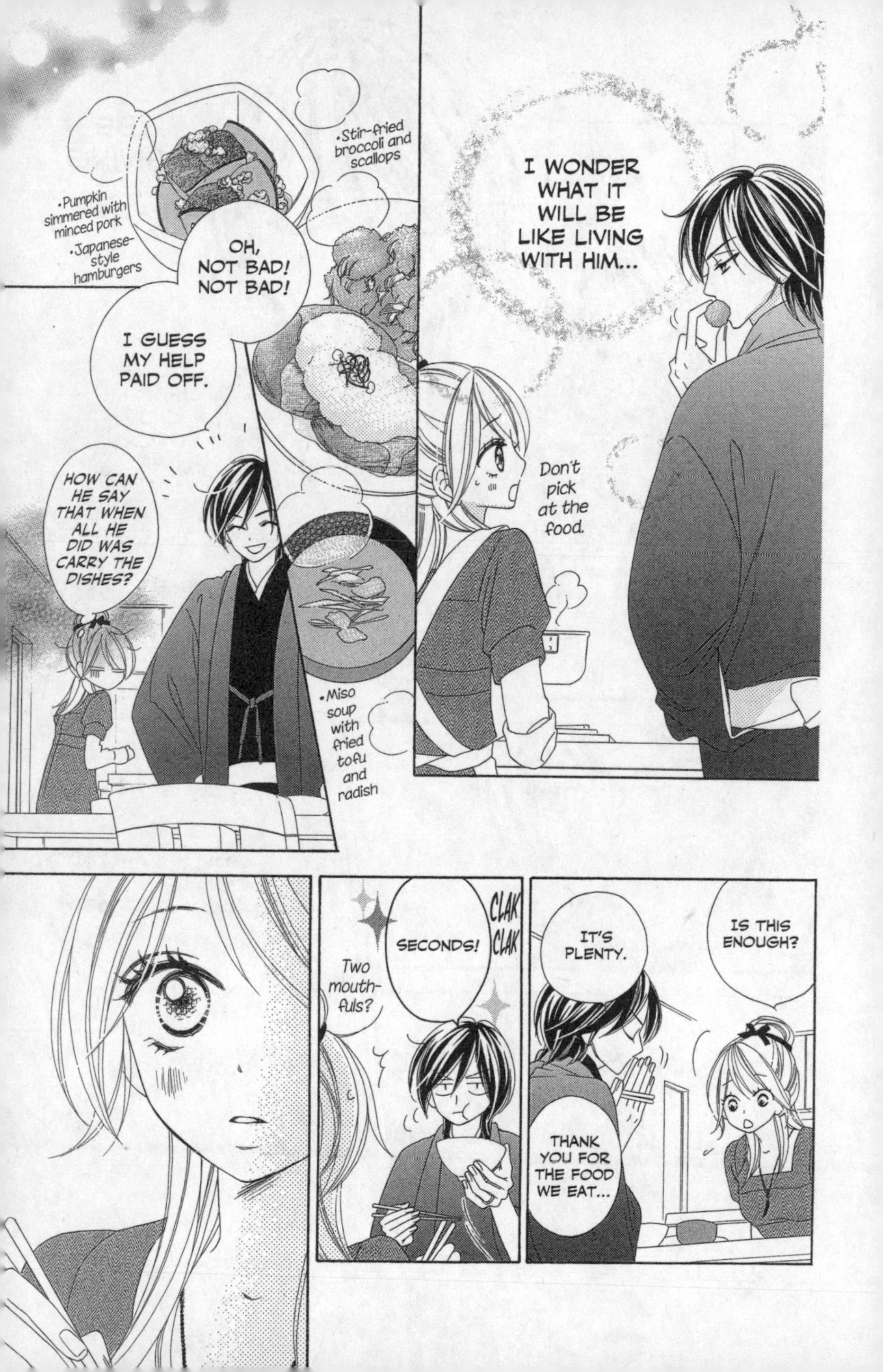
I WONDER WHAT IT WILL BE LIKE LIVING WITH HIM...
Don't pick at the food.
•Stir-fried broccoli and scallops
•Pumpkin simmered with minced pork
•Japanese-style hamburgers
OH, NOT BAD! NOT BAD!
I GUESS MY HELP PAID OFF.
HOW CAN HE SAY THAT WHEN ALL HE DID WAS CARRY THE DISHES?
•Miso soup with fried tofu and radish
IS THIS ENOUGH?
IT'S PLENTY.
THANK YOU FOR THE FOOD WE EAT...
CLAK CLAK
SECONDS!
Two mouth-fuls?

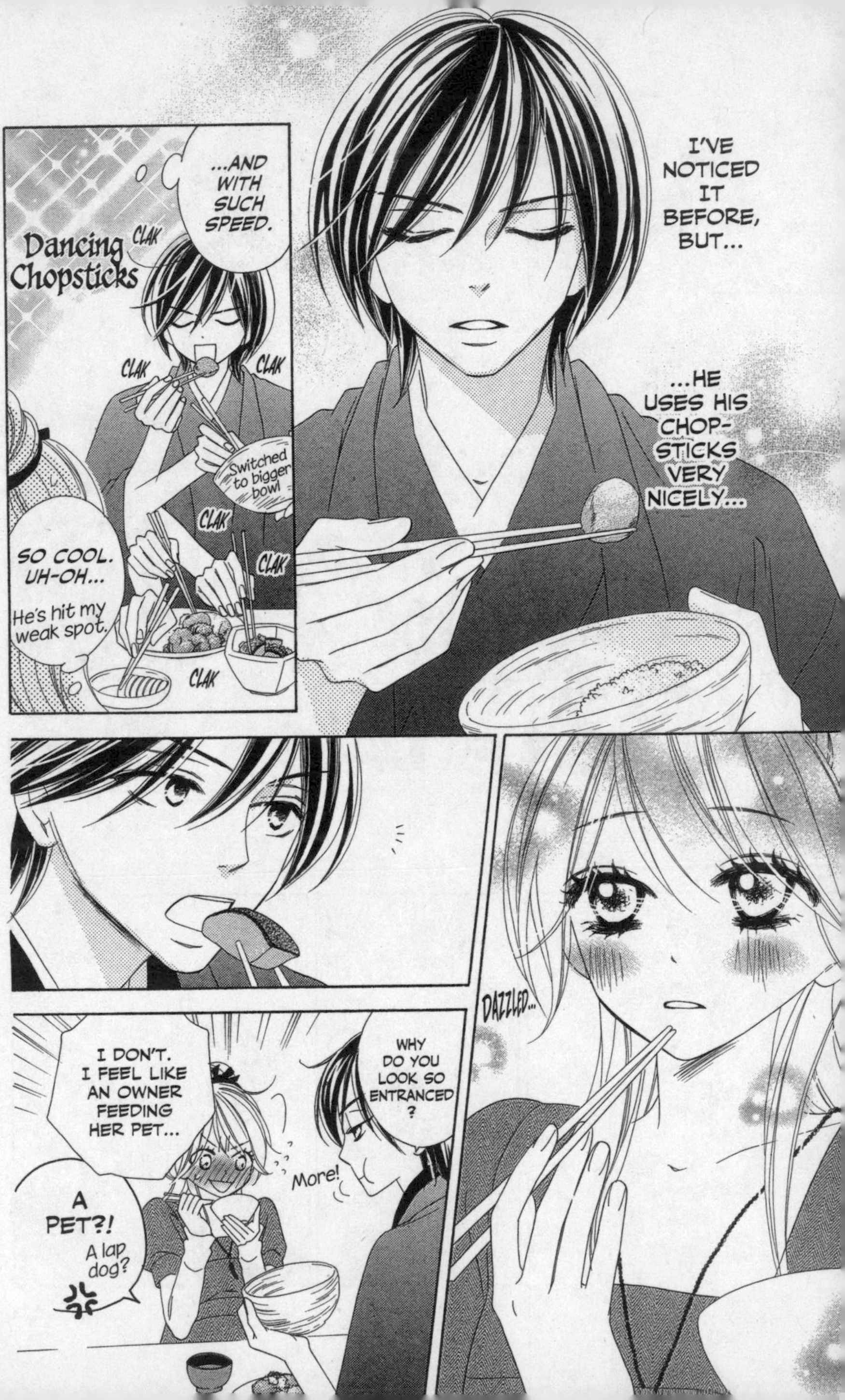
I'VE NOTICED IT BEFORE, BUT...
...HE USES HIS CHOP-STICKS VERY NICELY...
...AND WITH SUCH SPEED.
Dancing Chopsticks
CLAK
CLAK
CLAK
Switched to bigger bowl
CLAK
CLAK
CLAK
SO COOL. UH-OH...
He's hit my weak spot.
DAZZLED...
WHY DO YOU LOOK SO ENTRANCED?
More!
I DON'T. I FEEL LIKE AN OWNER FEEDING HER PET...
A PET?!
A lap dog?

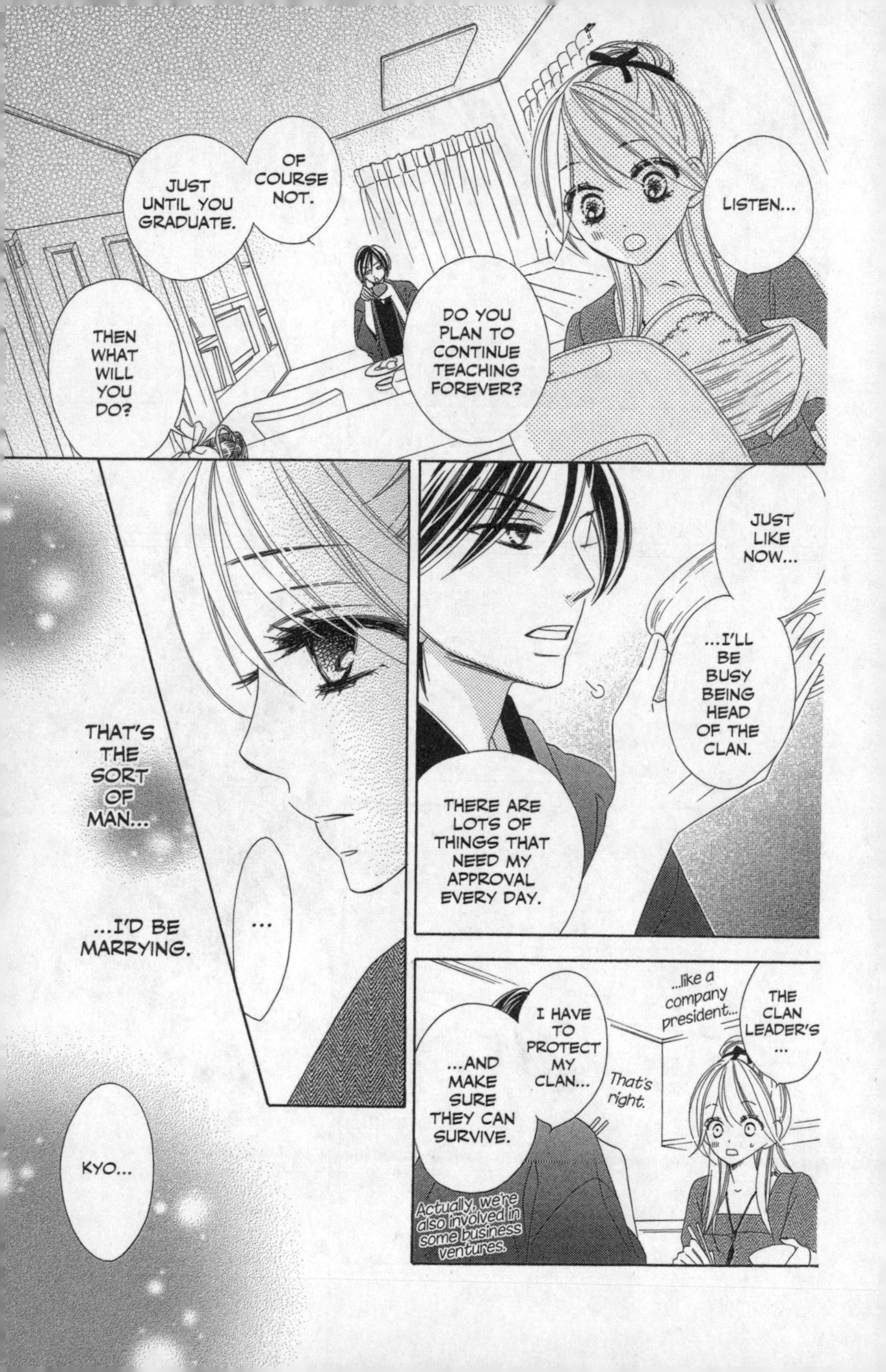
LISTEN...
DO YOU PLAN TO CONTINUE TEACHING FOREVER?
OF COURSE NOT.
JUST UNTIL YOU GRADUATE.
THEN WHAT WILL YOU DO?
JUST LIKE NOW...
...I'LL BE BUSY BEING HEAD OF THE CLAN.
THERE ARE LOTS OF THINGS THAT NEED MY APPROVAL EVERY DAY.
THE CLAN LEADER'S...
...like a company president...
That's right.
I HAVE TO PROTECT MY CLAN...
...AND MAKE SURE THEY CAN SURVIVE.
Actually, we're also involved in some business ventures.
...
THAT'S THE SORT OF MAN...
...I'D BE MARRYING.
KYO...

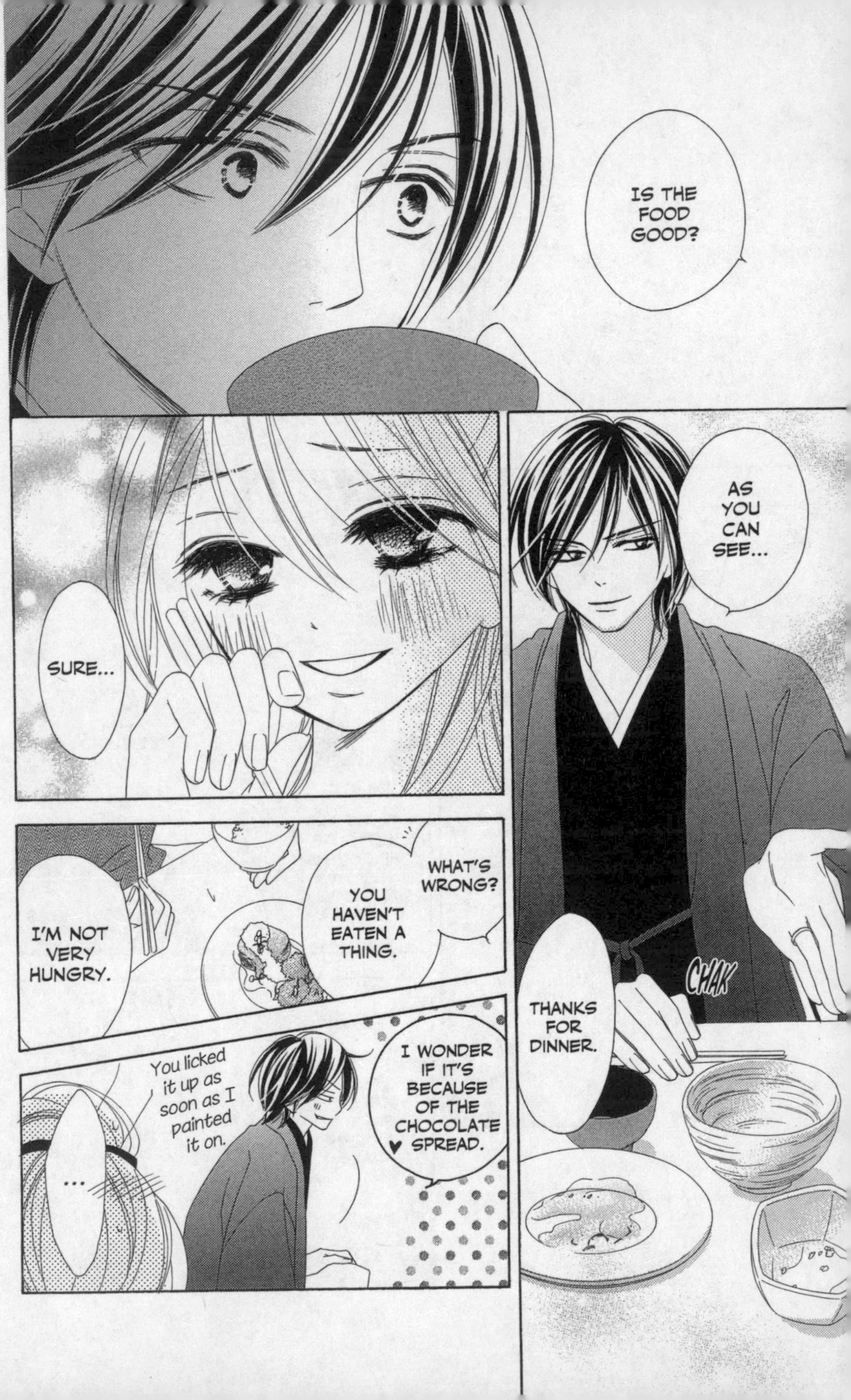
IS THE FOOD GOOD?
AS YOU CAN SEE...
CHAK
THANKS FOR DINNER.
SURE...
WHAT'S WRONG?
YOU HAVEN'T EATEN A THING.
I'M NOT VERY HUNGRY.
I WONDER IF IT'S BECAUSE OF THE CHOCOLATE SPREAD. ♥
You licked it up as soon as I painted it on.
...

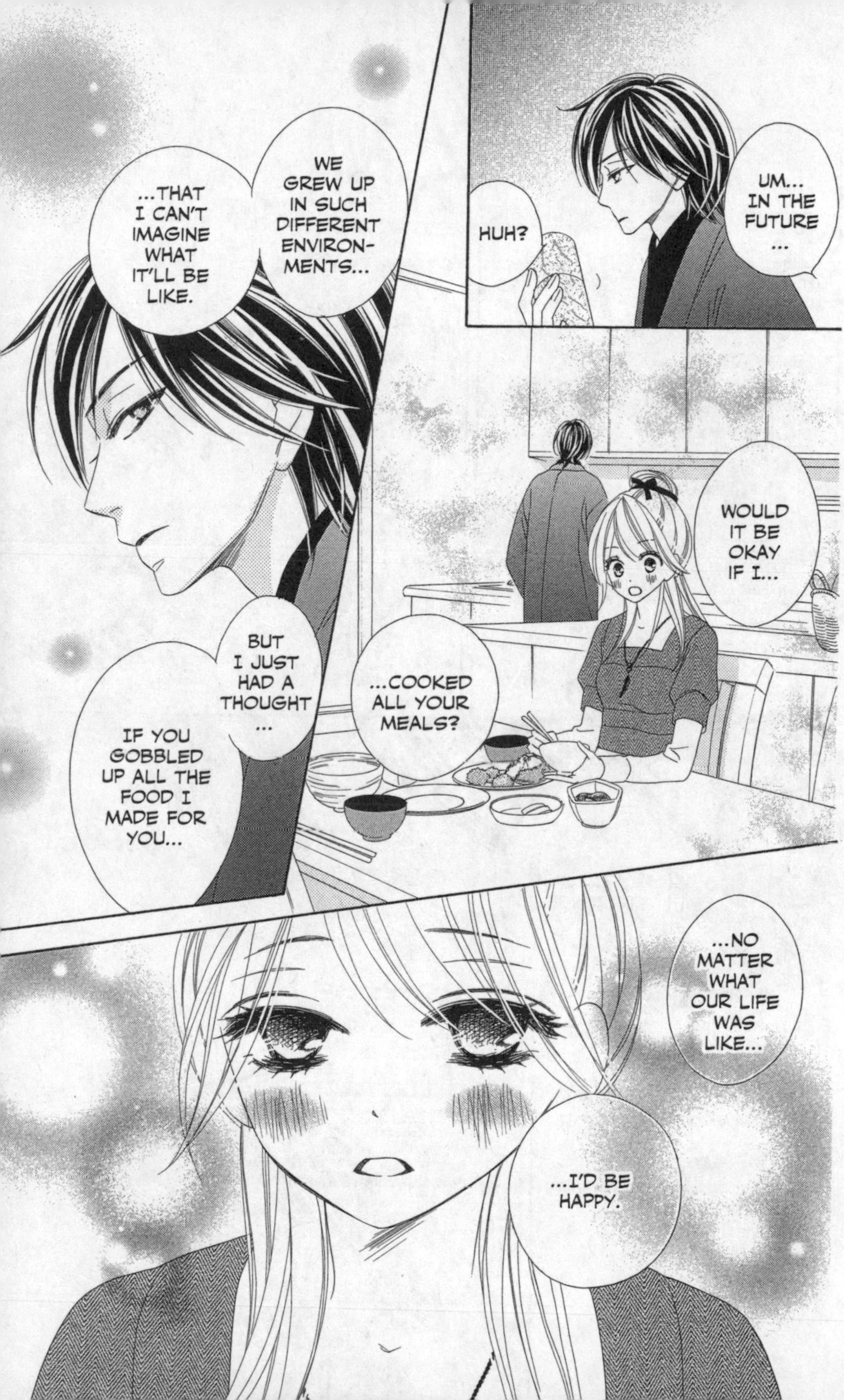
UM... IN THE FUTURE ...
HUH?
WOULD IT BE OKAY IF I...
...COOKED ALL YOUR MEALS?
WE GREW UP IN SUCH DIFFERENT ENVIRON-MENTS...
...THAT I CAN'T IMAGINE WHAT IT'LL BE LIKE.
BUT I JUST HAD A THOUGHT ...
IF YOU GOBBLED UP ALL THE FOOD I MADE FOR YOU...
...NO MATTER WHAT OUR LIFE WAS LIKE...
...I'D BE HAPPY.

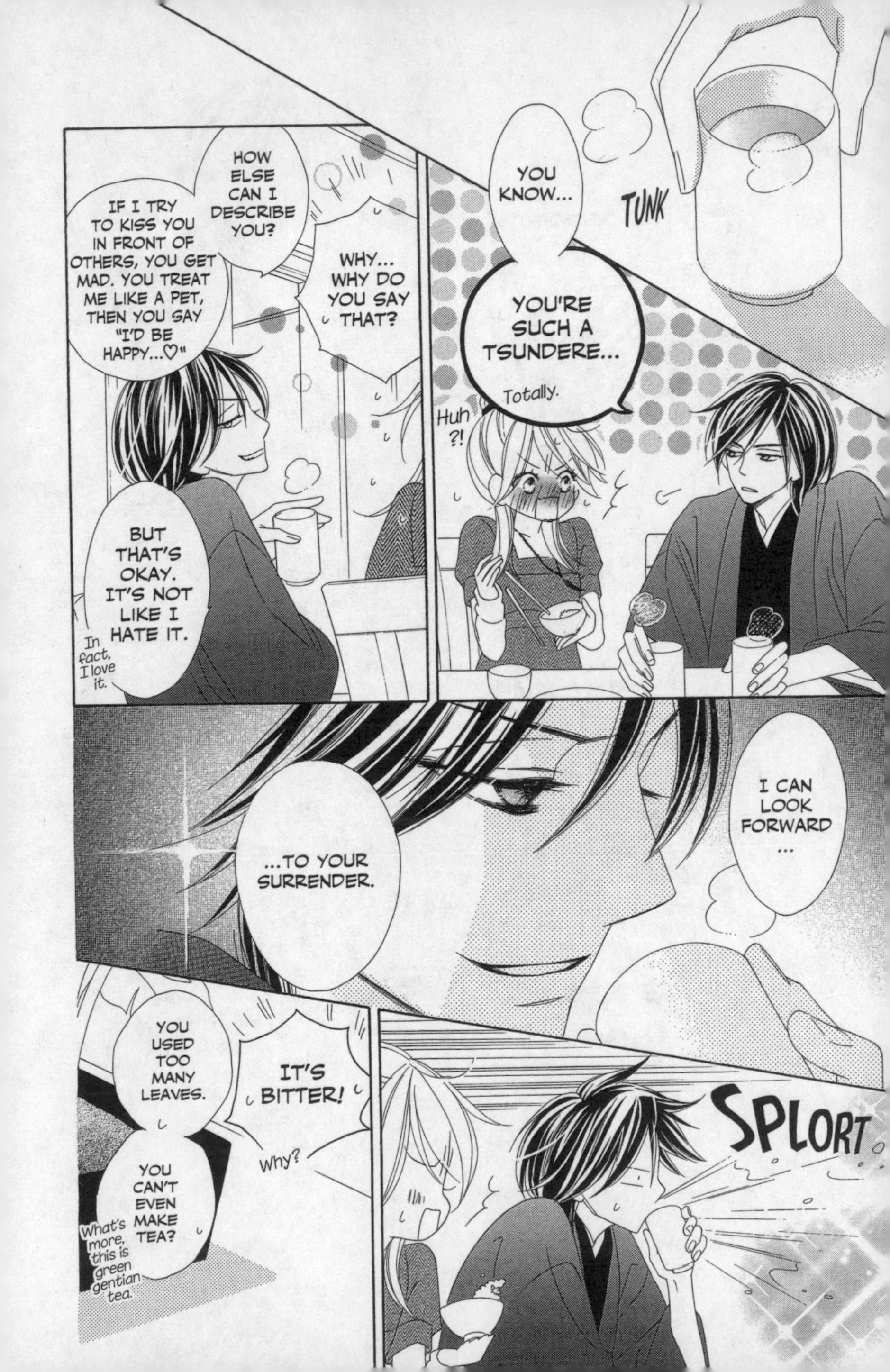
TUNK
YOU KNOW...
YOU'RE SUCH A TSUNDERE...
Totally.
Huh ?!
WHY... WHY DO YOU SAY THAT?
HOW ELSE CAN I DESCRIBE YOU?
IF I TRY TO KISS YOU IN FRONT OF OTHERS, YOU GET MAD. YOU TREAT ME LIKE A PET, THEN YOU SAY "I'D BE HAPPY...♡"
BUT THAT'S OKAY. IT'S NOT LIKE I HATE IT.
In fact, I love it.
I CAN LOOK FORWARD ...
...TO YOUR SURRENDER.
SPLORT
IT'S BITTER!
YOU USED TOO MANY LEAVES.
Why?
YOU CAN'T EVEN MAKE TEA?
What's more, this is green gentian tea.

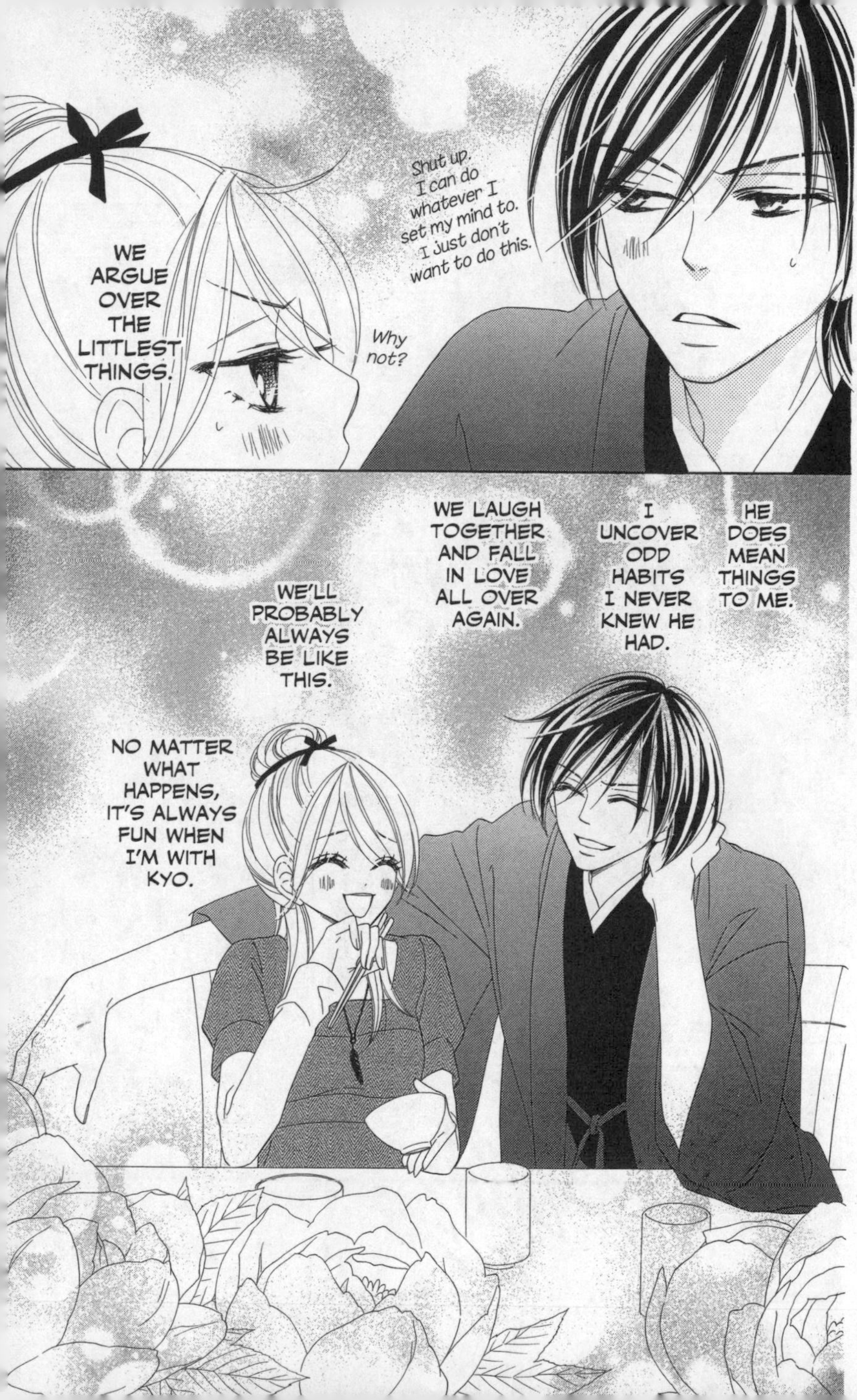
Shut up. I can do whatever I set my mind to. I just don't want to do this.
Why not?
WE ARGUE OVER THE LITTLEST THINGS.
HE DOES MEAN THINGS TO ME.
I UNCOVER ODD HABITS I NEVER KNEW HE HAD.
WE LAUGH TOGETHER AND FALL IN LOVE ALL OVER AGAIN.
WE'LL PROBABLY ALWAYS BE LIKE THIS.
NO MATTER WHAT HAPPENS, IT'S ALWAYS FUN WHEN I'M WITH KYO.

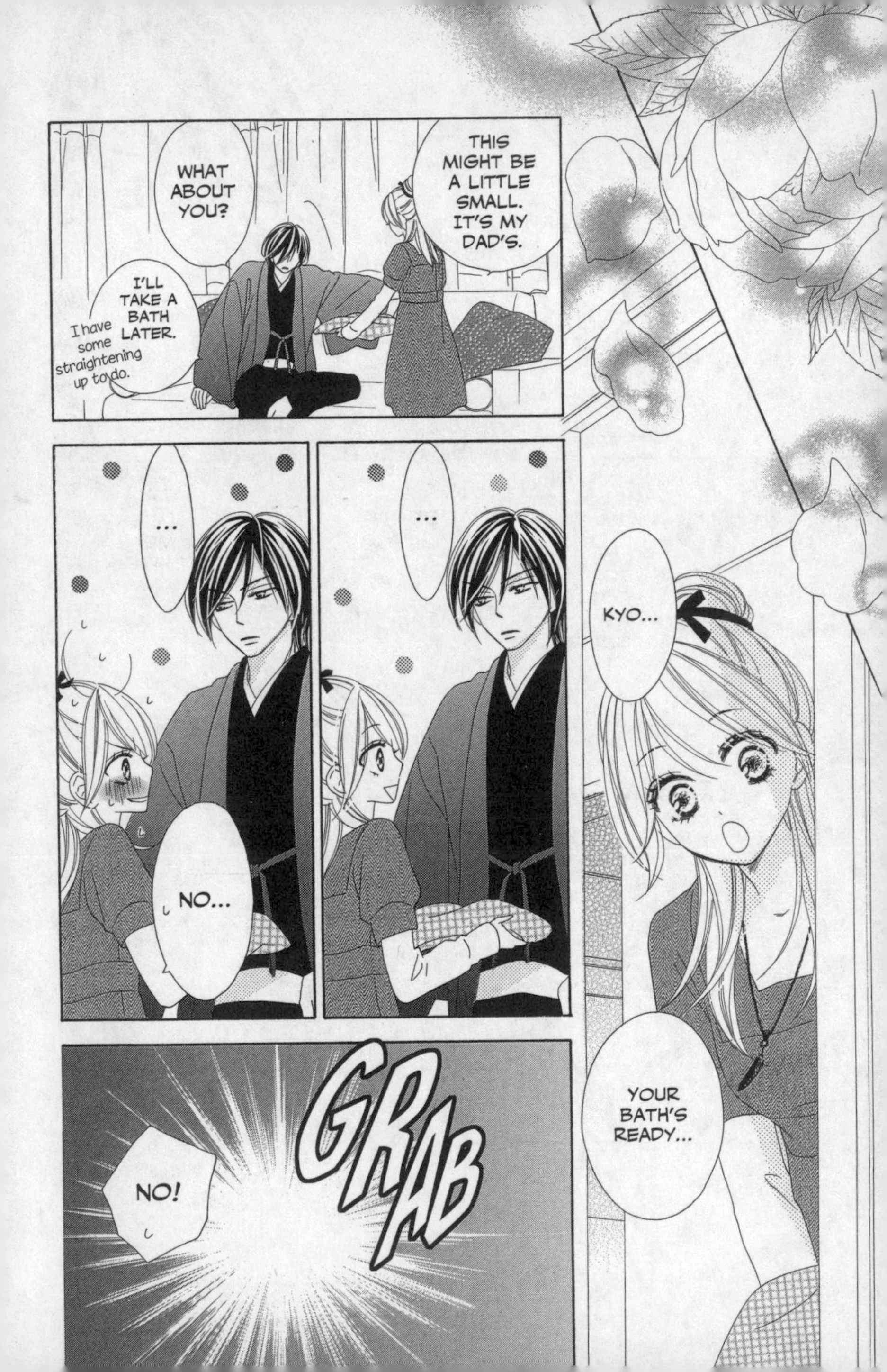
KYO...
YOUR BATH'S READY...
THIS MIGHT BE A LITTLE SMALL. IT'S MY DAD'S.
WHAT ABOUT YOU?
I'LL TAKE A BATH LATER.
I have some straightening up to do.
...
...
NO...
GRAB
NO!

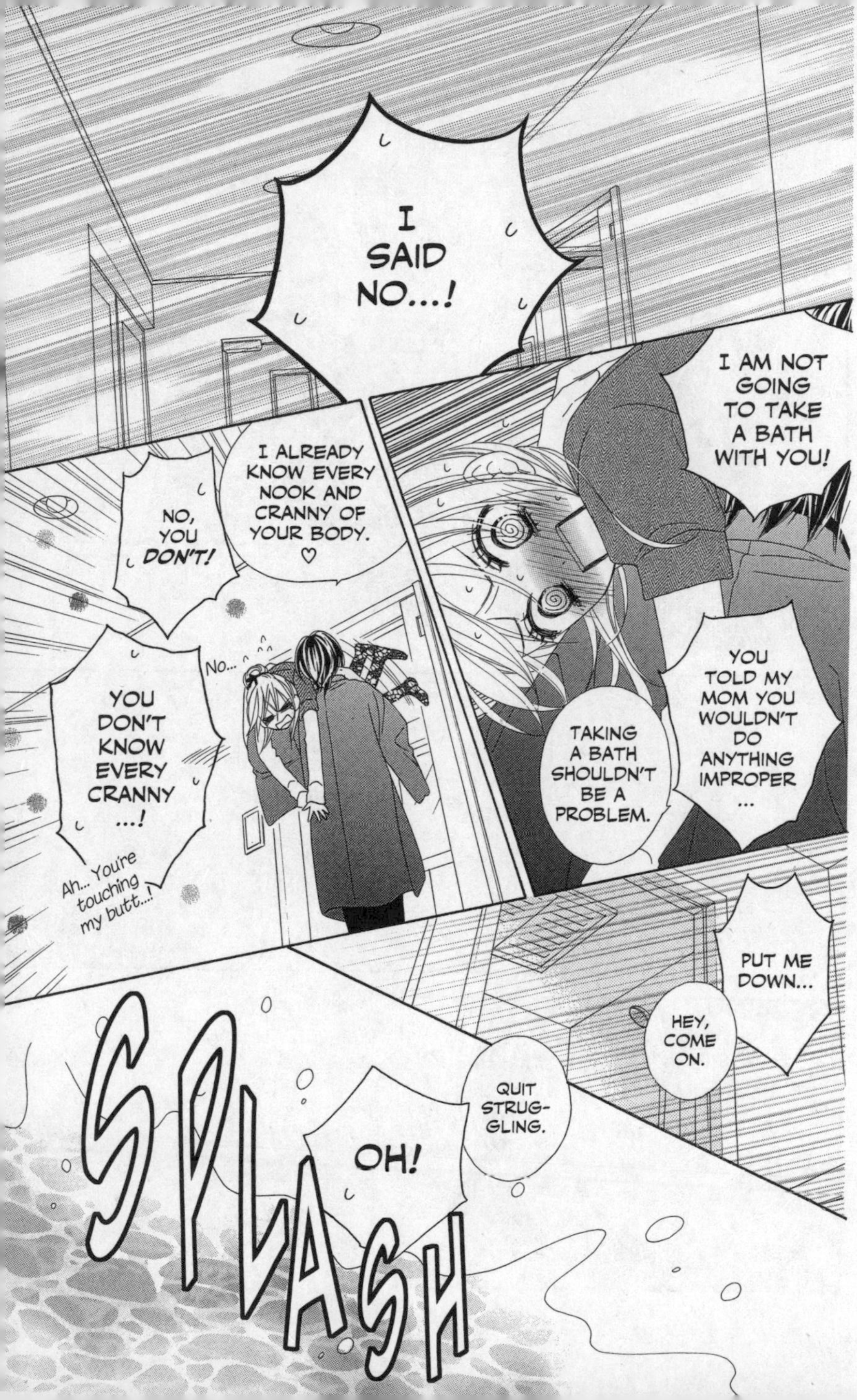
I SAID NO...!
I AM NOT GOING TO TAKE A BATH WITH YOU!
YOU TOLD MY MOM YOU WOULDN'T DO ANYTHING IMPROPER ...
TAKING A BATH SHOULDN'T BE A PROBLEM.
I ALREADY KNOW EVERY NOOK AND CRANNY OF YOUR BODY. ♡
NO, YOU DON'T!
No...
YOU DON'T KNOW EVERY CRANNY ...!
Ah... You're touching my butt...!
PUT ME DOWN...
HEY, COME ON.
QUIT STRUG-GLING.
OH!
SPLASH

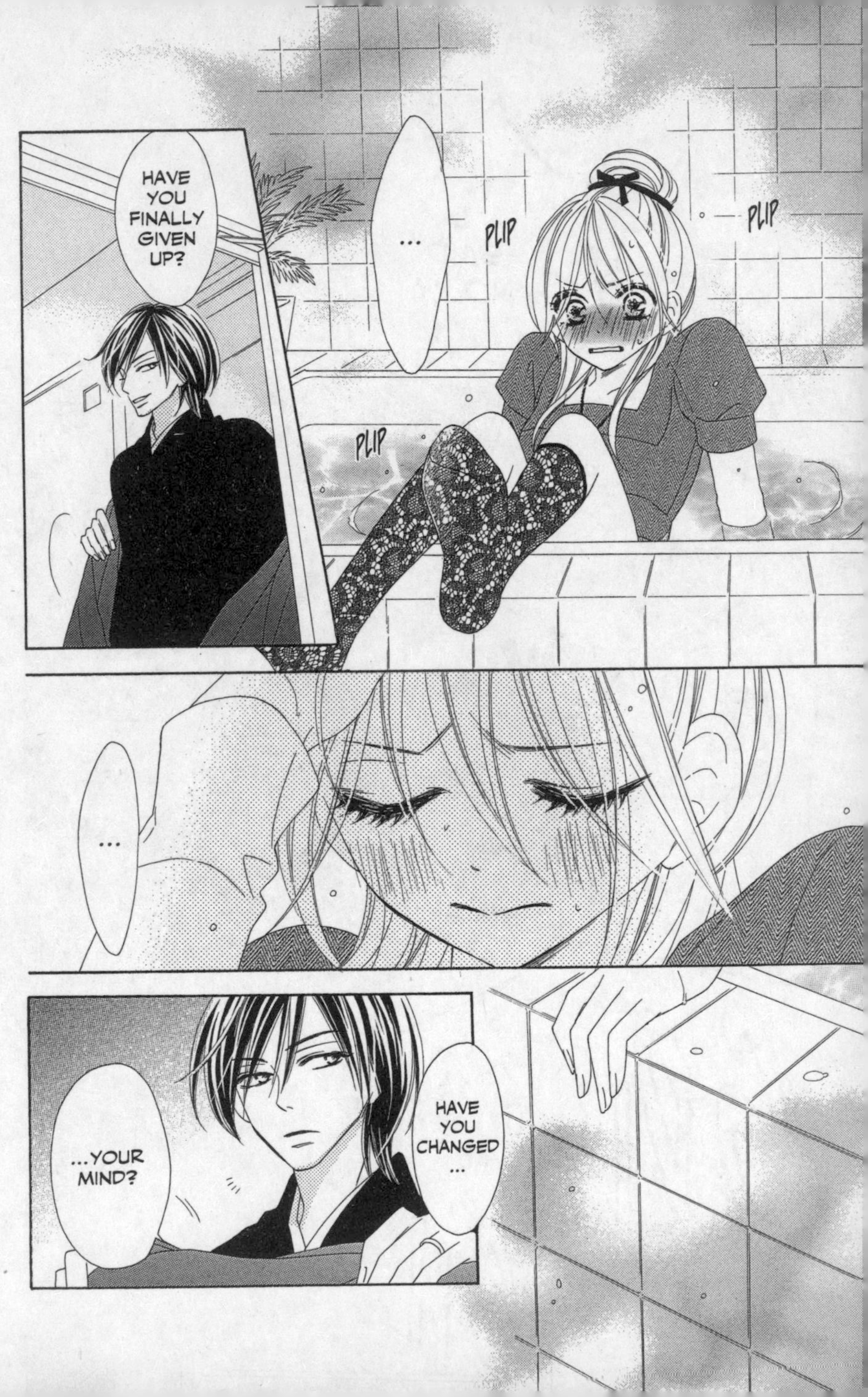
PLIP
PLIP
...
PLIP
HAVE YOU FINALLY GIVEN UP?
...
HAVE YOU CHANGED ...
...YOUR MIND?

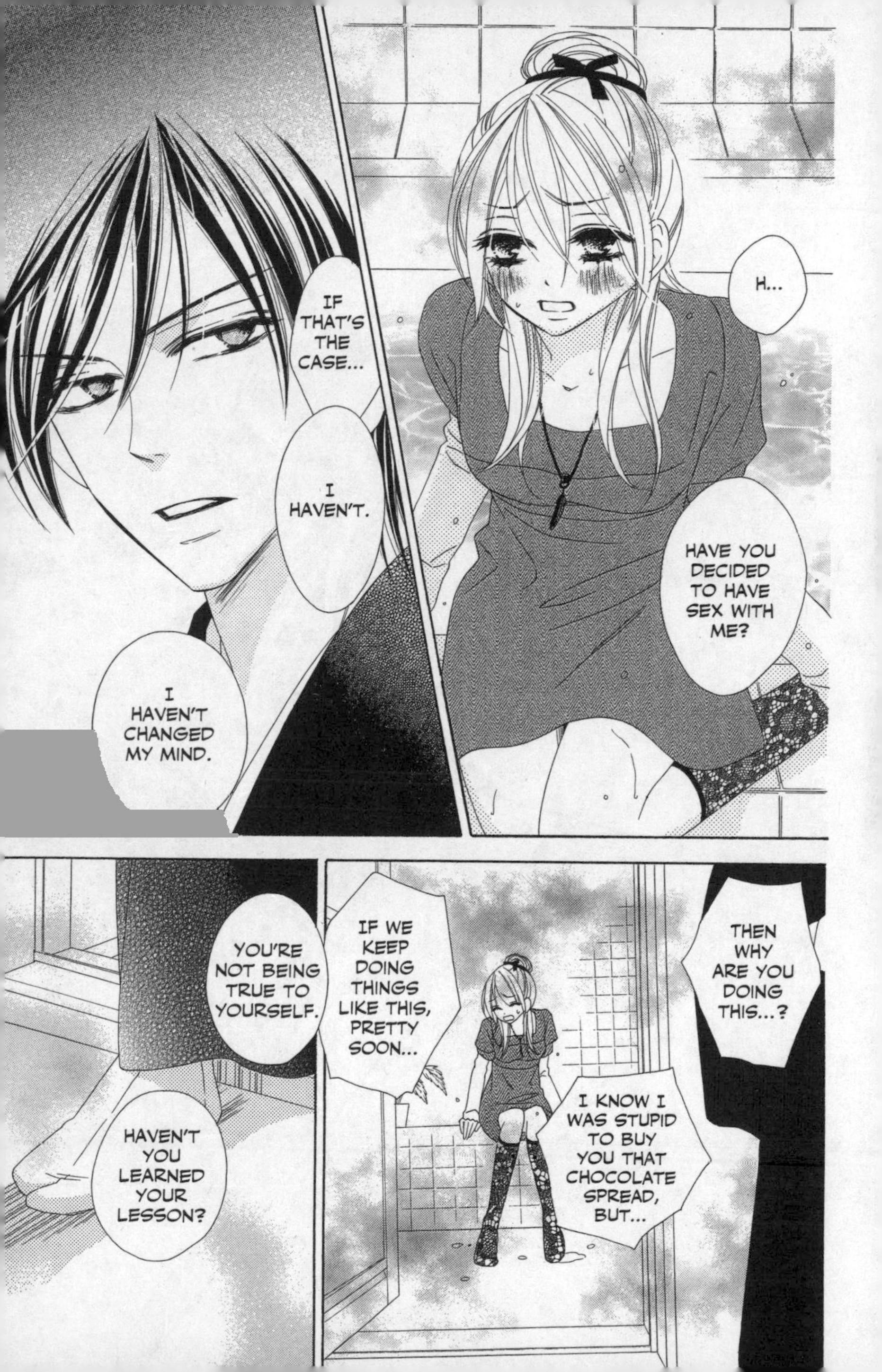

H...
HAVE YOU DECIDED TO HAVE SEX WITH ME?
IF THAT'S THE CASE...
I HAVEN'T.
I HAVEN'T CHANGED MY MIND.
THEN WHY ARE YOU DOING THIS...?
I KNOW I WAS STUPID TO BUY YOU THAT CHOCOLATE SPREAD, BUT...
IF WE KEEP DOING THINGS LIKE THIS, PRETTY SOON...
YOU'RE NOT BEING TRUE TO YOURSELF.
HAVEN'T YOU LEARNED YOUR LESSON?

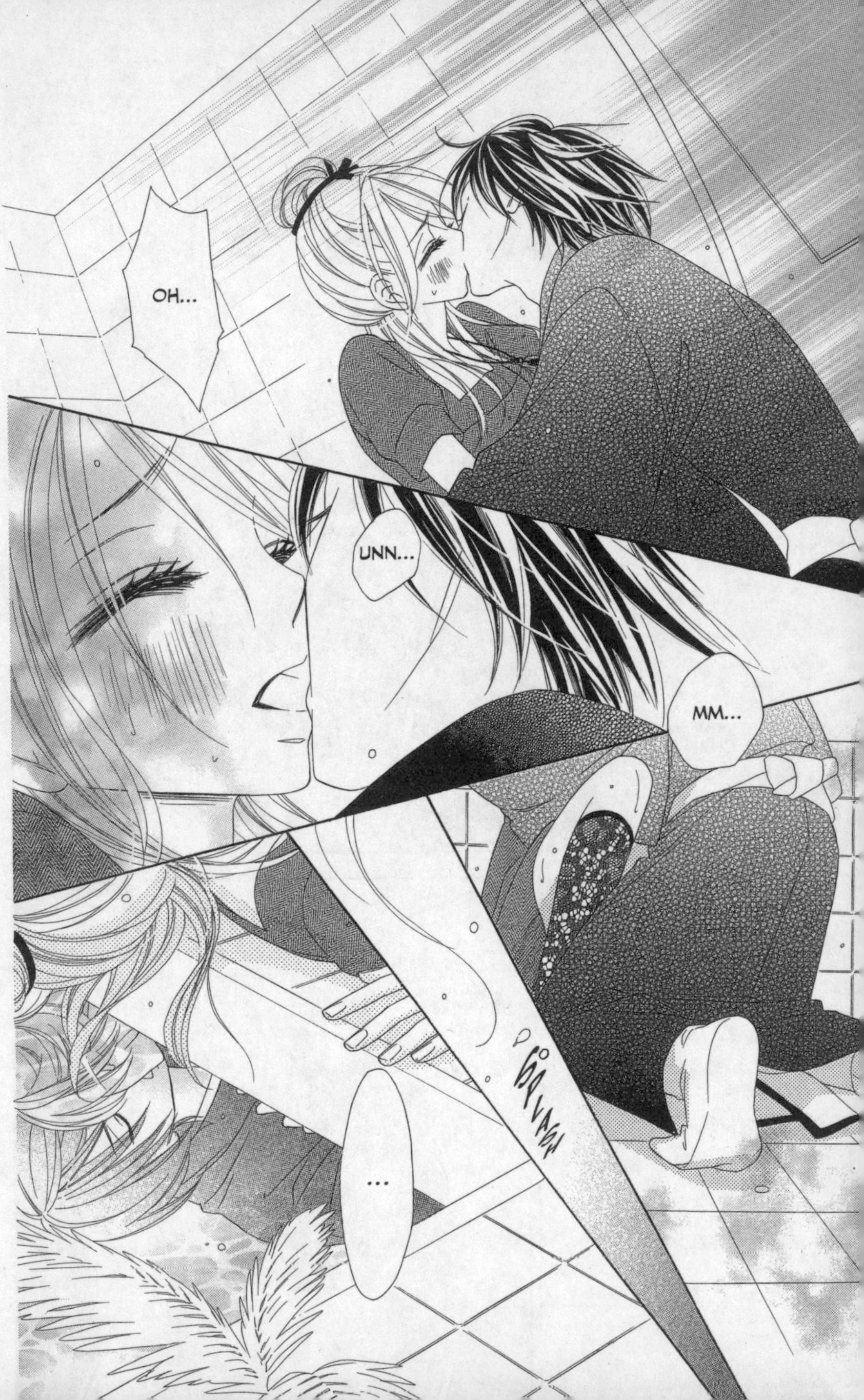
OH...
UNN...
MM...
...

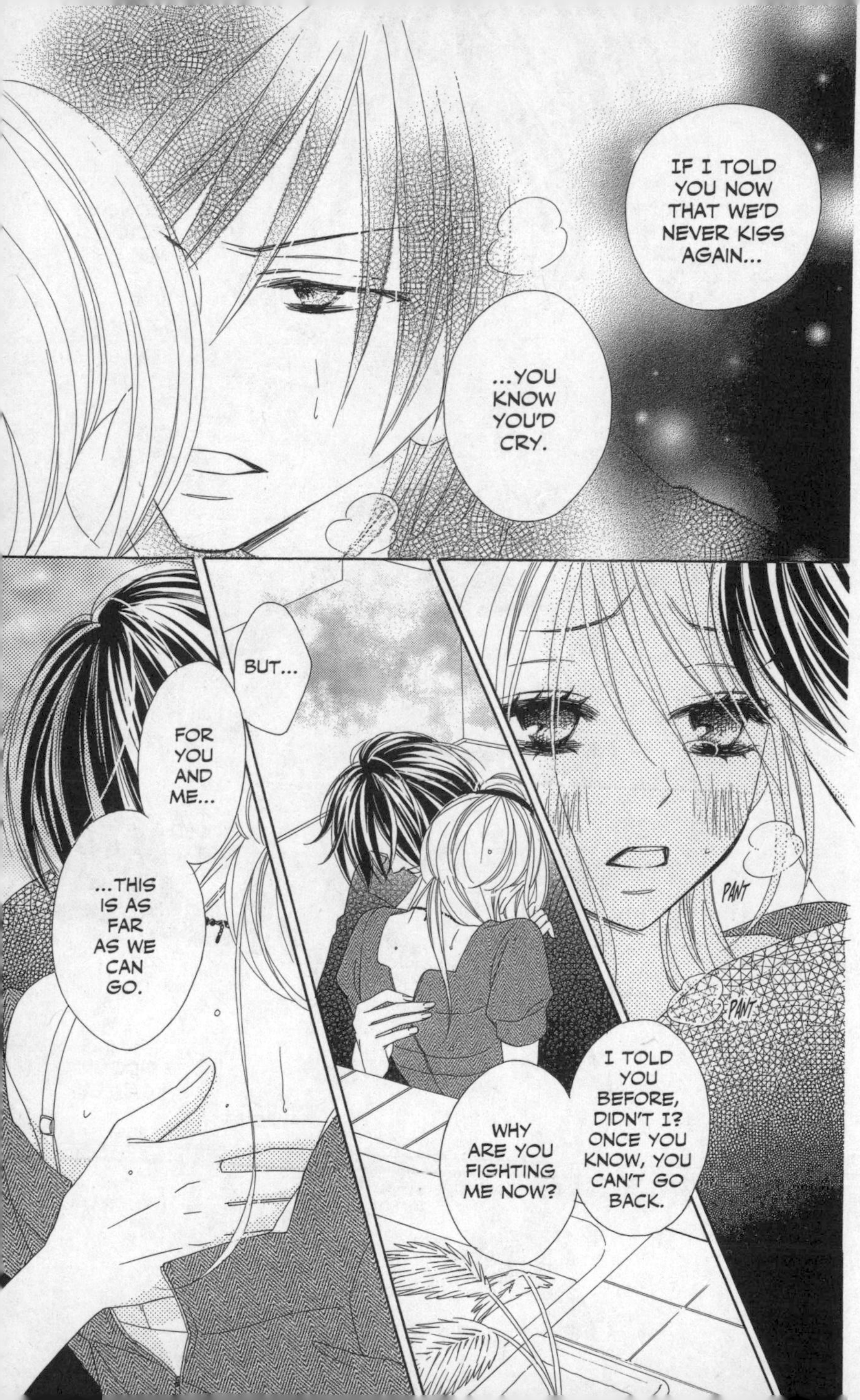
IF I TOLD YOU NOW THAT WE'D NEVER KISS AGAIN...
...YOU KNOW YOU'D CRY.
PANT
PANT
I TOLD YOU BEFORE, DIDN'T I? ONCE YOU KNOW, YOU CAN'T GO BACK.
WHY ARE YOU FIGHTING ME NOW?
BUT...
FOR YOU AND ME...
...THIS IS AS FAR AS WE CAN GO.

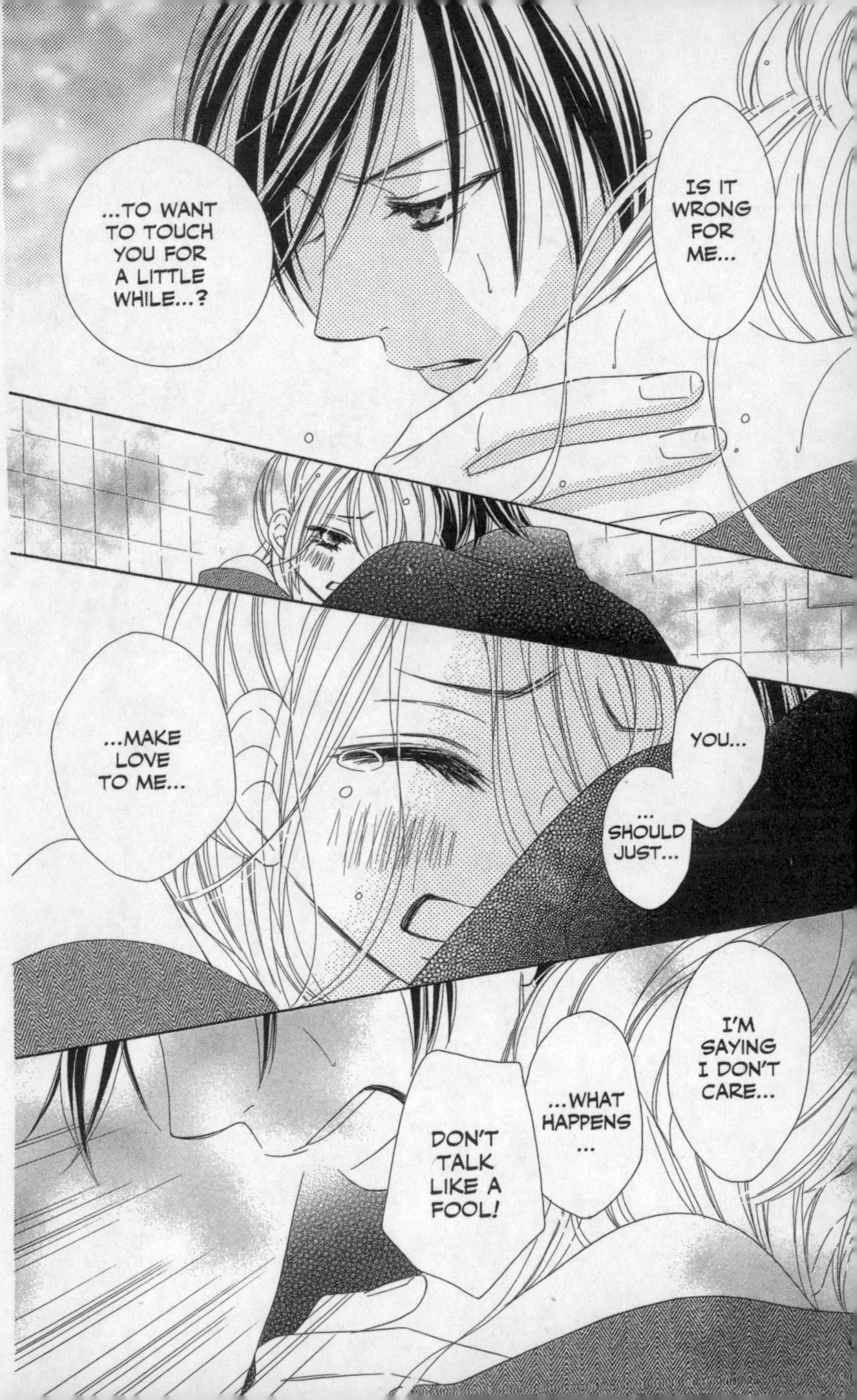
IS IT WRONG FOR ME...
...TO WANT TO TOUCH YOU FOR A LITTLE WHILE...?
YOU...
...SHOULD JUST...
...MAKE LOVE TO ME...
I'M SAYING I DON'T CARE...
...WHAT HAPPENS ...
DON'T TALK LIKE A FOOL!

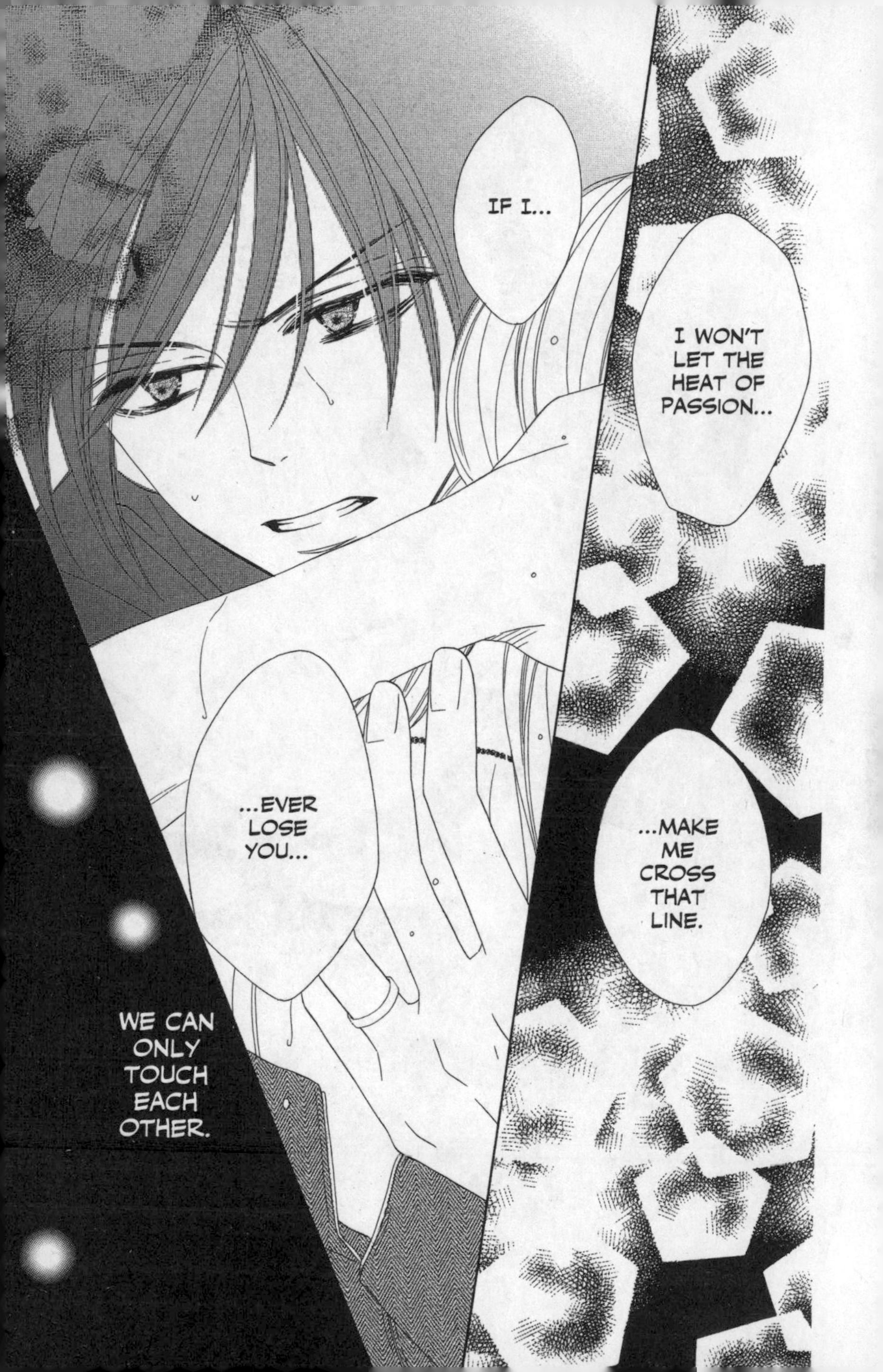
I WON'T LET THE HEAT OF PASSION...
...MAKE ME CROSS THAT LINE.
IF I...
...EVER LOSE YOU...
WE CAN ONLY TOUCH EACH OTHER.

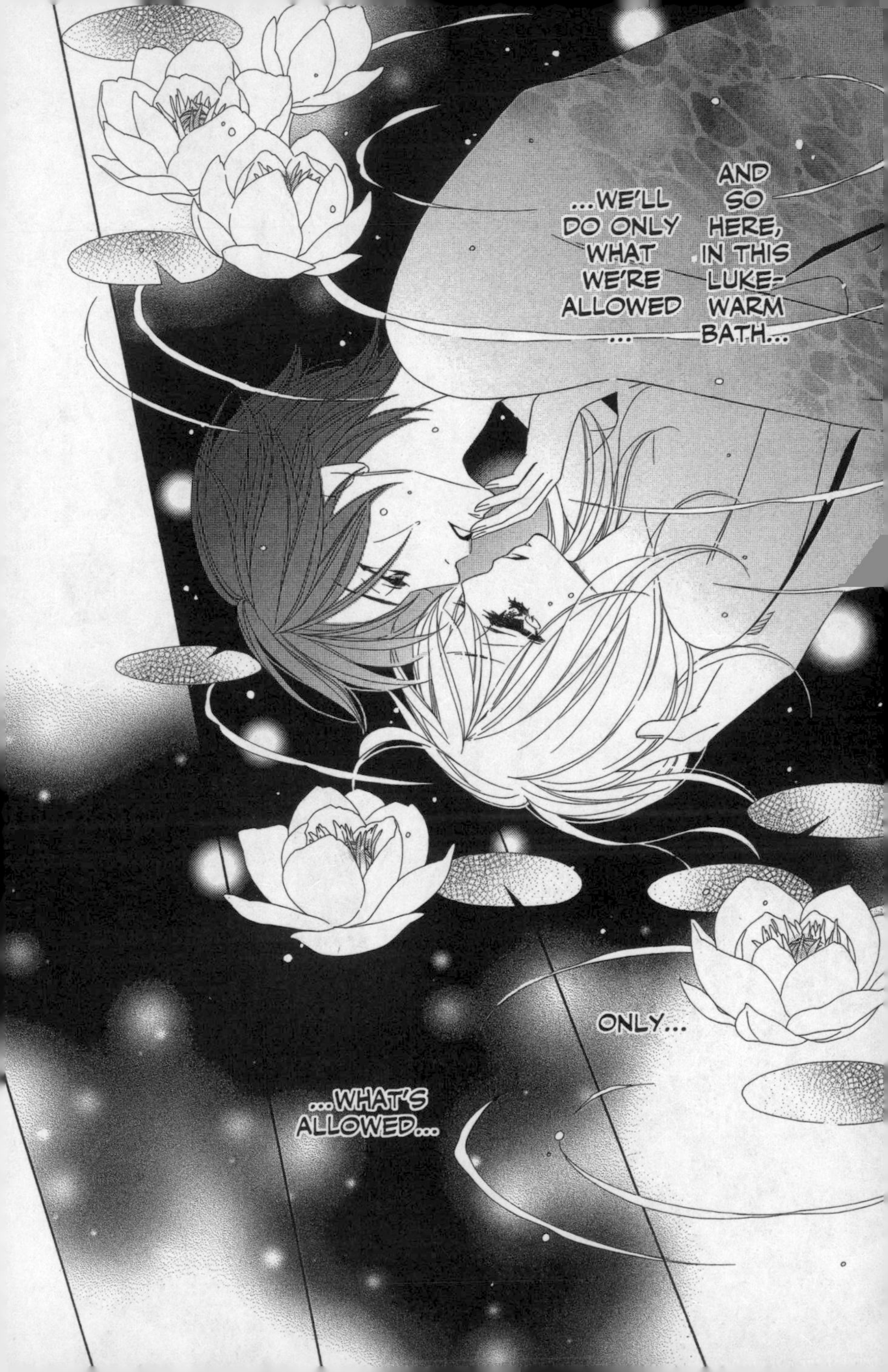
AND SO HERE, IN THIS LUKE-WARM BATH...
...WE'LL DO ONLY WHAT WE'RE ALLOWED...
ONLY...
...WHAT'S ALLOWED...

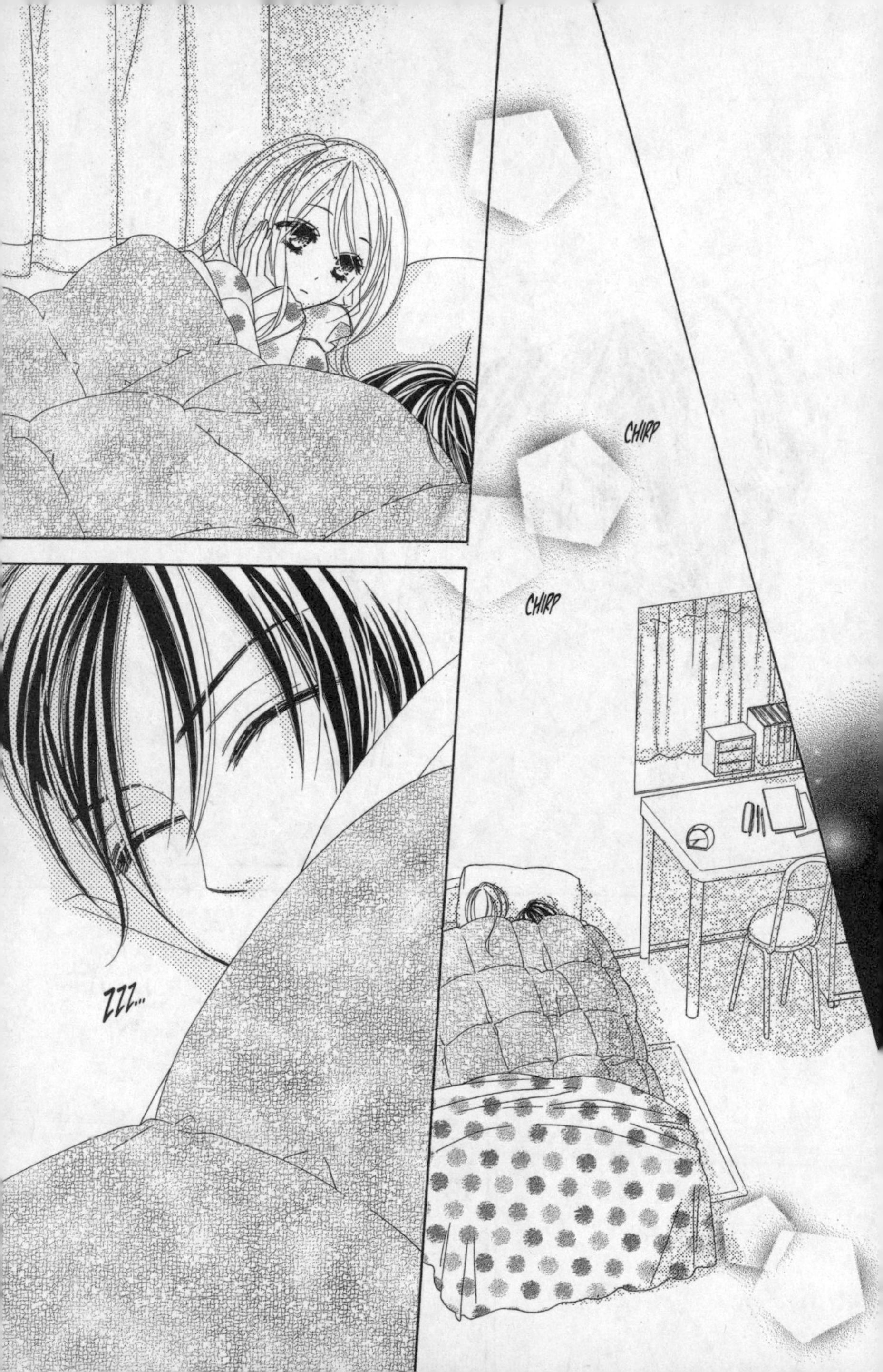
CHIRP
CHIRP
ZZZ...

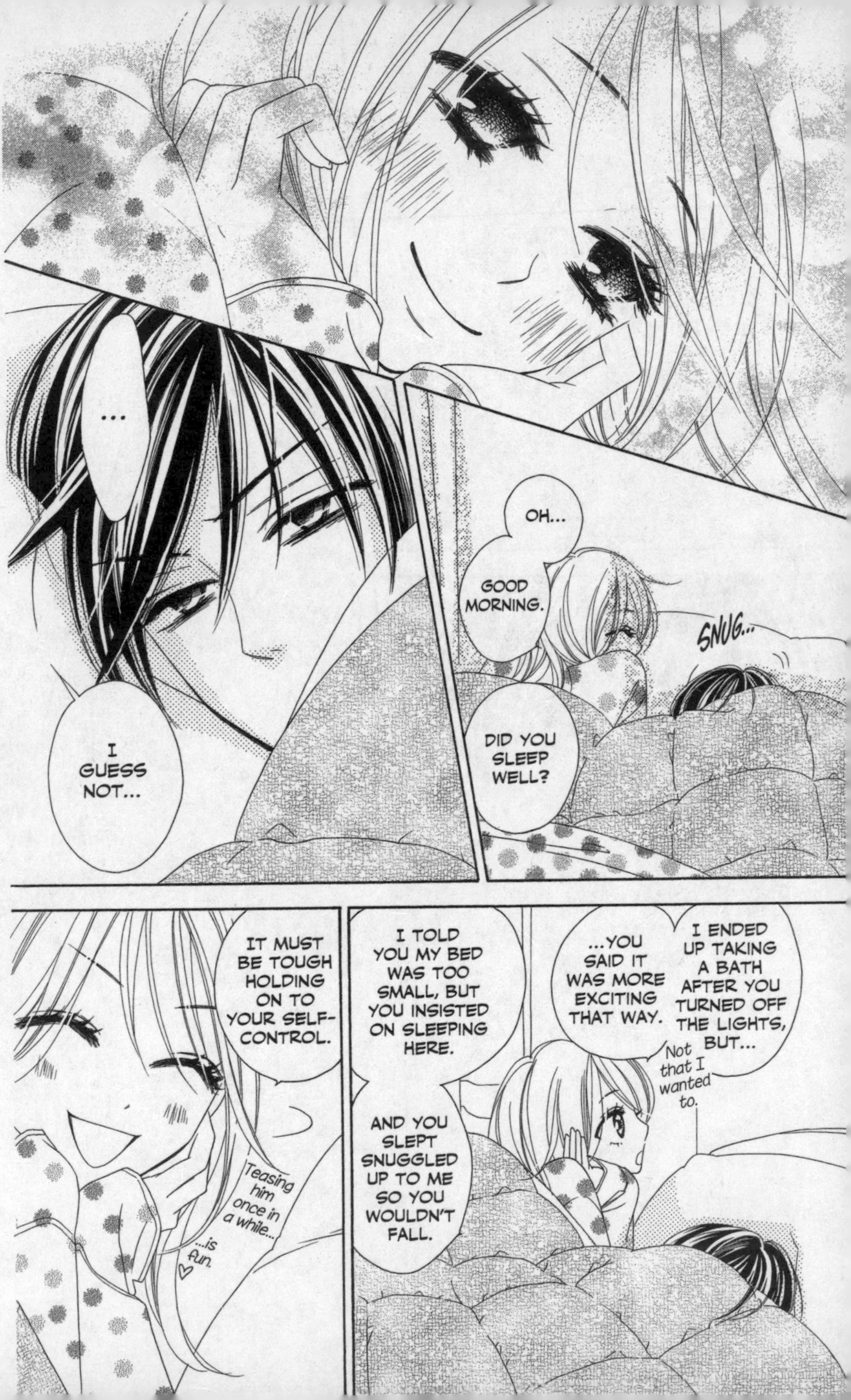
OH...
GOOD MORNING.
SNUG...
DID YOU SLEEP WELL?
...
I GUESS NOT...
I ENDED UP TAKING A BATH AFTER YOU TURNED OFF THE LIGHTS, BUT...
Not that I wanted to.
...YOU SAID IT WAS MORE EXCITING THAT WAY.
I TOLD YOU MY BED WAS TOO SMALL, BUT YOU INSISTED ON SLEEPING HERE.
AND YOU SLEPT SNUGGLED UP TO ME SO YOU WOULDN'T FALL.
IT MUST BE TOUGH HOLDING ON TO YOUR SELF-CONTROL.
Teasing him once in a while...
...is fun. ♡

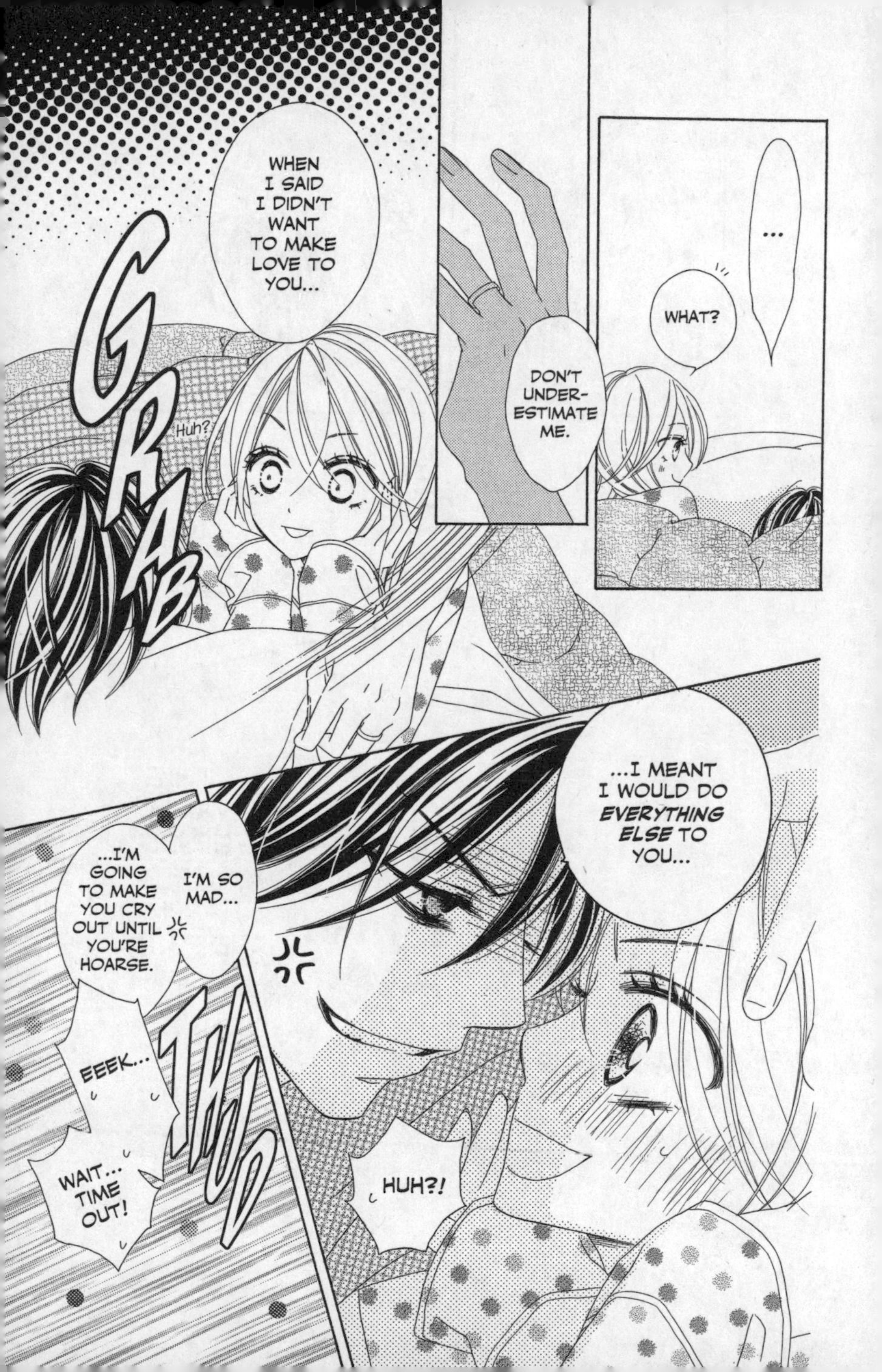
...
WHAT?
DON'T UNDER-ESTIMATE ME.
WHEN I SAID I DIDN'T WANT TO MAKE LOVE TO YOU...
Huh?
GRAB
...I MEANT I WOULD DO *EVERYTHING ELSE* TO YOU...
I'M SO MAD...
...I'M GOING TO MAKE YOU CRY OUT UNTIL YOU'RE HOARSE.
HUH?!
THUD
EEEK...
WAIT... TIME OUT!

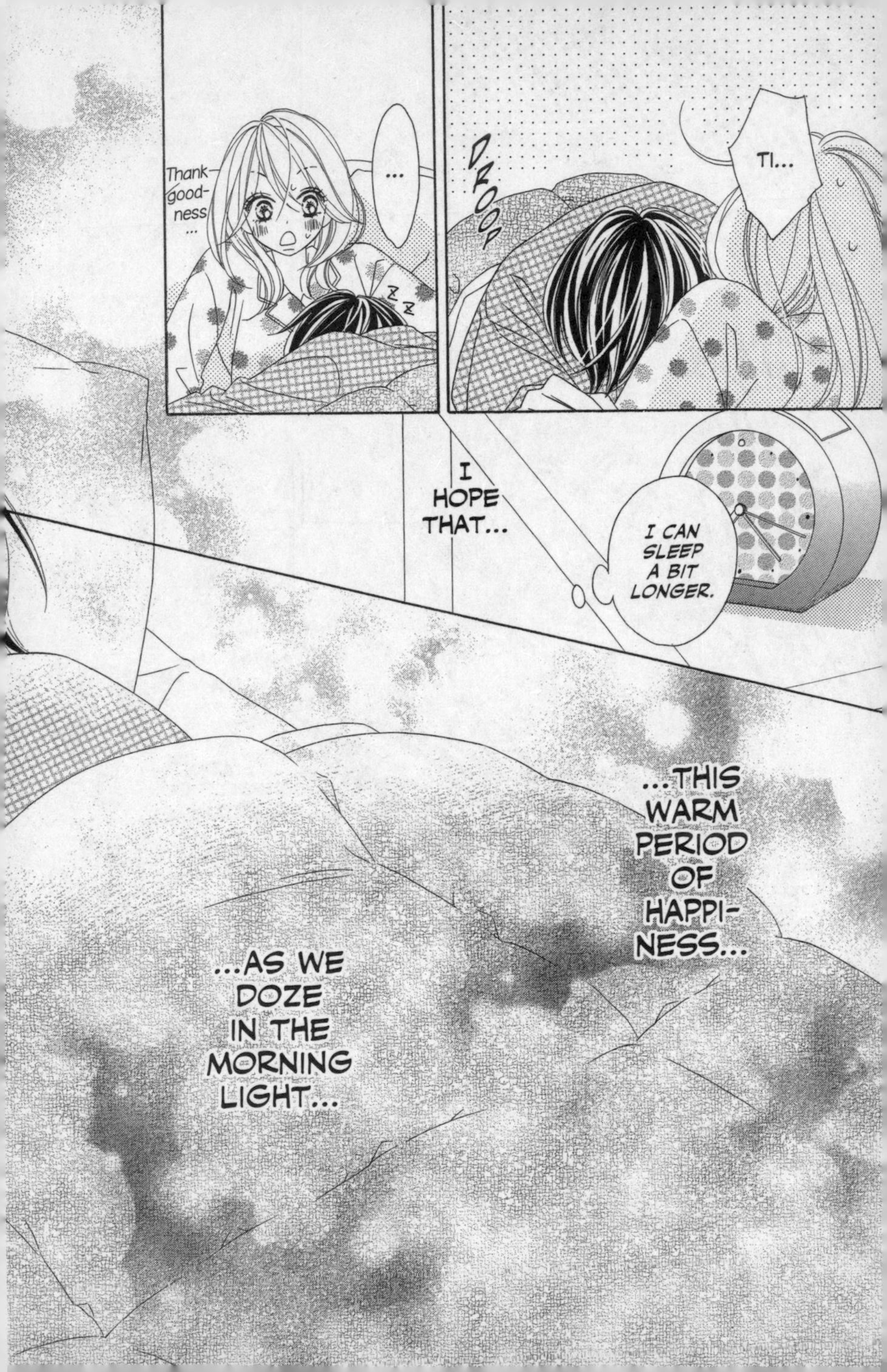
TI...
DROOP
...
Thank-goodness...
ZZZ
I CAN SLEEP A BIT LONGER.
I HOPE THAT...
...THIS WARM PERIOD OF HAPPINESS...
...AS WE DOZE IN THE MORNING LIGHT...

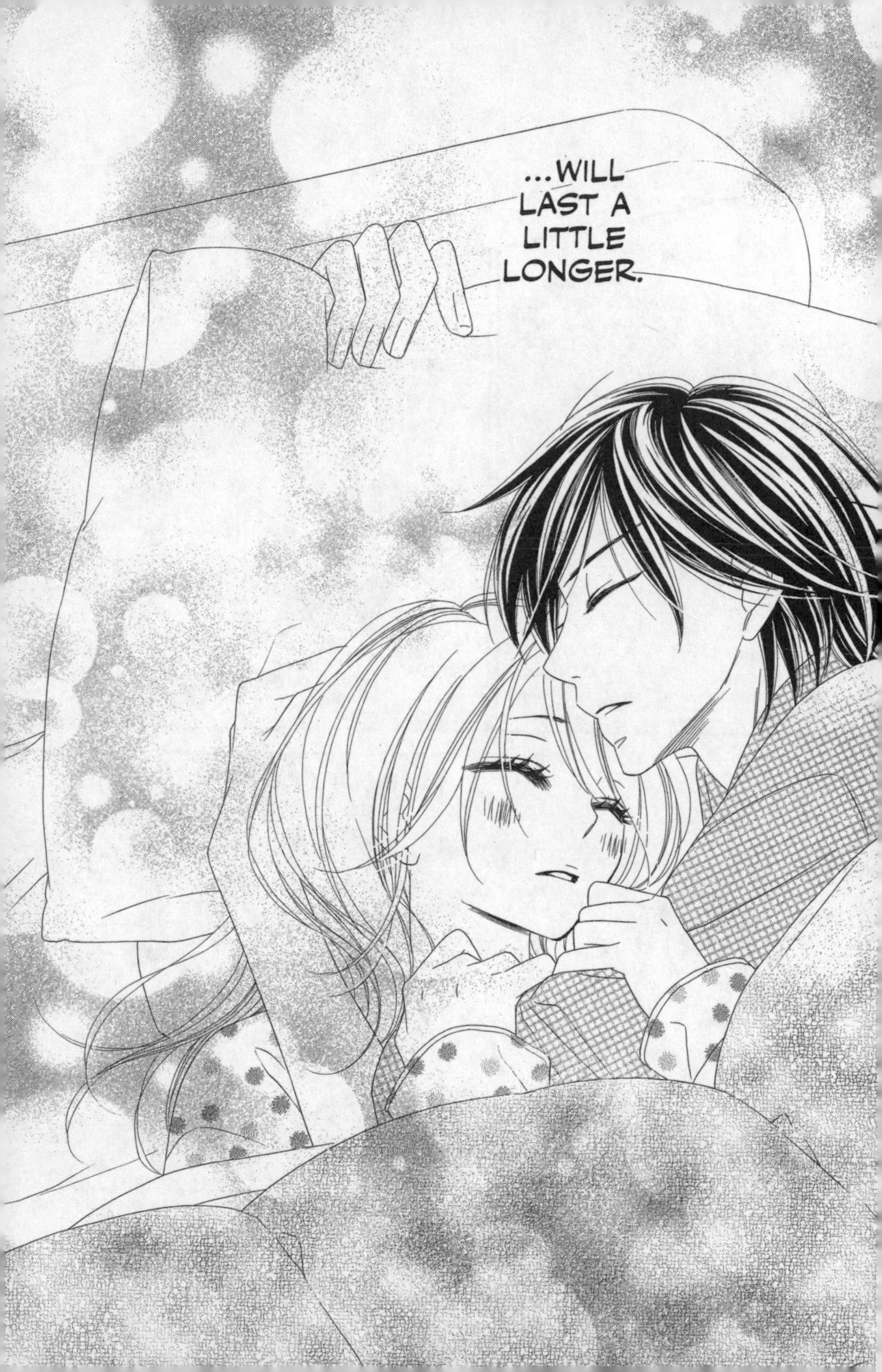
...WILL LAST A LITTLE LONGER.

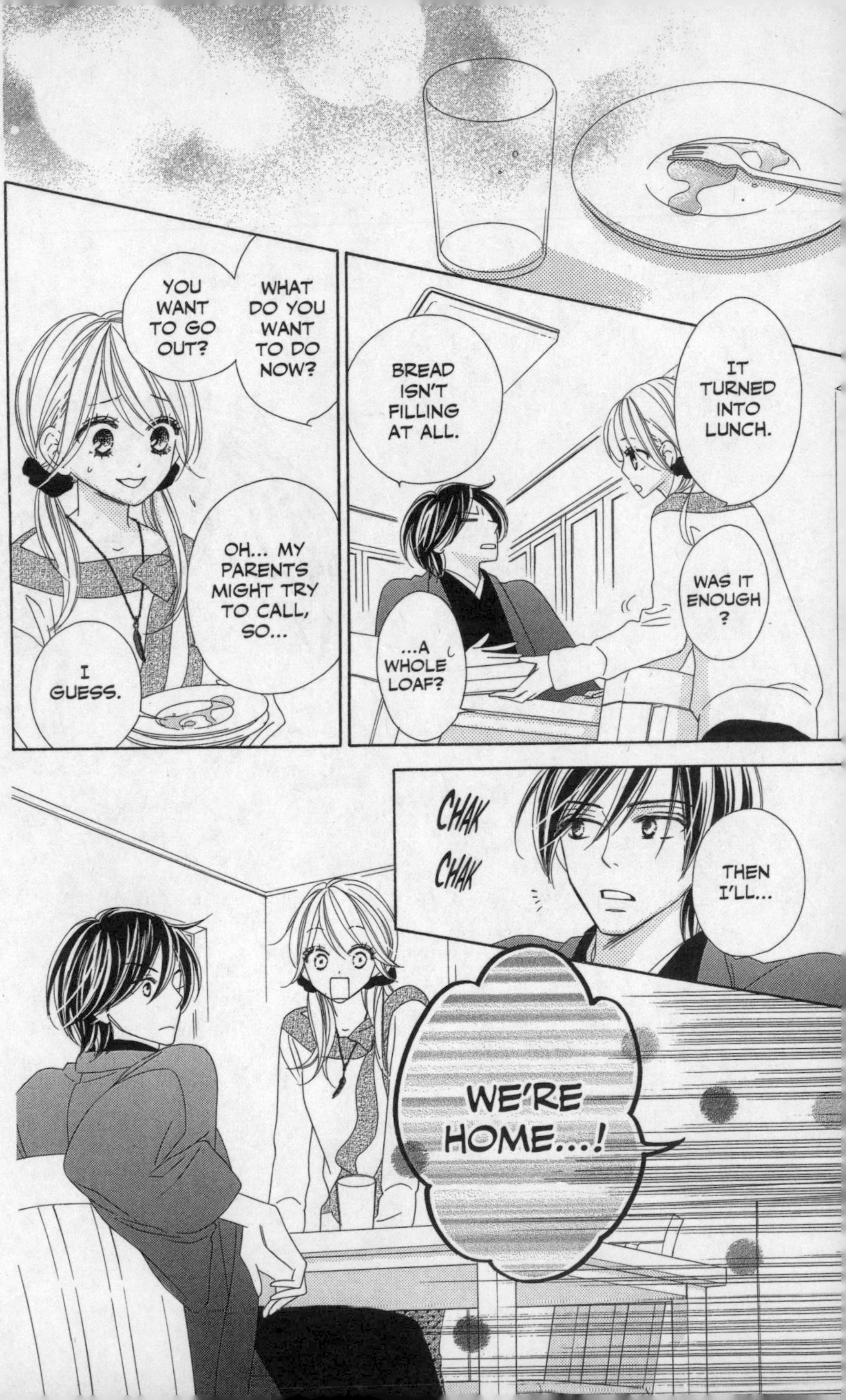
IT TURNED INTO LUNCH.
BREAD ISN'T FILLING AT ALL.
WAS IT ENOUGH?
...A WHOLE LOAF?
WHAT DO YOU WANT TO DO NOW?
YOU WANT TO GO OUT?
OH... MY PARENTS MIGHT TRY TO CALL, SO...
I GUESS.
CHAK
CHAK
THEN I'LL...
WE'RE HOME...!

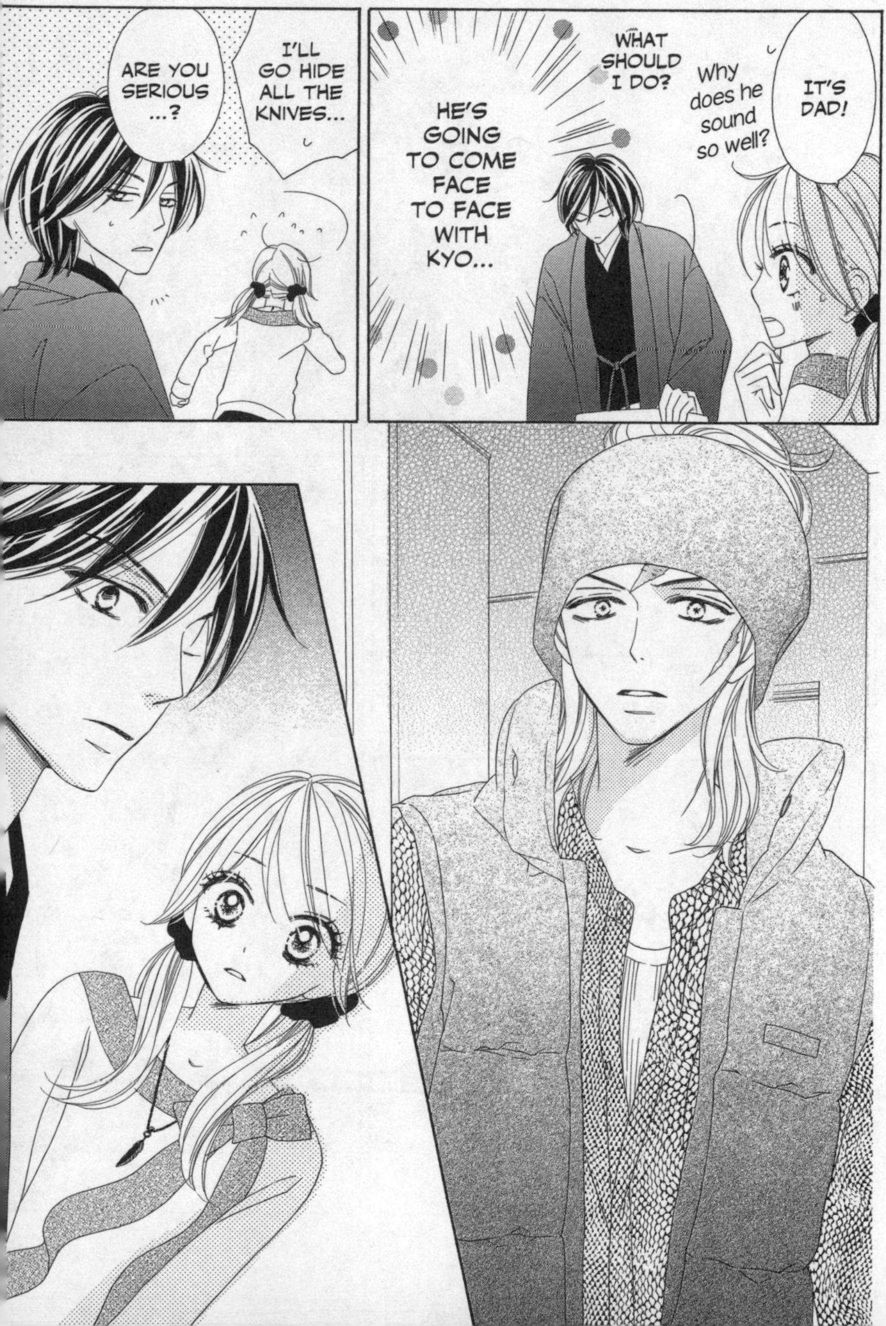
IT'S DAD!
Why does he sound so well?
WHAT SHOULD I DO?
HE'S GOING TO COME FACE TO FACE WITH KYO...
I'LL GO HIDE ALL THE KNIVES...
ARE YOU SERIOUS ...?

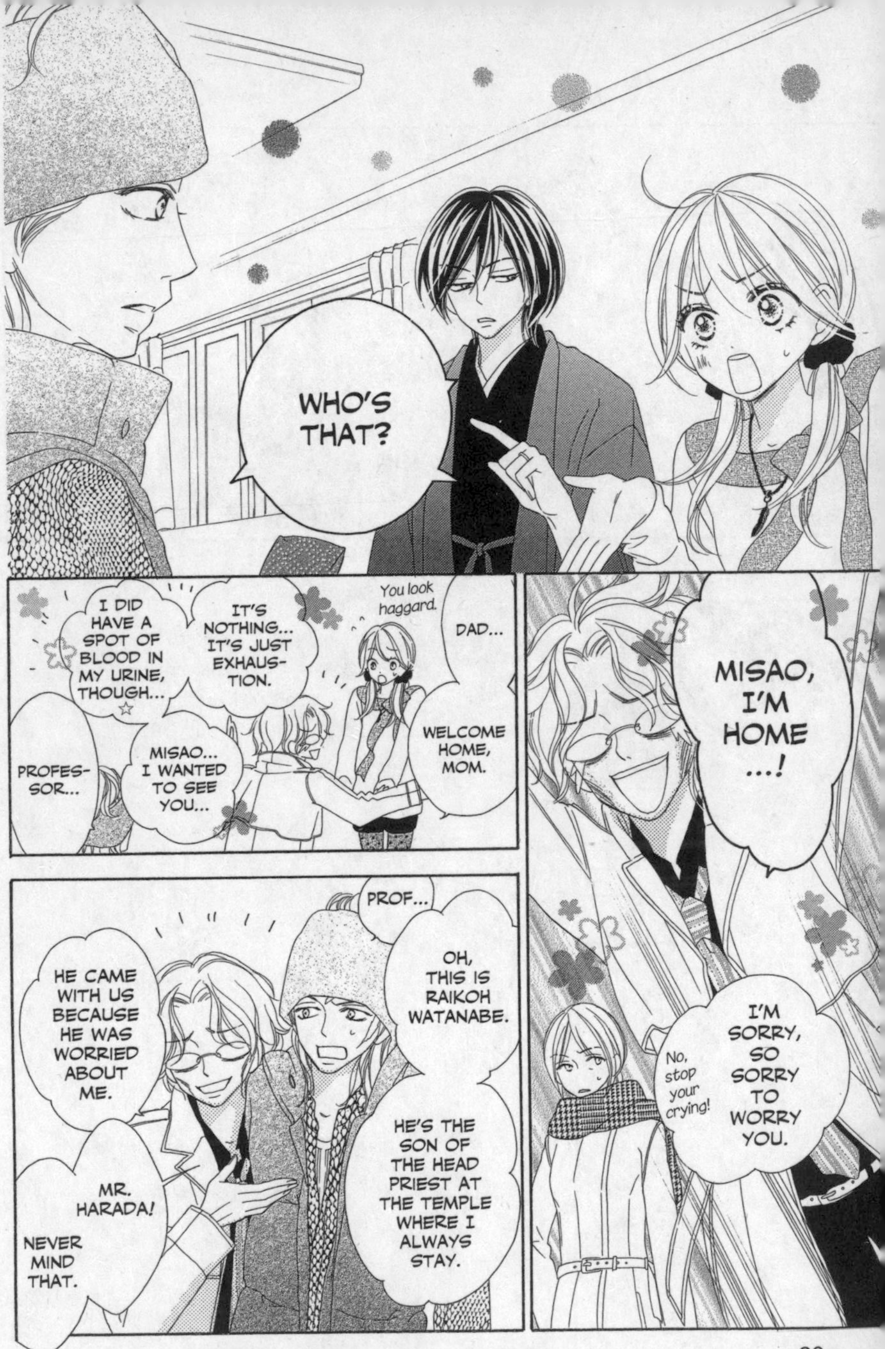
WHO'S THAT?
MISAO, I'M HOME ...!
I'M SORRY, SO SORRY TO WORRY YOU.
No, stop your crying!
DAD...
WELCOME HOME, MOM.
You look haggard.
IT'S NOTHING... IT'S JUST EXHAUSTION.
I DID HAVE A SPOT OF BLOOD IN MY URINE, THOUGH... ☆
MISAO... I WANTED TO SEE YOU...
PROFESSOR...
PROF...
OH, THIS IS RAIKOH WATANABE.
HE'S THE SON OF THE HEAD PRIEST AT THE TEMPLE WHERE I ALWAYS STAY.
HE CAME WITH US BECAUSE HE WAS WORRIED ABOUT ME.
MR. HARADA!
NEVER MIND THAT.

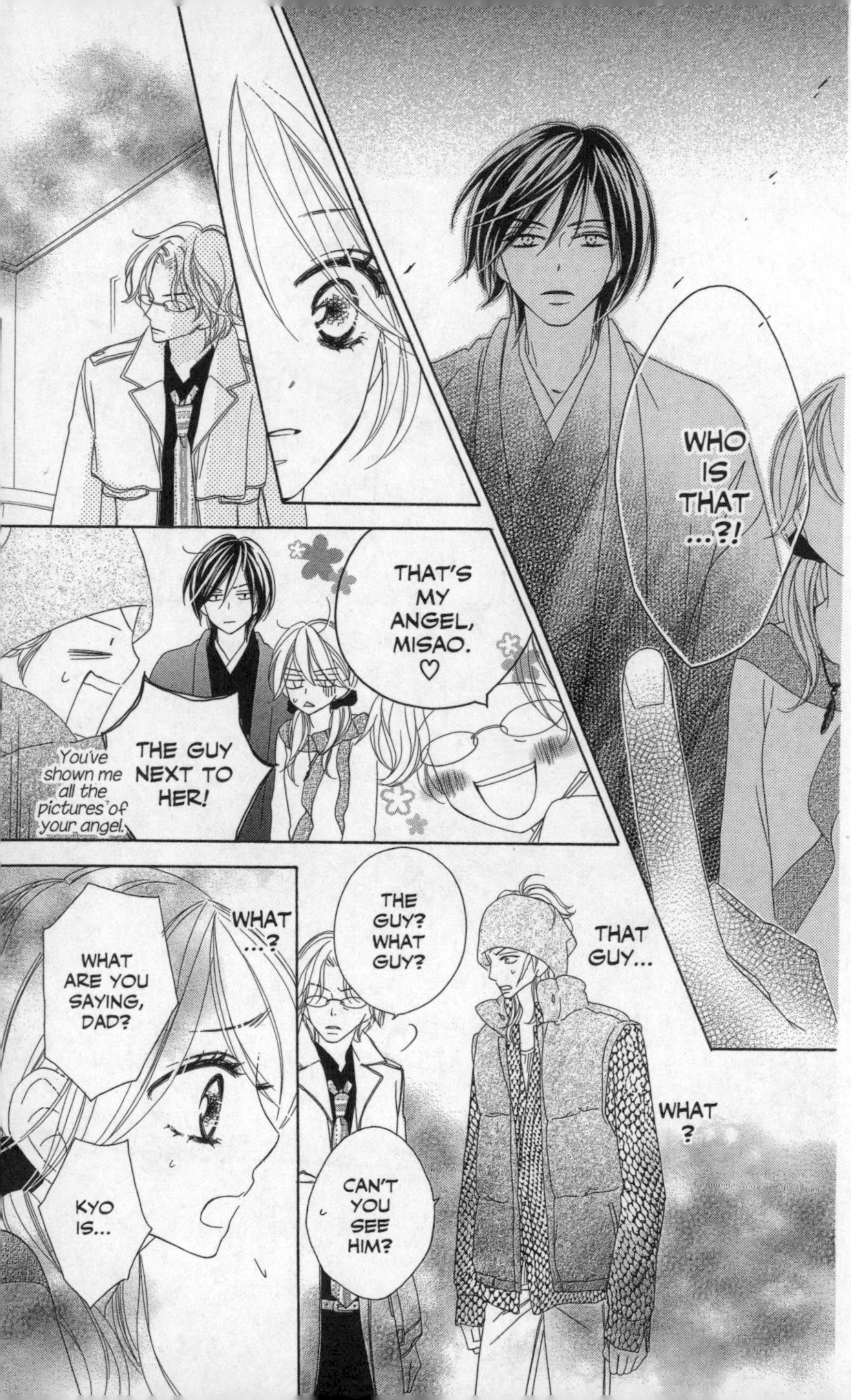
WHO IS THAT ...?!
THAT'S MY ANGEL, MISAO. ♡
THE GUY NEXT TO HER!
You've shown me all the pictures of your angel.
THAT GUY...
WHAT?
THE GUY? WHAT GUY?
CAN'T YOU SEE HIM?
WHAT ...?
WHAT ARE YOU SAYING, DAD?
KYO IS...

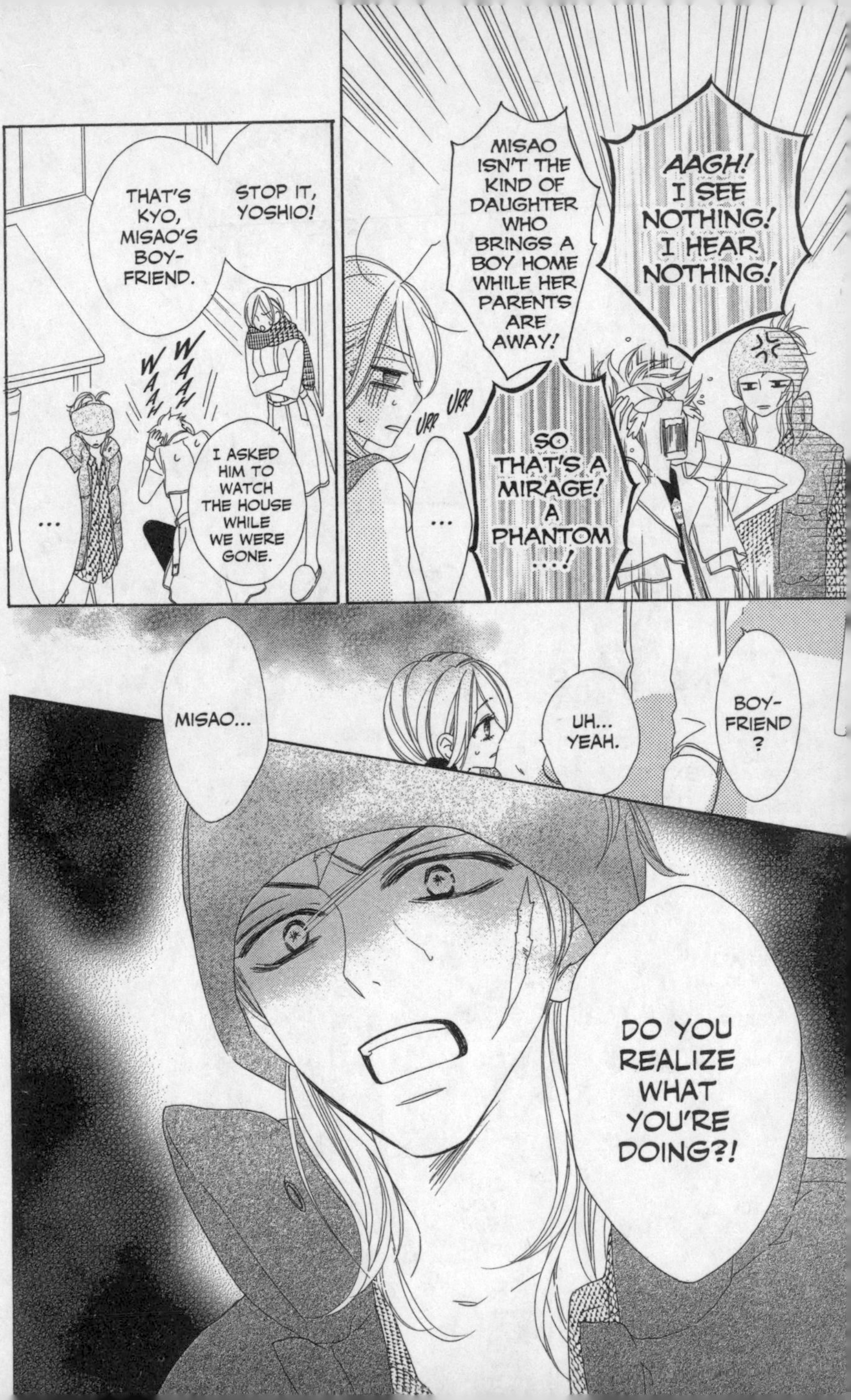
AAGH! I SEE NOTHING! I HEAR NOTHING!
MISAO ISN'T THE KIND OF DAUGHTER WHO BRINGS A BOY HOME WHILE HER PARENTS ARE AWAY!
SO THAT'S A MIRAGE! A PHANTOM...!
URR URR
...
STOP IT, YOSHIO!
THAT'S KYO, MISAO'S BOY-FRIEND.
WAAAH WAAAH
I ASKED HIM TO WATCH THE HOUSE WHILE WE WERE GONE.
...
BOY-FRIEND?
UH... YEAH.
MISAO...
DO YOU REALIZE WHAT YOU'RE DOING?!

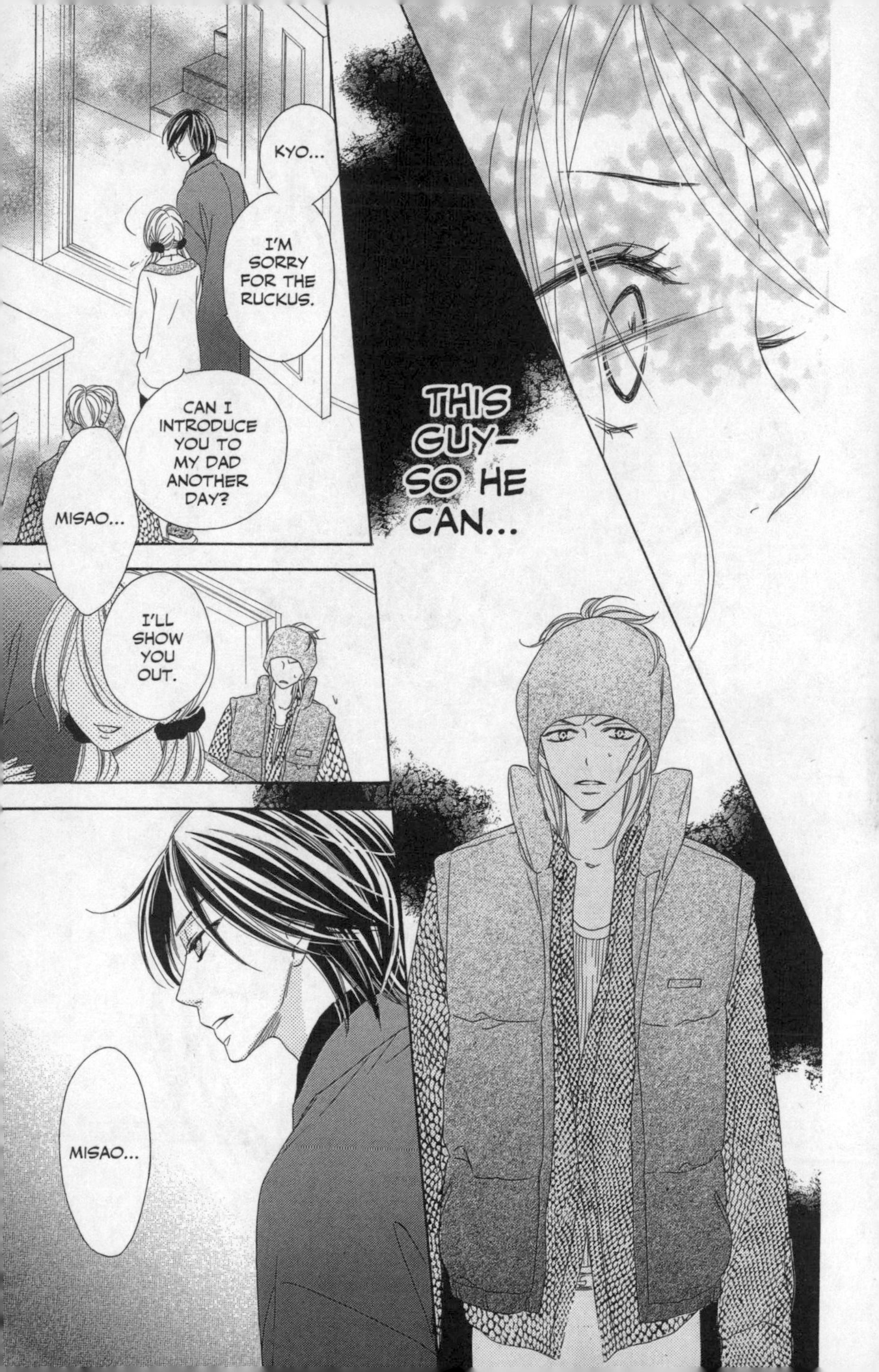
THIS GUY— SO HE CAN...
KYO...
I'M SORRY FOR THE RUCKUS.
CAN I INTRODUCE YOU TO MY DAD ANOTHER DAY?
MISAO...
I'LL SHOW YOU OUT.
MISAO...

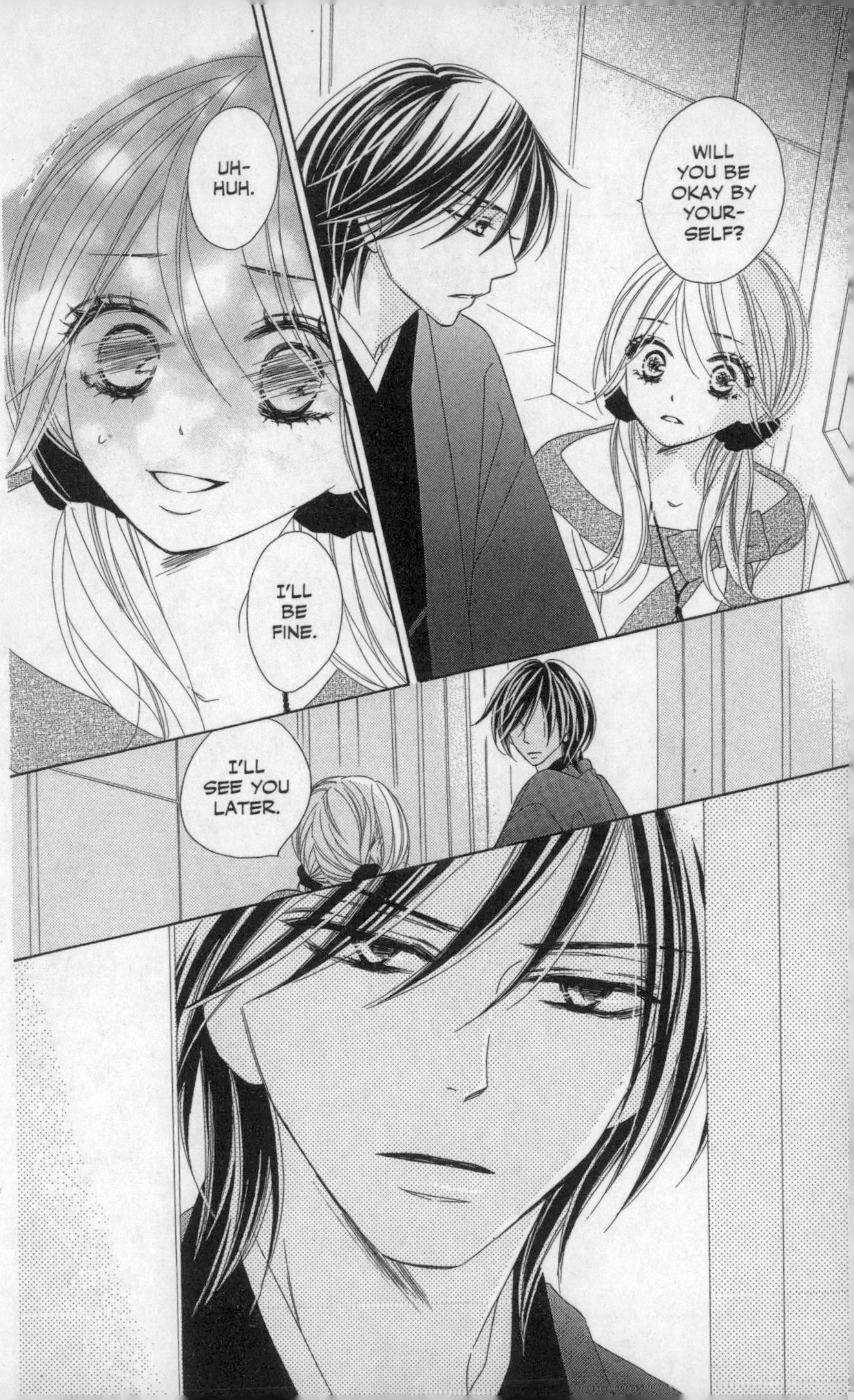
WILL YOU BE OKAY BY YOUR-SELF?
UH-HUH.
I'LL BE FINE.
I'LL SEE YOU LATER.

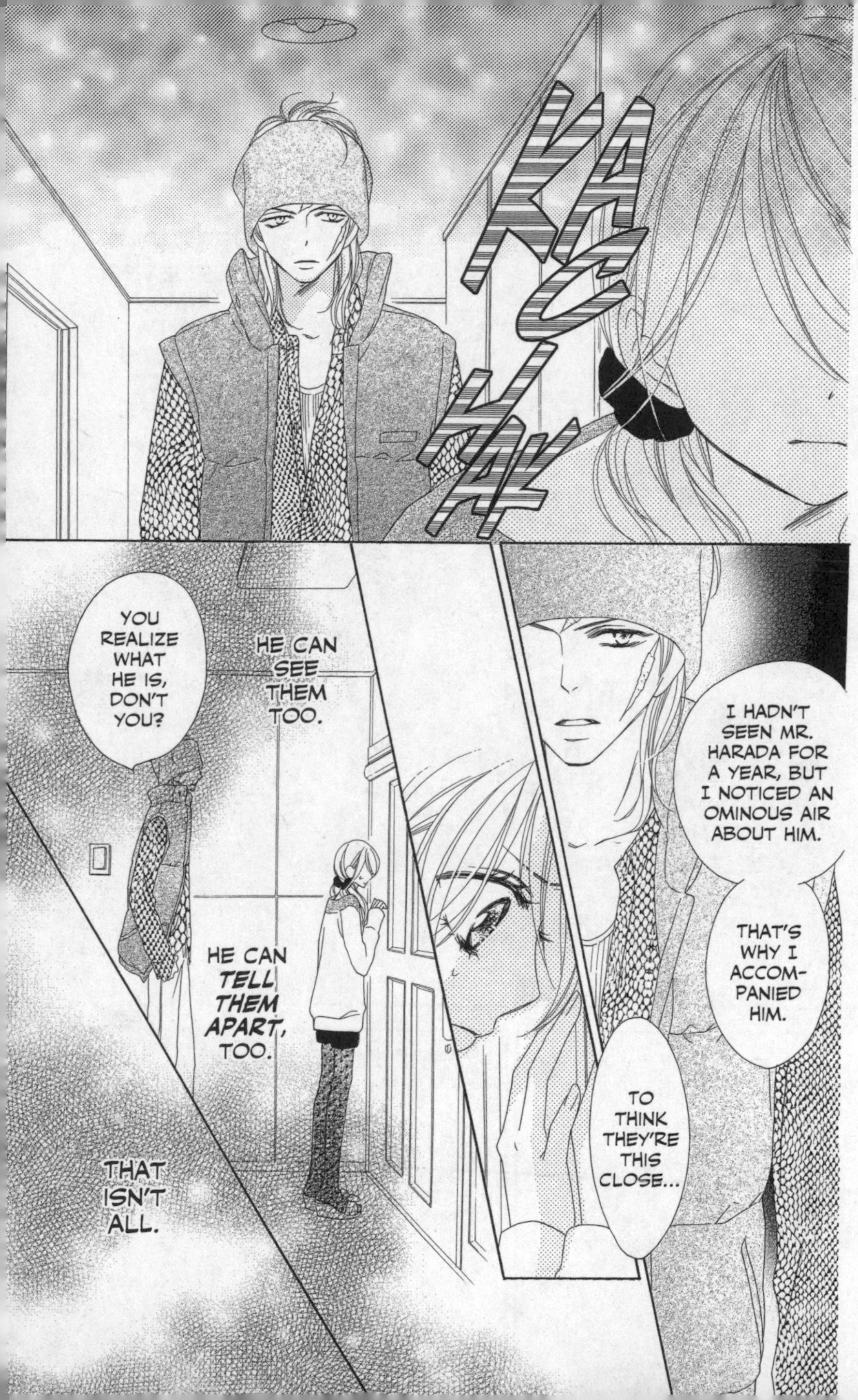
KACHAK
I HADN'T SEEN MR. HARADA FOR A YEAR, BUT I NOTICED AN OMINOUS AIR ABOUT HIM.
THAT'S WHY I ACCOMPANIED HIM.
TO THINK THEY'RE THIS CLOSE...
YOU REALIZE WHAT HE IS, DON'T YOU?
HE CAN SEE THEM TOO.
HE CAN *TELL THEM APART*, TOO.
THAT ISN'T ALL.

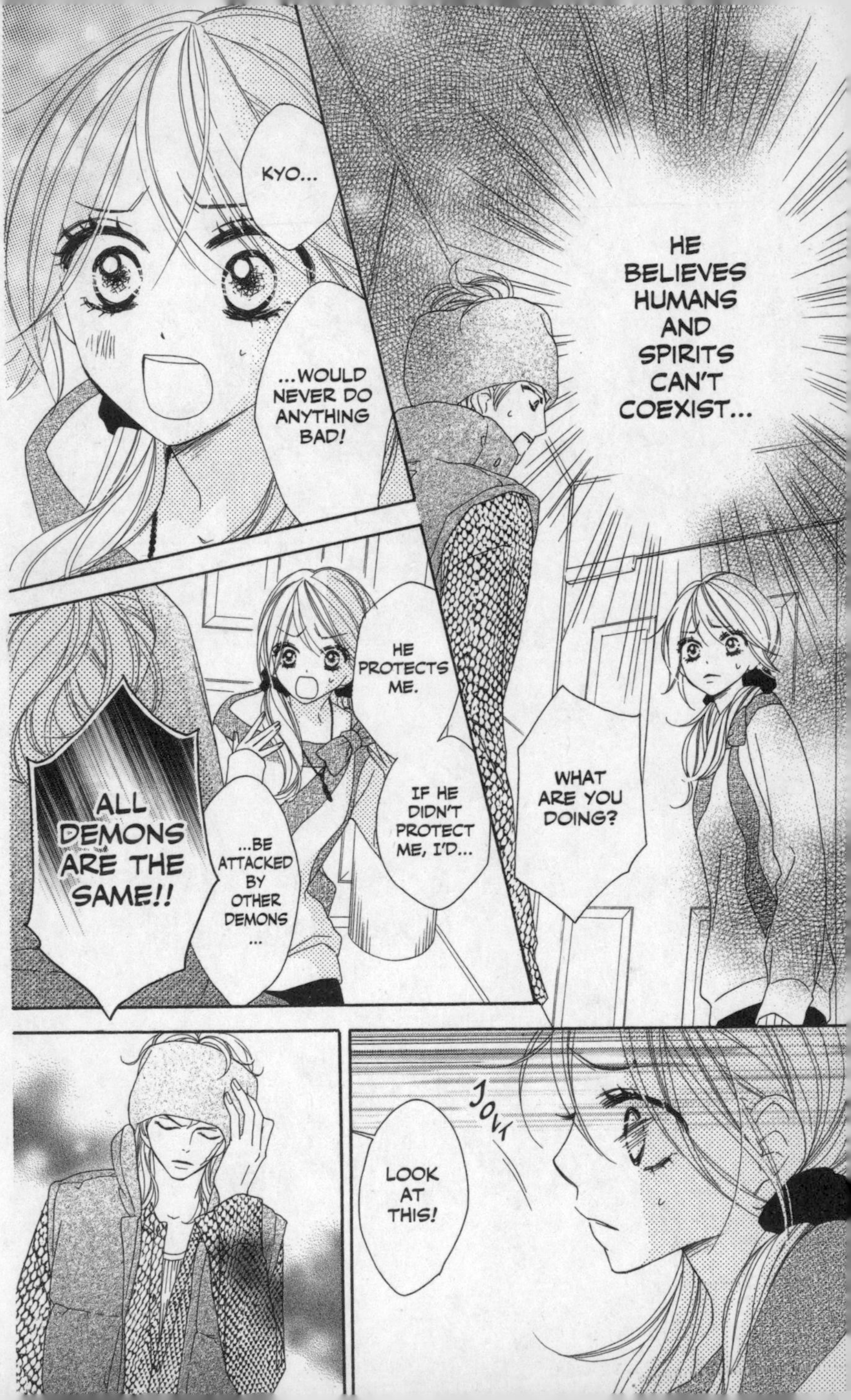
HE BELIEVES HUMANS AND SPIRITS CAN'T COEXIST...
WHAT ARE YOU DOING?
KYO...
...WOULD NEVER DO ANYTHING BAD!
HE PROTECTS ME.
IF HE DIDN'T PROTECT ME, I'D...
...BE ATTACKED BY OTHER DEMONS...
ALL DEMONS ARE THE SAME!!
JOLT
LOOK AT THIS!

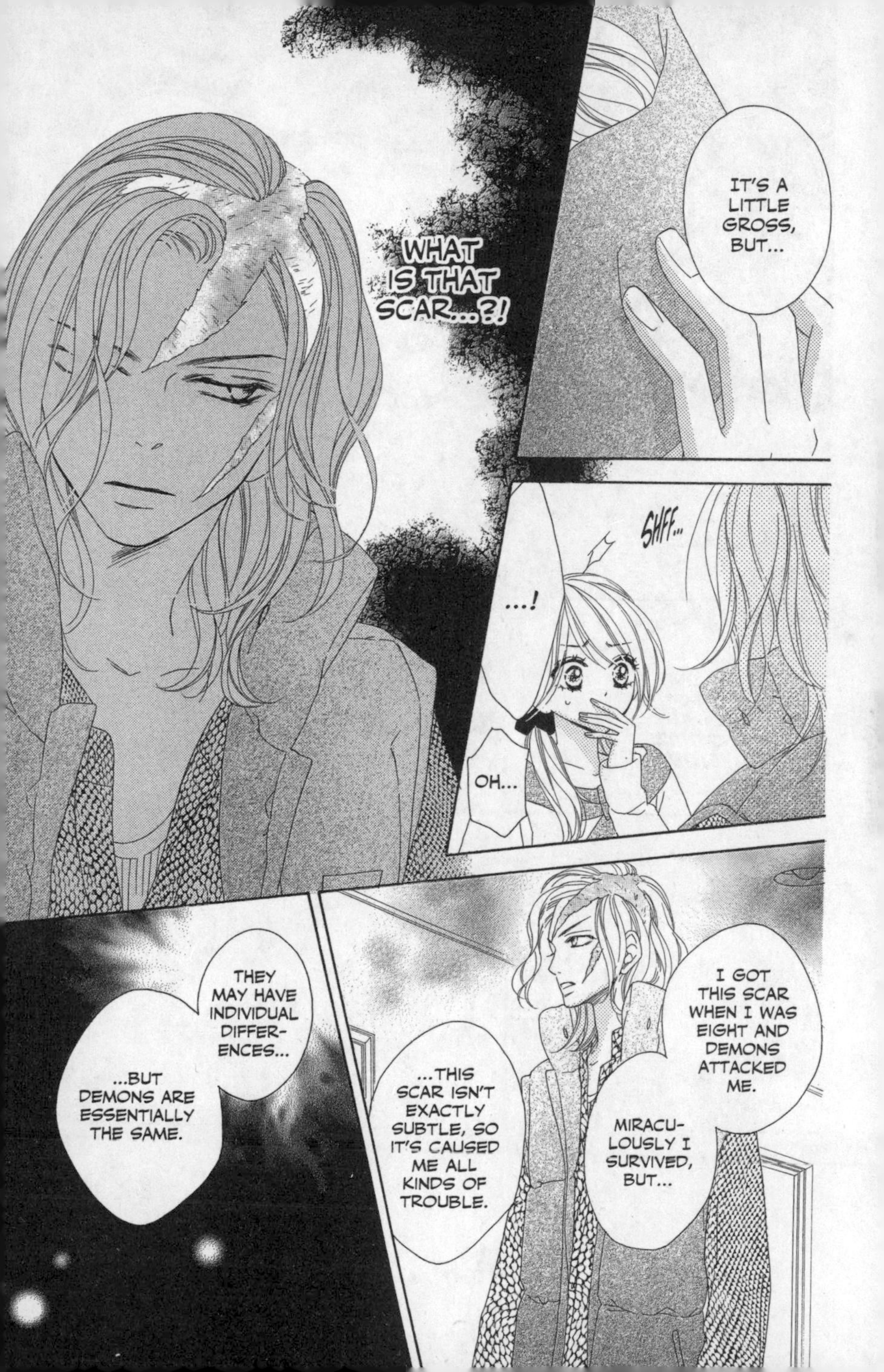
IT'S A LITTLE GROSS, BUT...
SHFF...
...!
OH...
WHAT IS THAT SCAR...?!
I GOT THIS SCAR WHEN I WAS EIGHT AND DEMONS ATTACKED ME.
MIRACU-LOUSLY I SURVIVED, BUT...
...THIS SCAR ISN'T EXACTLY SUBTLE, SO IT'S CAUSED ME ALL KINDS OF TROUBLE.
THEY MAY HAVE INDIVIDUAL DIFFER-ENCES...
...BUT DEMONS ARE ESSENTIALLY THE SAME.

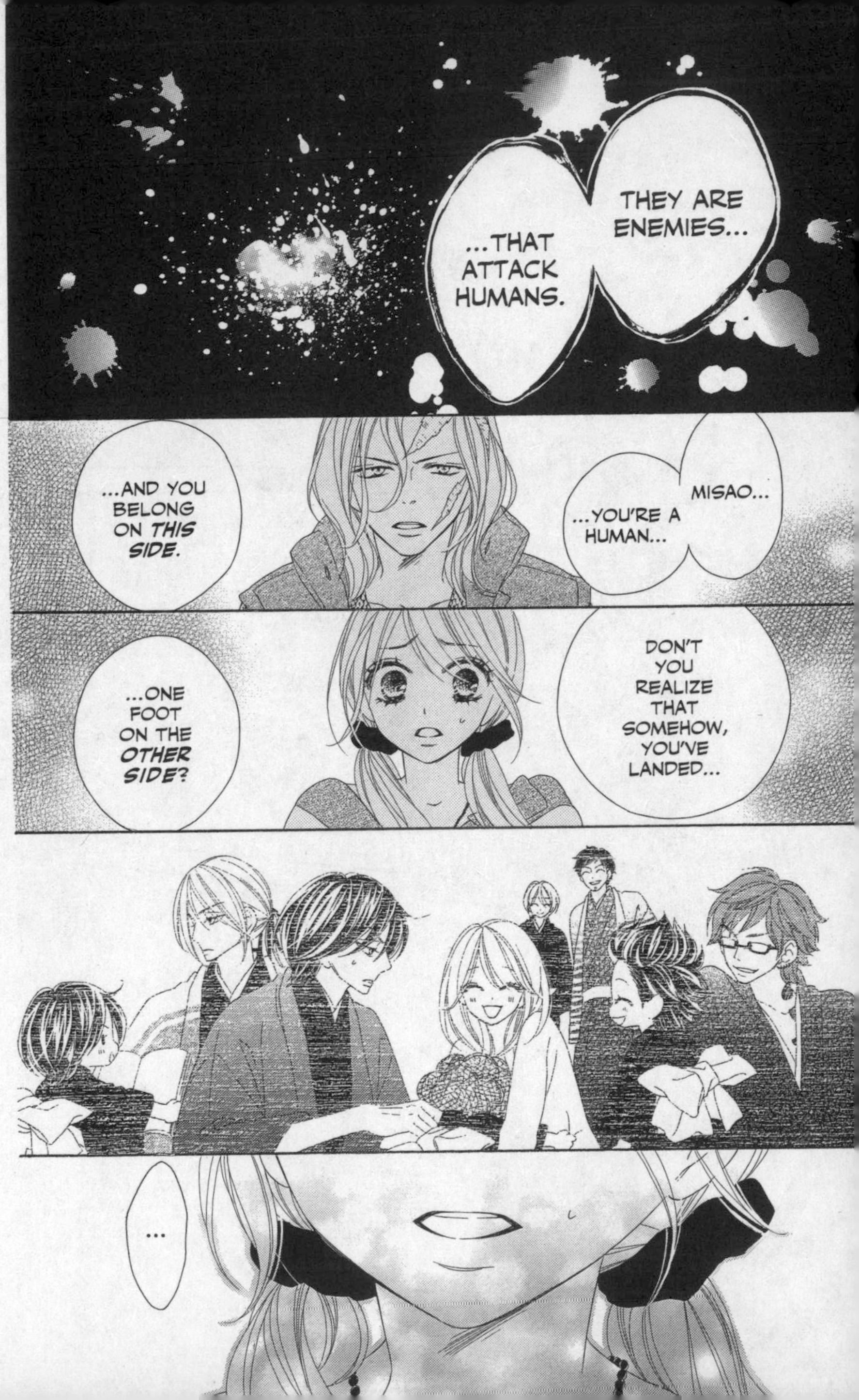
THEY ARE ENEMIES...
...THAT ATTACK HUMANS.
MISAO...
...YOU'RE A HUMAN...
...AND YOU BELONG ON *THIS SIDE*.
DON'T YOU REALIZE THAT SOMEHOW, YOU'VE LANDED...
...ONE FOOT ON THE *OTHER SIDE*?
...

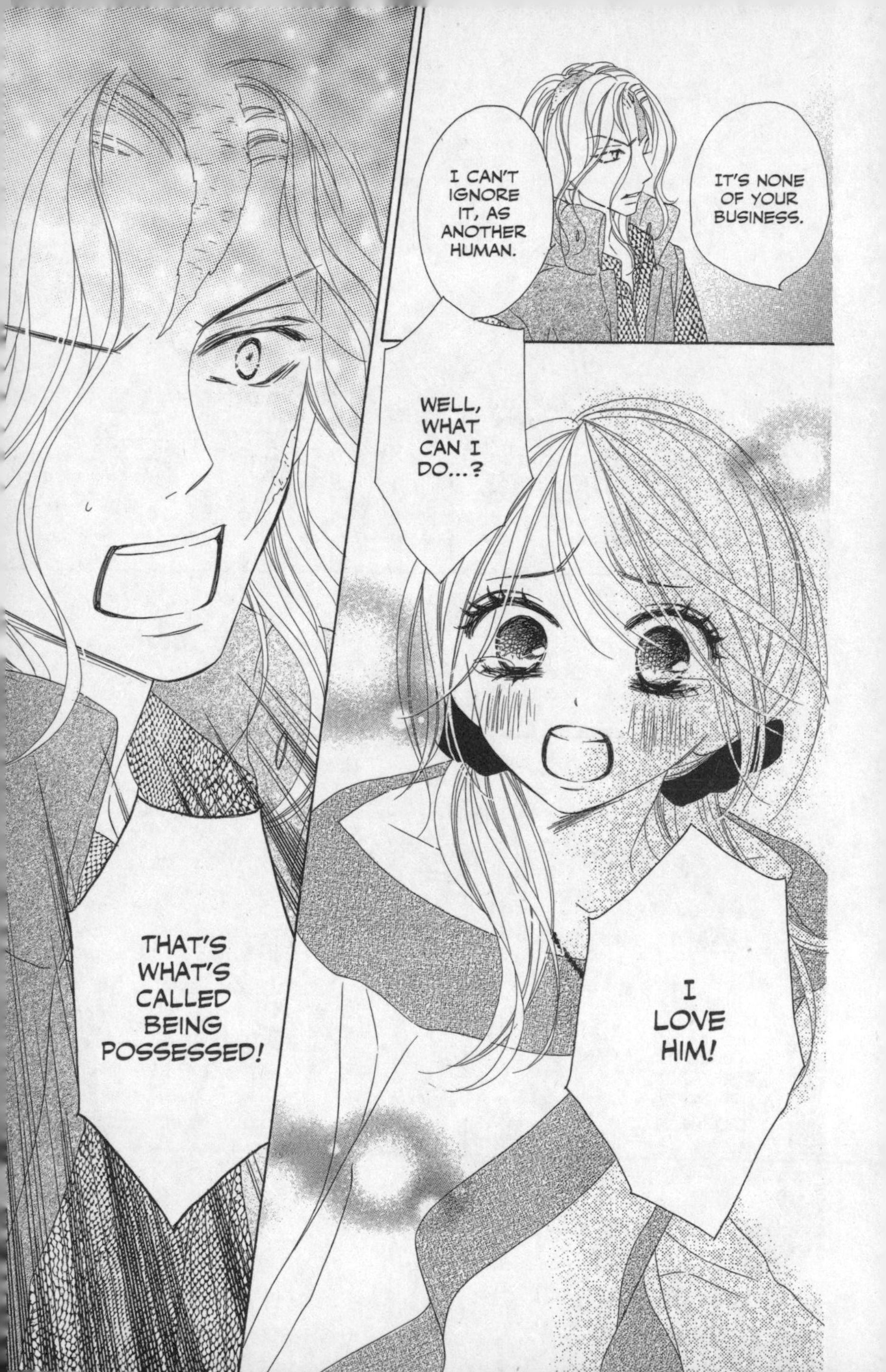
IT'S NONE OF YOUR BUSINESS.
I CAN'T IGNORE IT, AS ANOTHER HUMAN.
WELL, WHAT CAN I DO...?
I LOVE HIM!
THAT'S WHAT'S CALLED BEING POSSESSED!

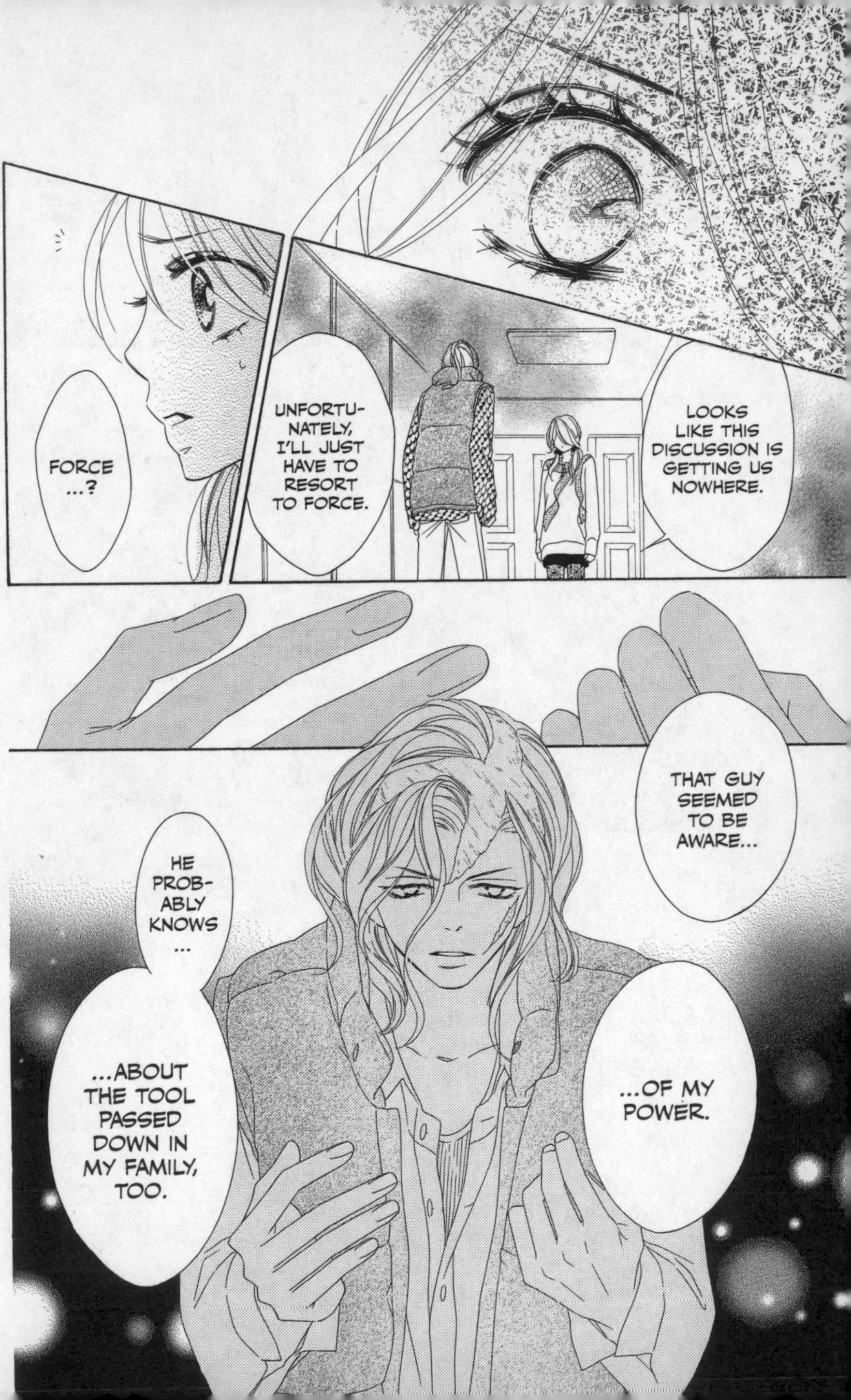
LOOKS LIKE THIS DISCUSSION IS GETTING US NOWHERE.
UNFORTU-NATELY, I'LL JUST HAVE TO RESORT TO FORCE.
FORCE ...?
THAT GUY SEEMED TO BE AWARE...
...OF MY POWER.
HE PROB-ABLY KNOWS ...
...ABOUT THE TOOL PASSED DOWN IN MY FAMILY, TOO.

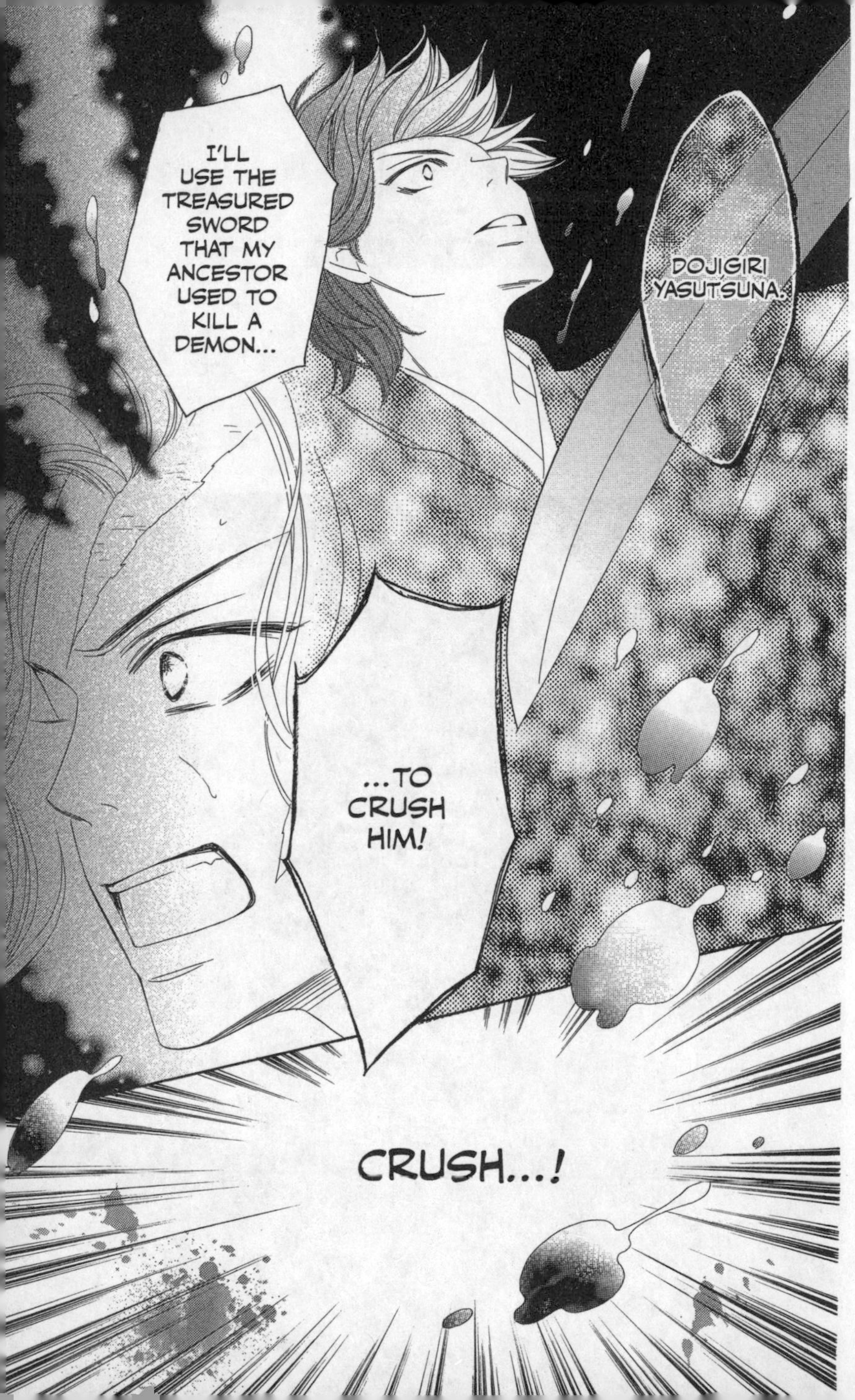
DOJIGIRI YASUTSUNA.
I'LL USE THE TREASURED SWORD THAT MY ANCESTOR USED TO KILL A DEMON...
...TO CRUSH HIM!
CRUSH...!

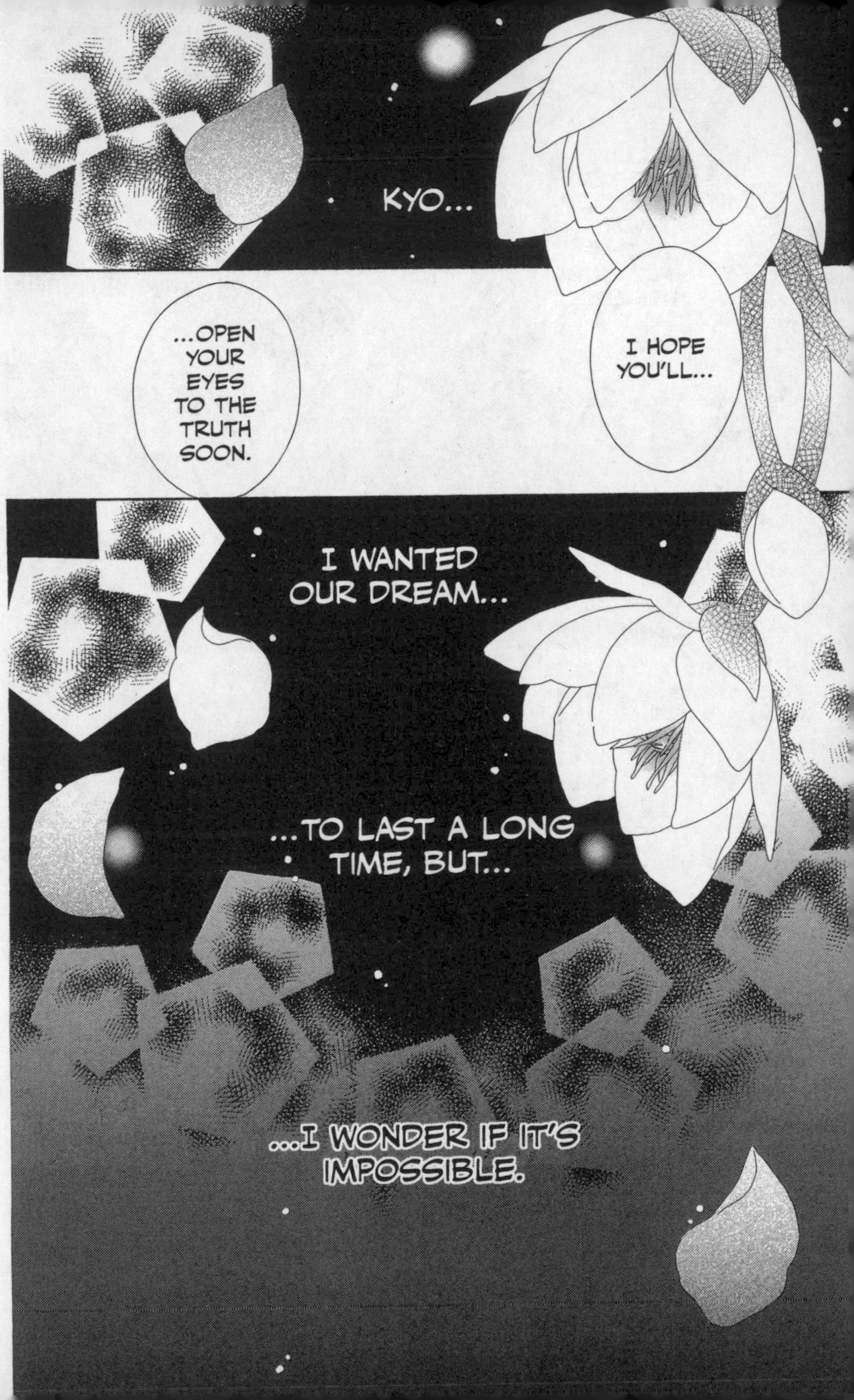
KYO...
I HOPE YOU'LL...
...OPEN YOUR EYES TO THE TRUTH SOON.
I WANTED OUR DREAM...
...TO LAST A LONG TIME, BUT...
...I WONDER IF IT'S IMPOSSIBLE.

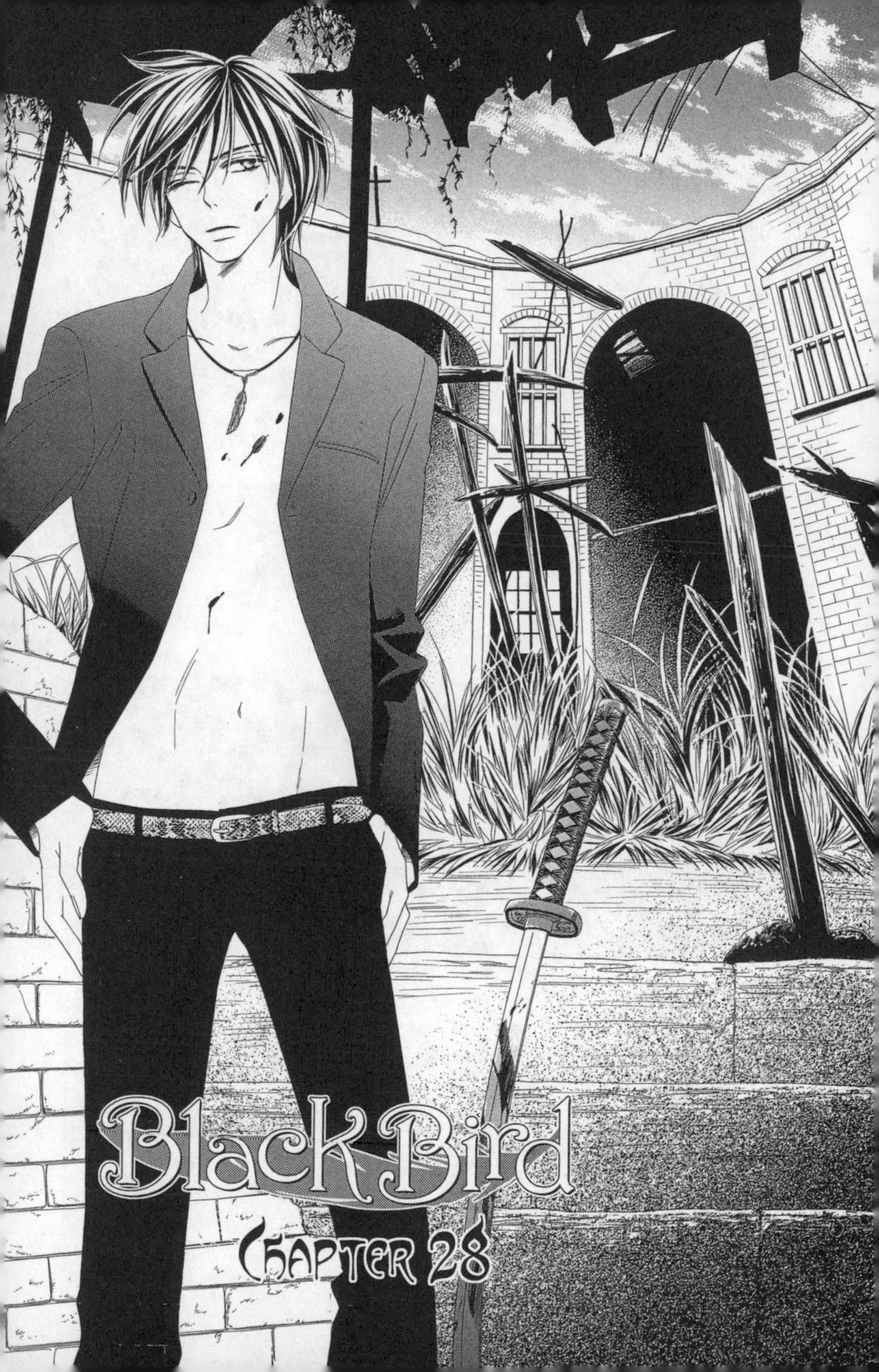
Black Bird
Chapter 28

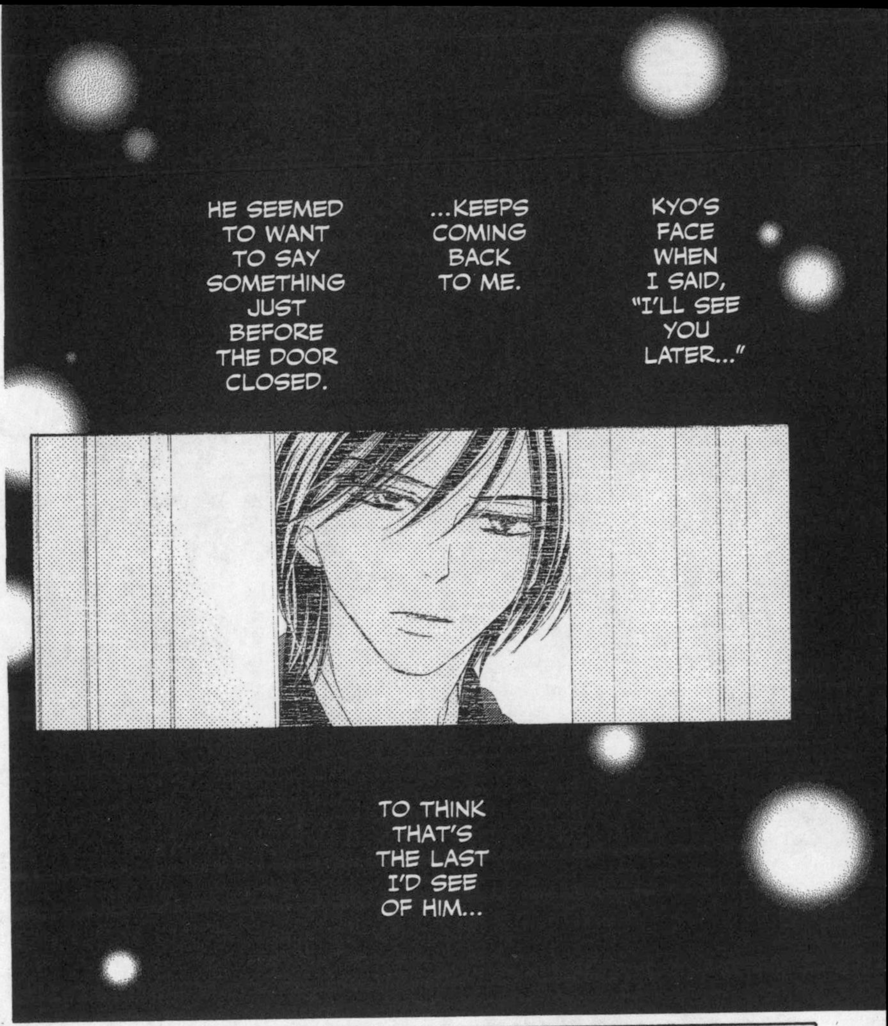
KYO'S FACE WHEN I SAID, "I'LL SEE YOU LATER..."
...KEEPS COMING BACK TO ME.
HE SEEMED TO WANT TO SAY SOMETHING JUST BEFORE THE DOOR CLOSED.
TO THINK THAT'S THE LAST I'D SEE OF HIM...

Raikoh Watanabe

Age: 18
Height: 177cm.

This name is easily recognizable!
I took it from Heian period monster buster Minamoto no Yorimitsu* and his retainer, Watanabe no Tsuna. The Dojigiri Yasutsuna is a real sword. The actual sword is stored away safely!
(Incidentally, "Doji" refers to the ogre Shuten-doji.)

I hope you will watch to see how his self-righteous actions will affect Misao and Kyo!

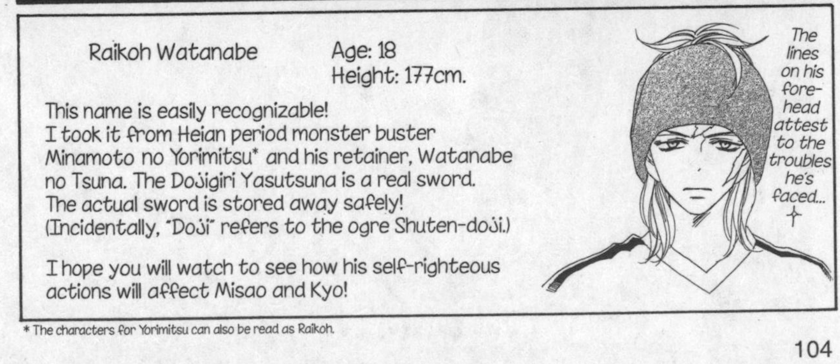
The lines on his fore-head attest to the troubles he's faced...

* The characters for Yorimitsu can also be read as Raikoh.

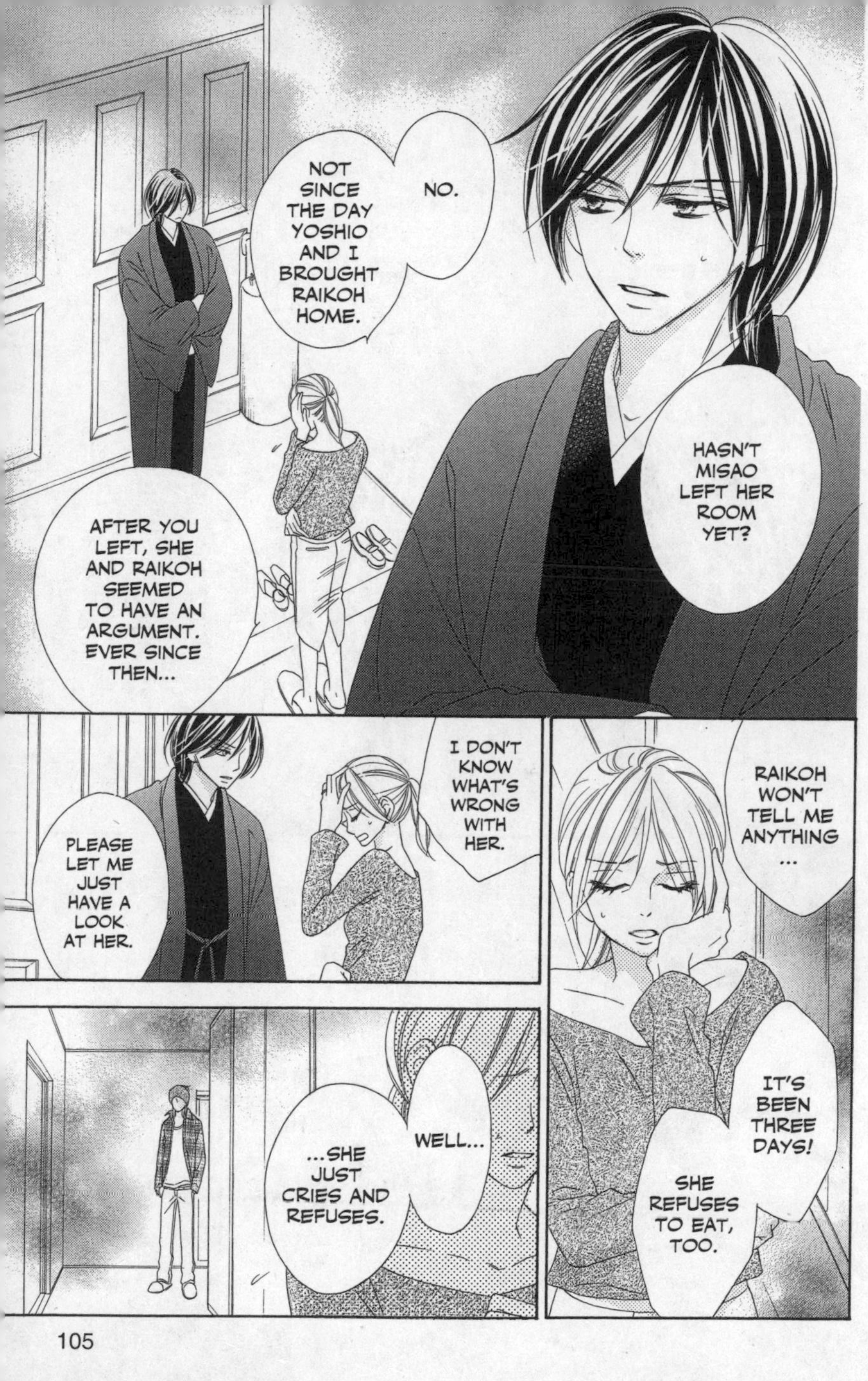
HASN'T MISAO LEFT HER ROOM YET?
NO.
NOT SINCE THE DAY YOSHIO AND I BROUGHT RAIKOH HOME.
AFTER YOU LEFT, SHE AND RAIKOH SEEMED TO HAVE AN ARGUMENT. EVER SINCE THEN...
RAIKOH WON'T TELL ME ANYTHING...
IT'S BEEN THREE DAYS!
SHE REFUSES TO EAT, TOO.
I DON'T KNOW WHAT'S WRONG WITH HER.
PLEASE LET ME JUST HAVE A LOOK AT HER.
WELL...
...SHE JUST CRIES AND REFUSES.

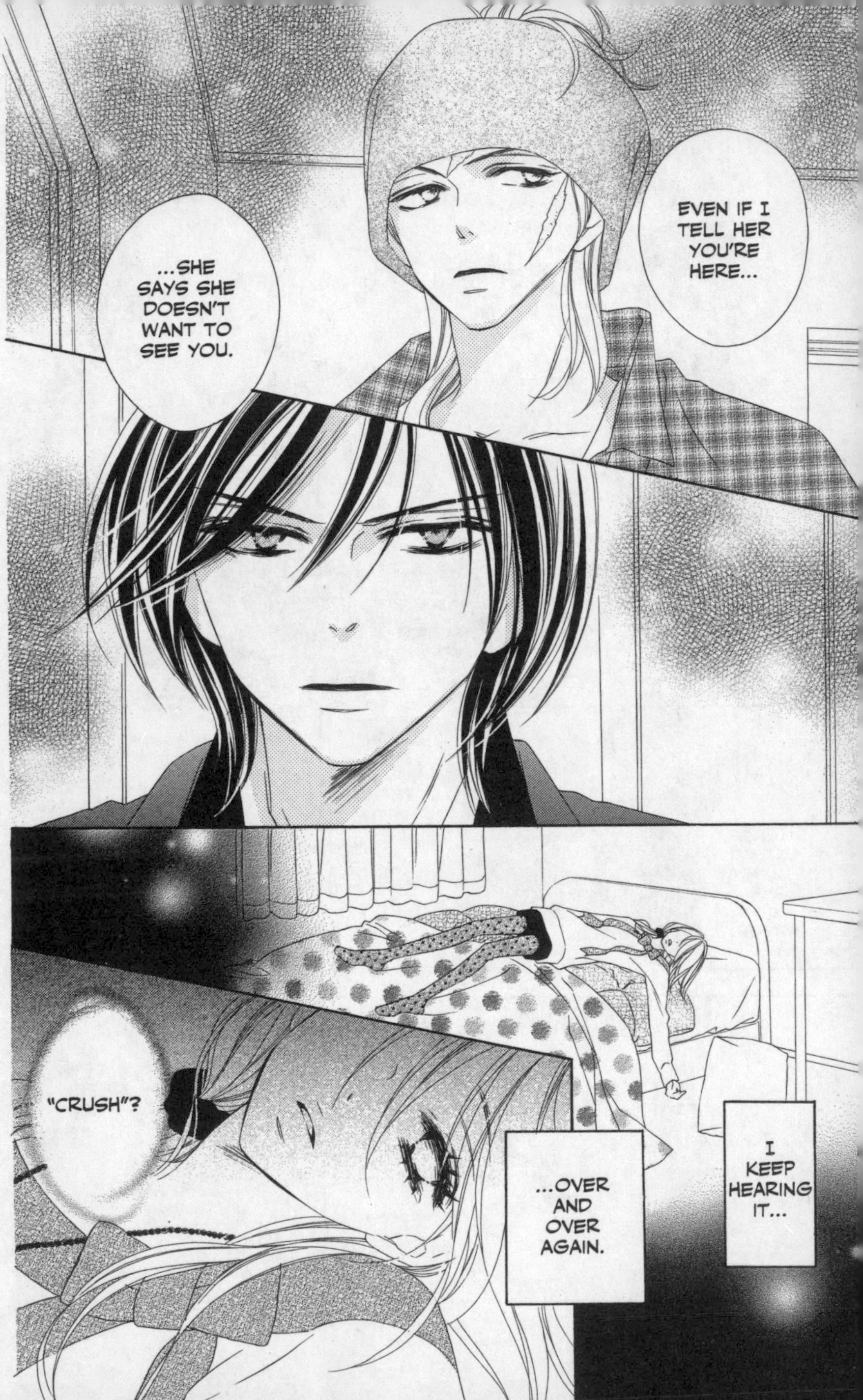
EVEN IF I TELL HER YOU'RE HERE...
...SHE SAYS SHE DOESN'T WANT TO SEE YOU.
I KEEP HEARING IT...
...OVER AND OVER AGAIN.
"CRUSH"?

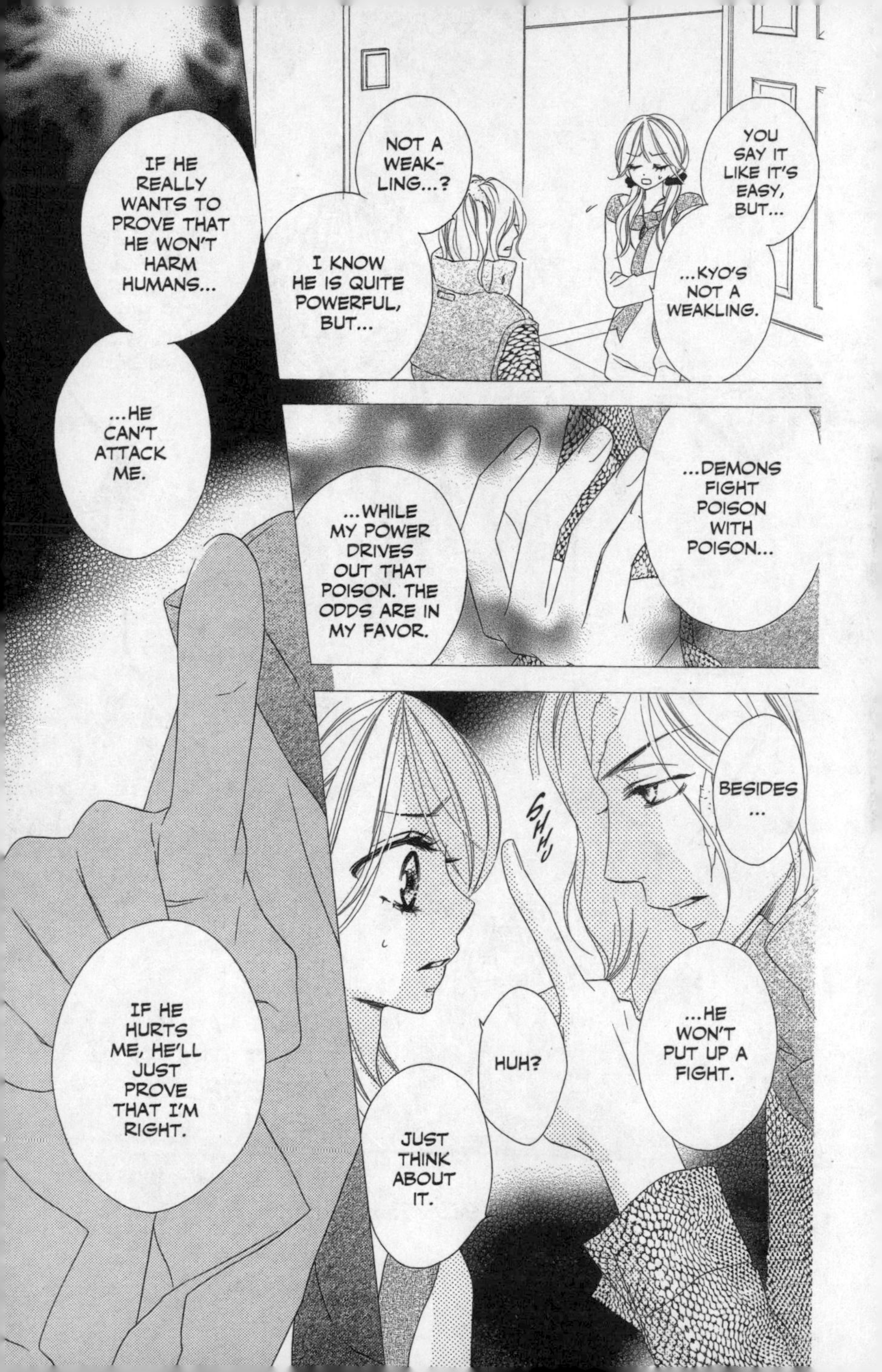
YOU SAY IT LIKE IT'S EASY, BUT...
...KYO'S NOT A WEAKLING.
NOT A WEAK-LING...?
I KNOW HE IS QUITE POWERFUL, BUT...
...DEMONS FIGHT POISON WITH POISON...
...WHILE MY POWER DRIVES OUT THAT POISON. THE ODDS ARE IN MY FAVOR.
BESIDES...
...HE WON'T PUT UP A FIGHT.
HUH?
JUST THINK ABOUT IT.
IF HE REALLY WANTS TO PROVE THAT HE WON'T HARM HUMANS...
...HE CAN'T ATTACK ME.
IF HE HURTS ME, HE'LL JUST PROVE THAT I'M RIGHT.

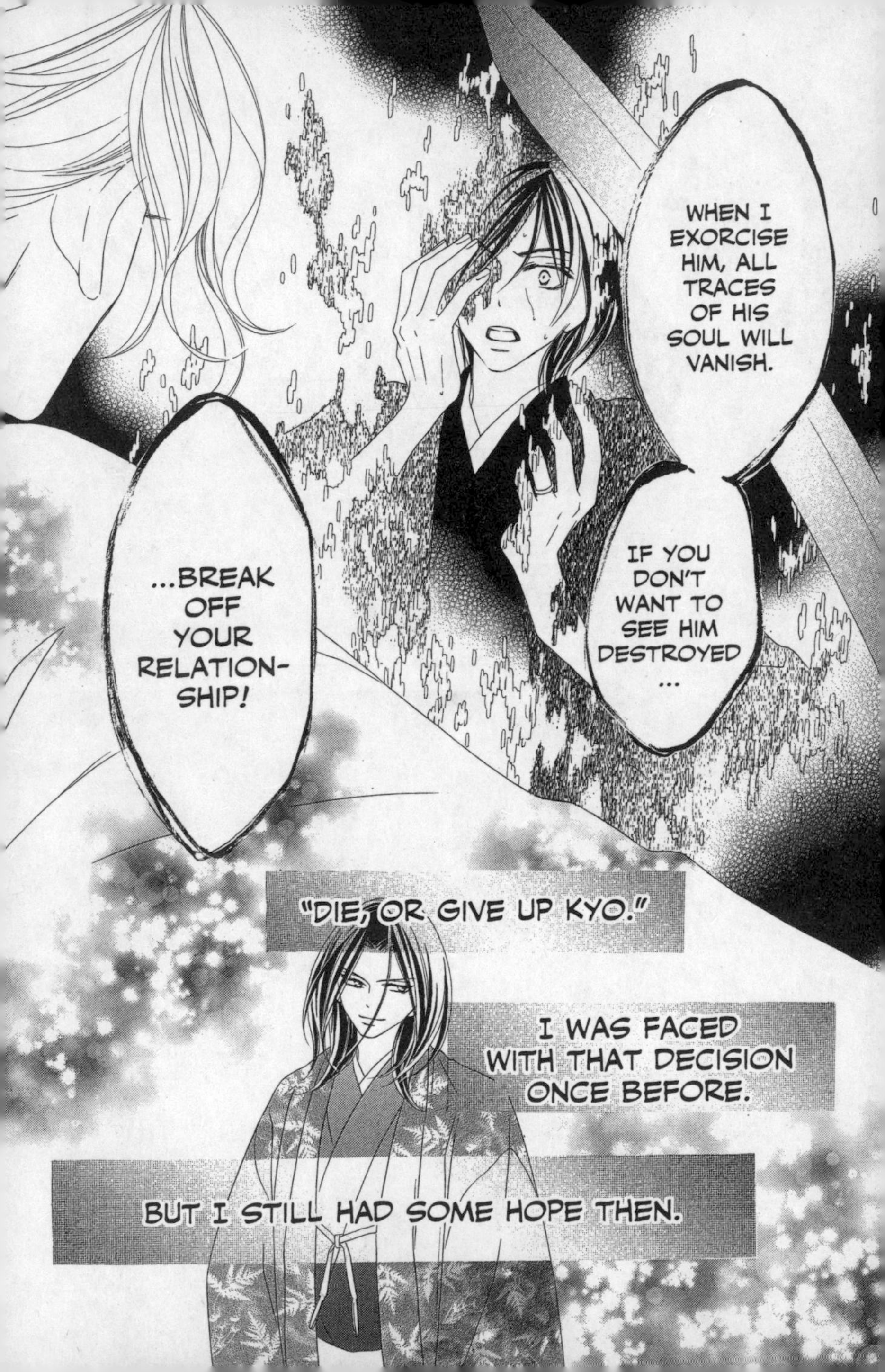
WHEN I EXORCISE HIM, ALL TRACES OF HIS SOUL WILL VANISH.
IF YOU DON'T WANT TO SEE HIM DESTROYED ...
...BREAK OFF YOUR RELATION-SHIP!
"DIE, OR GIVE UP KYO."
I WAS FACED WITH THAT DECISION ONCE BEFORE.
BUT I STILL HAD SOME HOPE THEN.

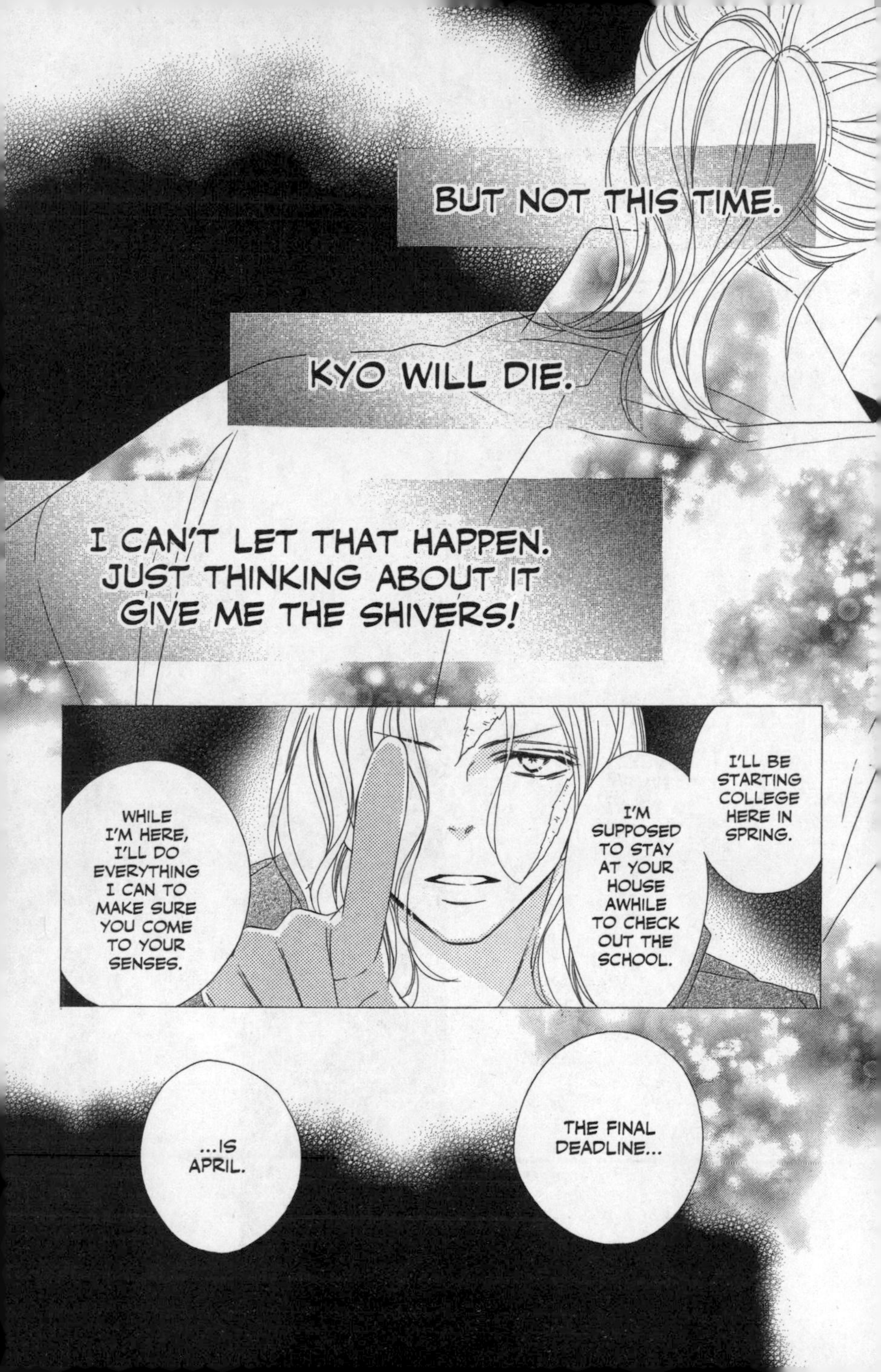
BUT NOT THIS TIME.
KYO WILL DIE.
I CAN'T LET THAT HAPPEN. JUST THINKING ABOUT IT GIVE ME THE SHIVERS!
I'LL BE STARTING COLLEGE HERE IN SPRING.
I'M SUPPOSED TO STAY AT YOUR HOUSE AWHILE TO CHECK OUT THE SCHOOL.
WHILE I'M HERE, I'LL DO EVERYTHING I CAN TO MAKE SURE YOU COME TO YOUR SENSES.
THE FINAL DEADLINE...
...IS APRIL.

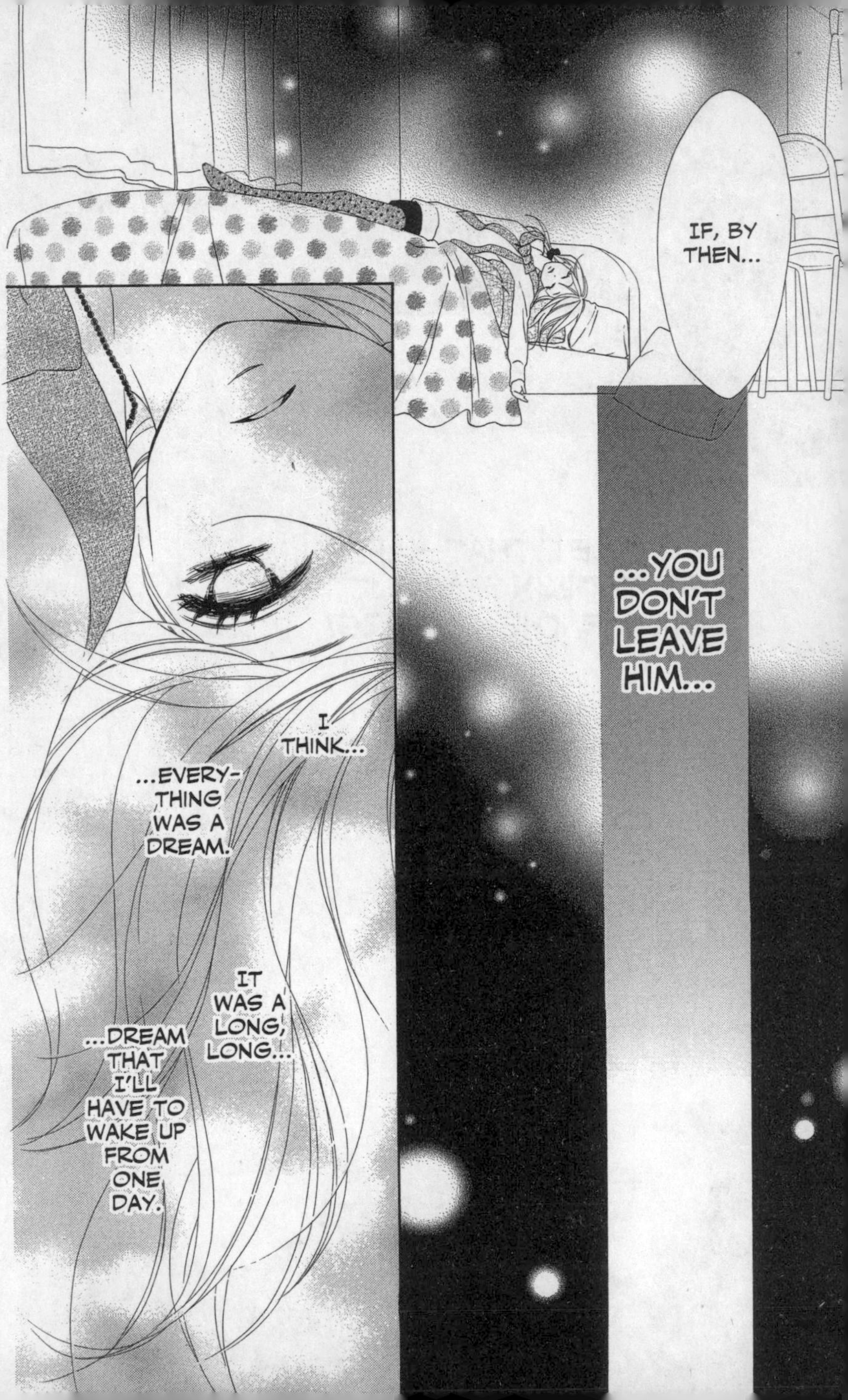
IF, BY THEN...
...YOU DON'T LEAVE HIM...
I THINK...
...EVERYTHING WAS A DREAM.
IT WAS A LONG, LONG...
...DREAM THAT I'LL HAVE TO WAKE UP FROM ONE DAY.

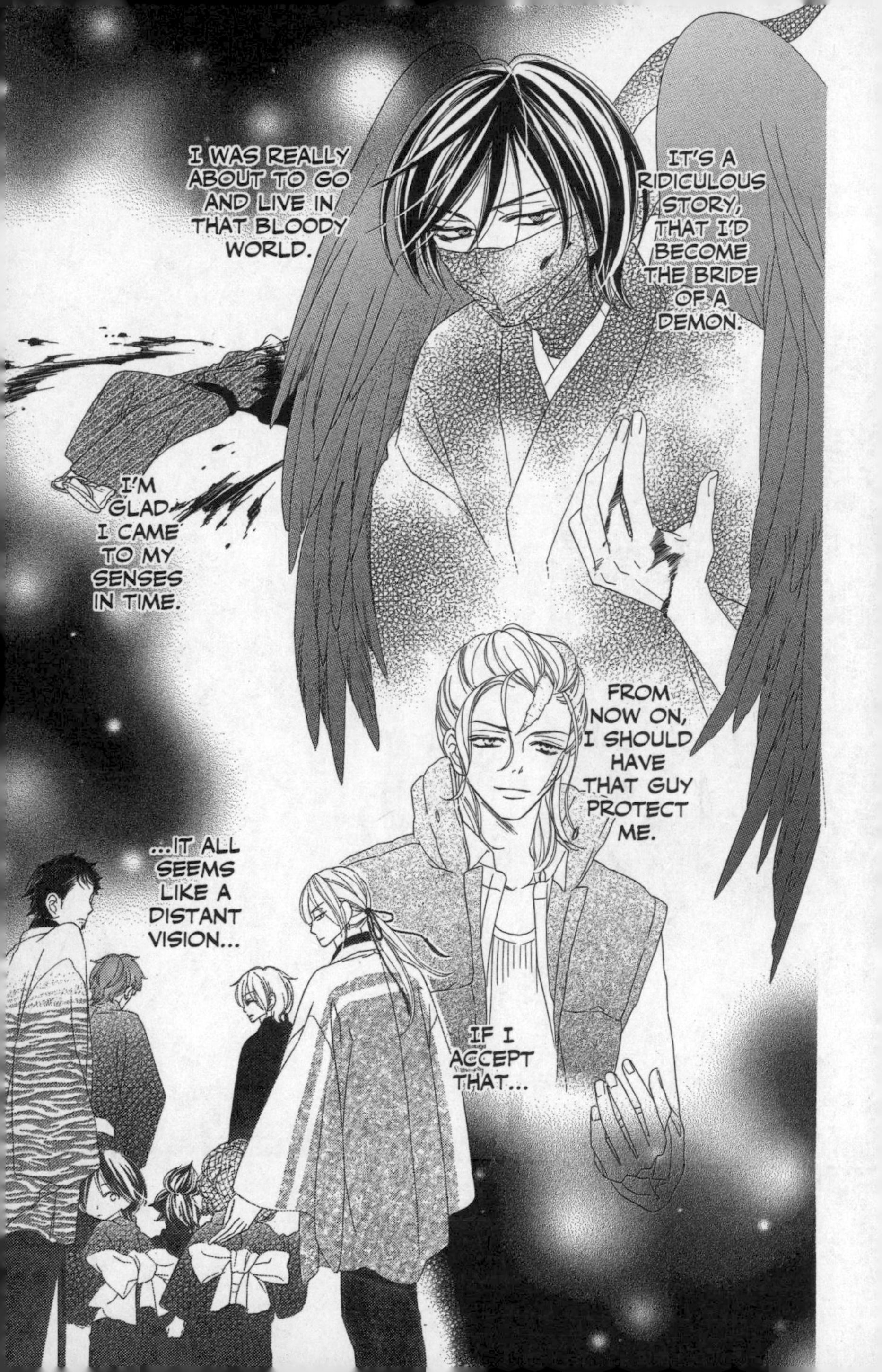
IT'S A RIDICULOUS STORY, THAT I'D BECOME THE BRIDE OF A DEMON.
I WAS REALLY ABOUT TO GO AND LIVE IN THAT BLOODY WORLD.
I'M GLAD I CAME TO MY SENSES IN TIME.
FROM NOW ON, I SHOULD HAVE THAT GUY PROTECT ME.
IF I ACCEPT THAT...
...IT ALL SEEMS LIKE A DISTANT VISION...

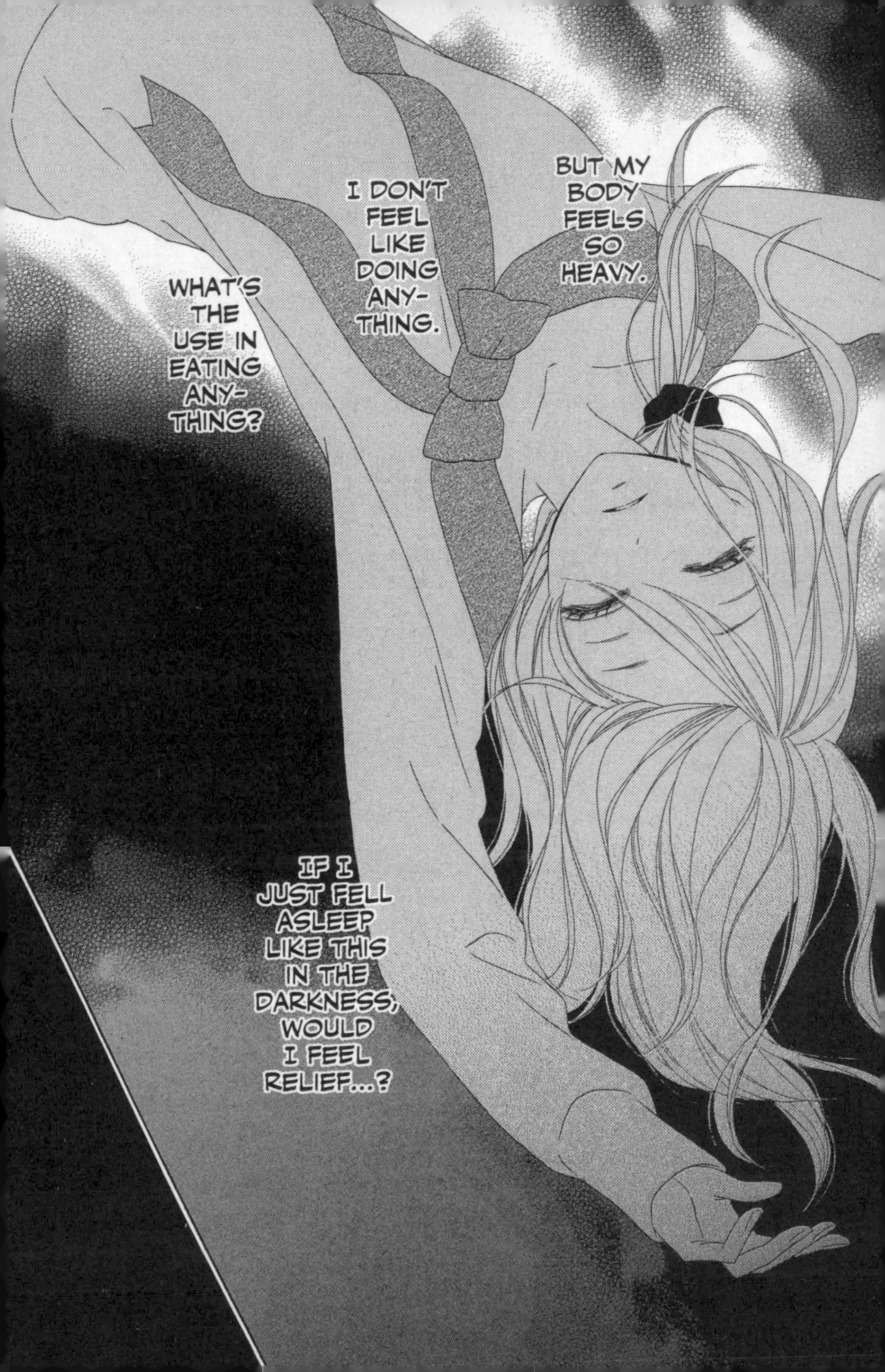
BUT MY BODY FEELS SO HEAVY.
I DON'T FEEL LIKE DOING ANY-THING.
WHAT'S THE USE IN EATING ANY-THING?
IF I JUST FELL ASLEEP LIKE THIS IN THE DARKNESS, WOULD I FEEL RELIEF...?

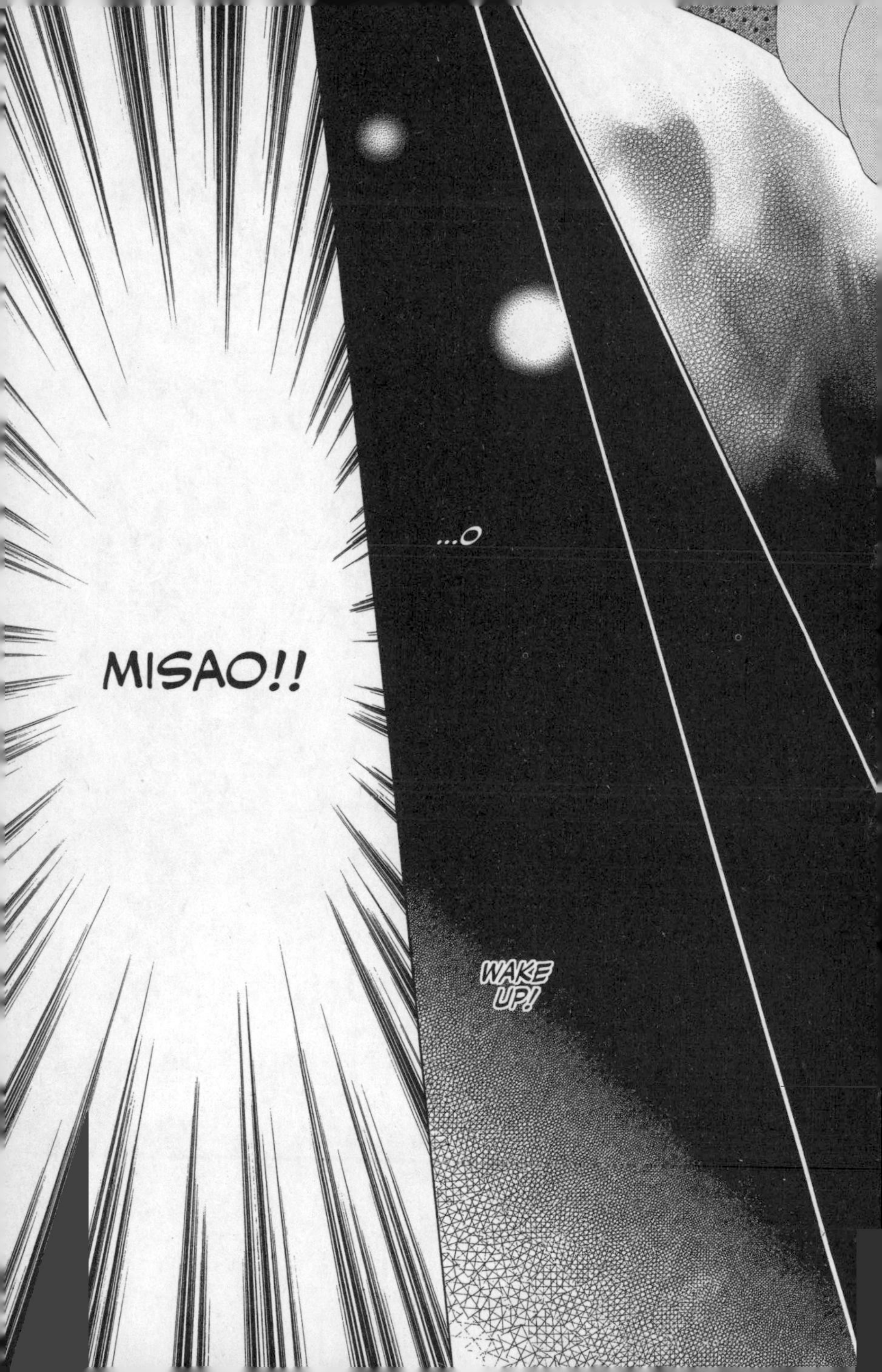
...O
WAKE UP!
MISAO!!

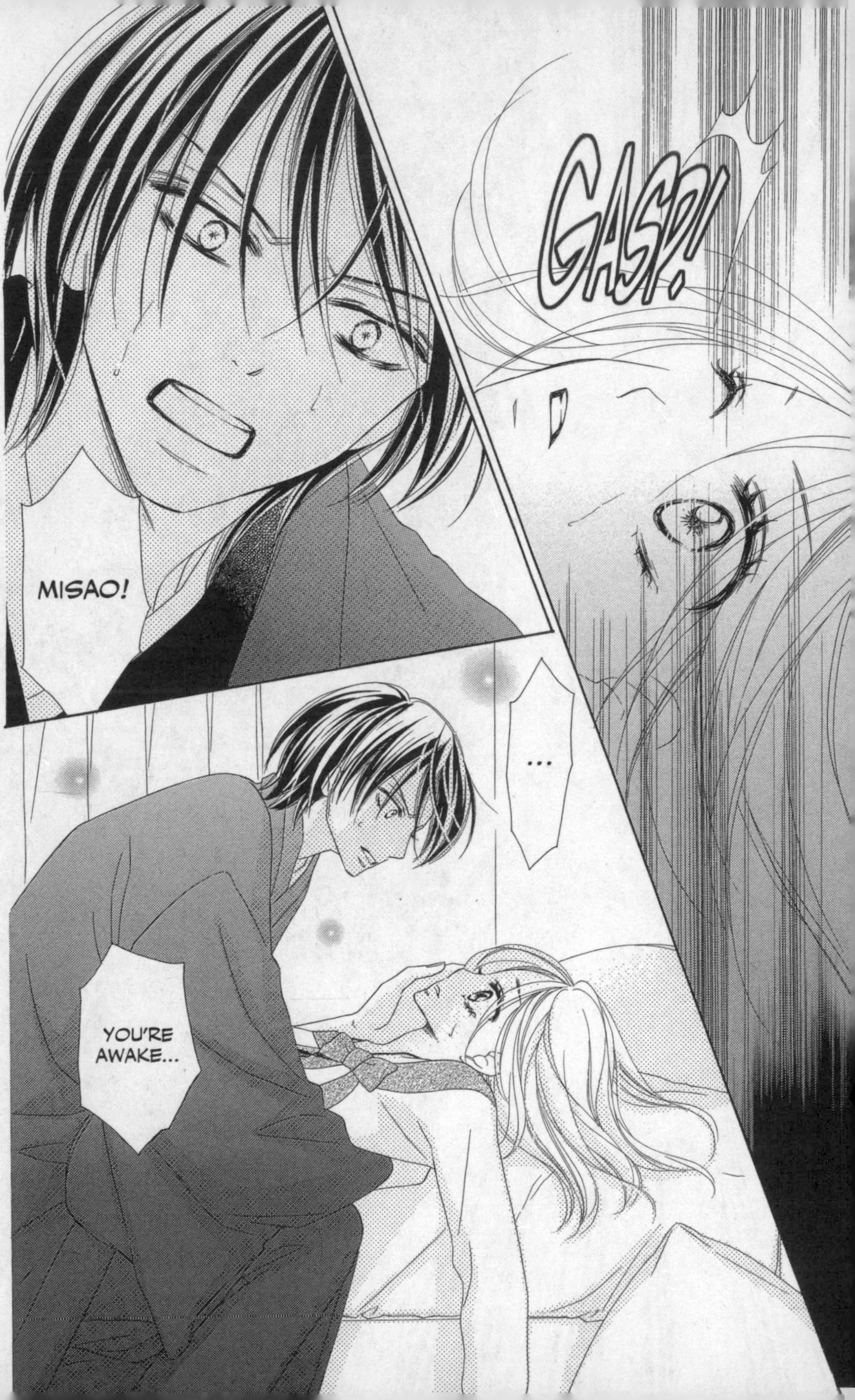
GASP!
MISAO!
...
YOU'RE AWAKE...

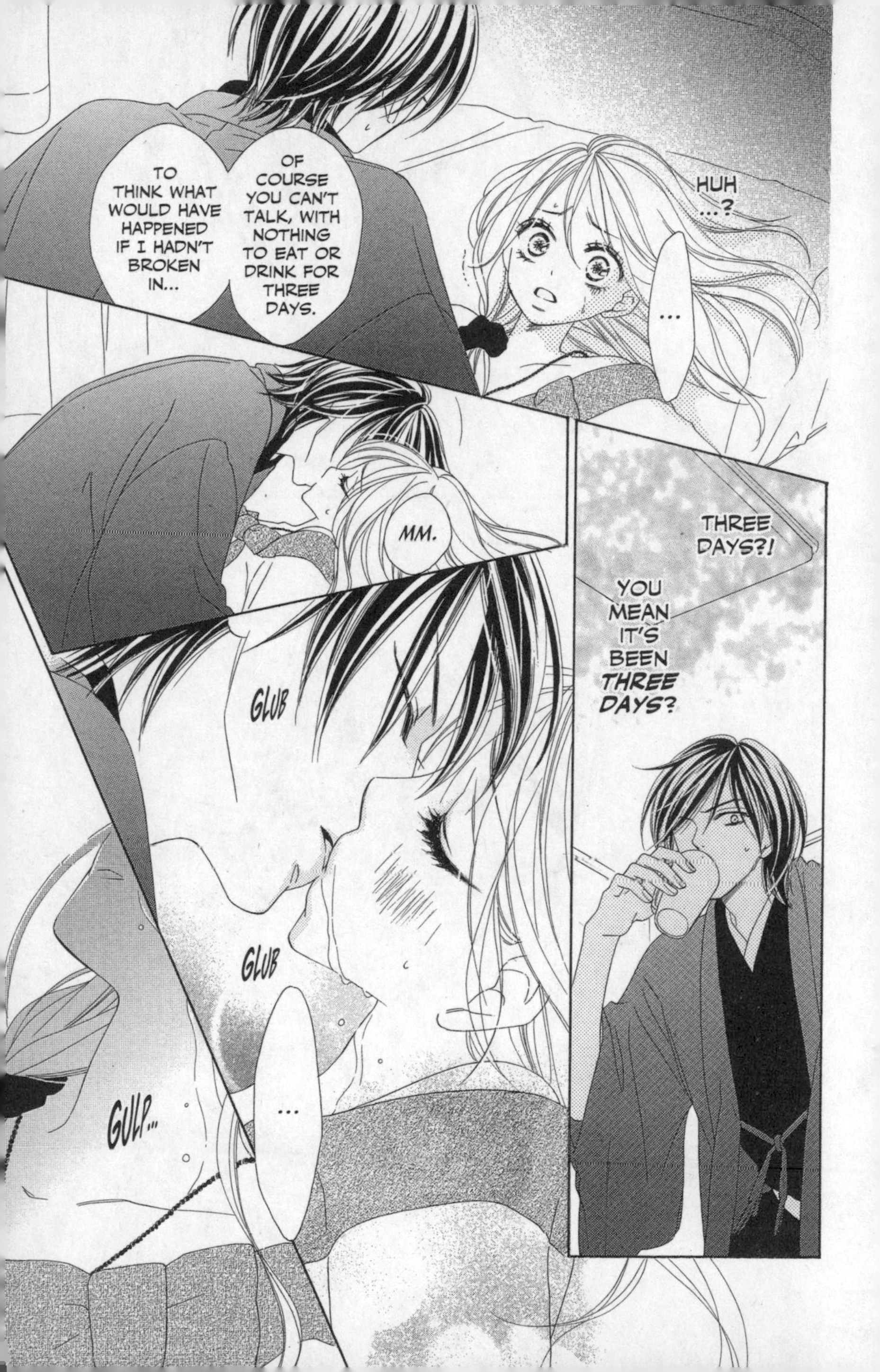
HUH ...?
...
OF COURSE YOU CAN'T TALK, WITH NOTHING TO EAT OR DRINK FOR THREE DAYS.
TO THINK WHAT WOULD HAVE HAPPENED IF I HADN'T BROKEN IN...
THREE DAYS?!
YOU MEAN IT'S BEEN THREE DAYS?
MM.
GLUB
GLUB
GULP...
...

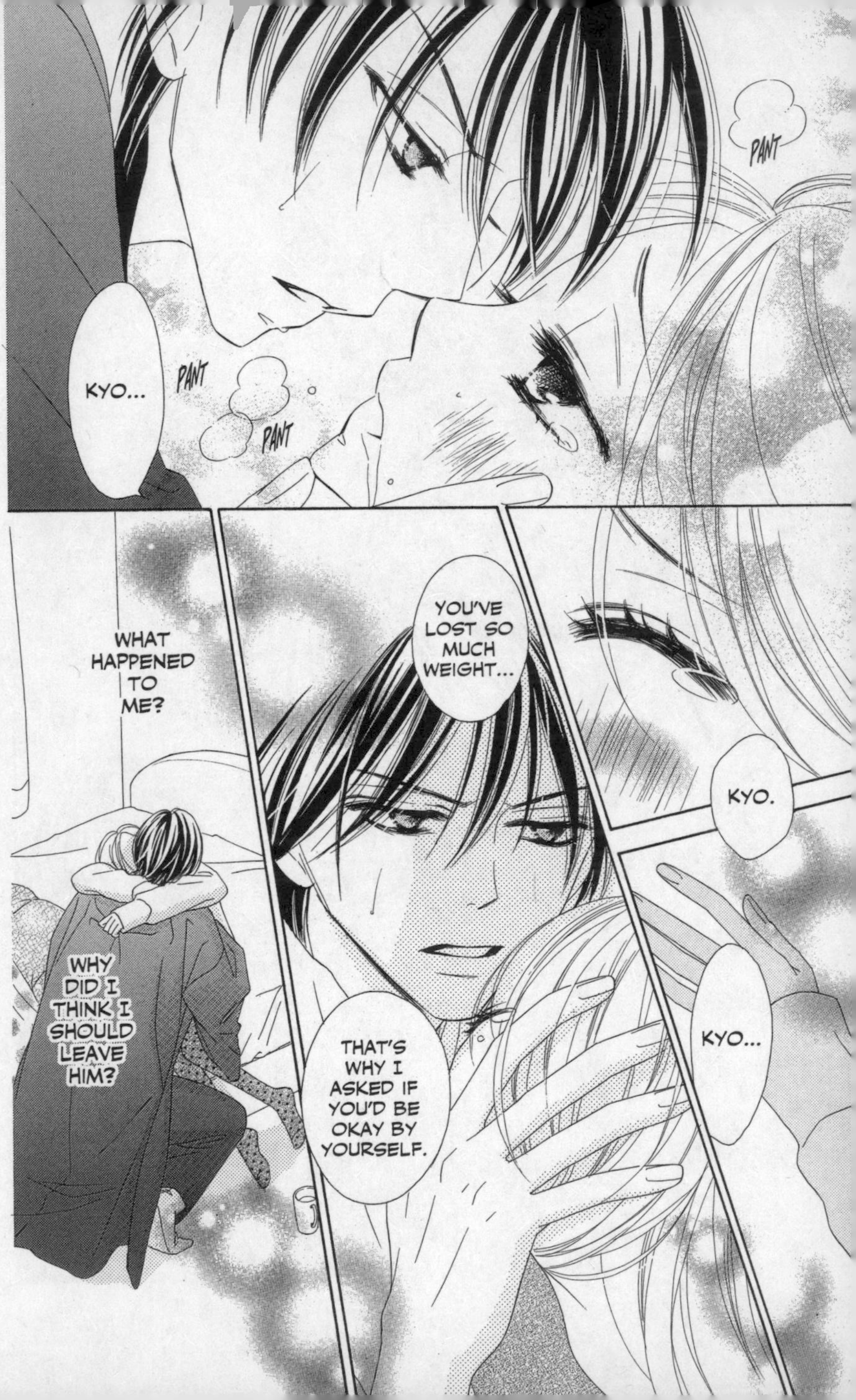
PANT
PANT
PANT
KYO...
KYO.
KYO...
YOU'VE LOST SO MUCH WEIGHT...
THAT'S WHY I ASKED IF YOU'D BE OKAY BY YOURSELF.
WHAT HAPPENED TO ME?
WHY DID I THINK I SHOULD LEAVE HIM?

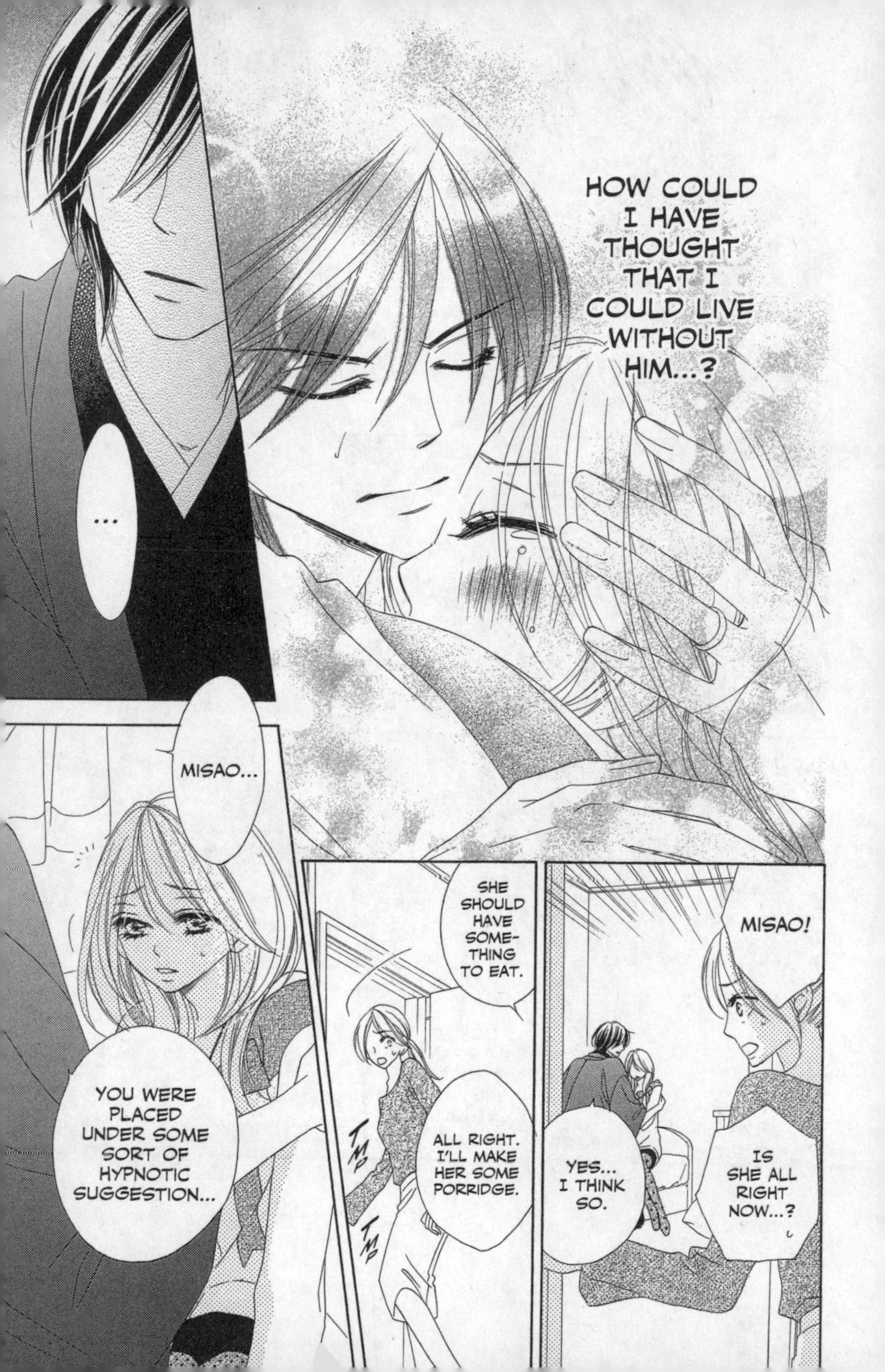
HOW COULD I HAVE THOUGHT THAT I COULD LIVE WITHOUT HIM...?
...
MISAO!
IS SHE ALL RIGHT NOW...?
YES... I THINK SO.
SHE SHOULD HAVE SOMETHING TO EAT.
ALL RIGHT. I'LL MAKE HER SOME PORRIDGE.
TMP
TMP
MISAO...
YOU WERE PLACED UNDER SOME SORT OF HYPNOTIC SUGGESTION...

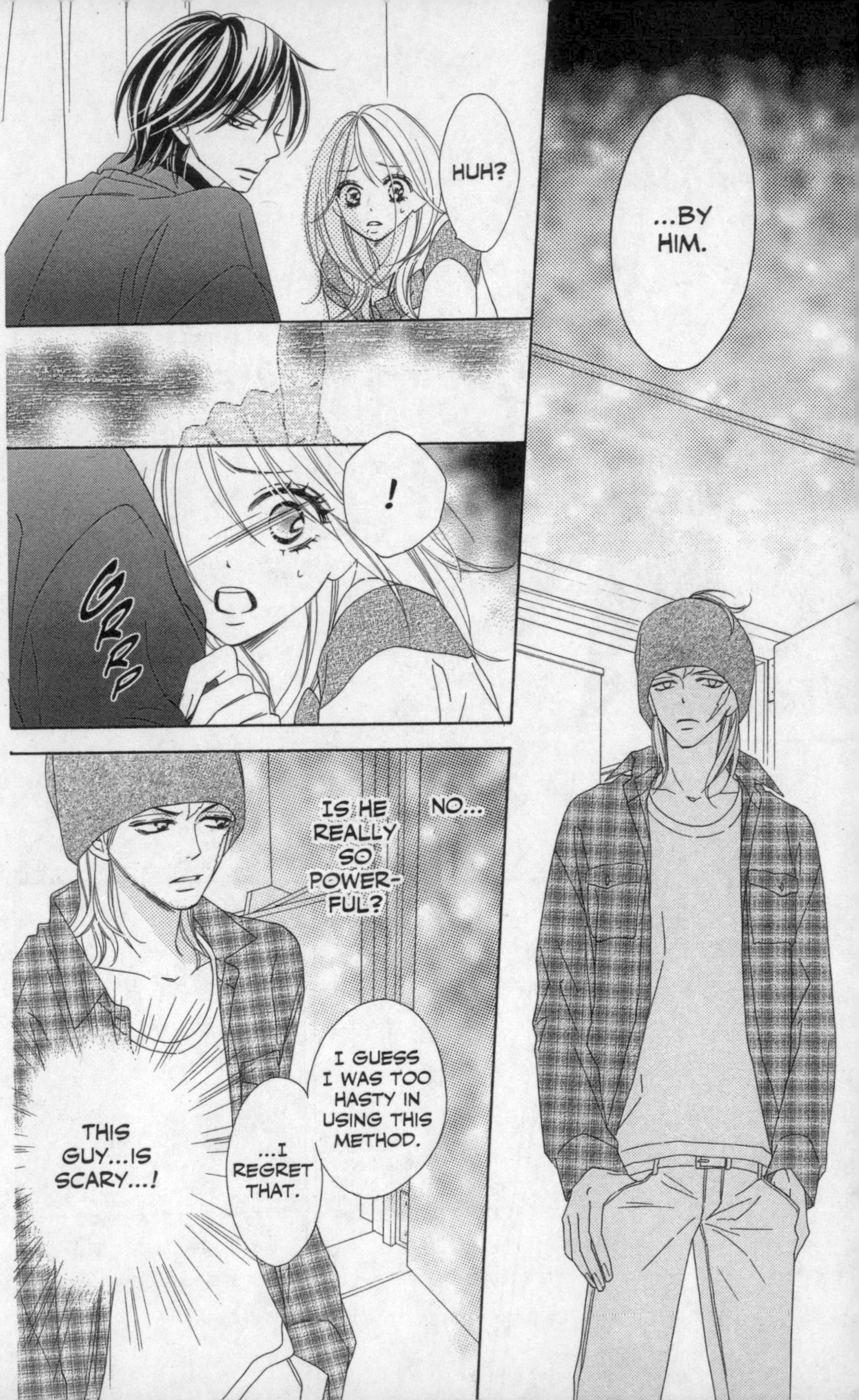

...BY HIM.
HUH?
!
NO...
IS HE REALLY SO POWERFUL?
I GUESS I WAS TOO HASTY IN USING THIS METHOD.
...I REGRET THAT.
THIS GUY...IS SCARY...!

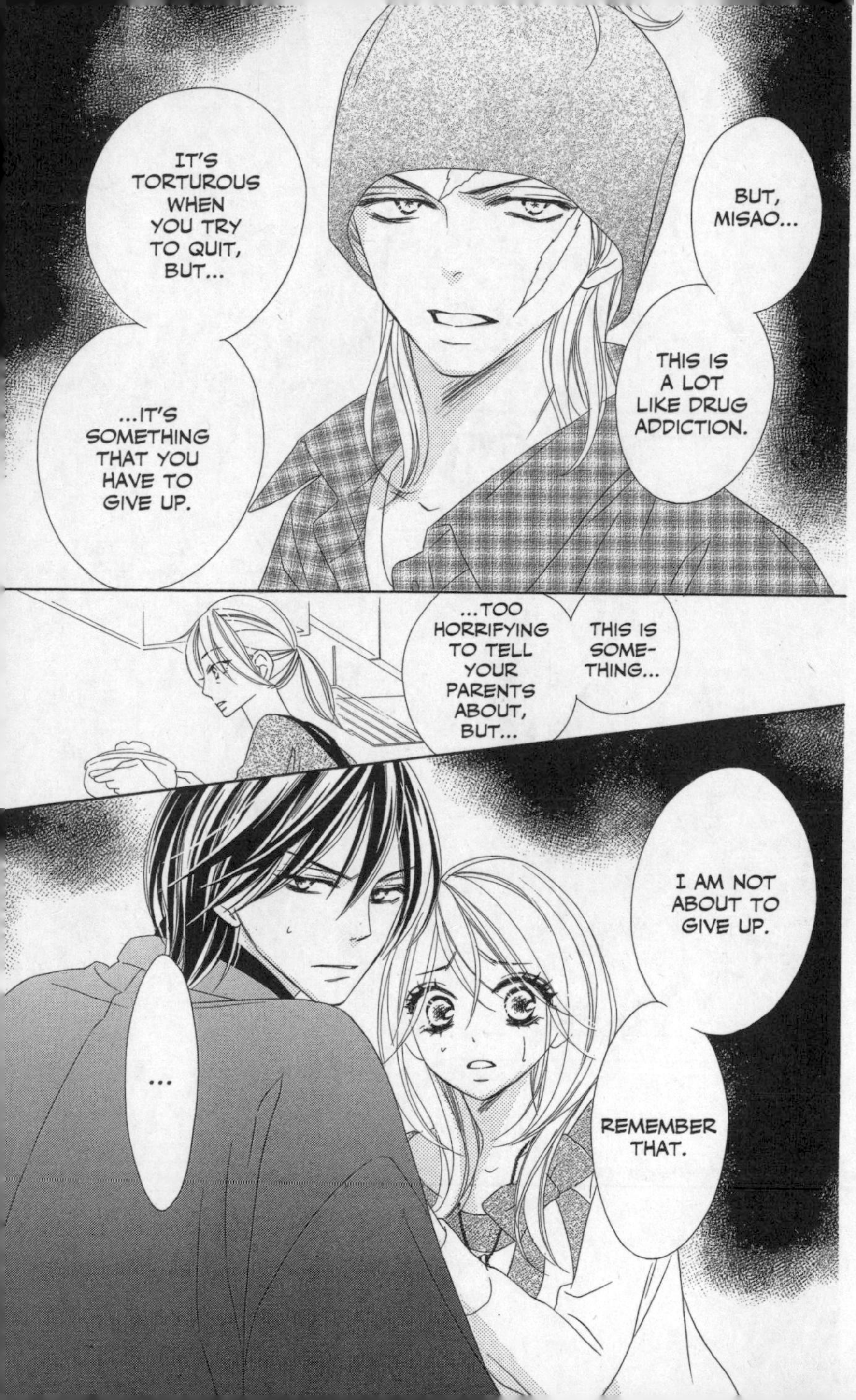
BUT, MISAO...
THIS IS A LOT LIKE DRUG ADDICTION.
IT'S TORTUROUS WHEN YOU TRY TO QUIT, BUT...
...IT'S SOMETHING THAT YOU HAVE TO GIVE UP.
THIS IS SOME-THING...
...TOO HORRIFYING TO TELL YOUR PARENTS ABOUT, BUT...
I AM NOT ABOUT TO GIVE UP.
REMEMBER THAT.
...

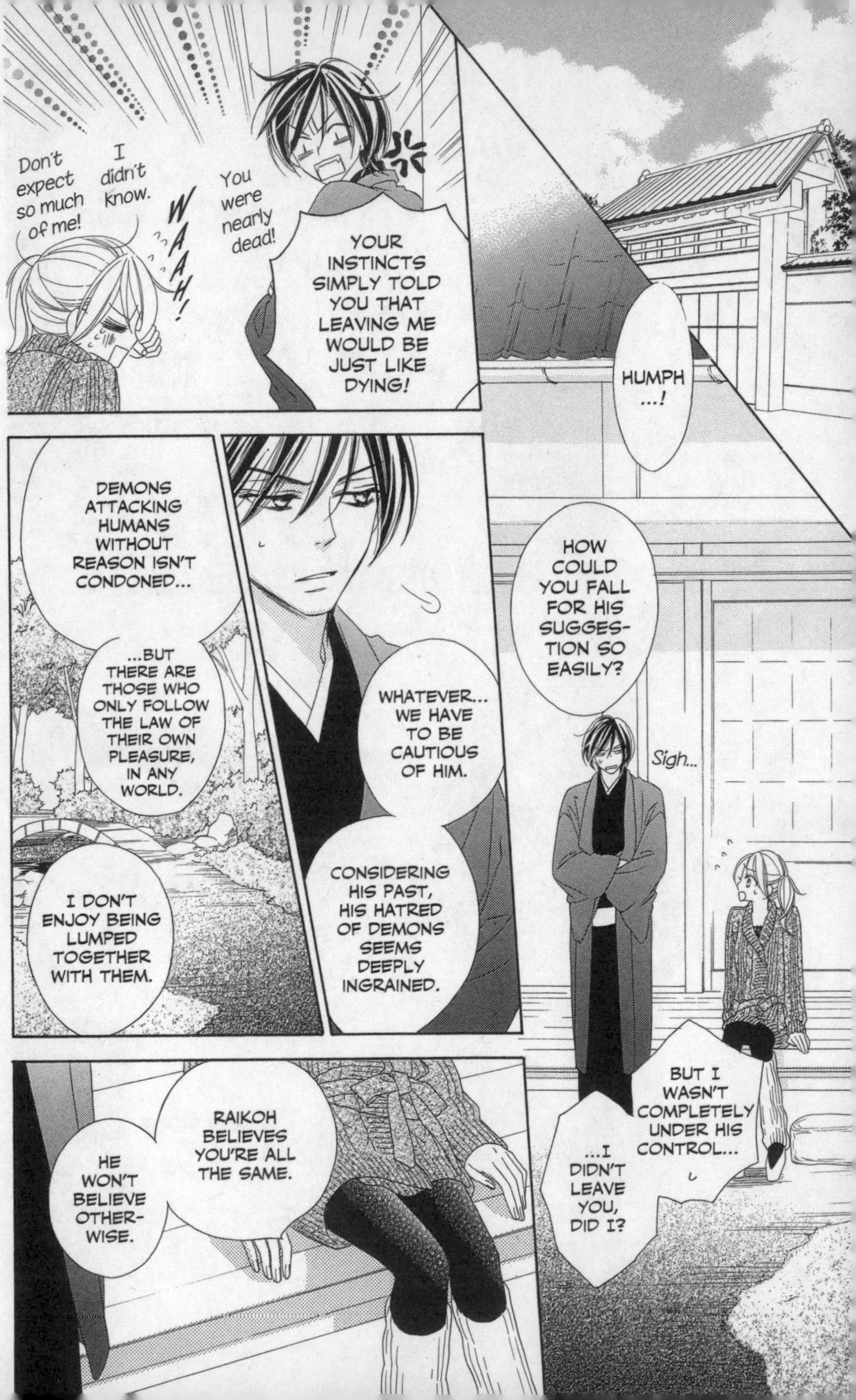
HUMPH ...!
HOW COULD YOU FALL FOR HIS SUGGESTION SO EASILY?
Sigh...
BUT I WASN'T COMPLETELY UNDER HIS CONTROL...
...I DIDN'T LEAVE YOU, DID I?
YOUR INSTINCTS SIMPLY TOLD YOU THAT LEAVING ME WOULD BE JUST LIKE DYING!
You were nearly dead!
WAAAH!
I didn't know.
Don't expect so much of me!
WHATEVER... WE HAVE TO BE CAUTIOUS OF HIM.
CONSIDERING HIS PAST, HIS HATRED OF DEMONS SEEMS DEEPLY INGRAINED.
DEMONS ATTACKING HUMANS WITHOUT REASON ISN'T CONDONED...
...BUT THERE ARE THOSE WHO ONLY FOLLOW THE LAW OF THEIR OWN PLEASURE, IN ANY WORLD.
I DON'T ENJOY BEING LUMPED TOGETHER WITH THEM.
RAIKOH BELIEVES YOU'RE ALL THE SAME.
HE WON'T BELIEVE OTHERWISE.

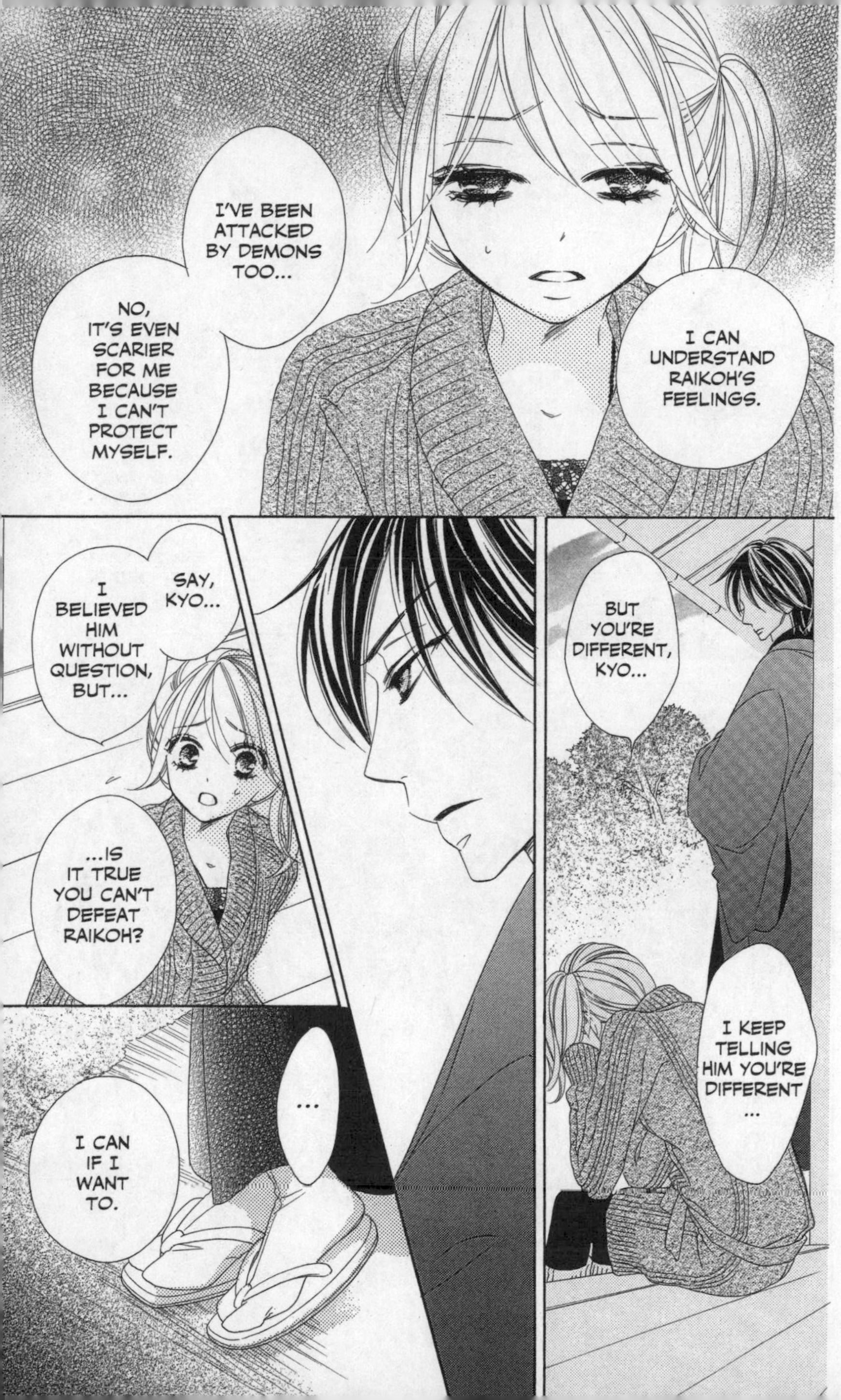
I CAN UNDERSTAND RAIKOH'S FEELINGS.
I'VE BEEN ATTACKED BY DEMONS TOO...
NO, IT'S EVEN SCARIER FOR ME BECAUSE I CAN'T PROTECT MYSELF.
BUT YOU'RE DIFFERENT, KYO...
I KEEP TELLING HIM YOU'RE DIFFERENT...
SAY, KYO...
I BELIEVED HIM WITHOUT QUESTION, BUT...
...IS IT TRUE YOU CAN'T DEFEAT RAIKOH?
...
I CAN IF I WANT TO.

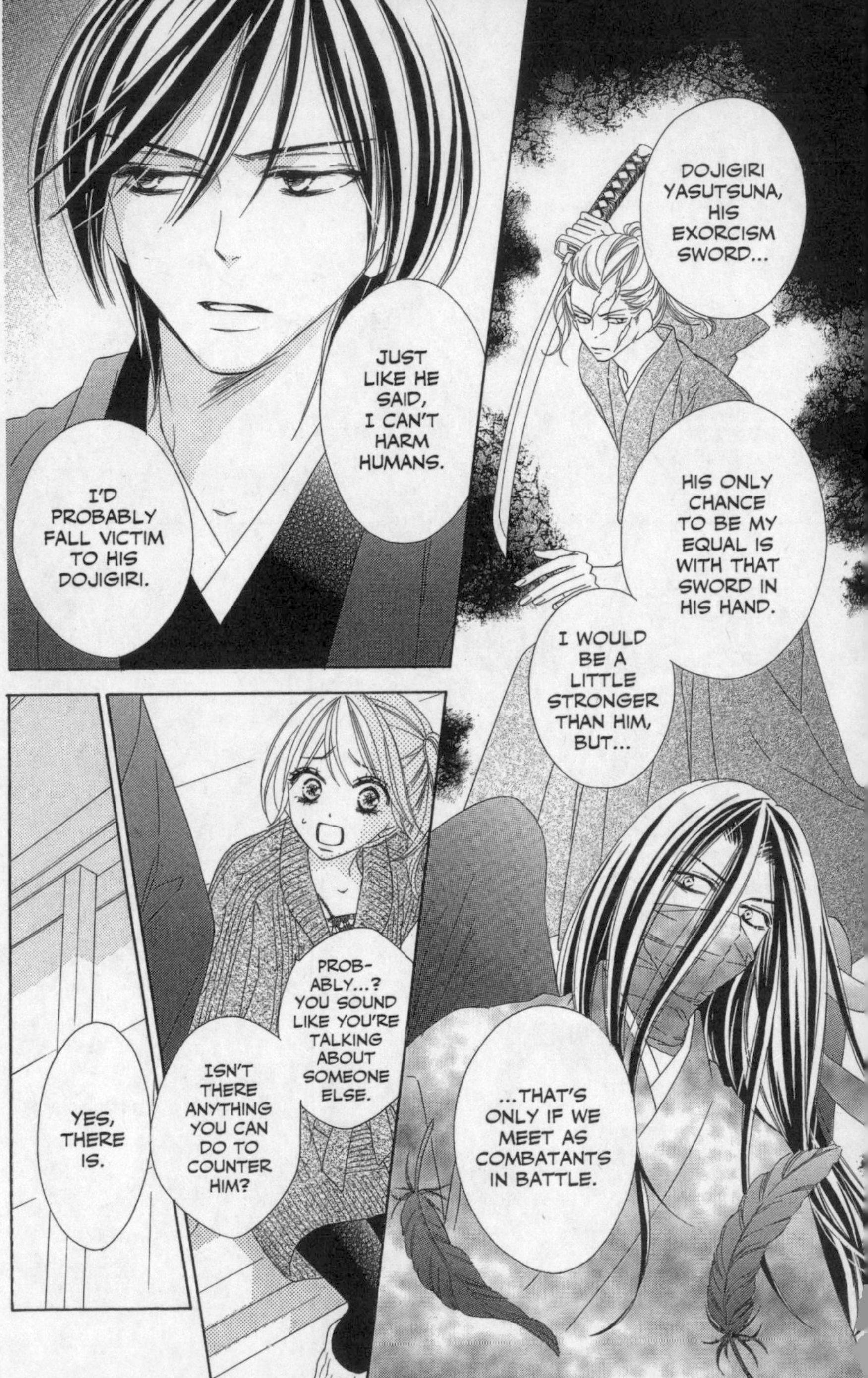
DOJIGIRI YASUTSUNA, HIS EXORCISM SWORD...
HIS ONLY CHANCE TO BE MY EQUAL IS WITH THAT SWORD IN HIS HAND.
I WOULD BE A LITTLE STRONGER THAN HIM, BUT...
...THAT'S ONLY IF WE MEET AS COMBATANTS IN BATTLE.
JUST LIKE HE SAID, I CAN'T HARM HUMANS.
I'D PROBABLY FALL VICTIM TO HIS DOJIGIRI.
PROB-ABLY...? YOU SOUND LIKE YOU'RE TALKING ABOUT SOMEONE ELSE.
ISN'T THERE ANYTHING YOU CAN DO TO COUNTER HIM?
YES, THERE IS.

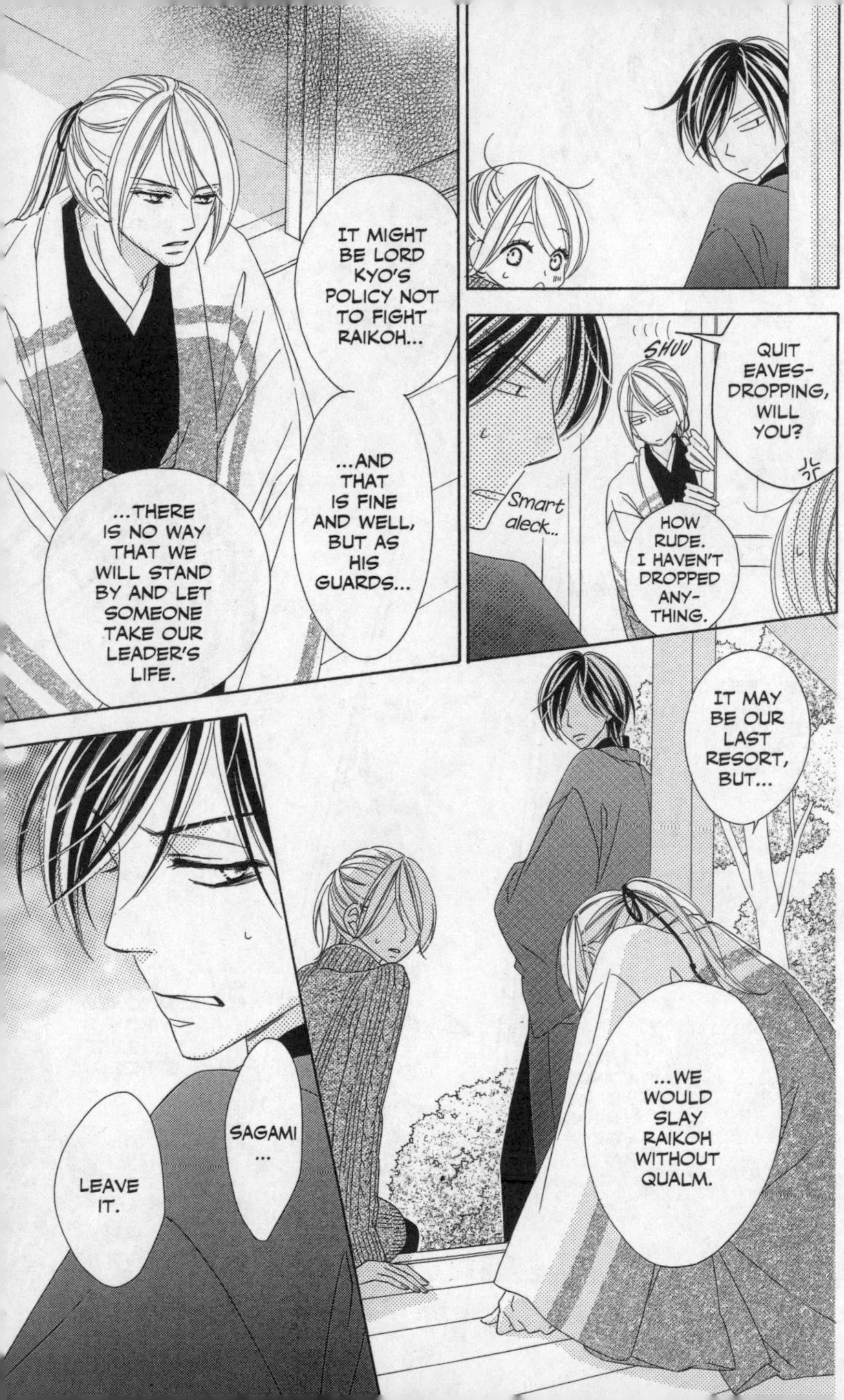
SHUU
QUIT EAVES-DROPPING, WILL YOU?
Smart aleck..
HOW RUDE. I HAVEN'T DROPPED ANY-THING.
IT MIGHT BE LORD KYO'S POLICY NOT TO FIGHT RAIKOH...
...AND THAT IS FINE AND WELL, BUT AS HIS GUARDS...
...THERE IS NO WAY THAT WE WILL STAND BY AND LET SOMEONE TAKE OUR LEADER'S LIFE.
IT MAY BE OUR LAST RESORT, BUT...
...WE WOULD SLAY RAIKOH WITHOUT QUALM.
SAGAMI...
LEAVE IT.

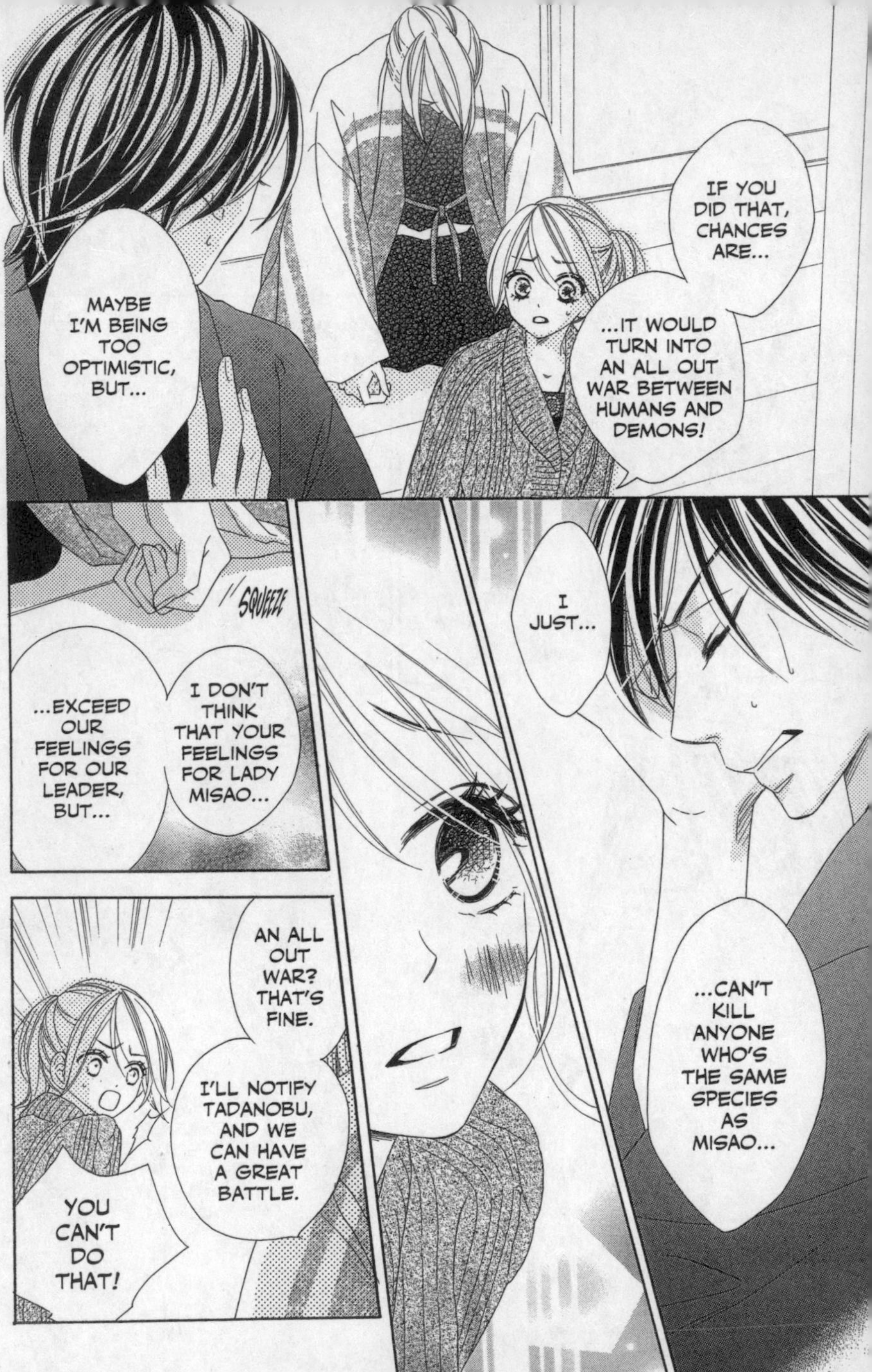
IF YOU DID THAT, CHANCES ARE...
...IT WOULD TURN INTO AN ALL OUT WAR BETWEEN HUMANS AND DEMONS!
MAYBE I'M BEING TOO OPTIMISTIC, BUT...
I JUST...
...CAN'T KILL ANYONE WHO'S THE SAME SPECIES AS MISAO...
SQUEEZE
I DON'T THINK THAT YOUR FEELINGS FOR LADY MISAO...
...EXCEED OUR FEELINGS FOR OUR LEADER, BUT...
AN ALL OUT WAR? THAT'S FINE.
I'LL NOTIFY TADANOBU, AND WE CAN HAVE A GREAT BATTLE.
YOU CAN'T DO THAT!

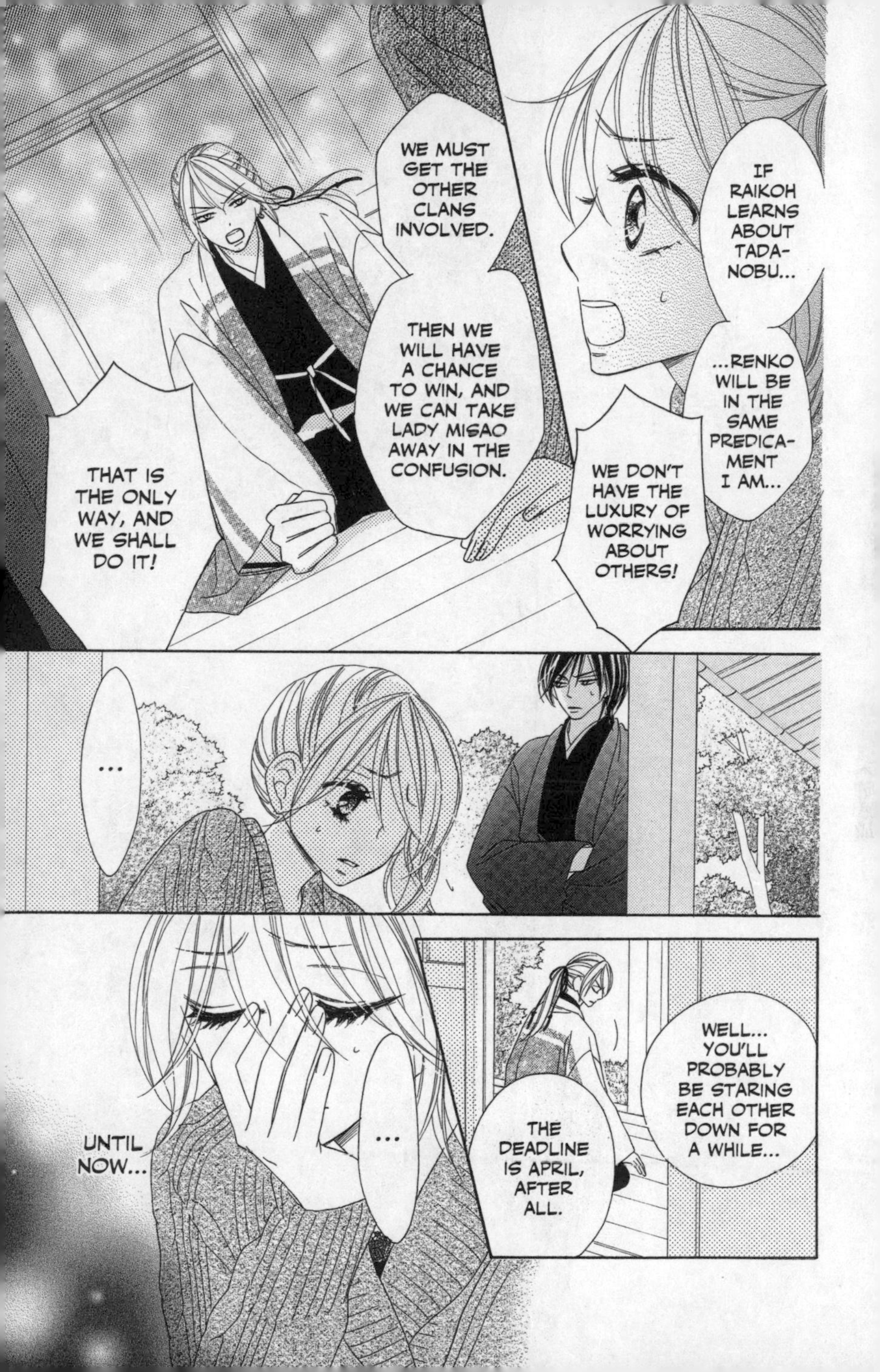
IF RAIKOH LEARNS ABOUT TADA-NOBU...
...RENKO WILL BE IN THE SAME PREDICA-MENT I AM...
WE DON'T HAVE THE LUXURY OF WORRYING ABOUT OTHERS!
WE MUST GET THE OTHER CLANS INVOLVED.
THEN WE WILL HAVE A CHANCE TO WIN, AND WE CAN TAKE LADY MISAO AWAY IN THE CONFUSION.
THAT IS THE ONLY WAY, AND WE SHALL DO IT!
...
WELL... YOU'LL PROBABLY BE STARING EACH OTHER DOWN FOR A WHILE...
THE DEADLINE IS APRIL, AFTER ALL.
...
UNTIL NOW...

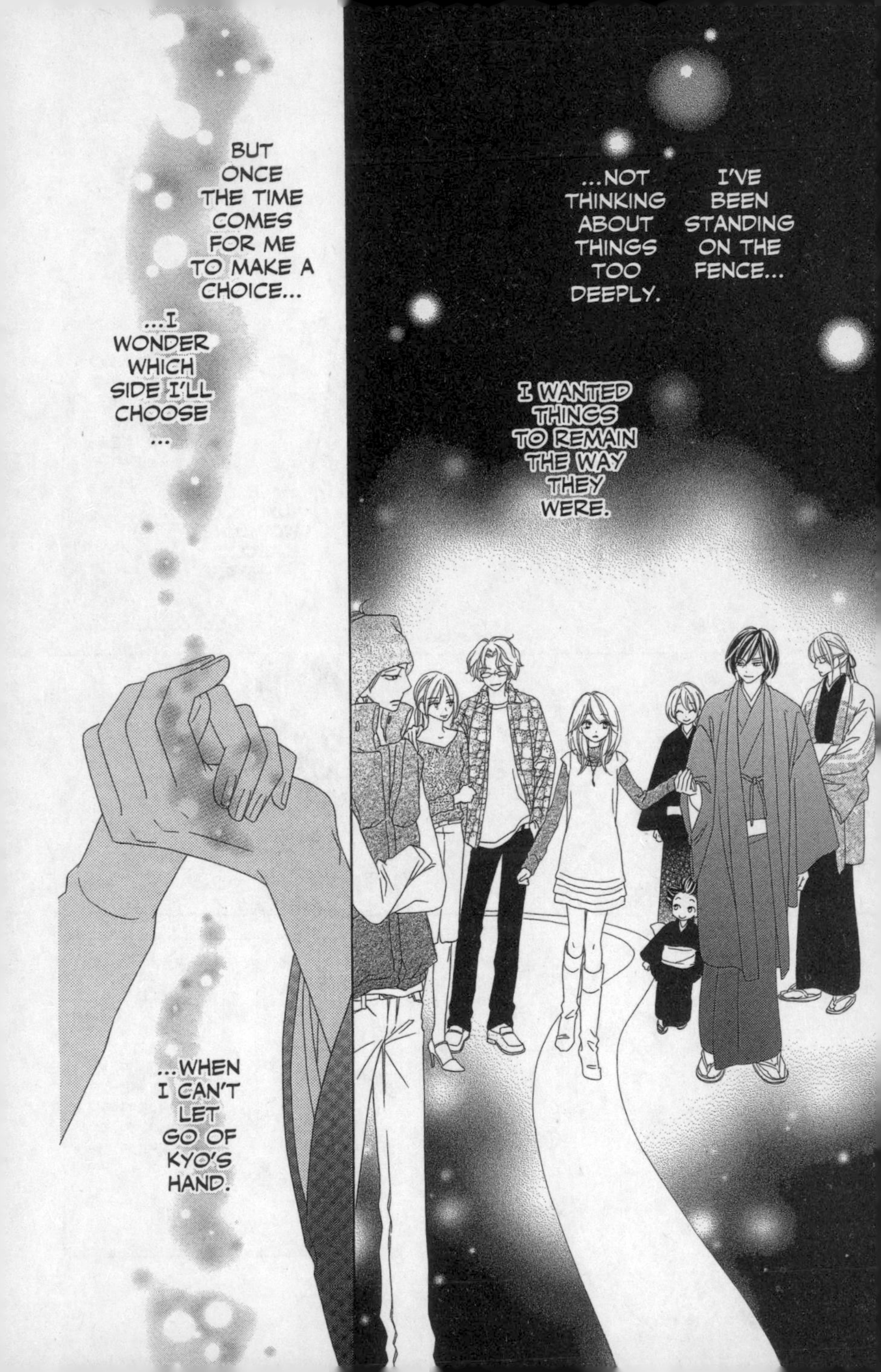
I'VE BEEN STANDING ON THE FENCE...
...NOT THINKING ABOUT THINGS TOO DEEPLY.
I WANTED THINGS TO REMAIN THE WAY THEY WERE.
BUT ONCE THE TIME COMES FOR ME TO MAKE A CHOICE...
...I WONDER WHICH SIDE I'LL CHOOSE...
...WHEN I CAN'T LET GO OF KYO'S HAND.

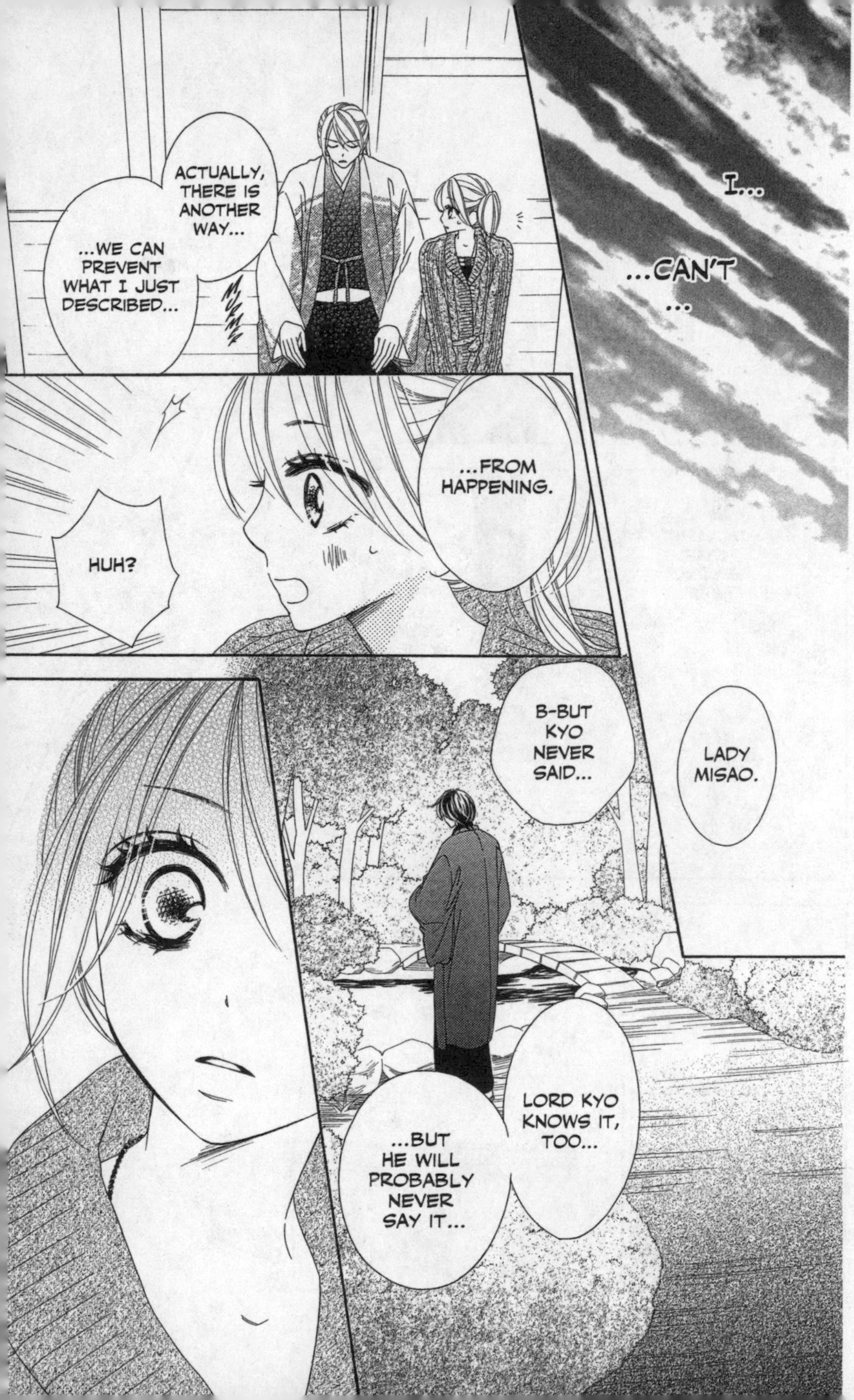
I...
...CAN'T ...
ACTUALLY, THERE IS ANOTHER WAY...
...WE CAN PREVENT WHAT I JUST DESCRIBED...
...FROM HAPPENING.
HUH?
LADY MISAO.
B-BUT KYO NEVER SAID...
LORD KYO KNOWS IT, TOO...
...BUT HE WILL PROBABLY NEVER SAY IT...

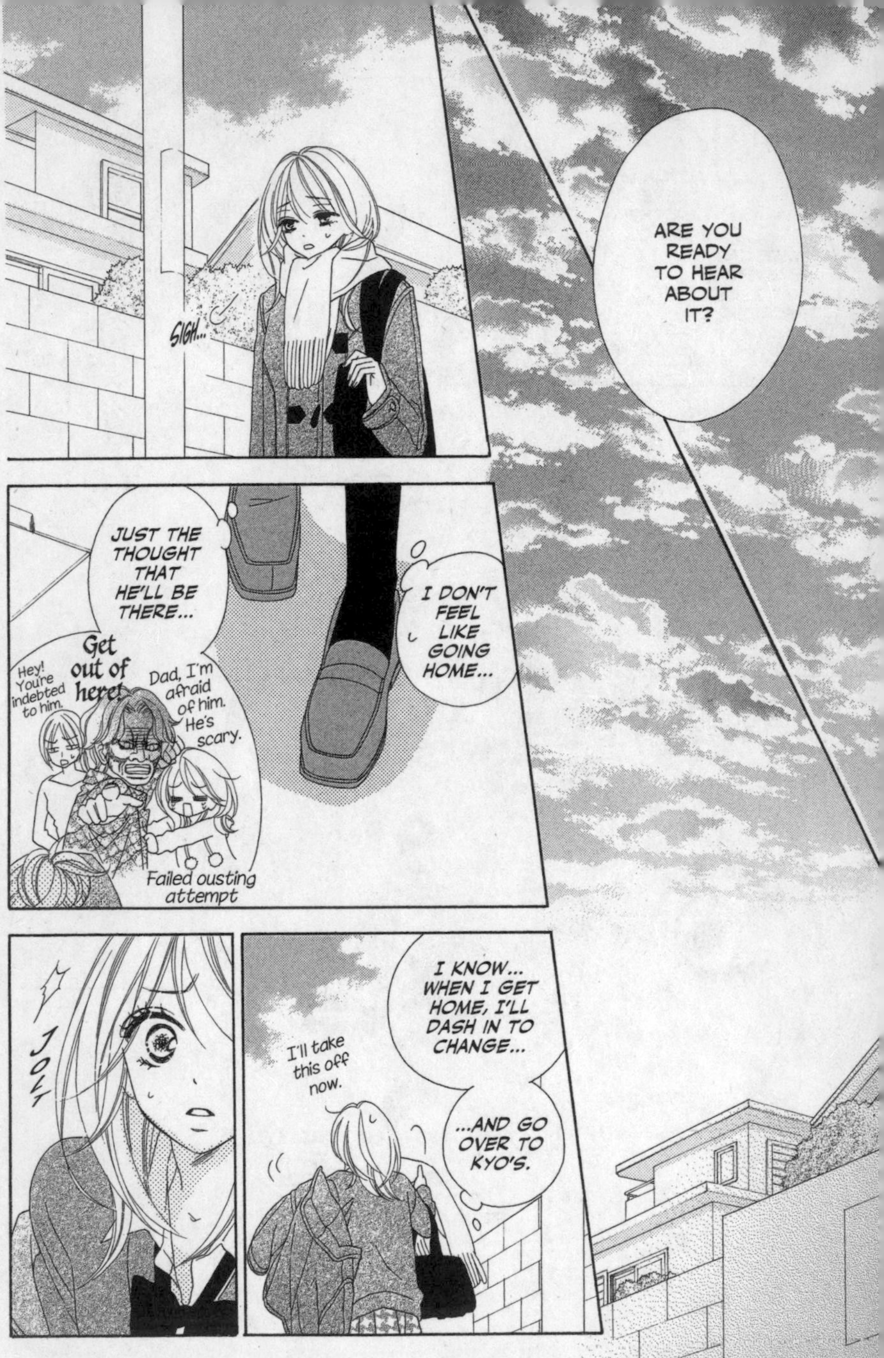
ARE YOU READY TO HEAR ABOUT IT?
SIGH...
I DON'T FEEL LIKE GOING HOME...
JUST THE THOUGHT THAT HE'LL BE THERE...
Dad, I'm afraid of him. He's scary.
Get out of here!
Hey! You're indebted to him.
Failed ousting attempt
I KNOW... WHEN I GET HOME, I'LL DASH IN TO CHANGE...
...AND GO OVER TO KYO'S.
I'll take this off now.
JOLT

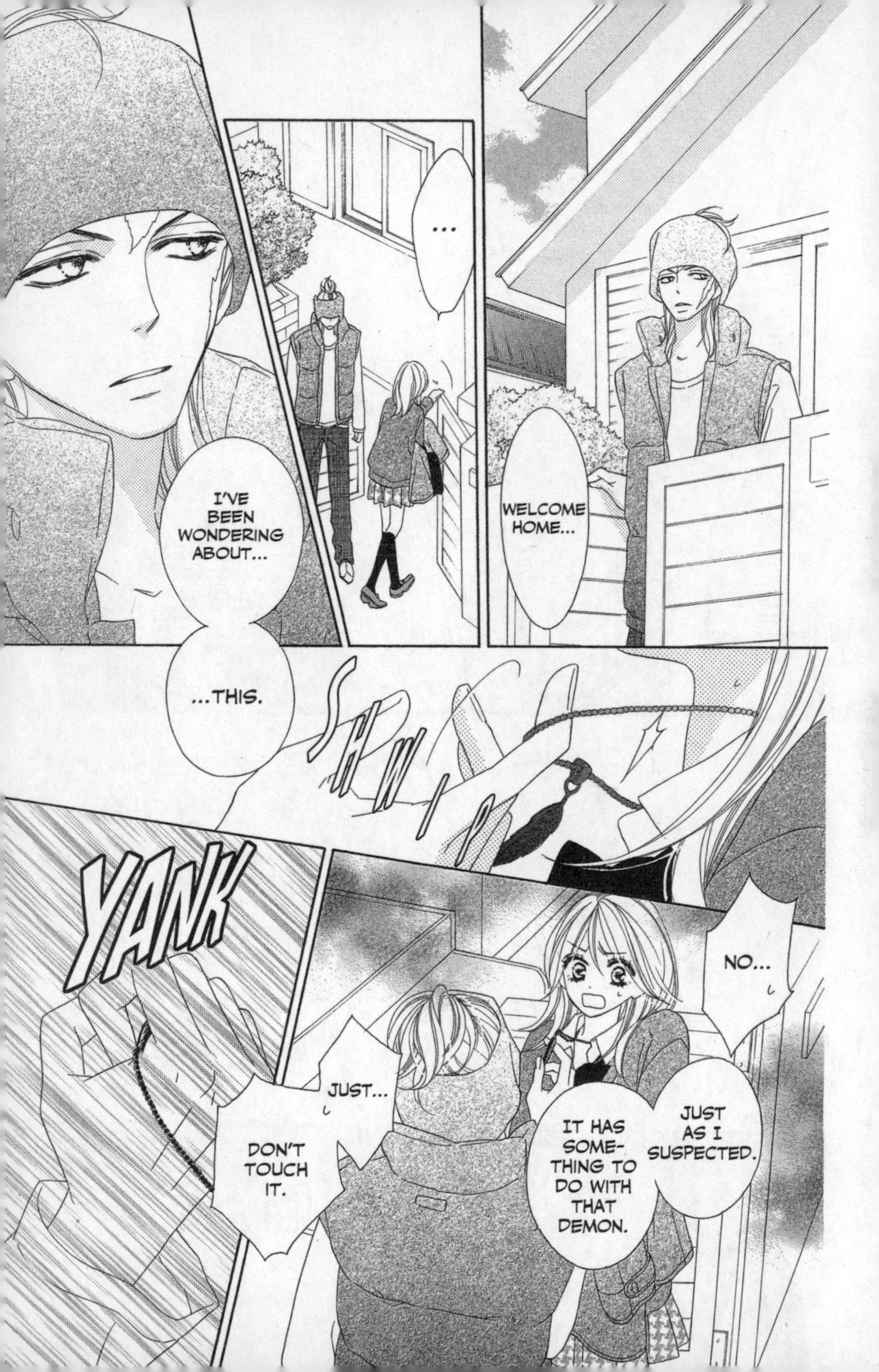
WELCOME HOME...
...
I'VE BEEN WONDERING ABOUT...
...THIS.
SHWIP
NO...
JUST AS I SUSPECTED.
IT HAS SOME-THING TO DO WITH THAT DEMON.
JUST...
DON'T TOUCH IT.
YANK

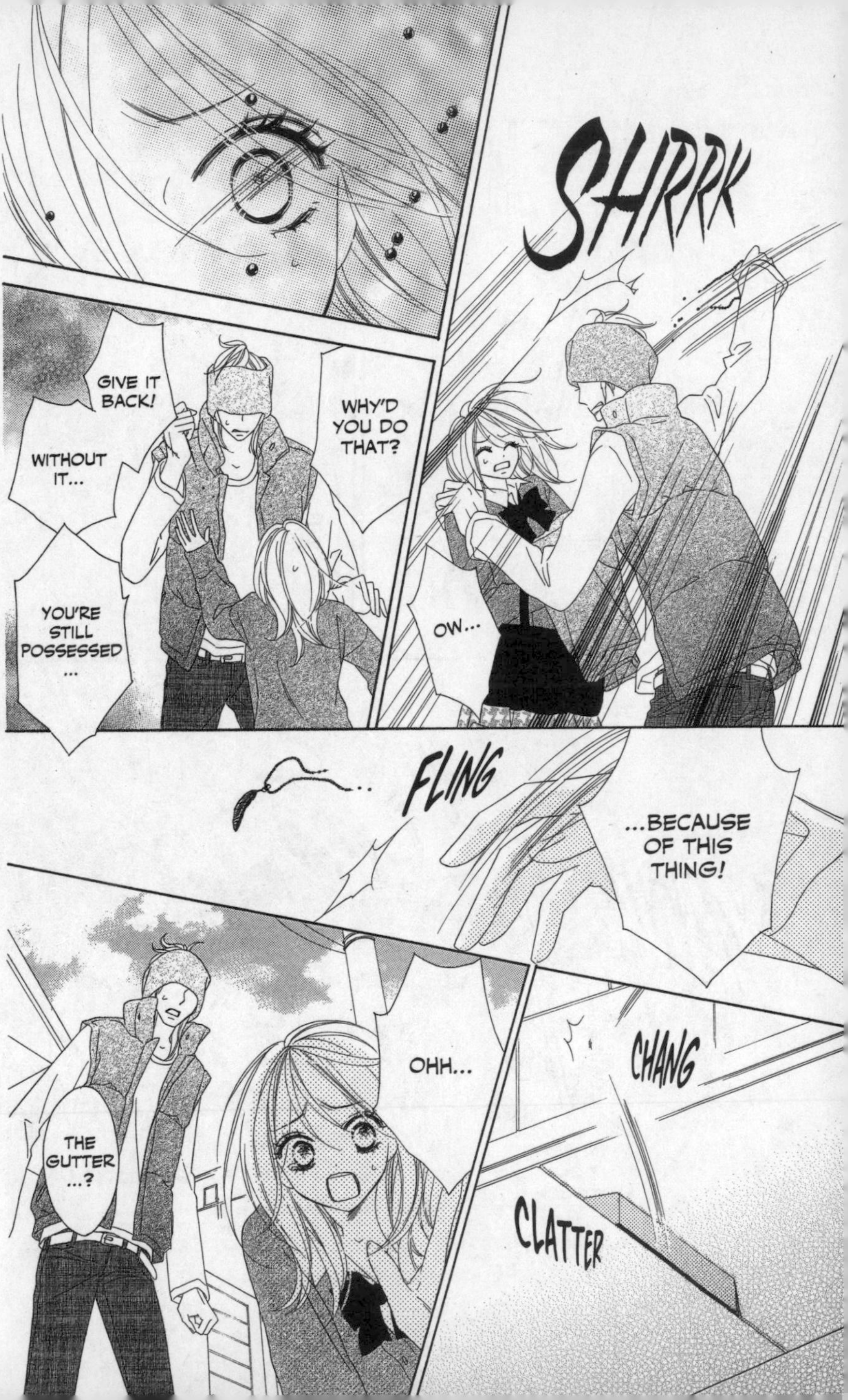
SHRRK
OW...
WHY'D YOU DO THAT?
GIVE IT BACK!
WITHOUT IT...
YOU'RE STILL POSSESSED...
...BECAUSE OF THIS THING!
FLING
CHANG
CLATTER
OHH...
THE GUTTER...?

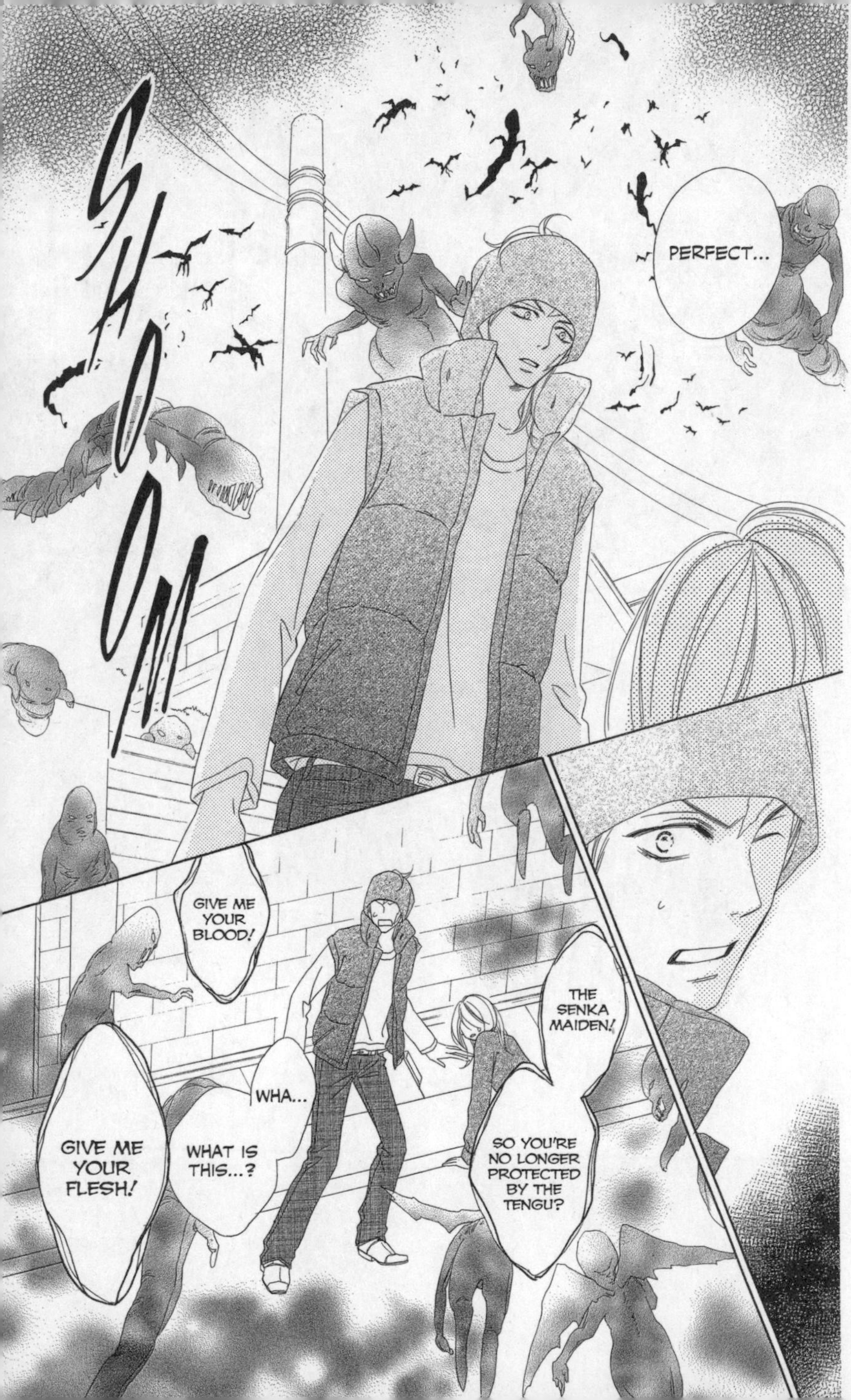

PERFECT...
SHOOM
THE SENKA MAIDEN!
SO YOU'RE NO LONGER PROTECTED BY THE TENGU?
GIVE ME YOUR BLOOD!
WHA...
WHAT IS THIS...?
GIVE ME YOUR FLESH!

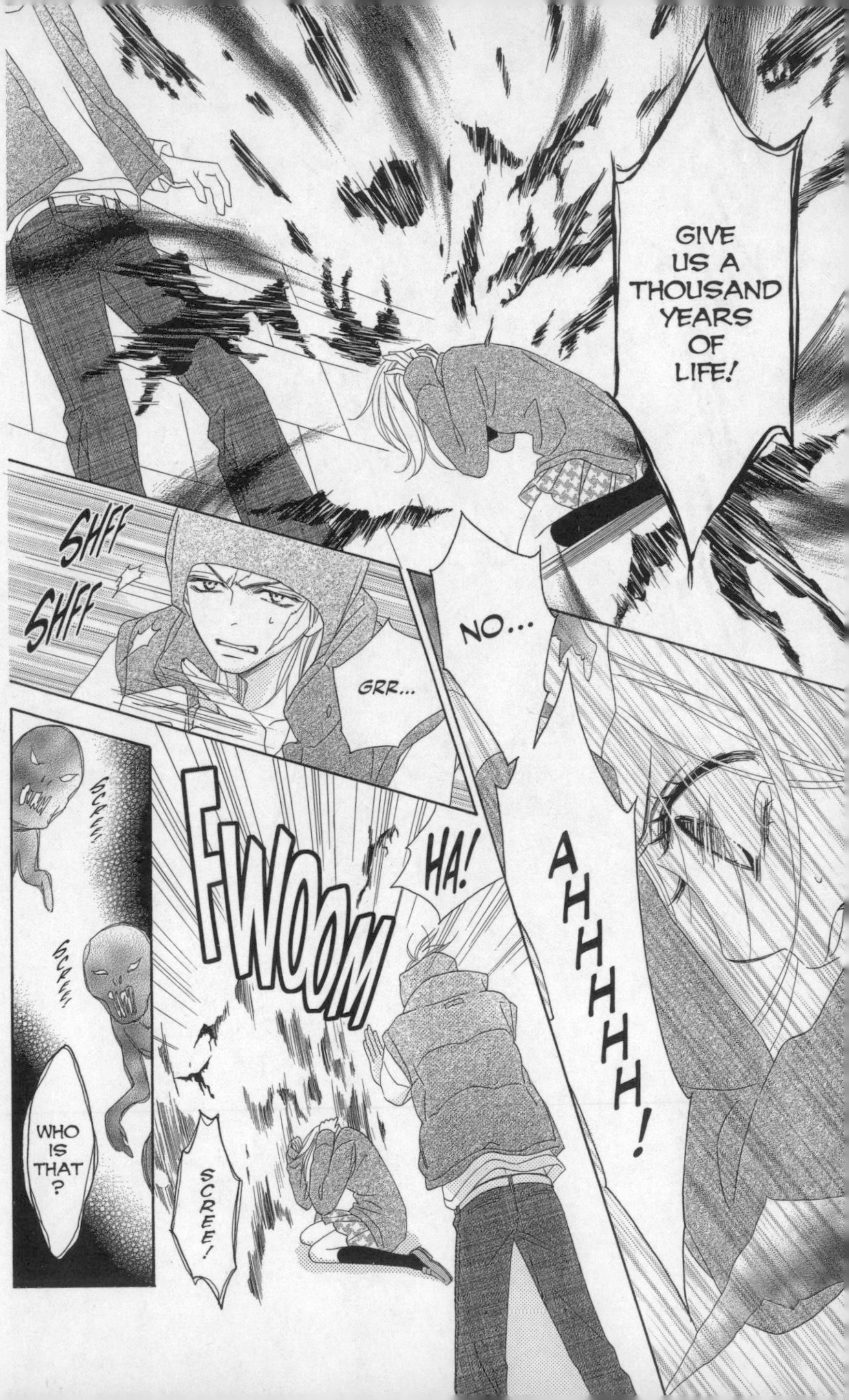
GIVE US A THOUSAND YEARS OF LIFE!
NO...
AHHHHHH!
SHFF SHFF
GRR...
FWOOM
HA!
SCREE!
WHO IS THAT?

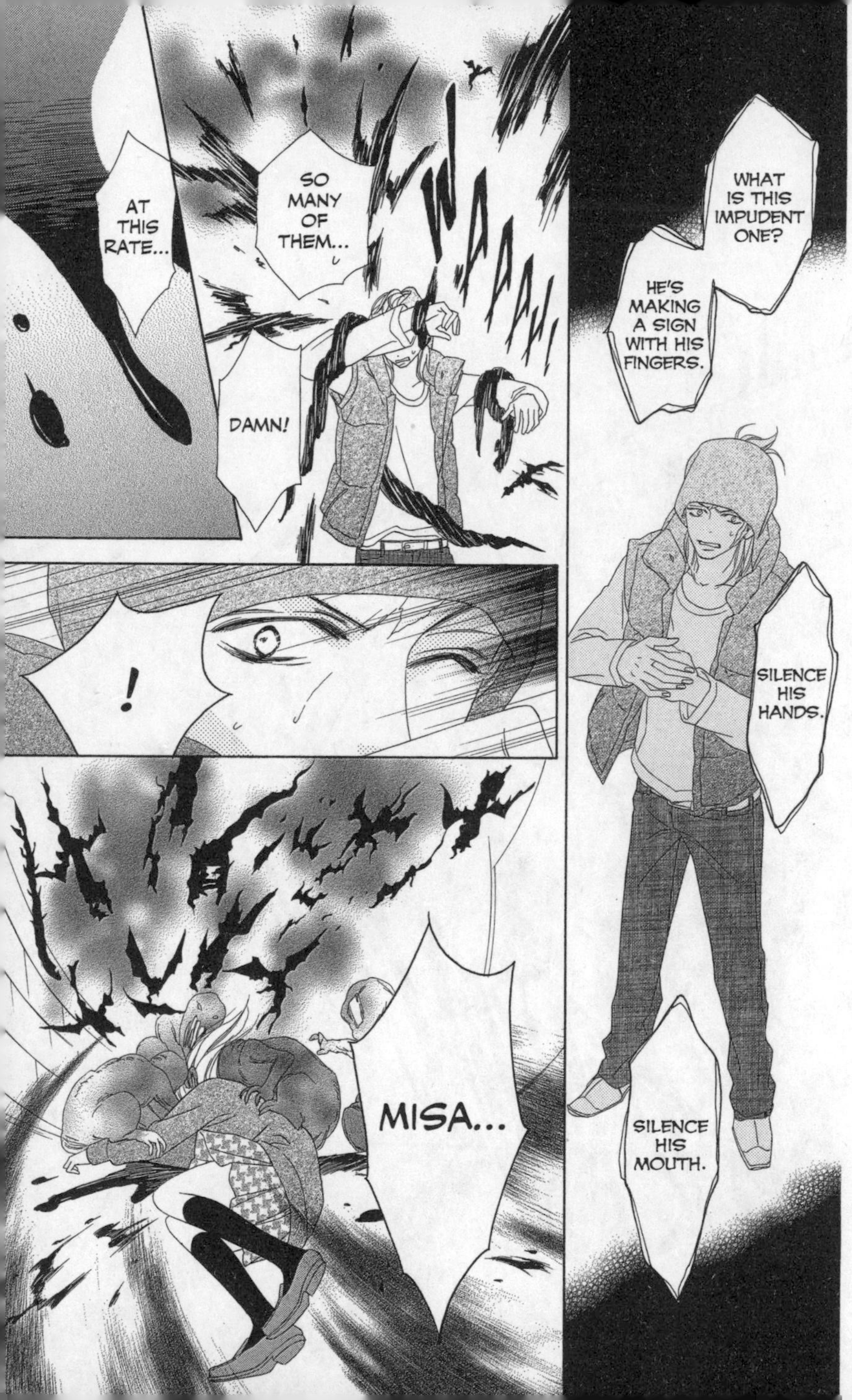
WHAT IS THIS IMPUDENT ONE?
HE'S MAKING A SIGN WITH HIS FINGERS.
SILENCE HIS HANDS.
SILENCE HIS MOUTH.
SO MANY OF THEM...
AT THIS RATE...
DAMN!
!
MISA...

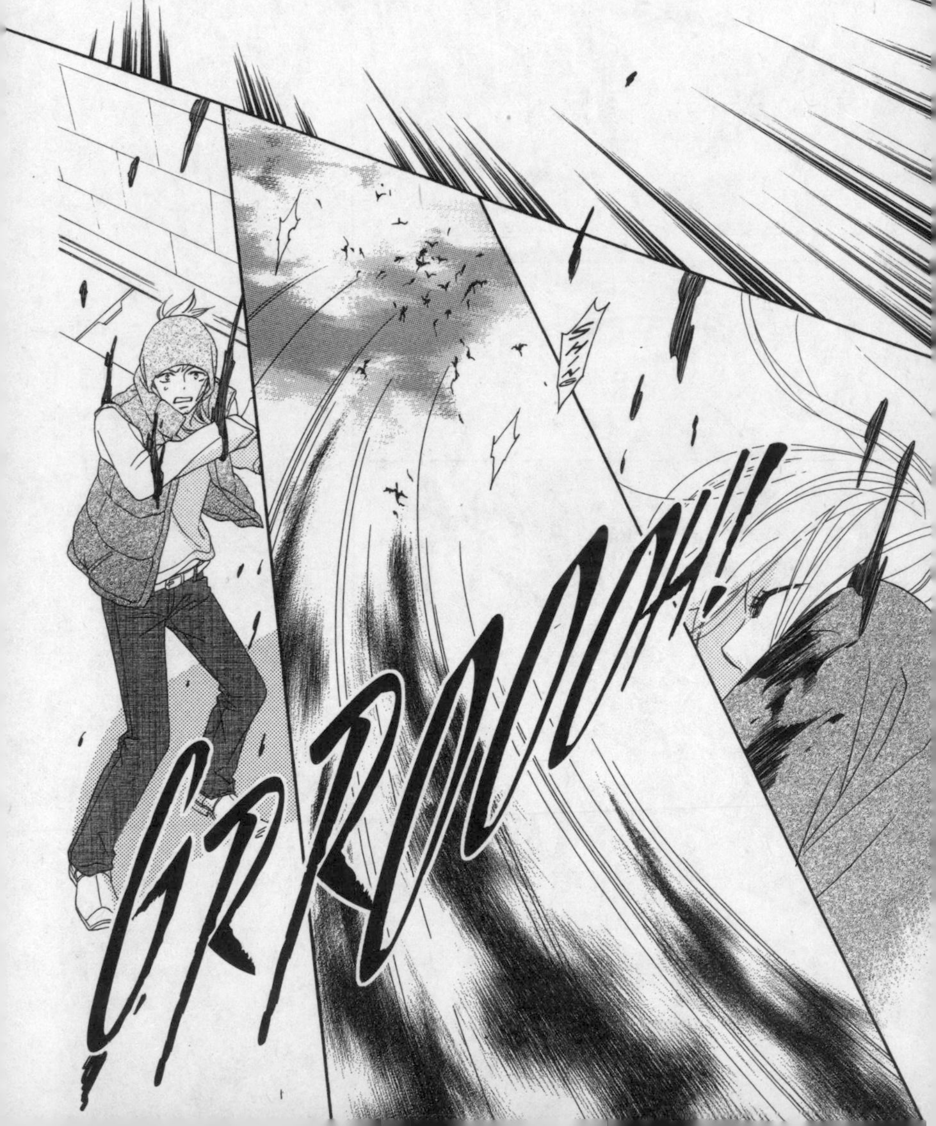
SHING
GRROOOH!!

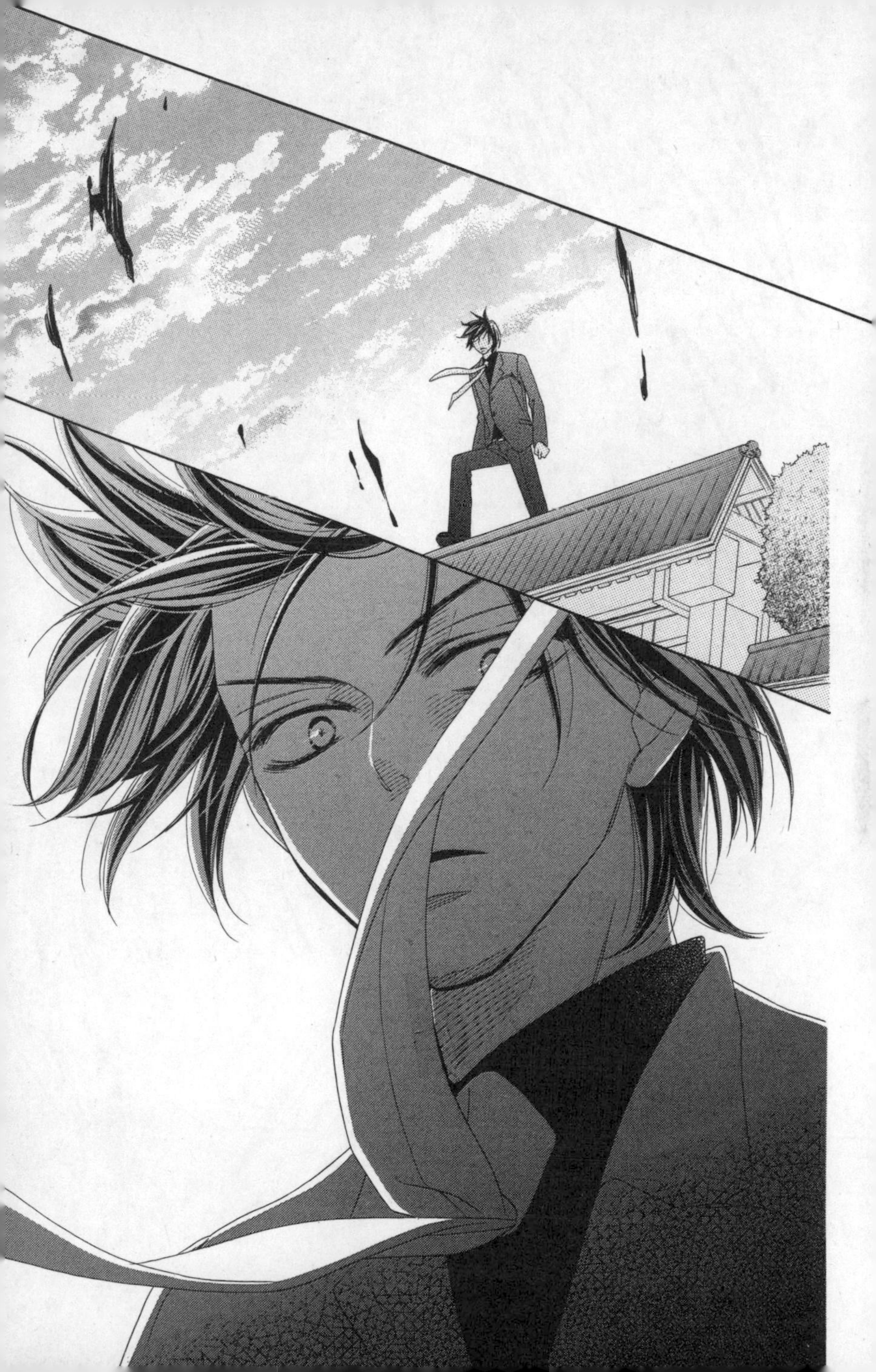

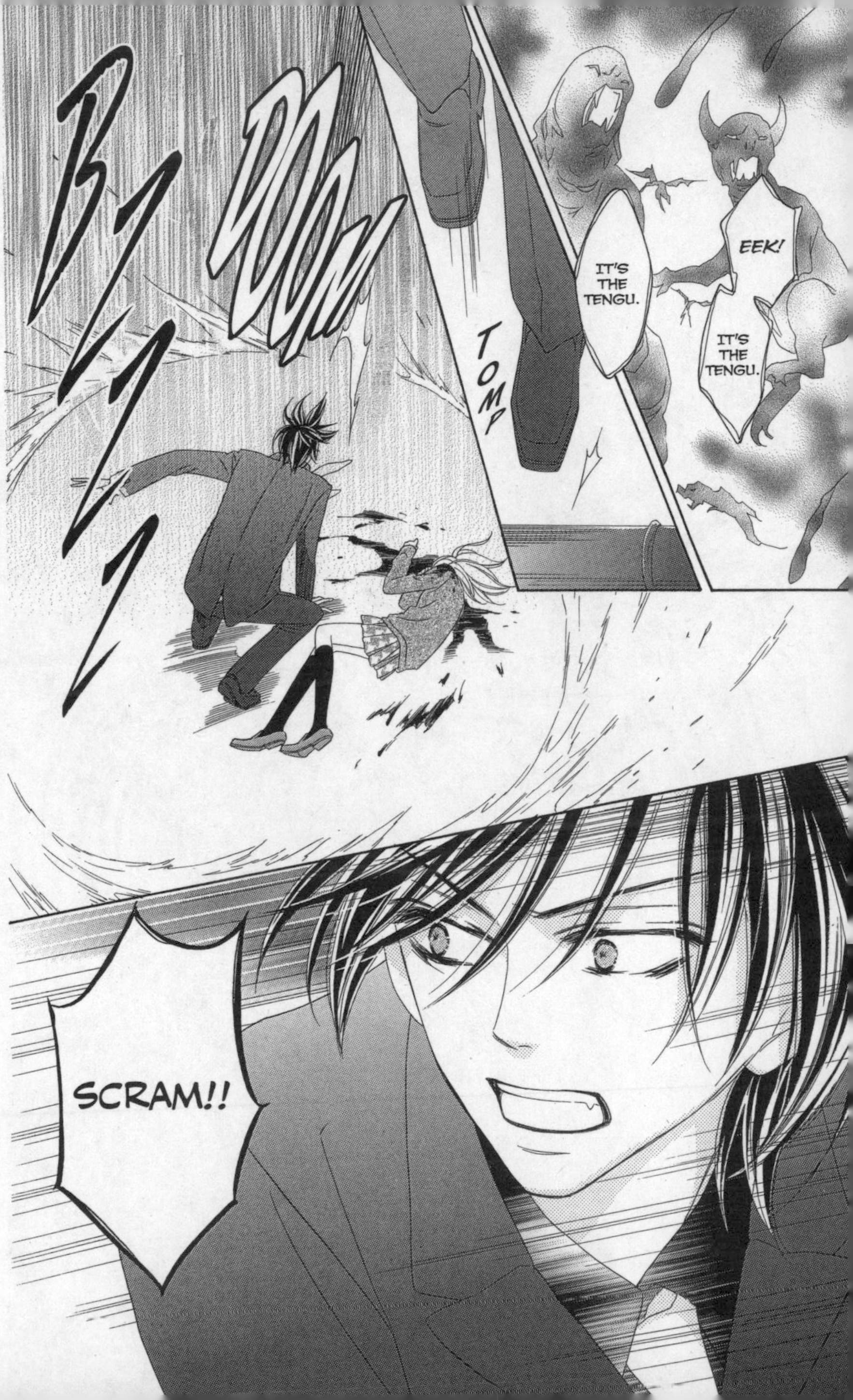
EEK!
IT'S THE TENGU.
IT'S THE TENGU.
TOMP
SCRAM!!

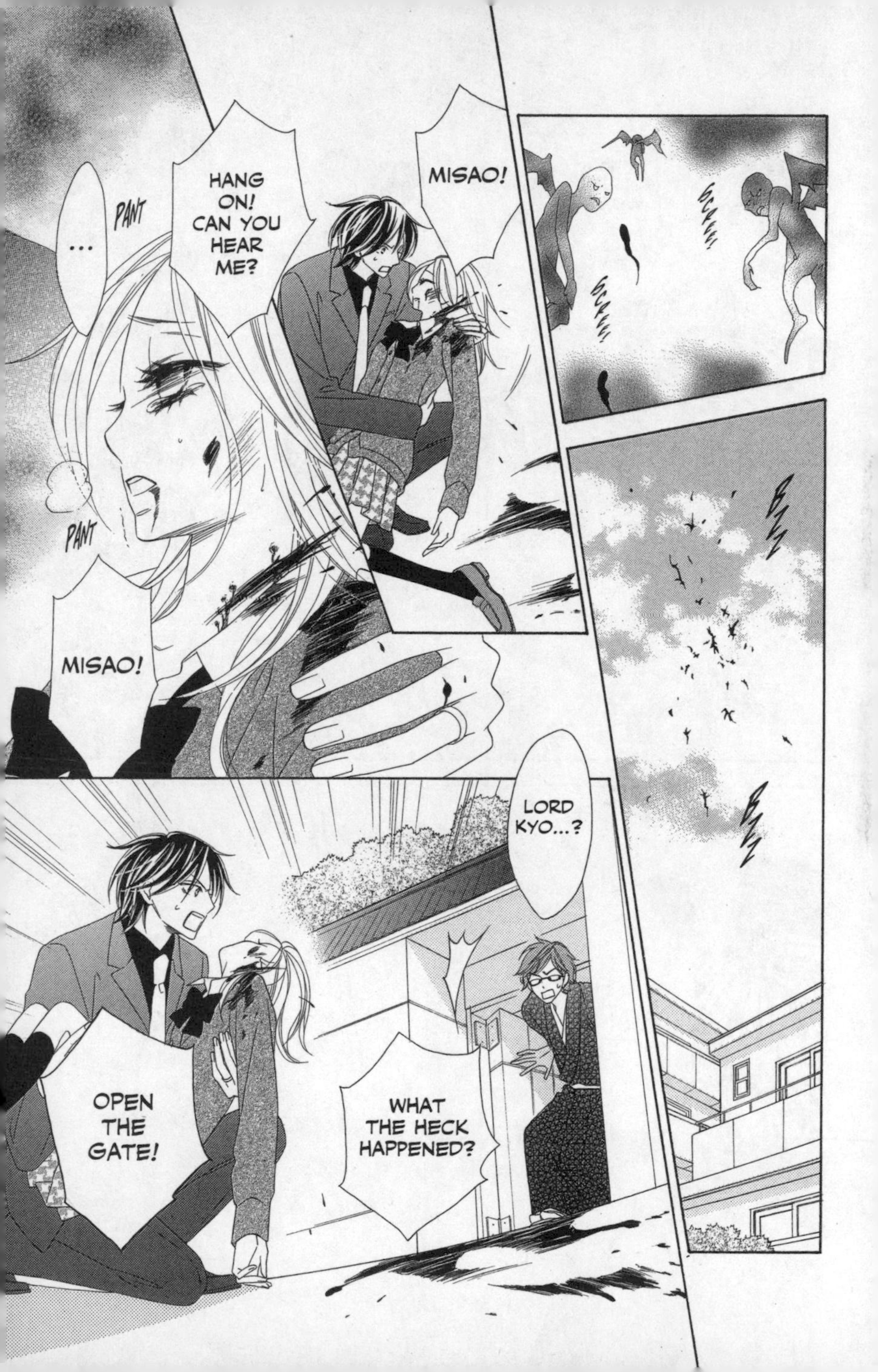
MISAO!
HANG ON! CAN YOU HEAR ME?
SCREEE!
SCREEE!
BZZZ
BZZZ
...
PANT
PANT
MISAO!
LORD KYO...?
WHAT THE HECK HAPPENED?
OPEN THE GATE!

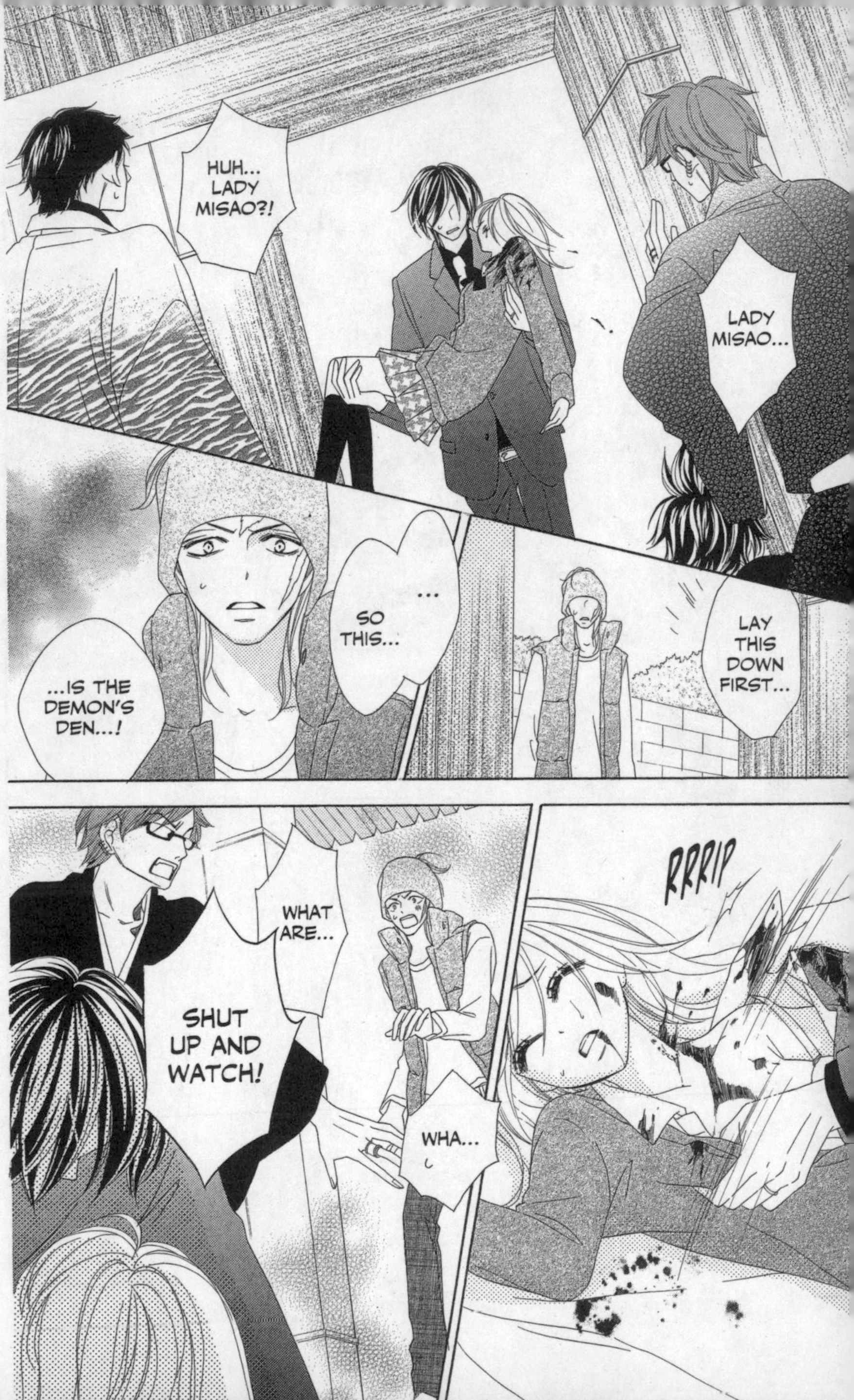
LADY MISAO...
HUH... LADY MISAO?!
LAY THIS DOWN FIRST...
...
SO THIS...
...IS THE DEMON'S DEN...!
RRRIP
WHA...
WHAT ARE...
SHUT UP AND WATCH!

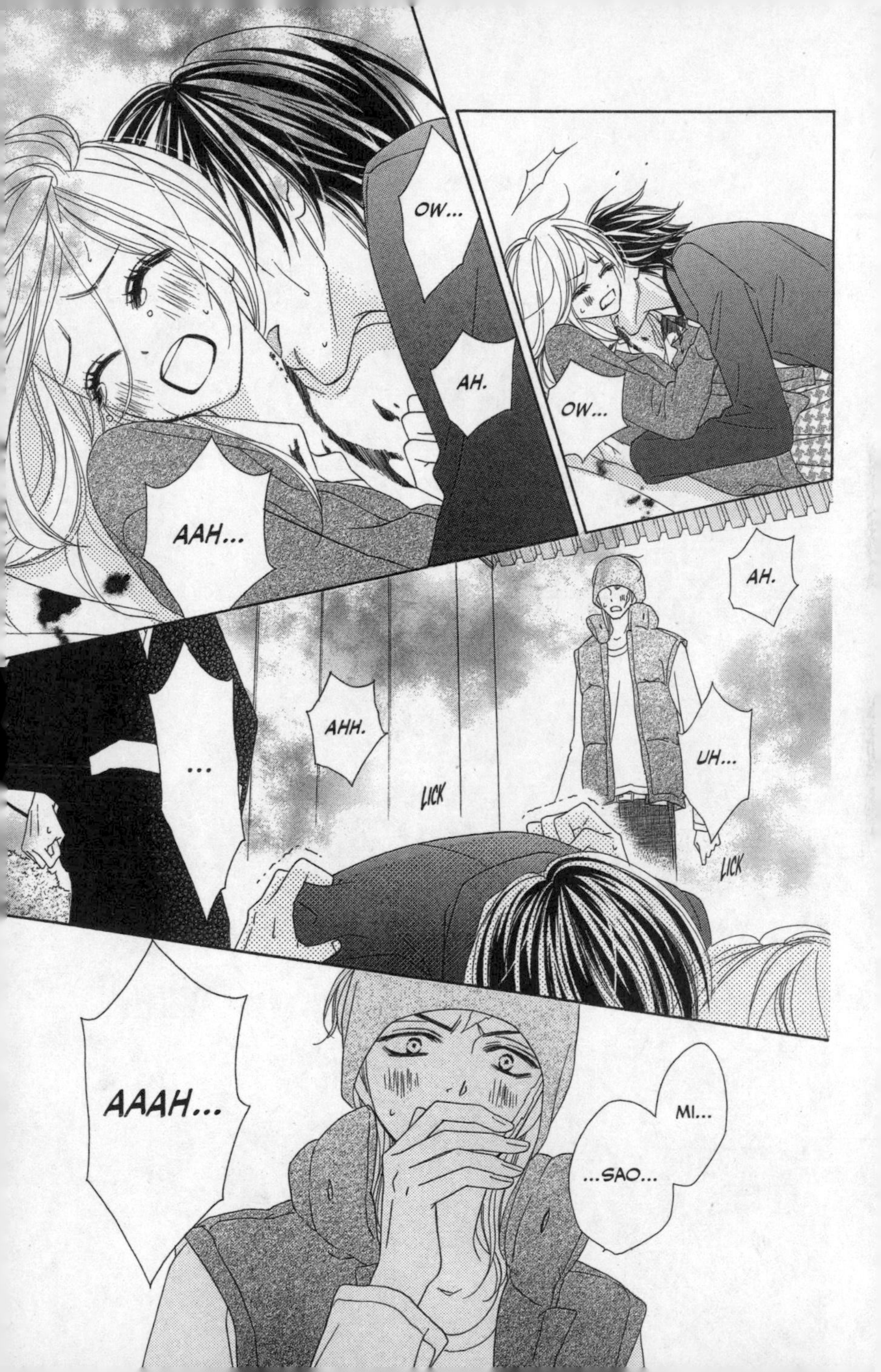
OW...
OW...
AH.
AAH...
AH.
UH...
LICK
LICK
AHH.
...
MI...
...SAO...
AAAH...

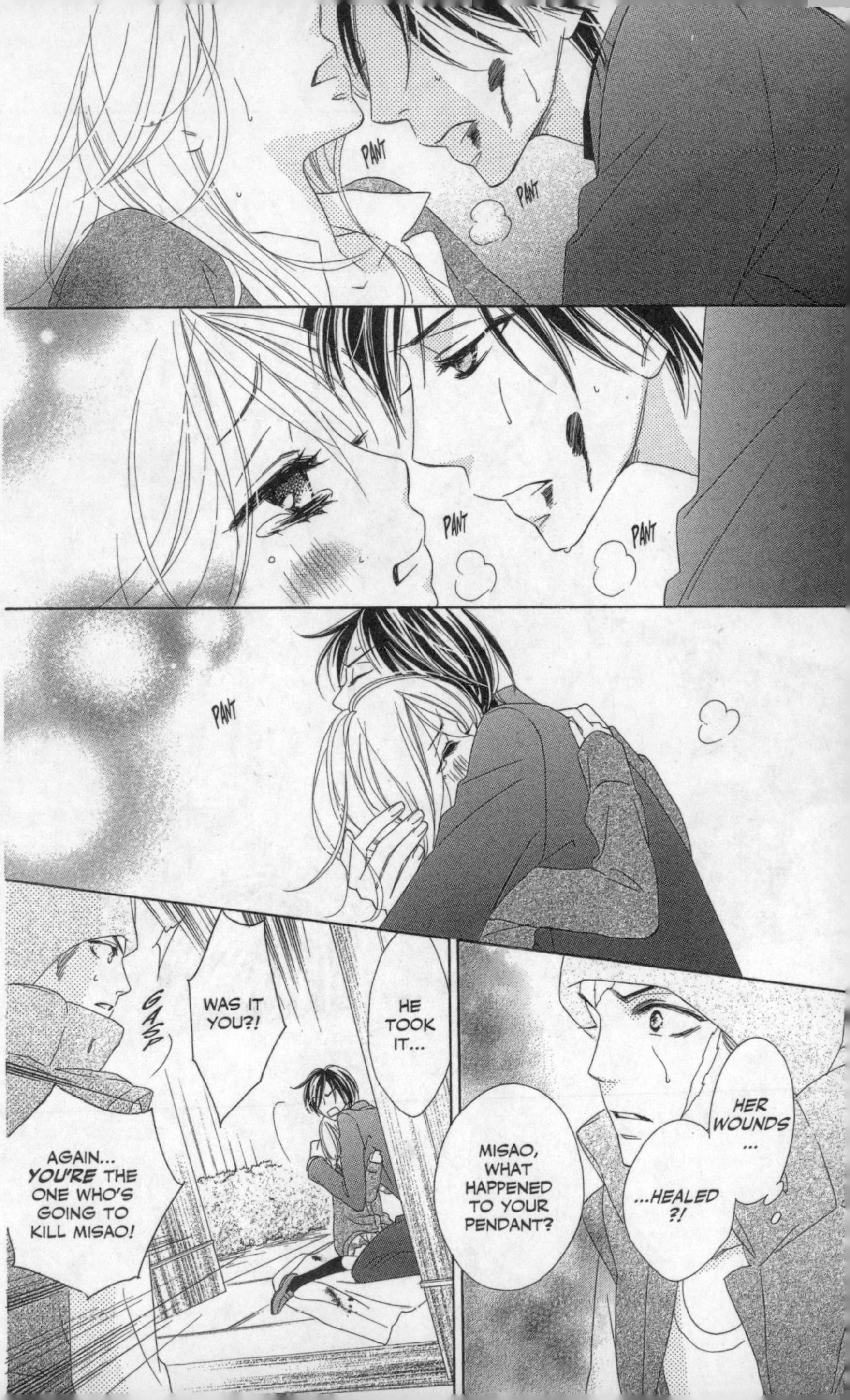
PANT
PANT
PANT
PANT
PANT
HER WOUNDS...
...HEALED?!
MISAO, WHAT HAPPENED TO YOUR PENDANT?
HE TOOK IT...
WAS IT YOU?!
GASP
AGAIN... ***YOU'RE*** THE ONE WHO'S GOING TO KILL MISAO!

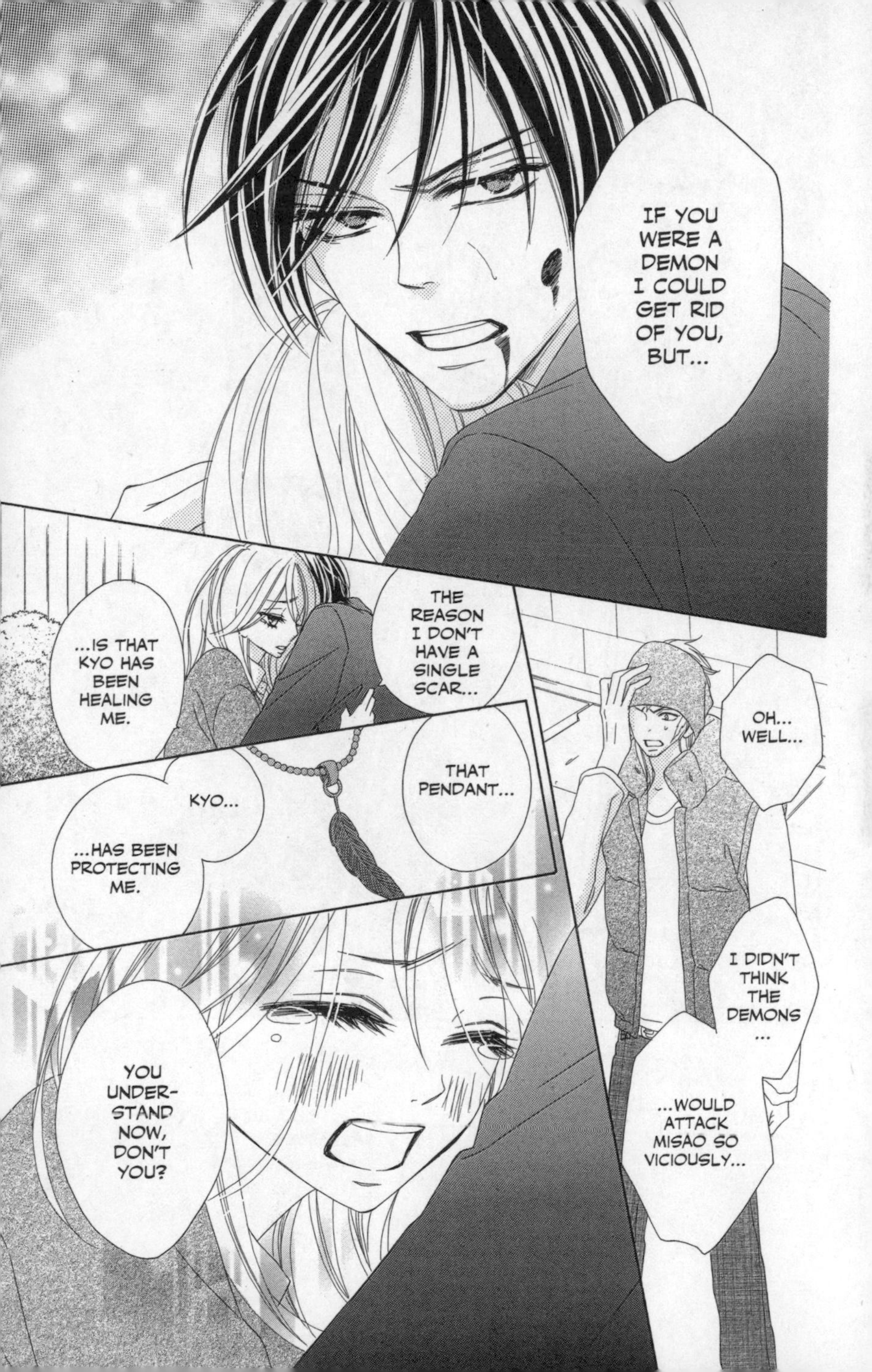
IF YOU WERE A DEMON I COULD GET RID OF YOU, BUT...
OH... WELL...
I DIDN'T THINK THE DEMONS ...
...WOULD ATTACK MISAO SO VICIOUSLY...
THE REASON I DON'T HAVE A SINGLE SCAR...
...IS THAT KYO HAS BEEN HEALING ME.
THAT PENDANT...
KYO...
...HAS BEEN PROTECTING ME.
YOU UNDER-STAND NOW, DON'T YOU?

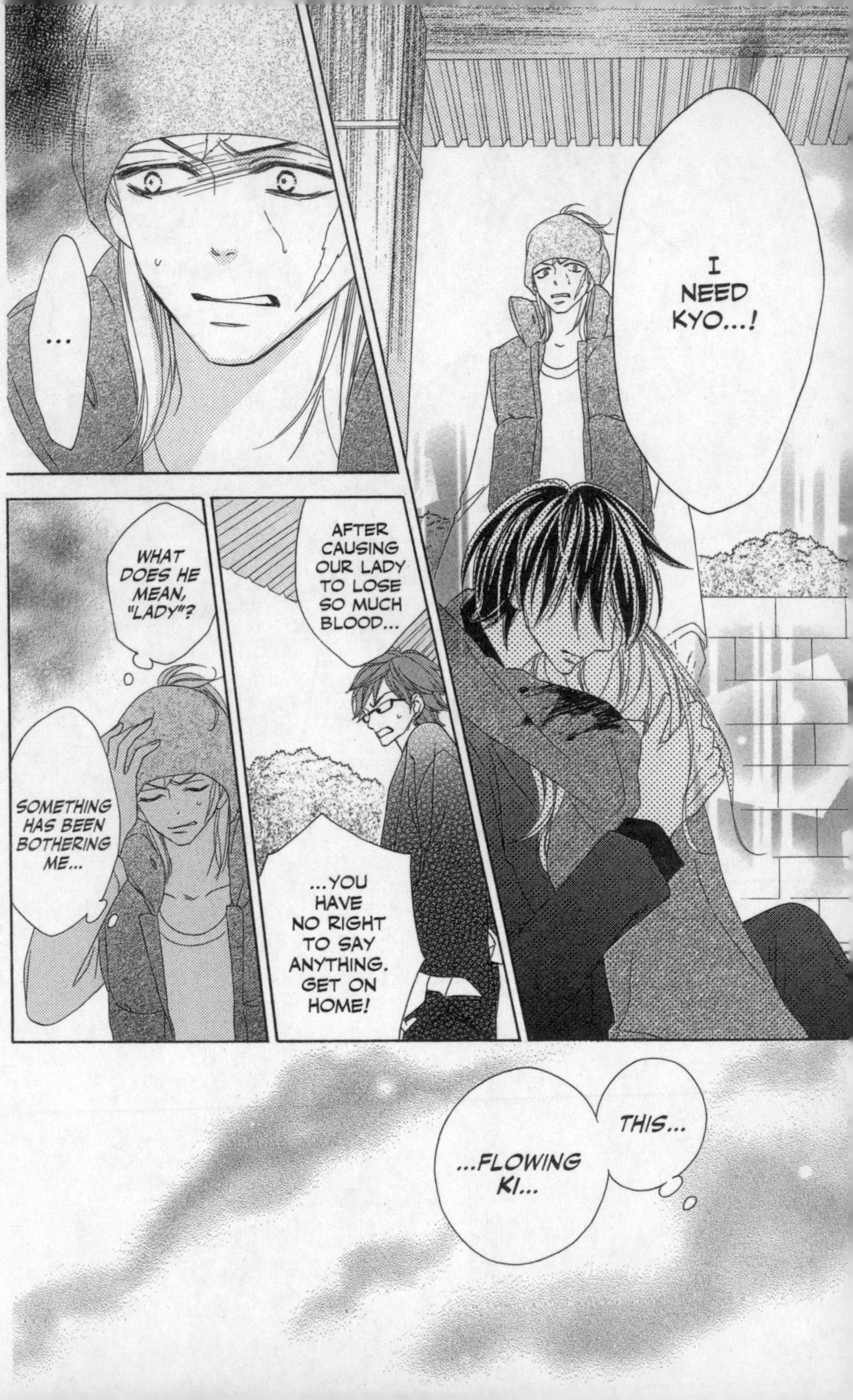
I NEED KYO...!
...
AFTER CAUSING OUR LADY TO LOSE SO MUCH BLOOD...
...YOU HAVE NO RIGHT TO SAY ANYTHING. GET ON HOME!
WHAT DOES HE MEAN, "LADY"?
SOMETHING HAS BEEN BOTHERING ME...
THIS...
...FLOWING KI...

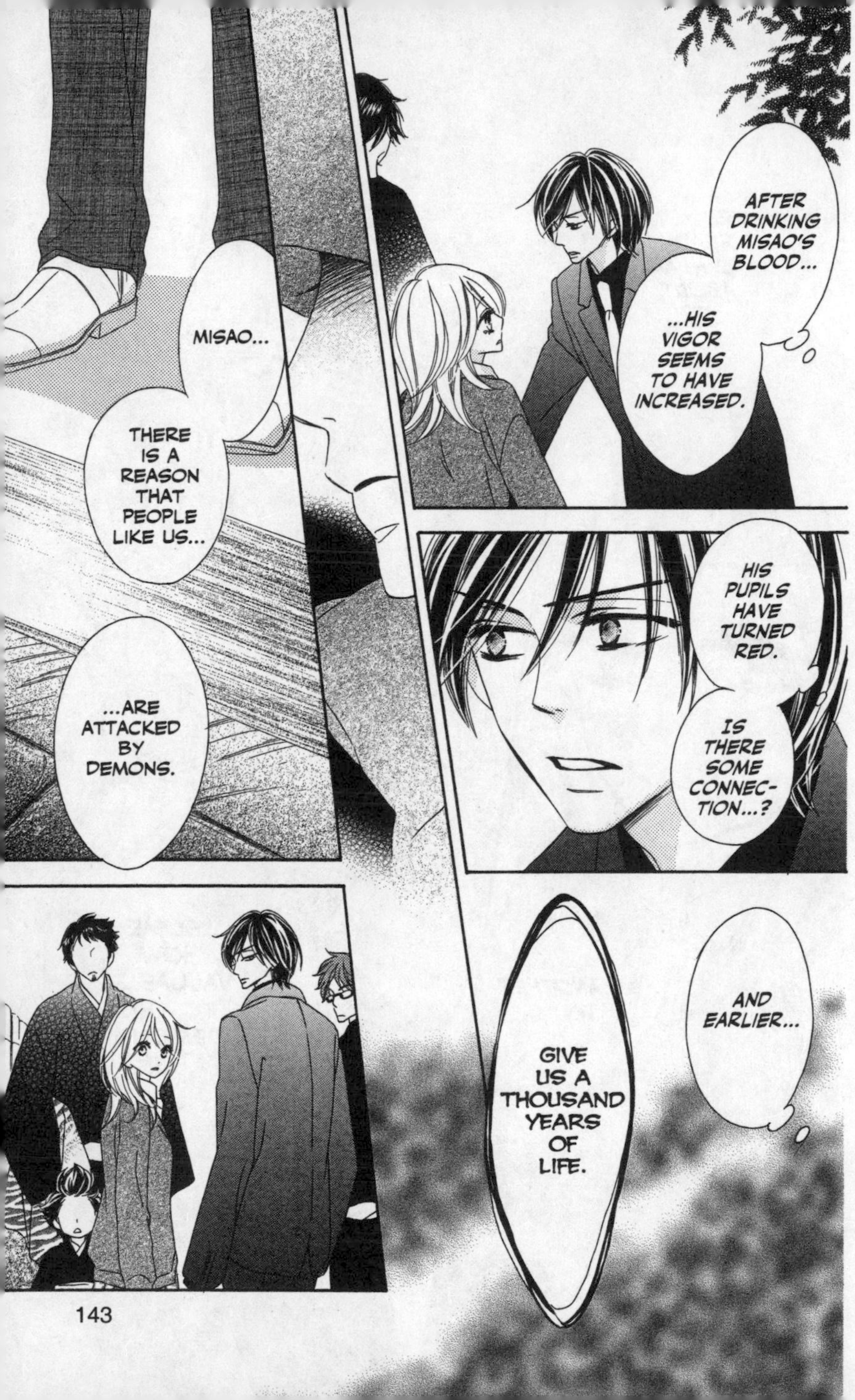
AFTER DRINKING MISAO'S BLOOD...
...HIS VIGOR SEEMS TO HAVE INCREASED.
HIS PUPILS HAVE TURNED RED.
IS THERE SOME CONNEC-TION...?
MISAO...
THERE IS A REASON THAT PEOPLE LIKE US...
...ARE ATTACKED BY DEMONS.
AND EARLIER...
GIVE US A THOUSAND YEARS OF LIFE.

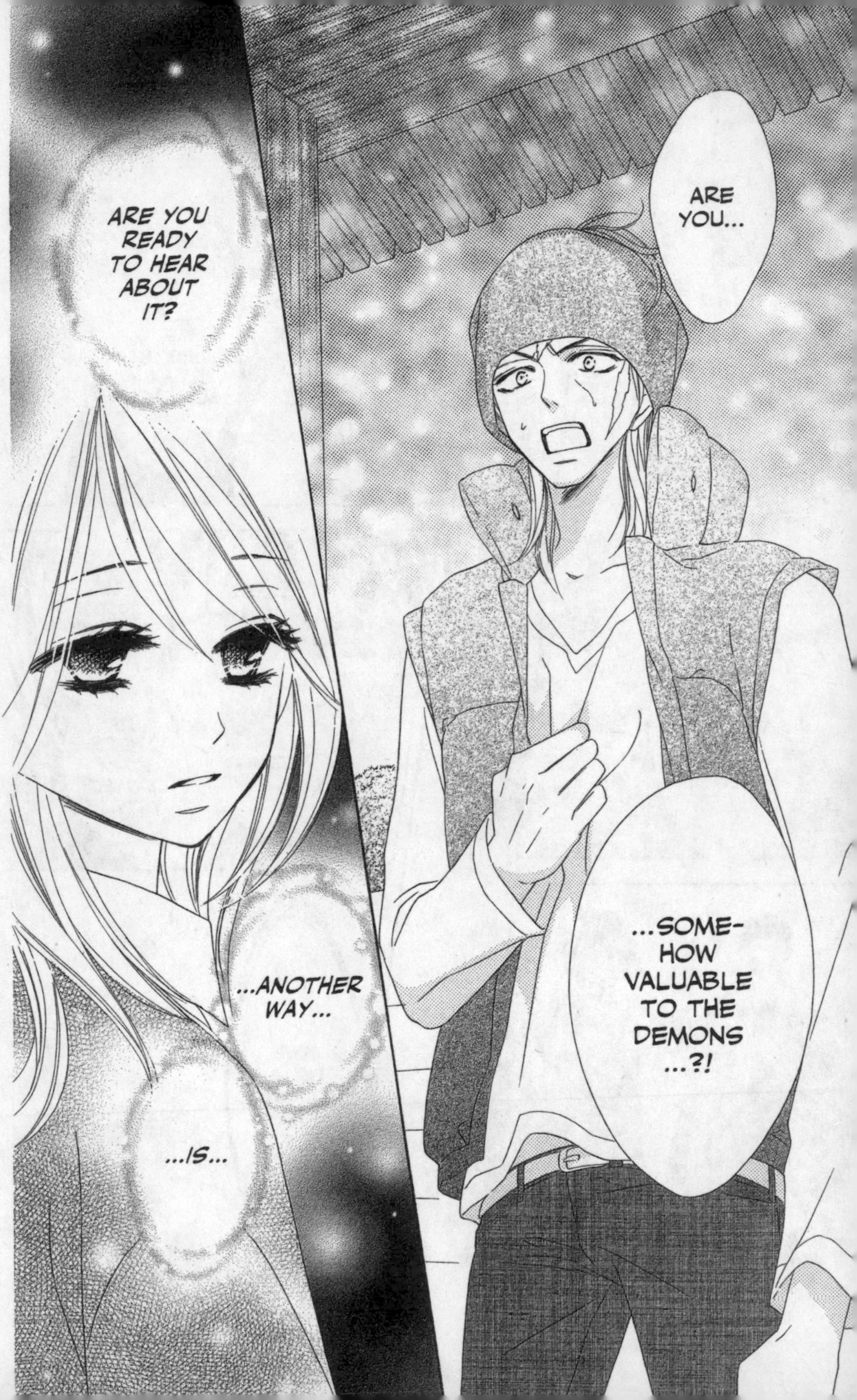
ARE YOU...
...SOME-HOW VALUABLE TO THE DEMONS ...?!
ARE YOU READY TO HEAR ABOUT IT?
...ANOTHER WAY...
...IS...

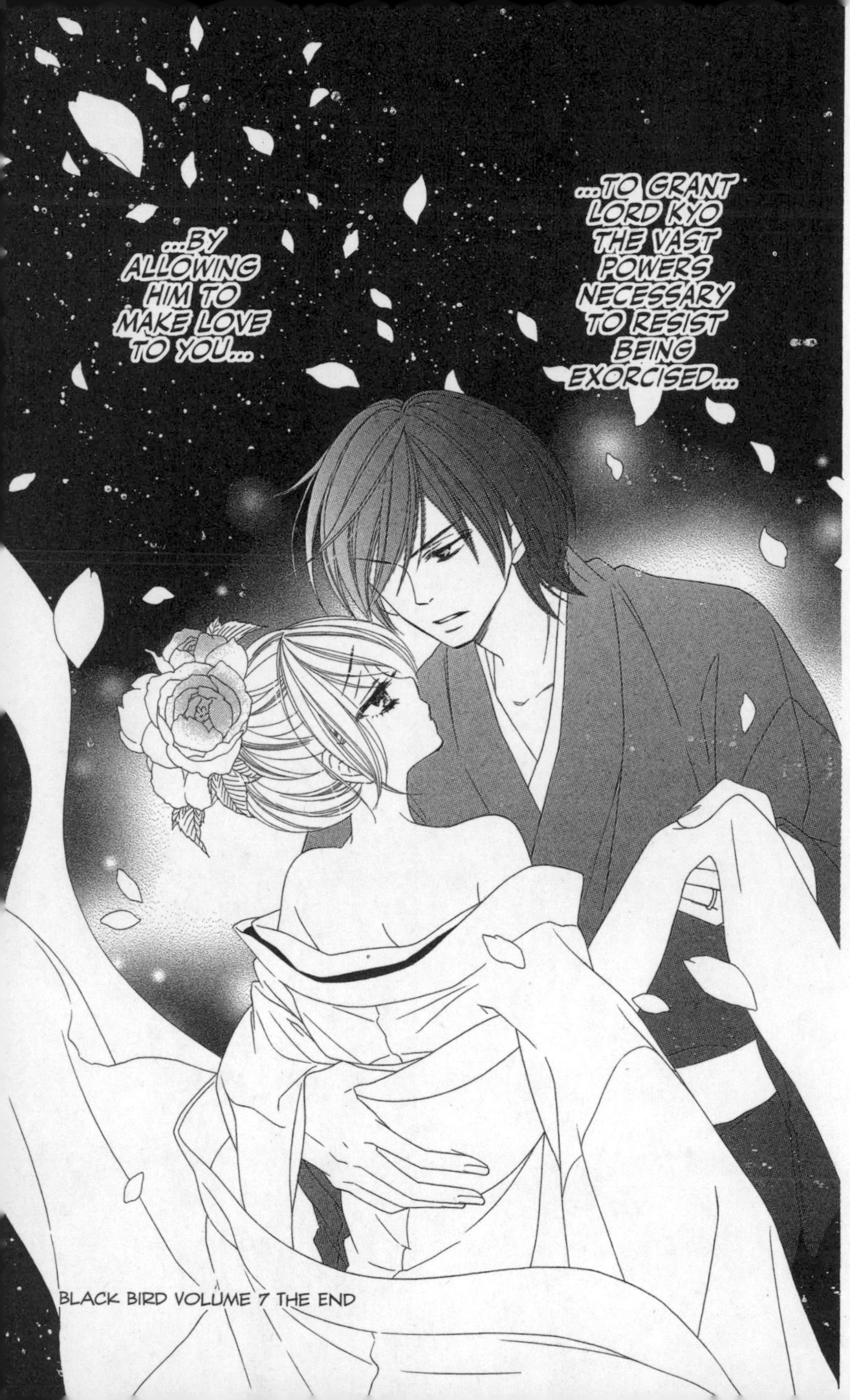
...TO GRANT LORD KYO THE VAST POWERS NECESSARY TO RESIST BEING EXORCISED...
...BY ALLOWING HIM TO MAKE LOVE TO YOU...
BLACK BIRD VOLUME 7 THE END

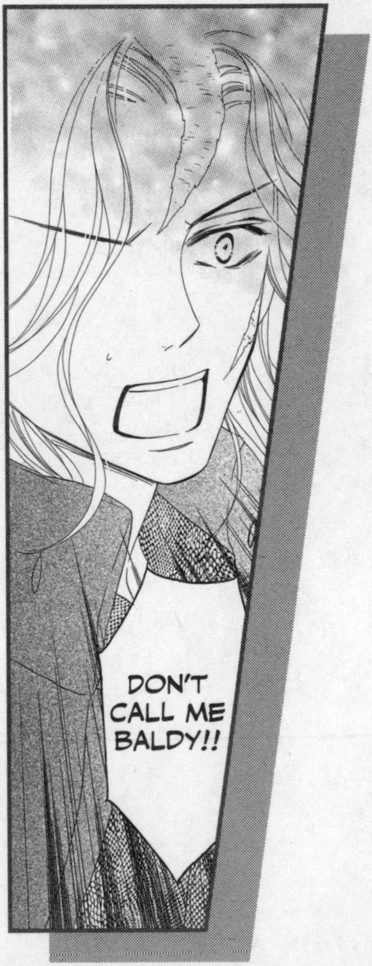
DON'T CALL ME BALDY!!

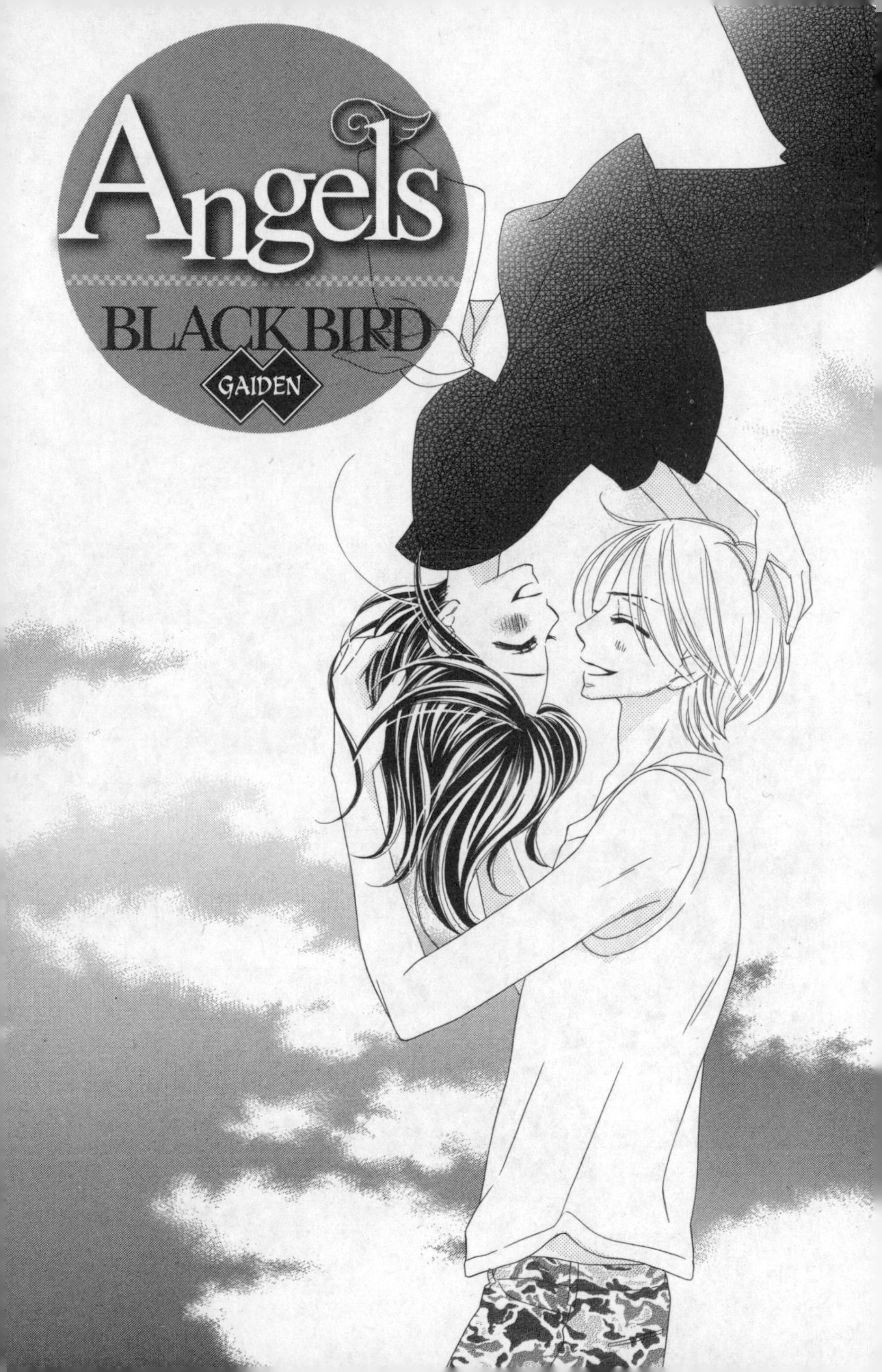
Angels
BLACK BIRD
GAIDEN

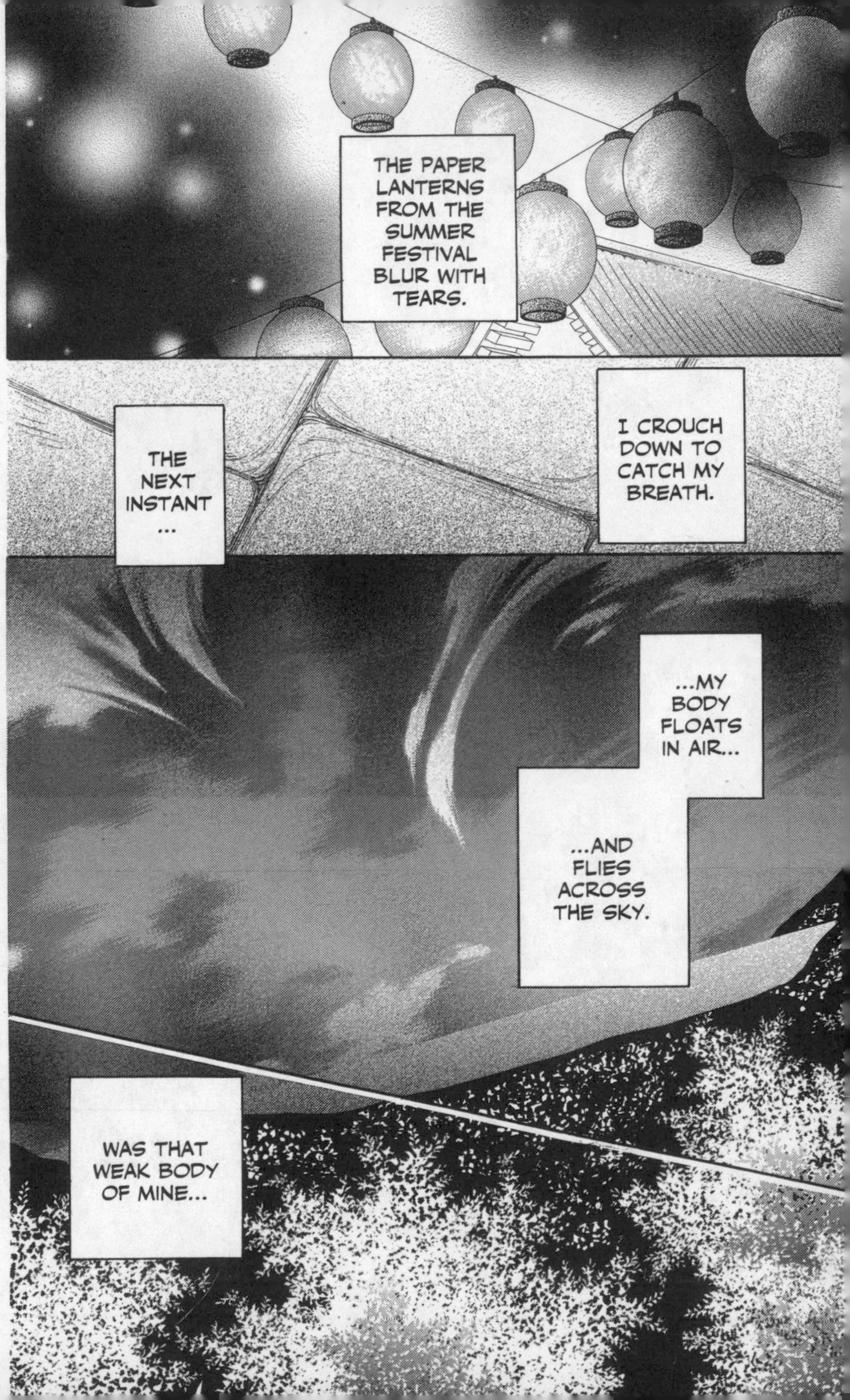
THE PAPER LANTERNS FROM THE SUMMER FESTIVAL BLUR WITH TEARS.
I CROUCH DOWN TO CATCH MY BREATH.
THE NEXT INSTANT ...
...MY BODY FLOATS IN AIR...
...AND FLIES ACROSS THE SKY.
WAS THAT WEAK BODY OF MINE...

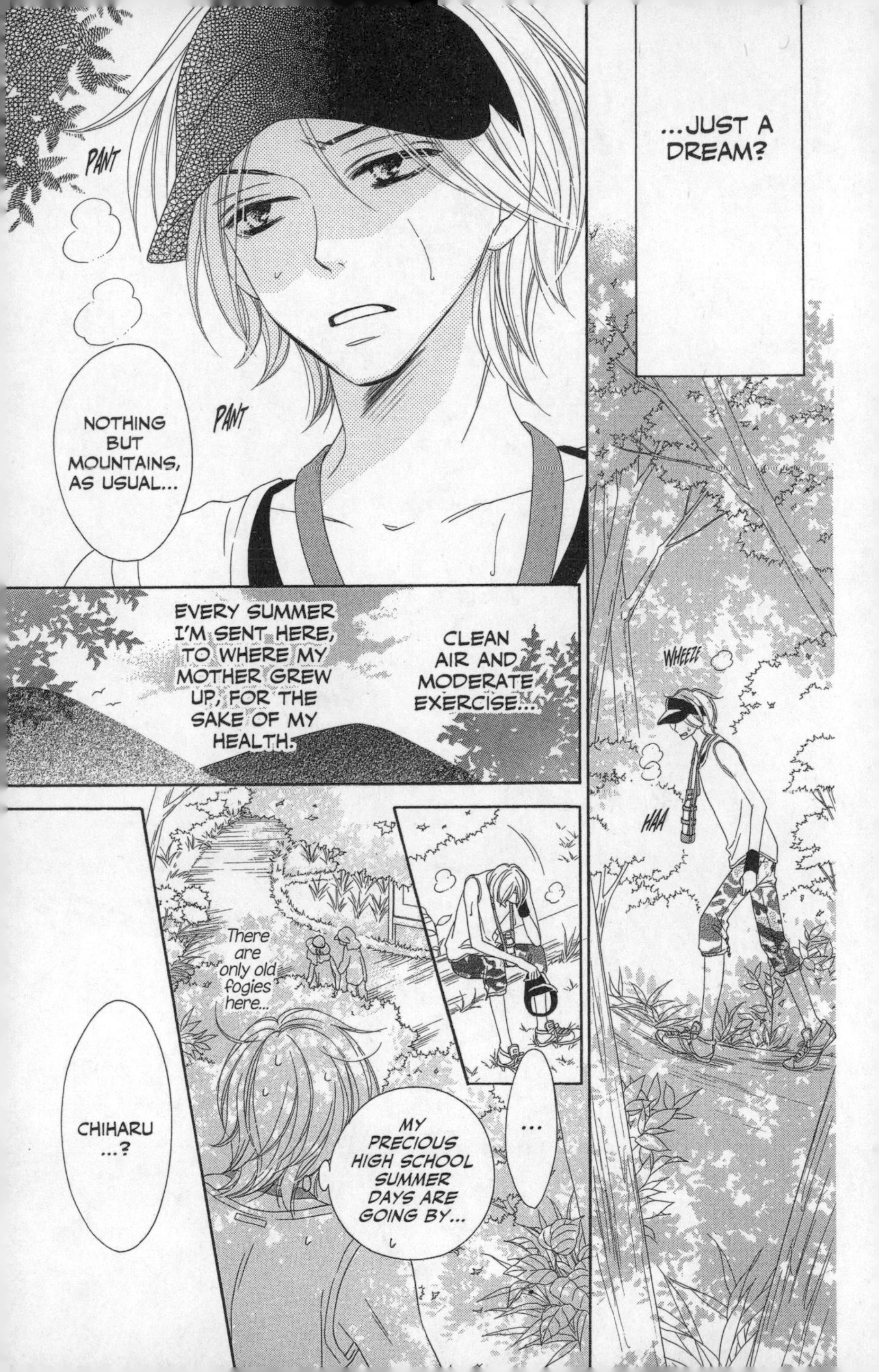
...JUST A DREAM?
WHEEZE
HAA
PANT
PANT
NOTHING BUT MOUNTAINS, AS USUAL...
EVERY SUMMER I'M SENT HERE, TO WHERE MY MOTHER GREW UP, FOR THE SAKE OF MY HEALTH.
CLEAN AIR AND MODERATE EXERCISE...
...
There are only old fogies here...
MY PRECIOUS HIGH SCHOOL SUMMER DAYS ARE GOING BY...
CHIHARU ...?

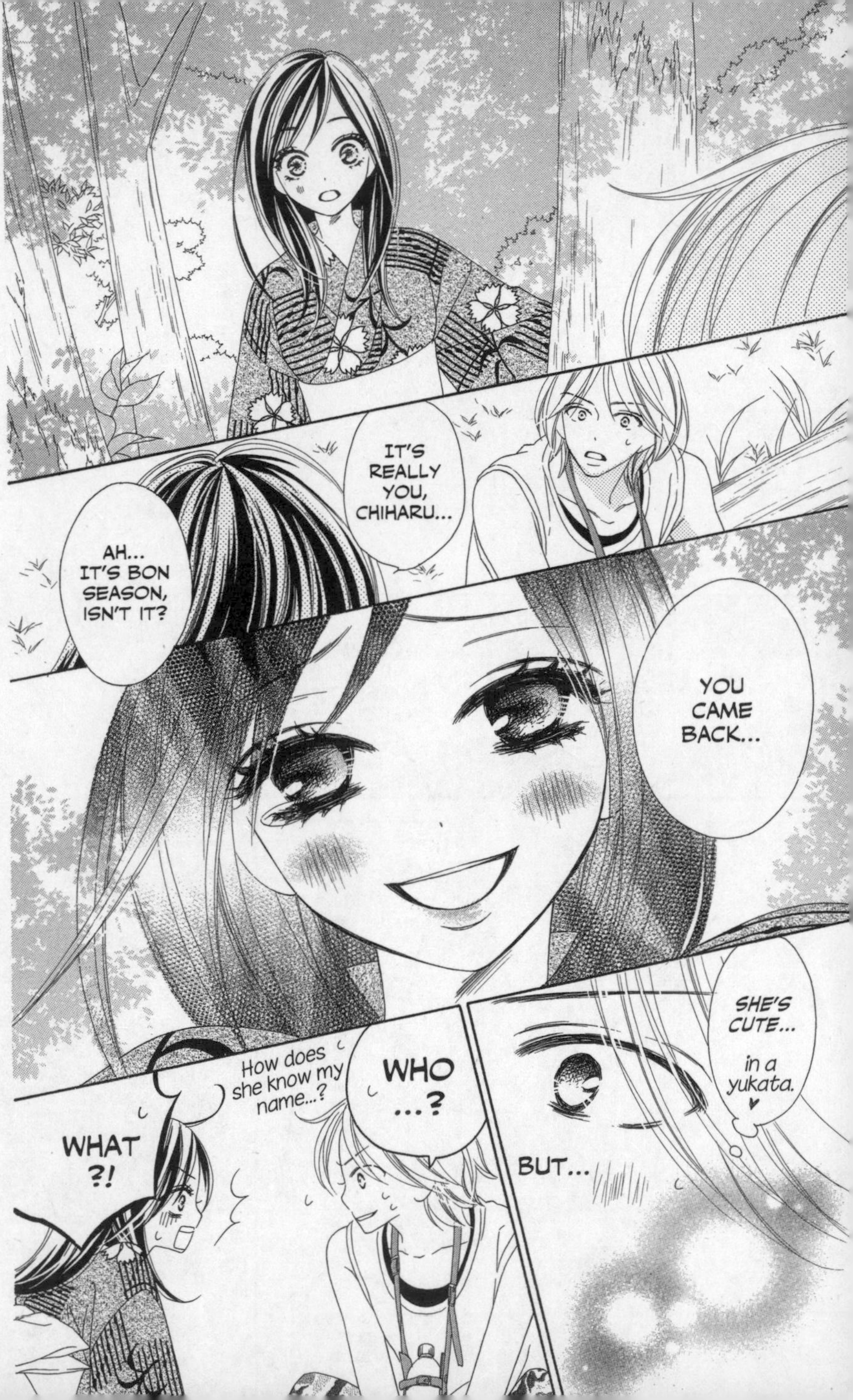

IT'S REALLY YOU, CHIHARU...
AH... IT'S BON SEASON, ISN'T IT?
YOU CAME BACK...
SHE'S CUTE...
in a yukata. ♥
BUT...
WHO ...?
How does she know my name...?
WHAT ?!

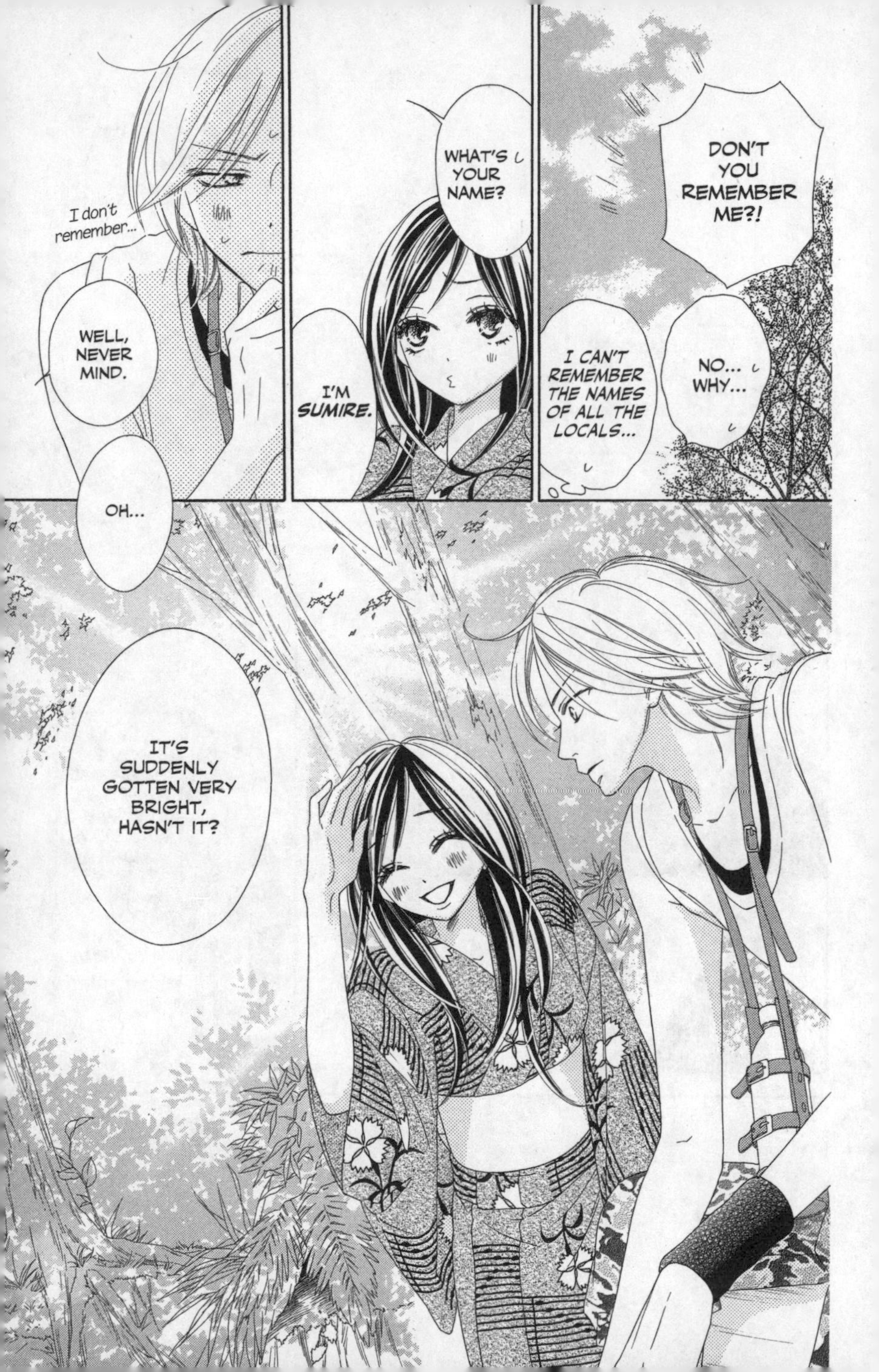
DON'T YOU REMEMBER ME?!
NO... WHY...
I CAN'T REMEMBER THE NAMES OF ALL THE LOCALS...
WHAT'S YOUR NAME?
I'M *SUMIRE.*
I don't remember...
WELL, NEVER MIND.
OH...
IT'S SUDDENLY GOTTEN VERY BRIGHT, HASN'T IT?

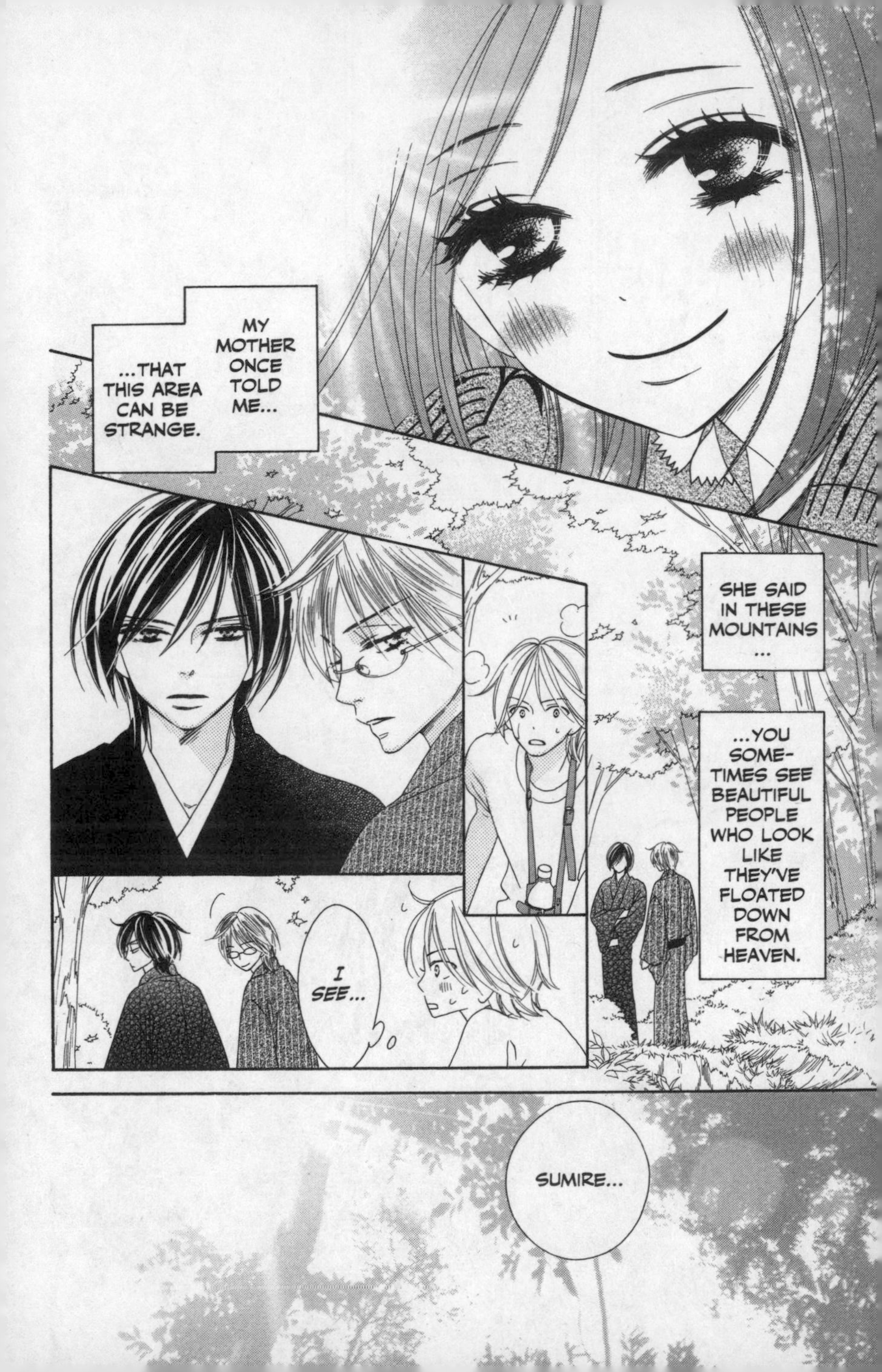
MY MOTHER ONCE TOLD ME...
...THAT THIS AREA CAN BE STRANGE.
SHE SAID IN THESE MOUNTAINS...
...YOU SOMETIMES SEE BEAUTIFUL PEOPLE WHO LOOK LIKE THEY'VE FLOATED DOWN FROM HEAVEN.
I SEE...
SUMIRE...

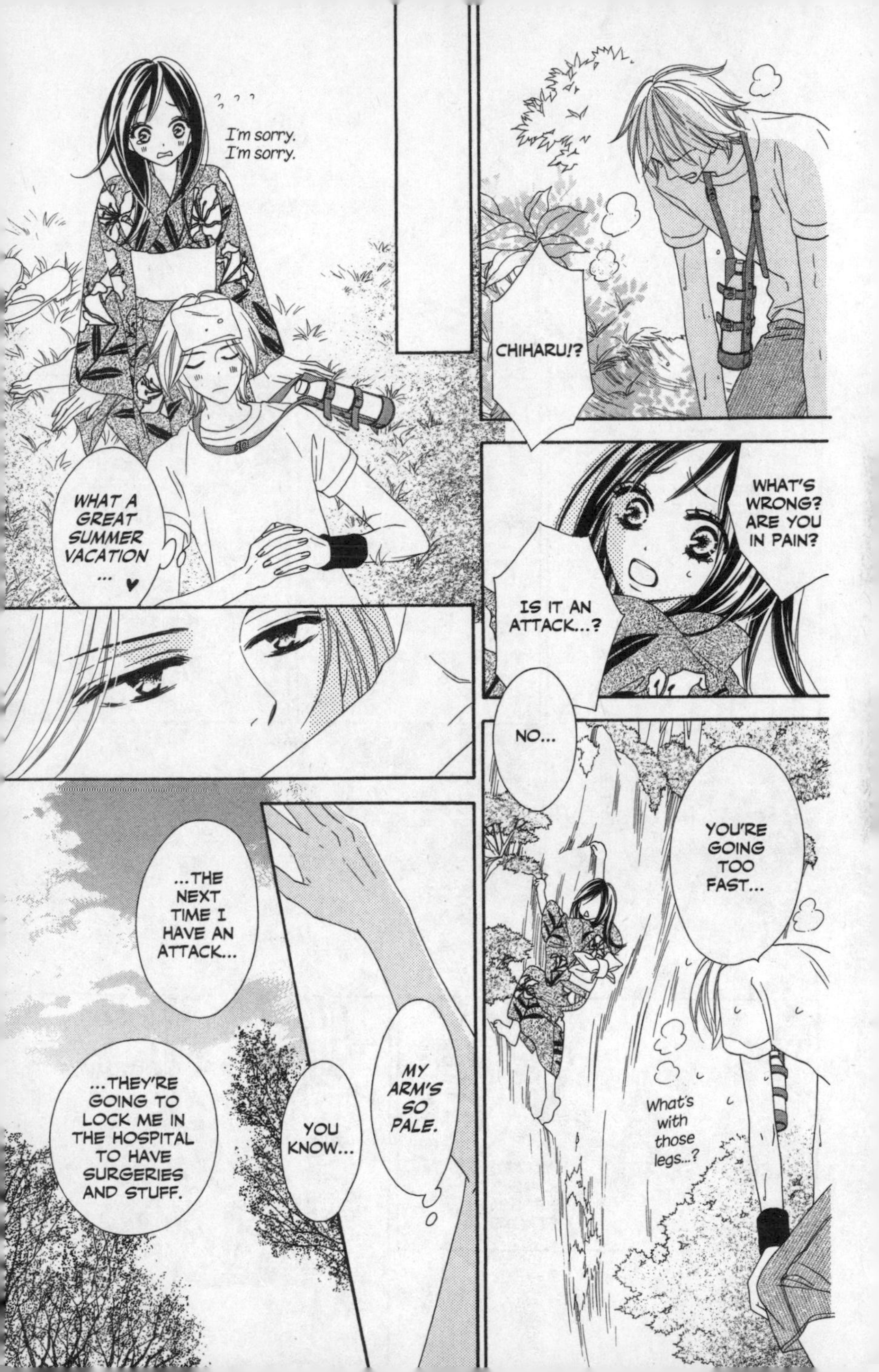
CHIHARU!?
WHAT'S WRONG? ARE YOU IN PAIN?
IS IT AN ATTACK...?
NO...
YOU'RE GOING TOO FAST...
What's with those legs...?
I'm sorry. I'm sorry.
WHAT A GREAT SUMMER VACATION... ♥
...THE NEXT TIME I HAVE AN ATTACK...
MY ARM'S SO PALE.
YOU KNOW...
...THEY'RE GOING TO LOCK ME IN THE HOSPITAL TO HAVE SURGERIES AND STUFF.

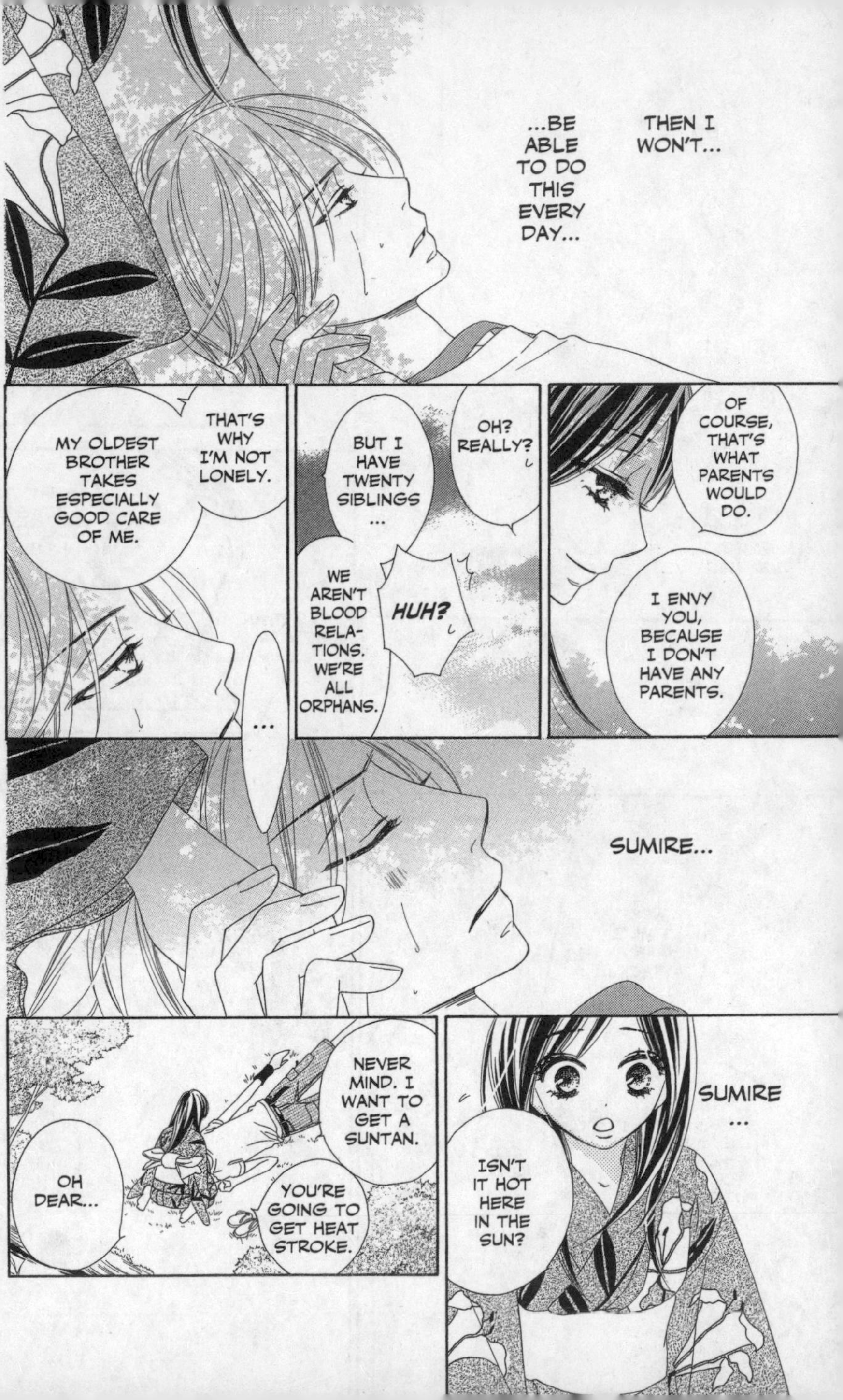
THEN I WON'T...
...BE ABLE TO DO THIS EVERY DAY...
OF COURSE, THAT'S WHAT PARENTS WOULD DO.
I ENVY YOU, BECAUSE I DON'T HAVE ANY PARENTS.
OH? REALLY?
BUT I HAVE TWENTY SIBLINGS...
HUH?
WE AREN'T BLOOD RELA-TIONS. WE'RE ALL ORPHANS.
THAT'S WHY I'M NOT LONELY.
MY OLDEST BROTHER TAKES ESPECIALLY GOOD CARE OF ME.
...
SUMIRE...
SUMIRE...
ISN'T IT HOT HERE IN THE SUN?
NEVER MIND. I WANT TO GET A SUNTAN.
YOU'RE GOING TO GET HEAT STROKE.
OH DEAR...

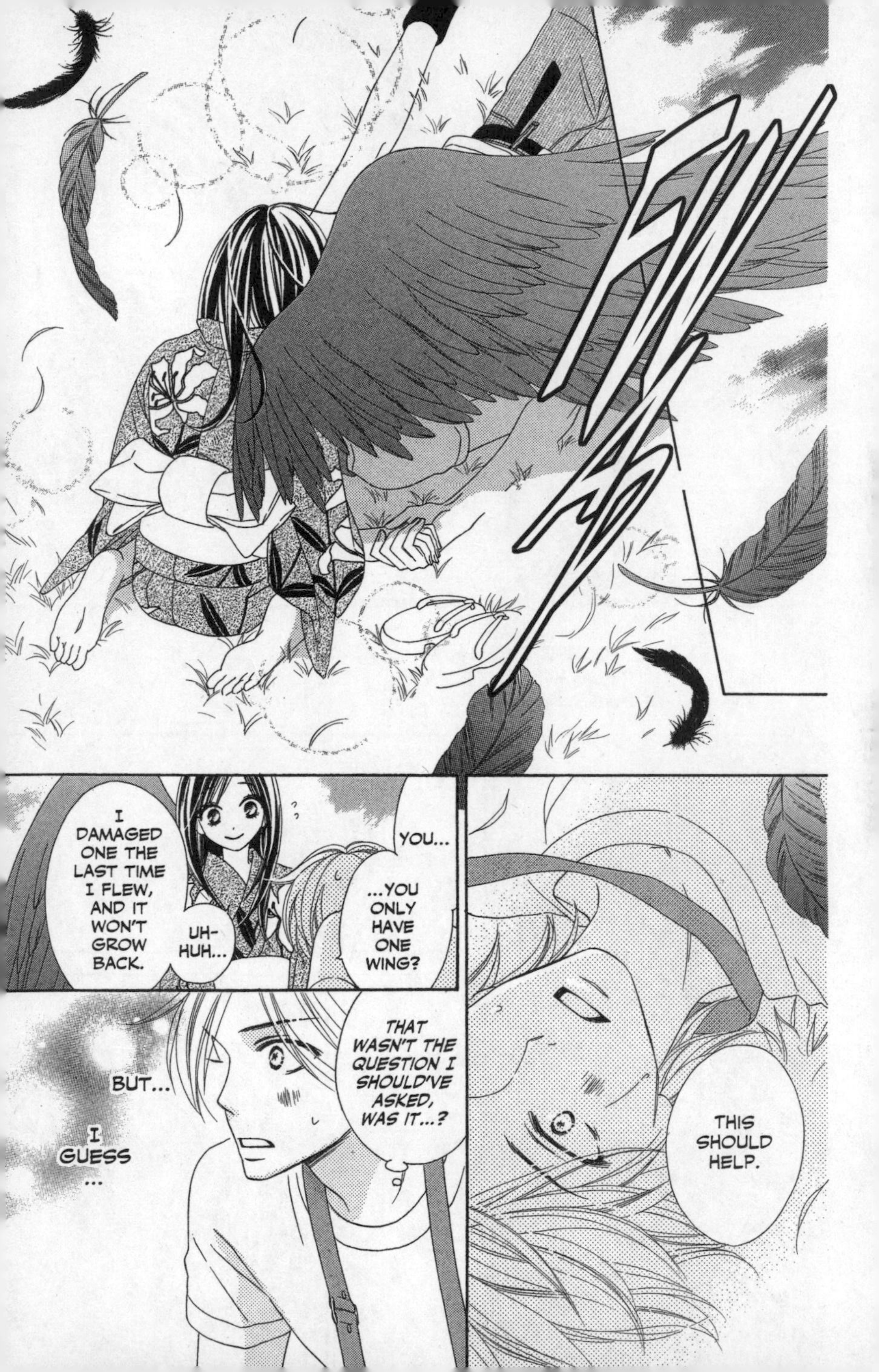
THIS SHOULD HELP.
YOU...
...YOU ONLY HAVE ONE WING?
UH-HUH...
I DAMAGED ONE THE LAST TIME I FLEW, AND IT WON'T GROW BACK.
THAT WASN'T THE QUESTION I SHOULD'VE ASKED, WAS IT...?
BUT...
I GUESS ...

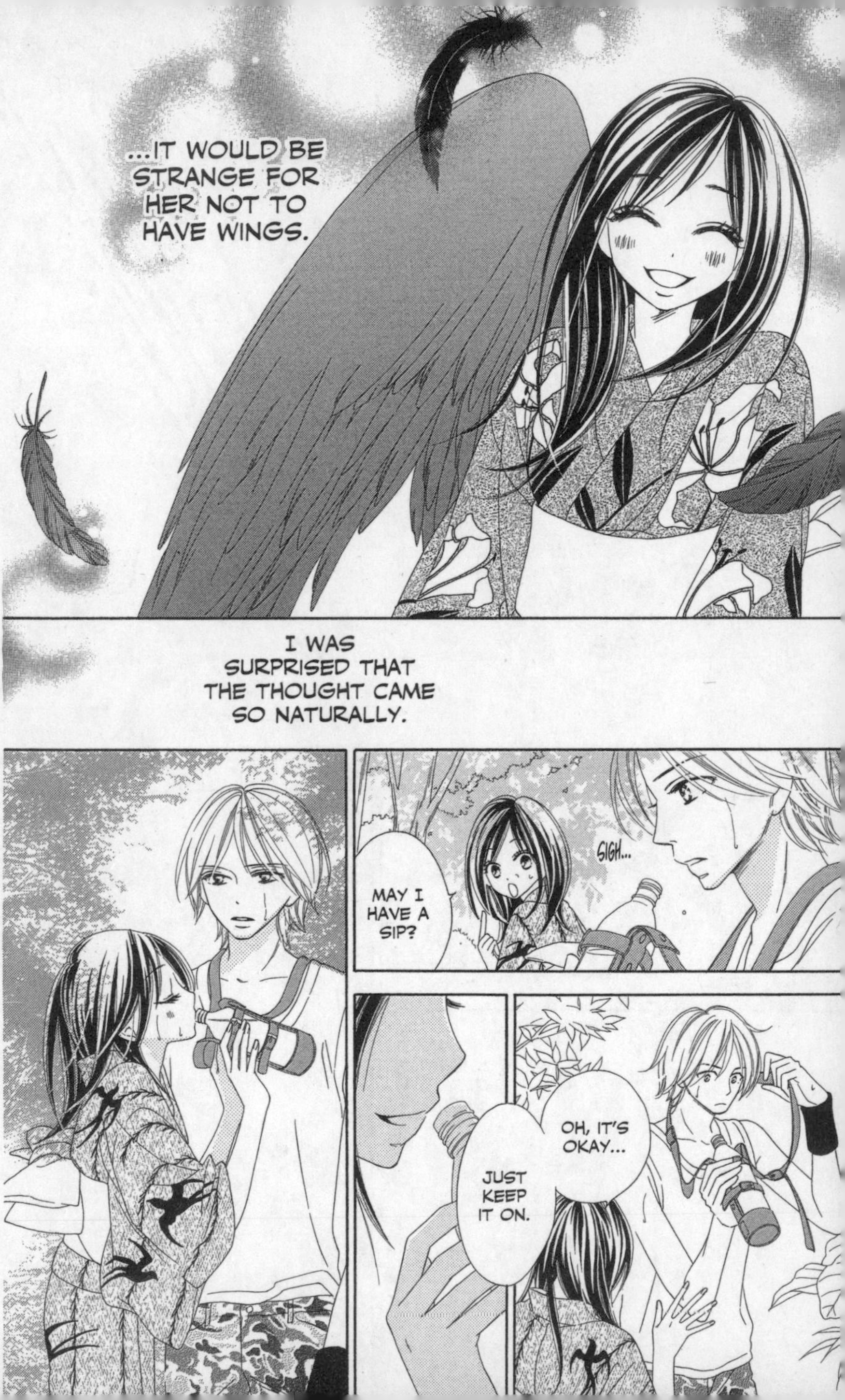
...IT WOULD BE STRANGE FOR HER NOT TO HAVE WINGS.
I WAS SURPRISED THAT THE THOUGHT CAME SO NATURALLY.
SIGH...
MAY I HAVE A SIP?
OH, IT'S OKAY...
JUST KEEP IT ON.

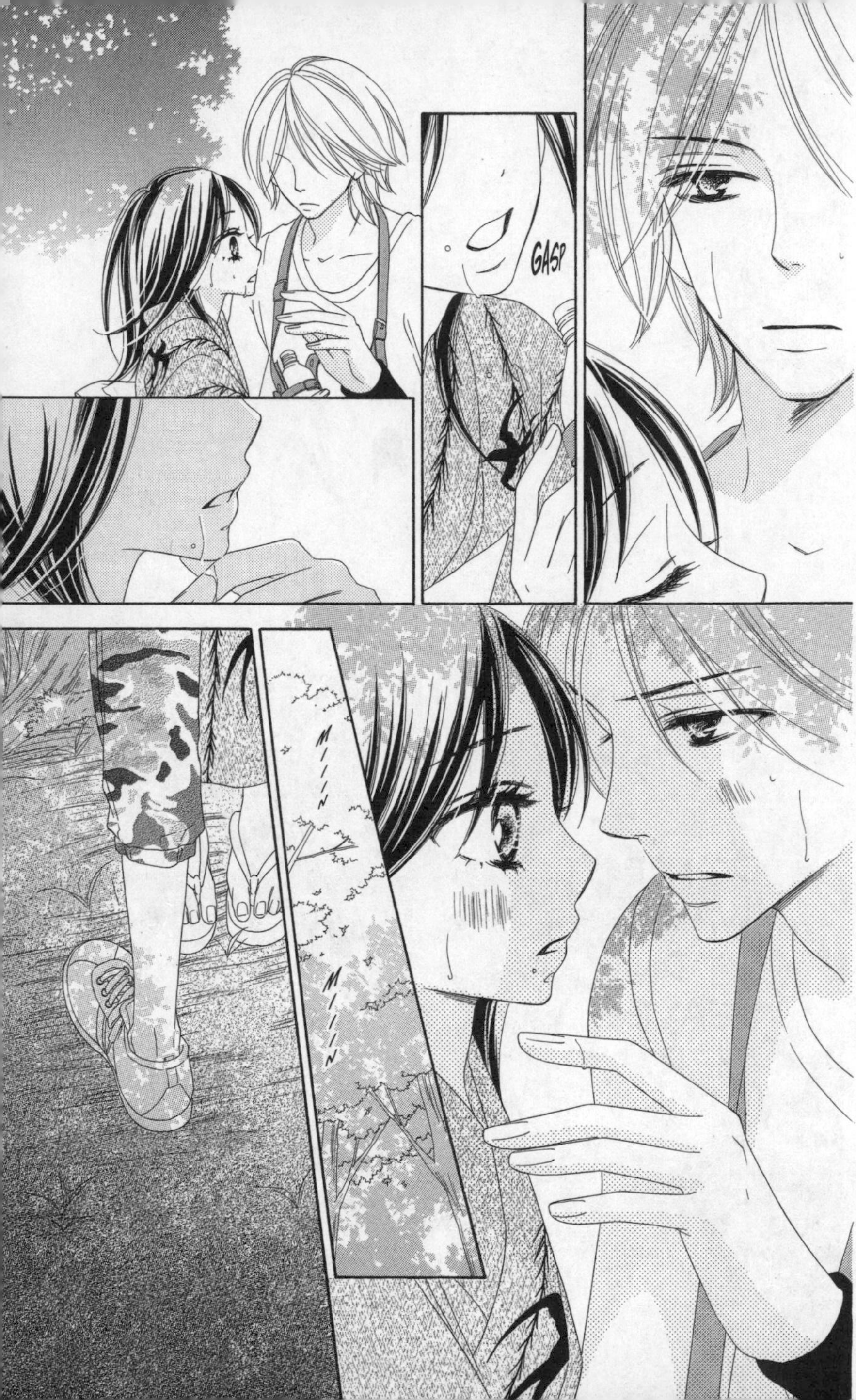
GASP
MIIIN
MIIIN

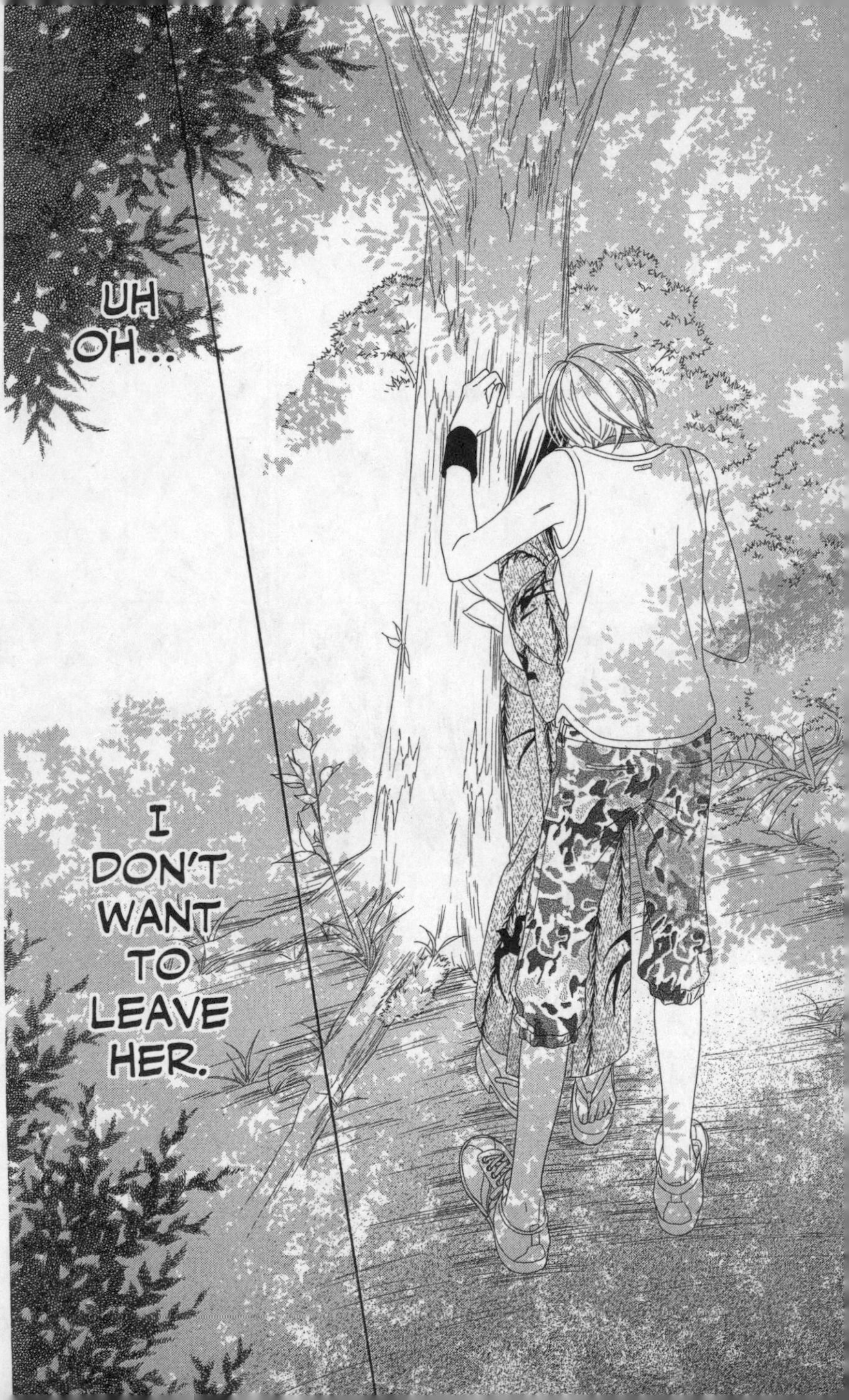
UH OH...
I DON'T WANT TO LEAVE HER.

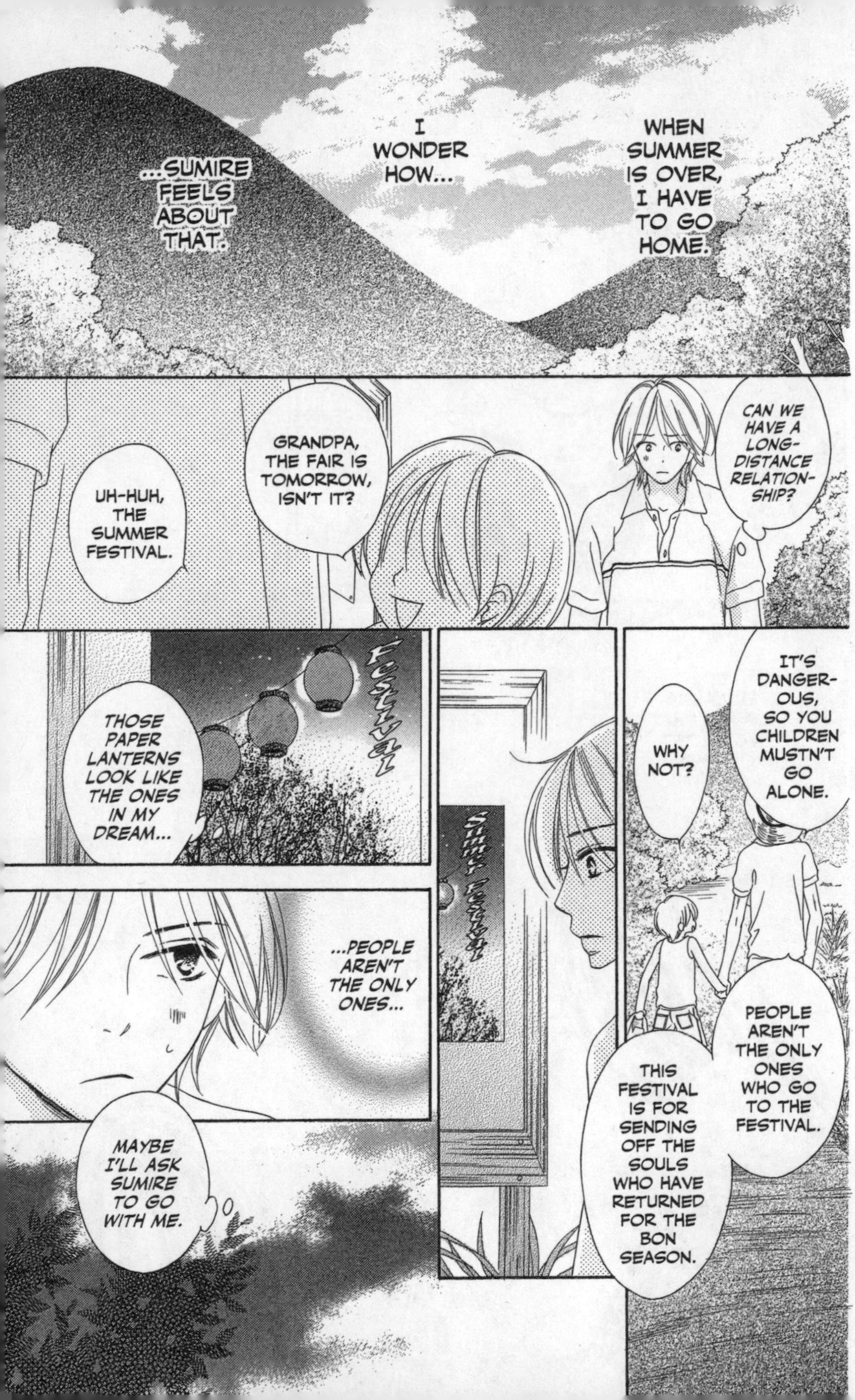
WHEN SUMMER IS OVER, I HAVE TO GO HOME.
I WONDER HOW...
...SUMIRE FEELS ABOUT THAT.
CAN WE HAVE A LONG-DISTANCE RELATIONSHIP?
GRANDPA, THE FAIR IS TOMORROW, ISN'T IT?
UH-HUH, THE SUMMER FESTIVAL.
IT'S DANGEROUS, SO YOU CHILDREN MUSTN'T GO ALONE.
WHY NOT?
PEOPLE AREN'T THE ONLY ONES WHO GO TO THE FESTIVAL.
THIS FESTIVAL IS FOR SENDING OFF THE SOULS WHO HAVE RETURNED FOR THE BON SEASON.
Summer Festival
FESTIVAL
THOSE PAPER LANTERNS LOOK LIKE THE ONES IN MY DREAM...
...PEOPLE AREN'T THE ONLY ONES...
MAYBE I'LL ASK SUMIRE TO GO WITH ME.

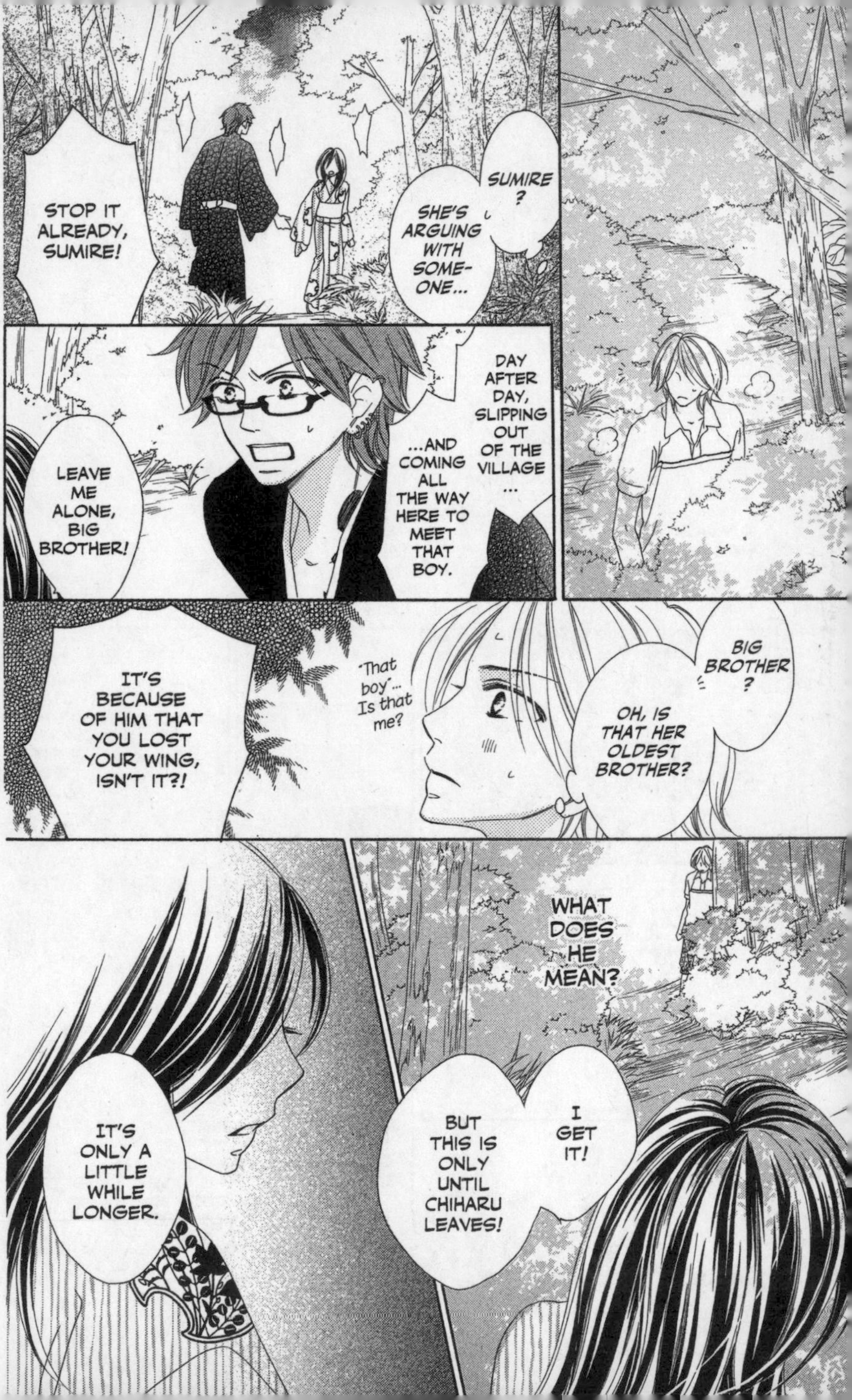
SUMIRE?
SHE'S ARGUING WITH SOME-ONE...
STOP IT ALREADY, SUMIRE!
DAY AFTER DAY, SLIPPING OUT OF THE VILLAGE...
...AND COMING ALL THE WAY HERE TO MEET THAT BOY.
LEAVE ME ALONE, BIG BROTHER!
BIG BROTHER?
OH, IS THAT HER OLDEST BROTHER?
"That boy"... Is that me?
IT'S BECAUSE OF HIM THAT YOU LOST YOUR WING, ISN'T IT?!
WHAT DOES HE MEAN?
I GET IT!
BUT THIS IS ONLY UNTIL CHIHARU LEAVES!
IT'S ONLY A LITTLE WHILE LONGER.

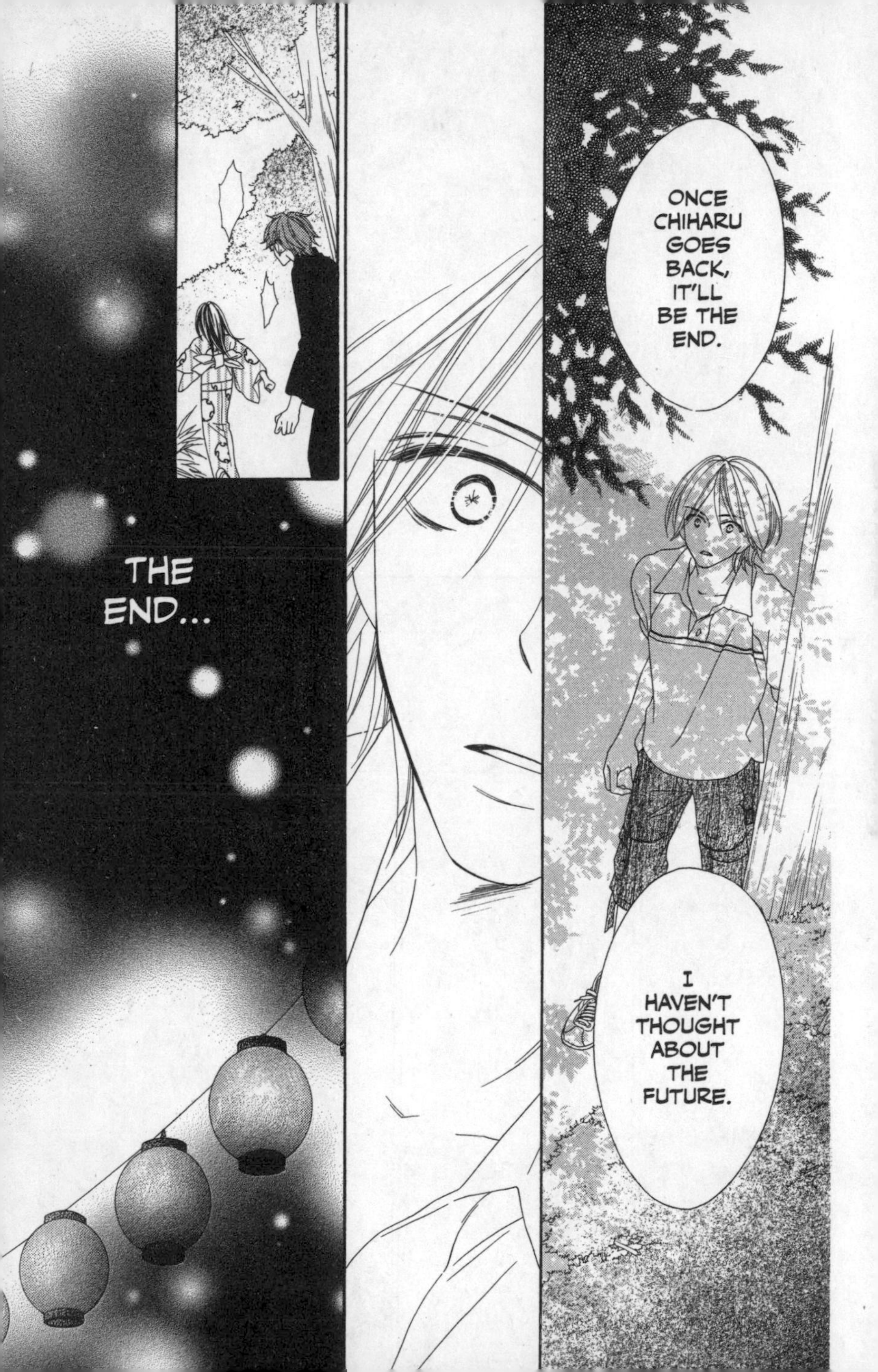
ONCE CHIHARU GOES BACK, IT'LL BE THE END.
I HAVEN'T THOUGHT ABOUT THE FUTURE.
THE END...

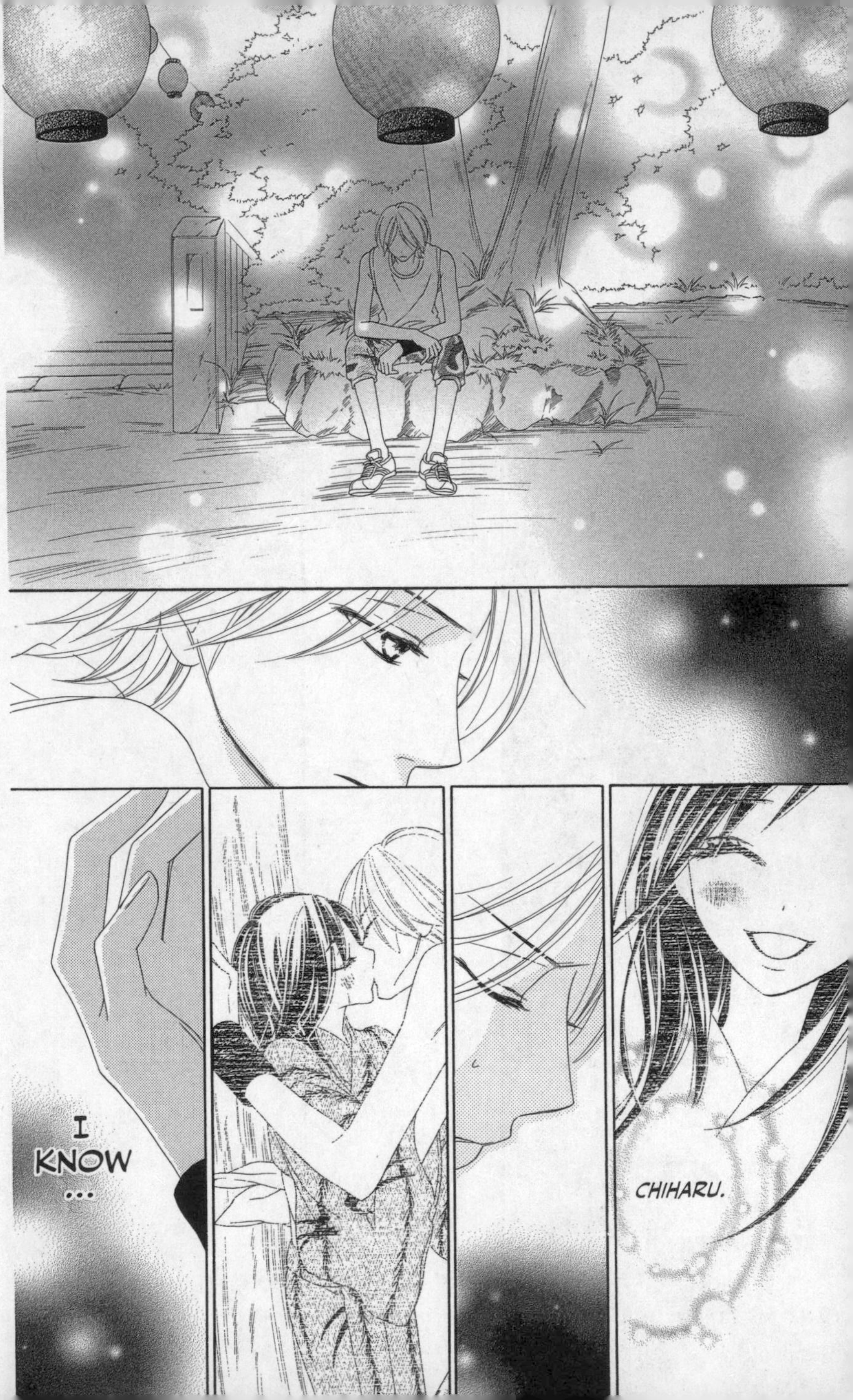
CHIHARU.
I KNOW ...

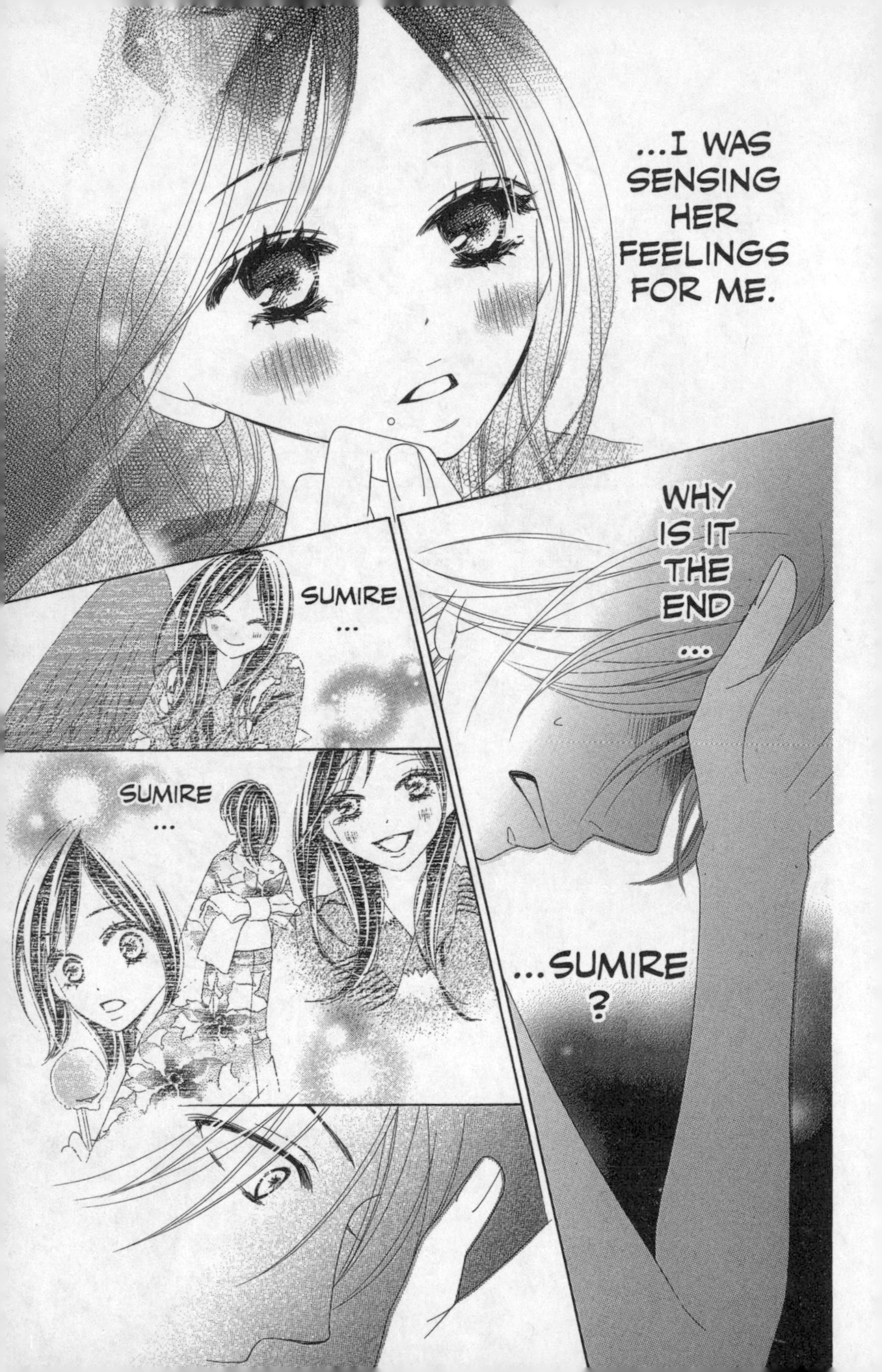
...I WAS SENSING HER FEELINGS FOR ME.
WHY IS IT THE END ...
...SUMIRE ?
SUMIRE ...
SUMIRE ...

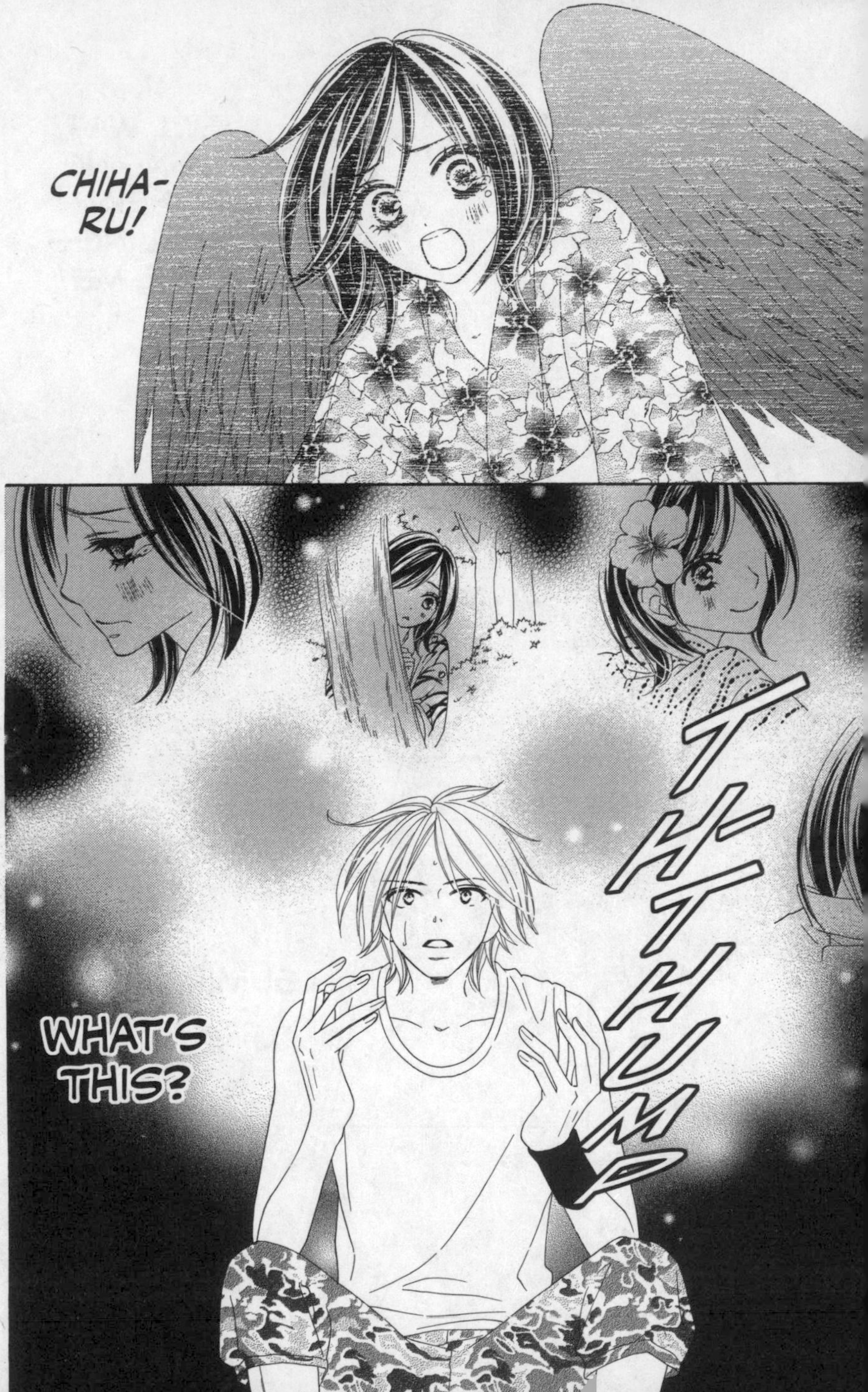
CHIHA-
RU!
THHUMP
WHAT'S
THIS?

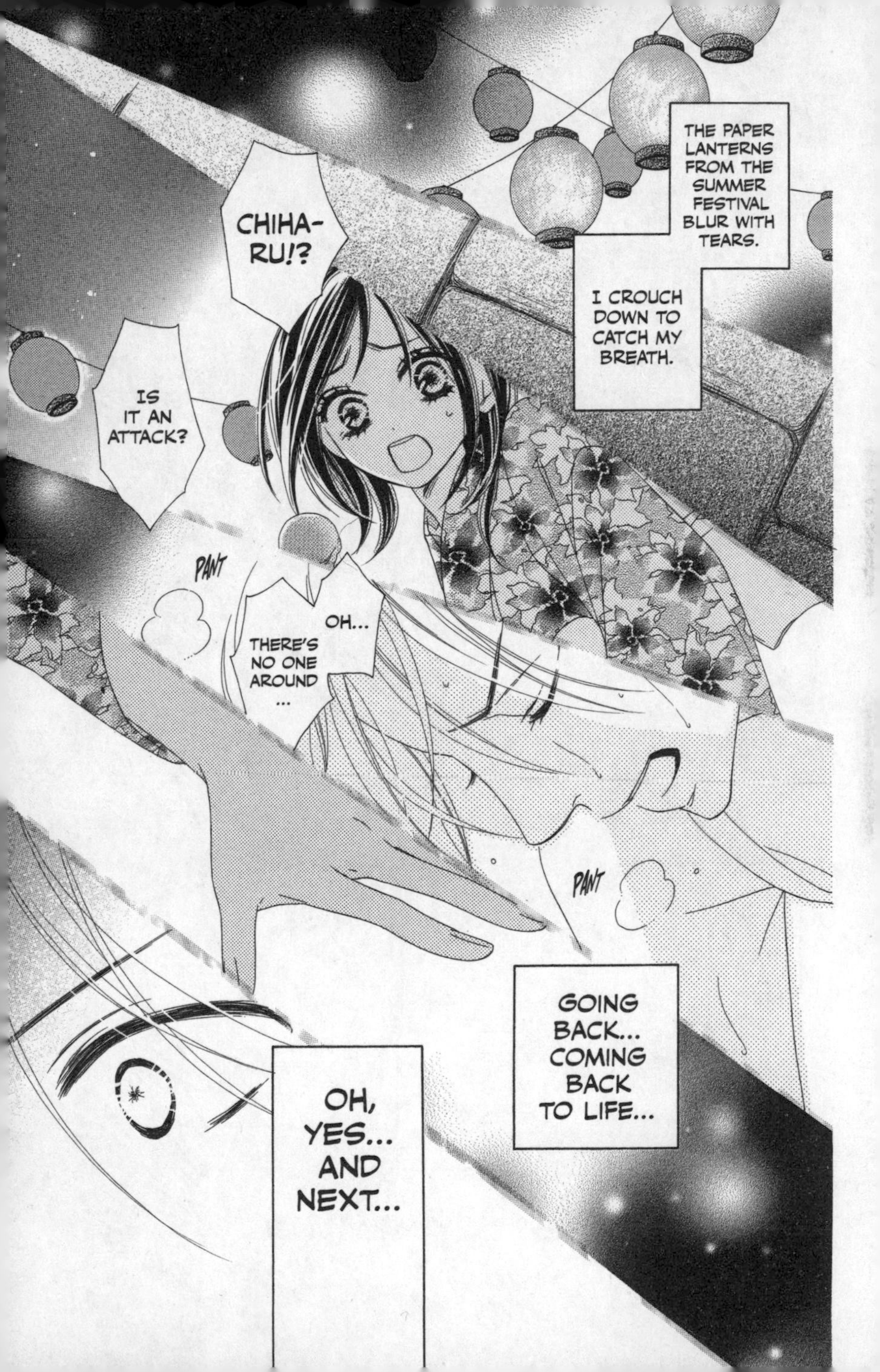
THE PAPER LANTERNS FROM THE SUMMER FESTIVAL BLUR WITH TEARS.
I CROUCH DOWN TO CATCH MY BREATH.
CHIHA-RU!?
IS IT AN ATTACK?
PANT
OH... THERE'S NO ONE AROUND...
PANT
GOING BACK... COMING BACK TO LIFE...
OH, YES... AND NEXT...

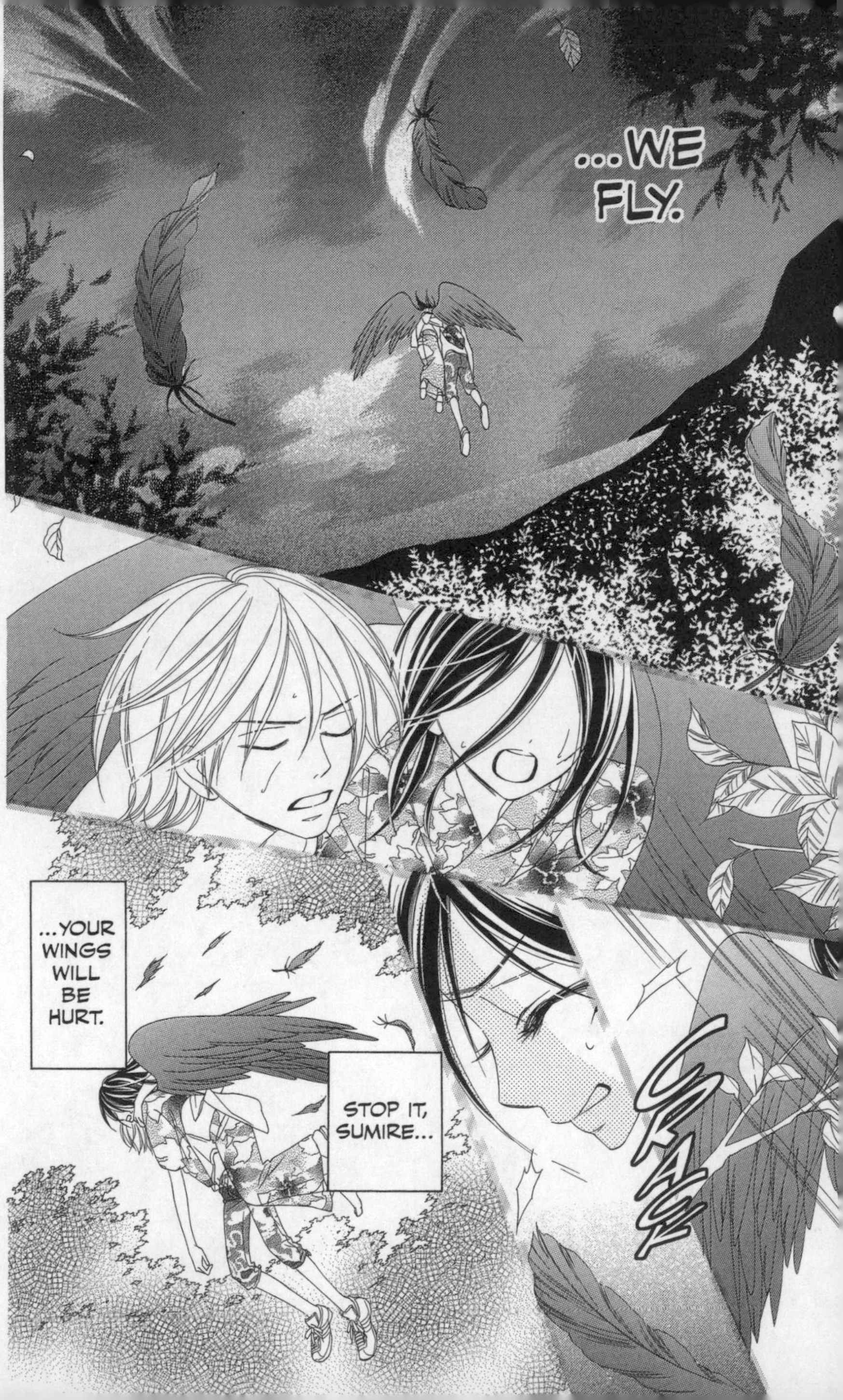
...WE FLY.
STOP IT, SUMIRE...
...YOUR WINGS WILL BE HURT.

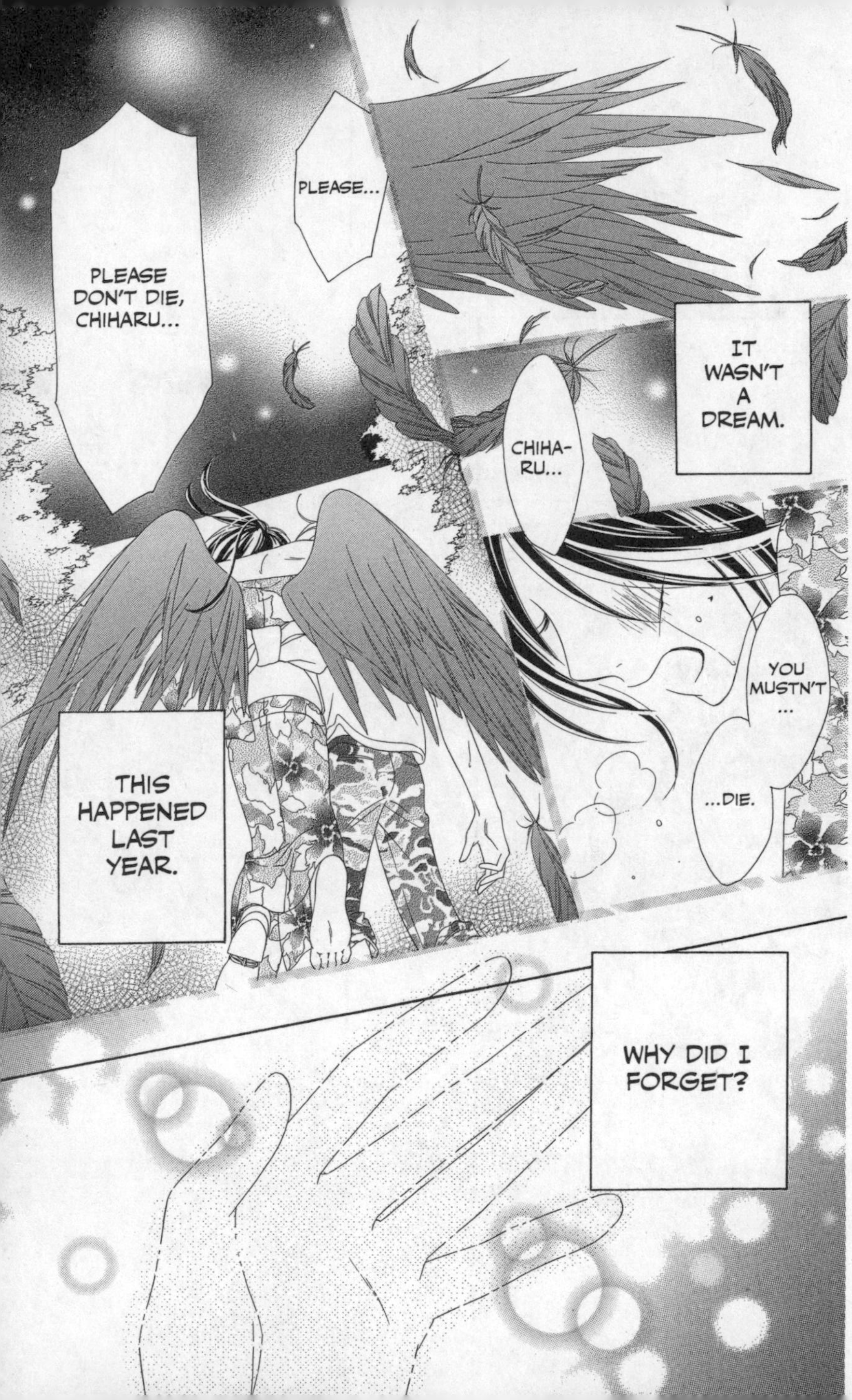
PLEASE...
PLEASE DON'T DIE, CHIHARU...
IT WASN'T A DREAM.
CHIHARU...
YOU MUSTN'T...
...DIE.
THIS HAPPENED LAST YEAR.
WHY DID I FORGET?

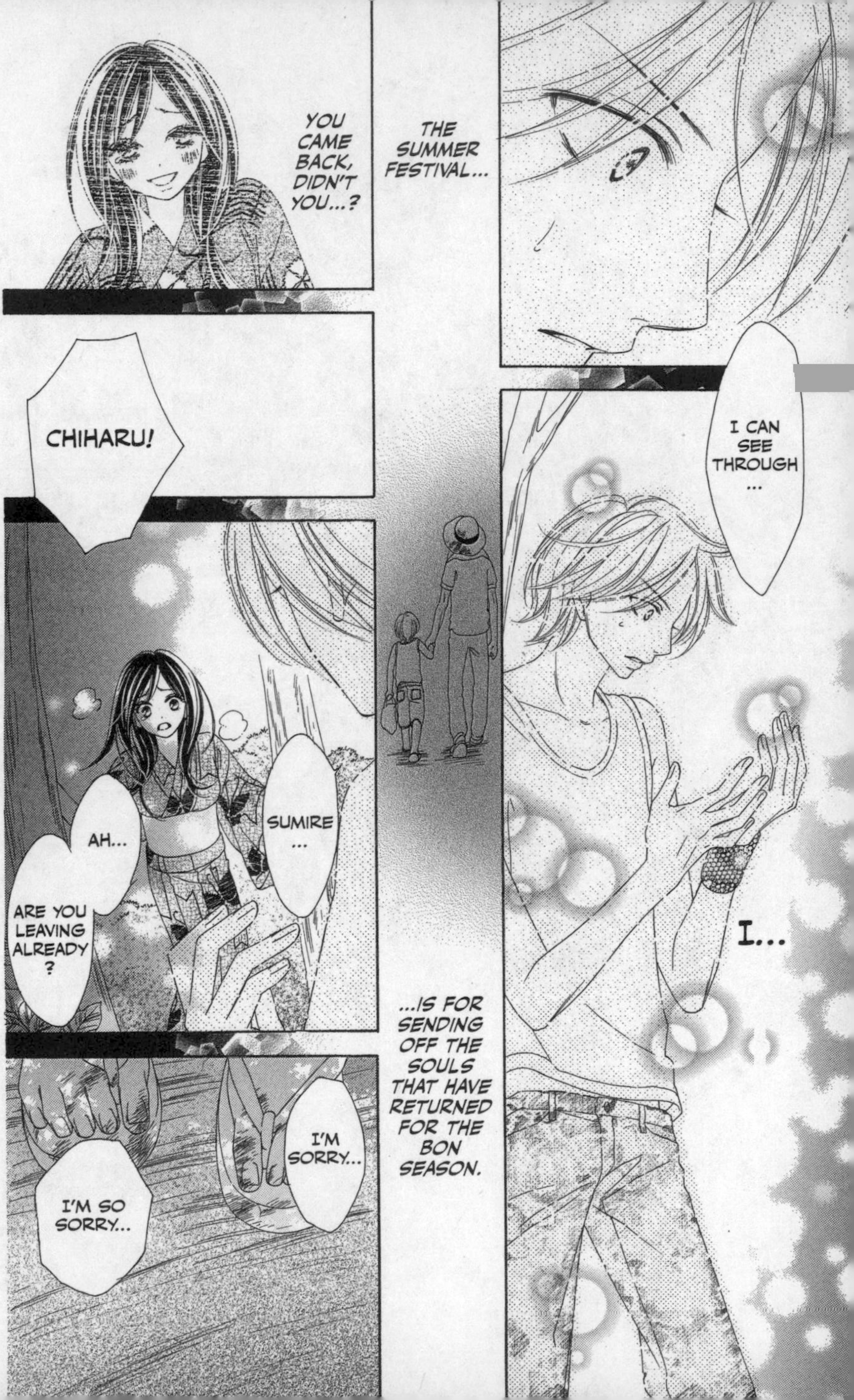
I CAN SEE THROUGH...
I...
THE SUMMER FESTIVAL...
...IS FOR SENDING OFF THE SOULS THAT HAVE RETURNED FOR THE BON SEASON.
YOU CAME BACK, DIDN'T YOU...?
CHIHARU!
SUMIRE...
AH...
ARE YOU LEAVING ALREADY?
I'M SORRY...
I'M SO SORRY...

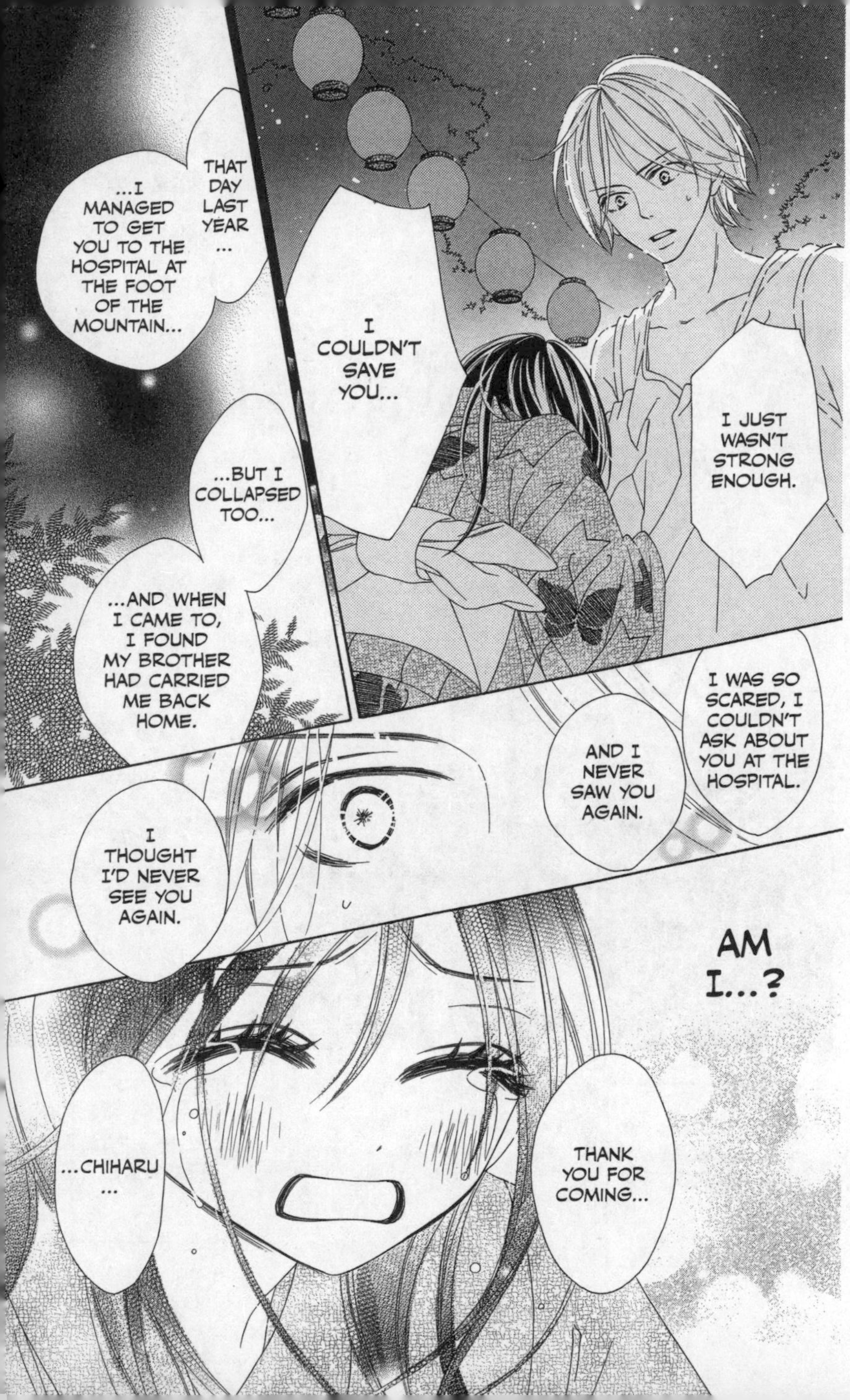
I COULDN'T SAVE YOU...
I JUST WASN'T STRONG ENOUGH.
THAT DAY LAST YEAR...
...I MANAGED TO GET YOU TO THE HOSPITAL AT THE FOOT OF THE MOUNTAIN...
...BUT I COLLAPSED TOO...
...AND WHEN I CAME TO, I FOUND MY BROTHER HAD CARRIED ME BACK HOME.
I WAS SO SCARED, I COULDN'T ASK ABOUT YOU AT THE HOSPITAL.
AND I NEVER SAW YOU AGAIN.
I THOUGHT I'D NEVER SEE YOU AGAIN.
AM I...?
THANK YOU FOR COMING...
...CHIHARU...

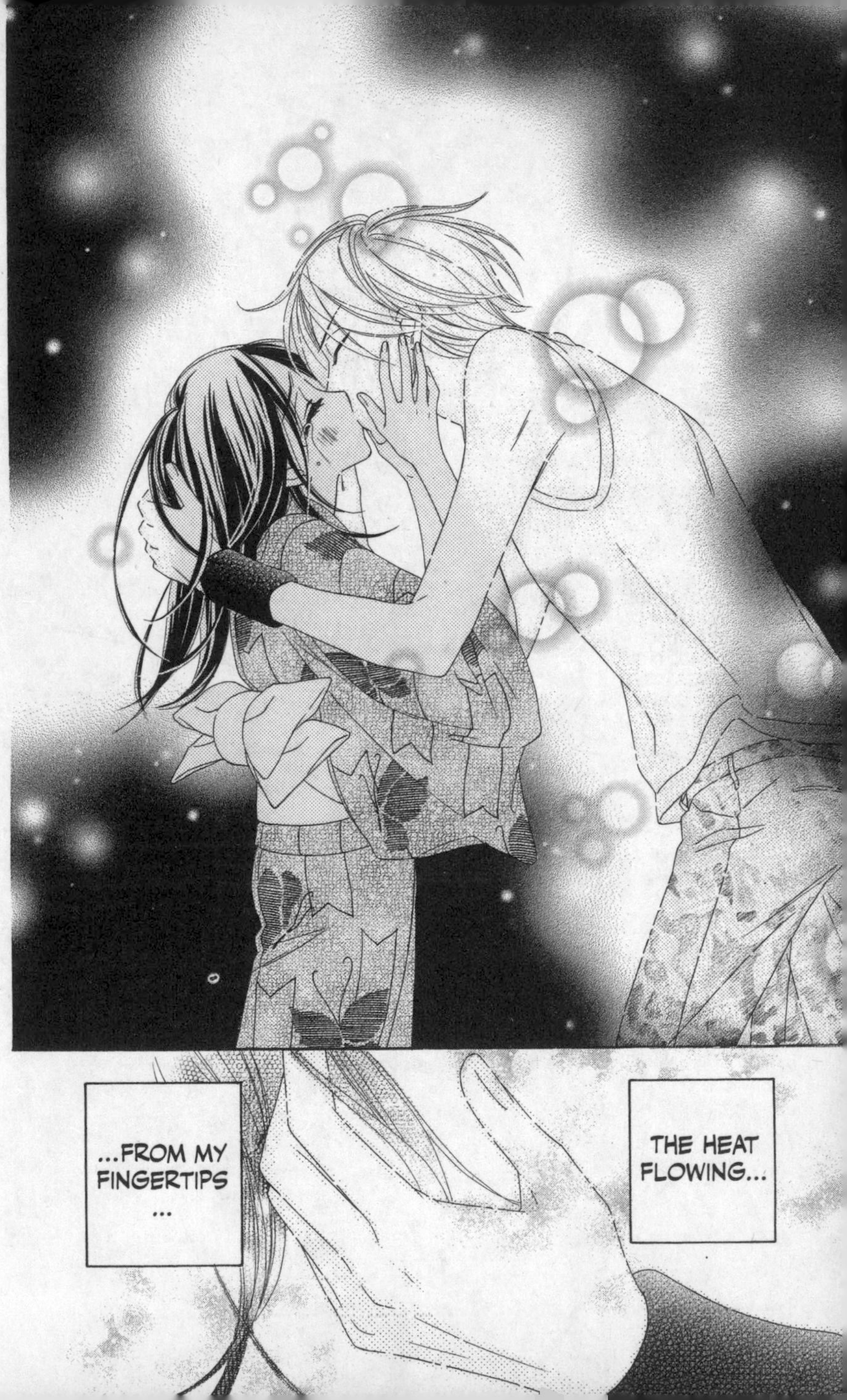
THE HEAT FLOWING...
...FROM MY FINGERTIPS ...

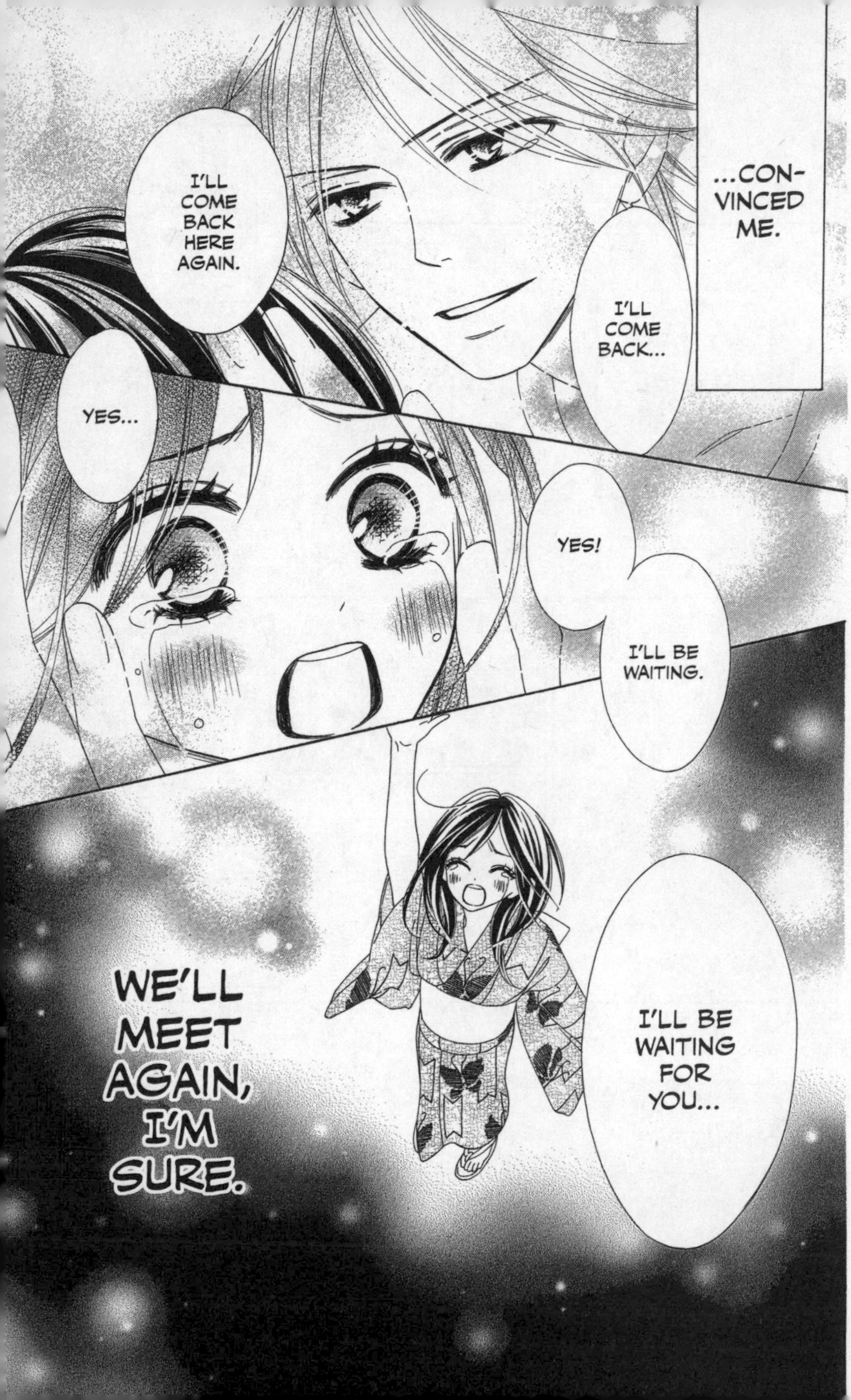
...CON-VINCED ME.
I'LL COME BACK...
I'LL COME BACK HERE AGAIN.
YES...
YES!
I'LL BE WAITING.
I'LL BE WAITING FOR YOU...
WE'LL MEET AGAIN, I'M SURE.

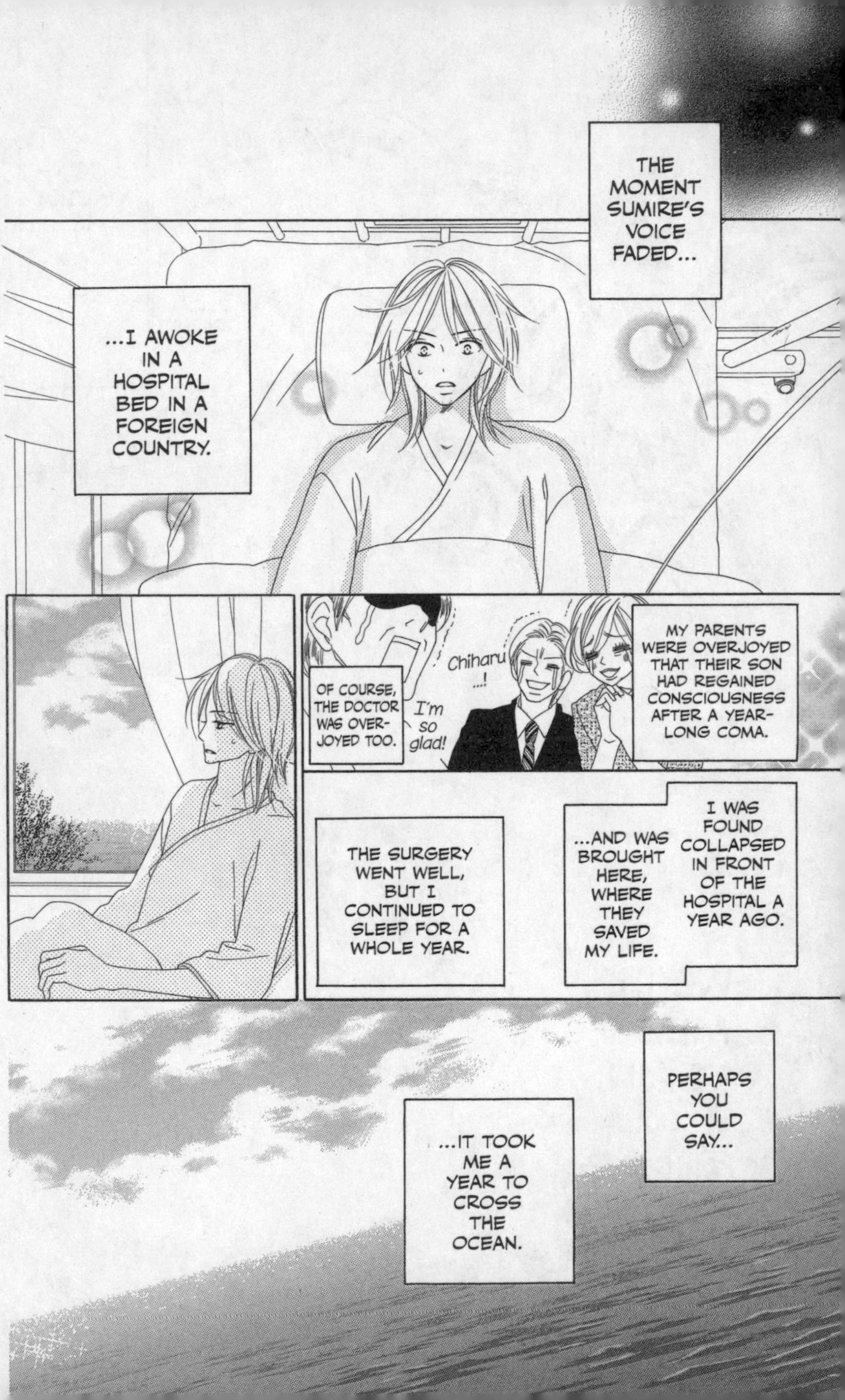
THE MOMENT SUMIRE'S VOICE FADED...
...I AWOKE IN A HOSPITAL BED IN A FOREIGN COUNTRY.
MY PARENTS WERE OVERJOYED THAT THEIR SON HAD REGAINED CONSCIOUSNESS AFTER A YEAR-LONG COMA.
Chiharu...!
I'm so glad!
OF COURSE, THE DOCTOR WAS OVER-JOYED TOO.
I WAS FOUND COLLAPSED IN FRONT OF THE HOSPITAL A YEAR AGO.
...AND WAS BROUGHT HERE, WHERE THEY SAVED MY LIFE.
THE SURGERY WENT WELL, BUT I CONTINUED TO SLEEP FOR A WHOLE YEAR.
PERHAPS YOU COULD SAY...
...IT TOOK ME A YEAR TO CROSS THE OCEAN.

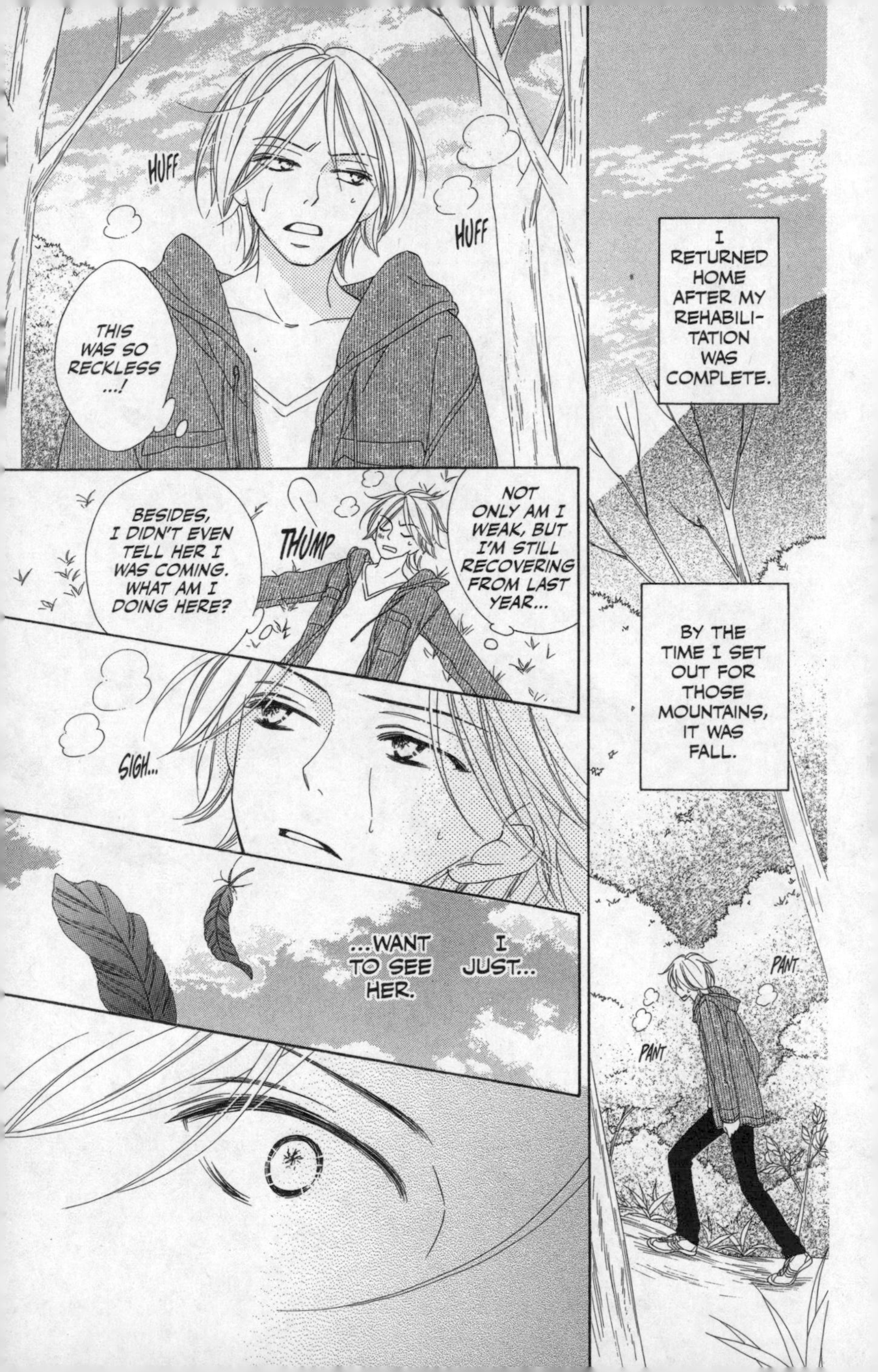
I RETURNED HOME AFTER MY REHABILITATION WAS COMPLETE.
BY THE TIME I SET OUT FOR THOSE MOUNTAINS, IT WAS FALL.
PANT
PANT
HUFF
HUFF
THIS WAS SO RECKLESS ...!
NOT ONLY AM I WEAK, BUT I'M STILL RECOVERING FROM LAST YEAR...
THUMP
BESIDES, I DIDN'T EVEN TELL HER I WAS COMING. WHAT AM I DOING HERE?
SIGH...
I JUST...
...WANT TO SEE HER.

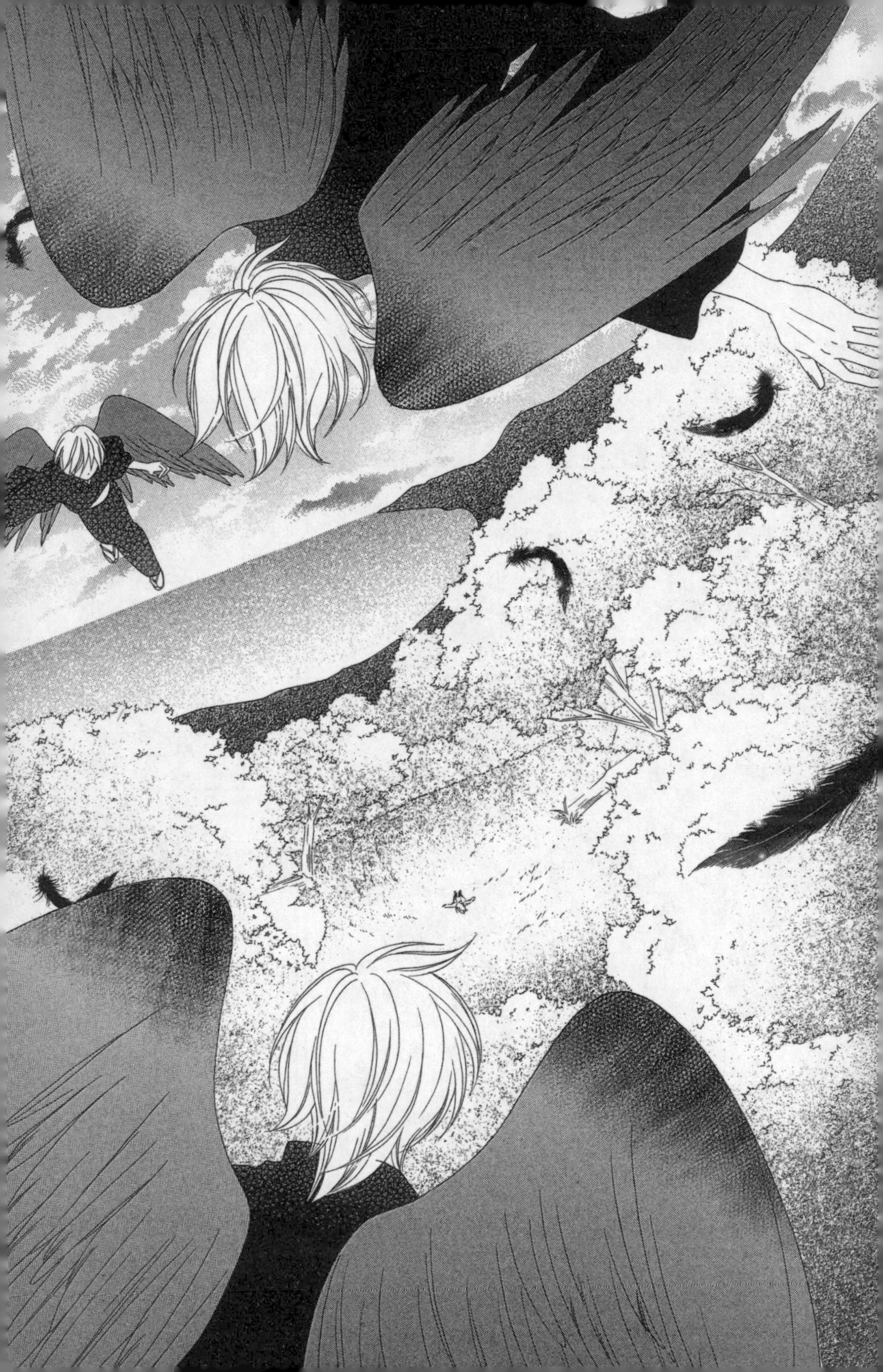

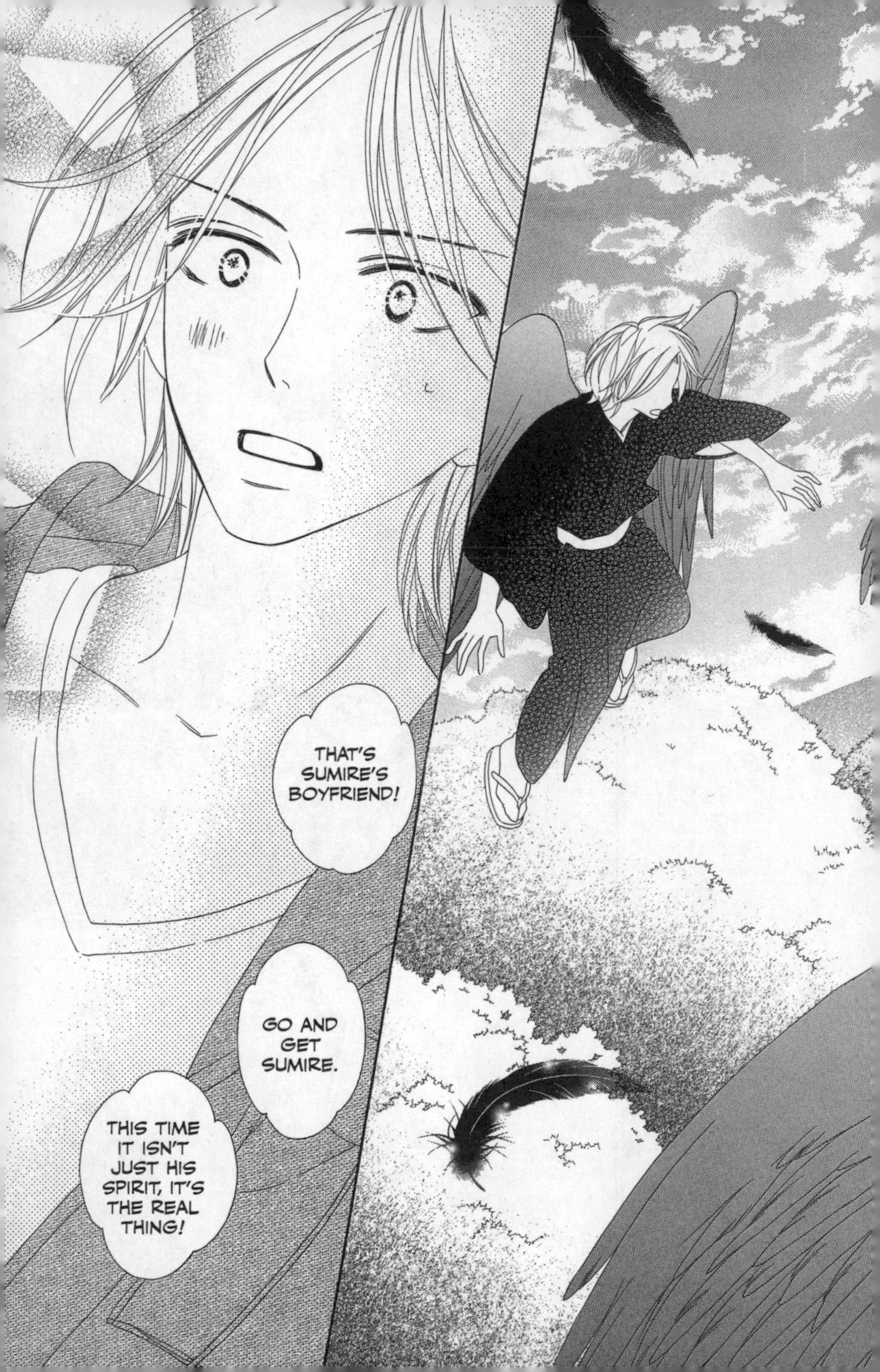
THAT'S SUMIRE'S BOYFRIEND!
GO AND GET SUMIRE.
THIS TIME IT ISN'T JUST HIS SPIRIT, IT'S THE REAL THING!

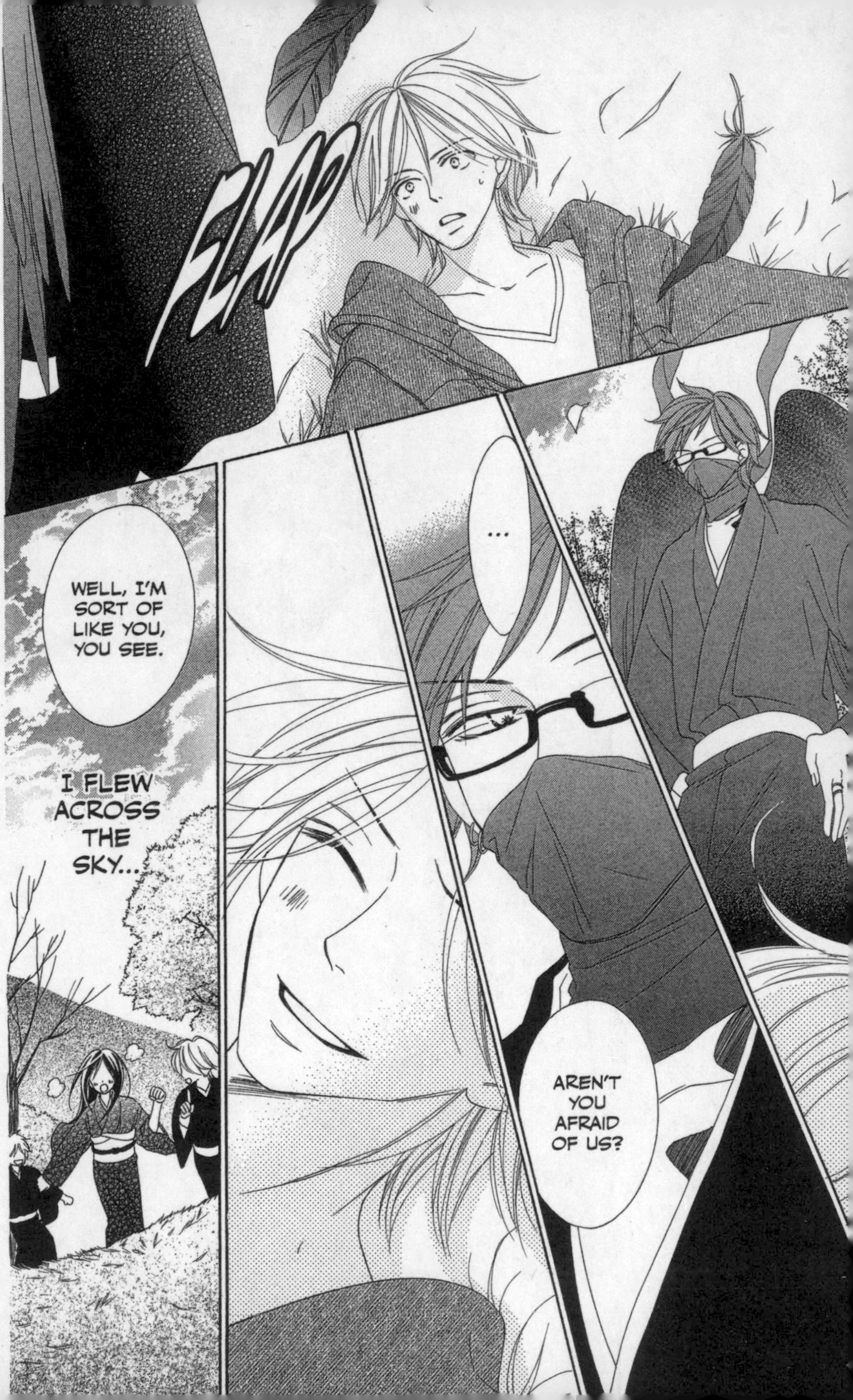
...
AREN'T YOU AFRAID OF US?
WELL, I'M SORT OF LIKE YOU, YOU SEE.
I FLEW ACROSS THE SKY...

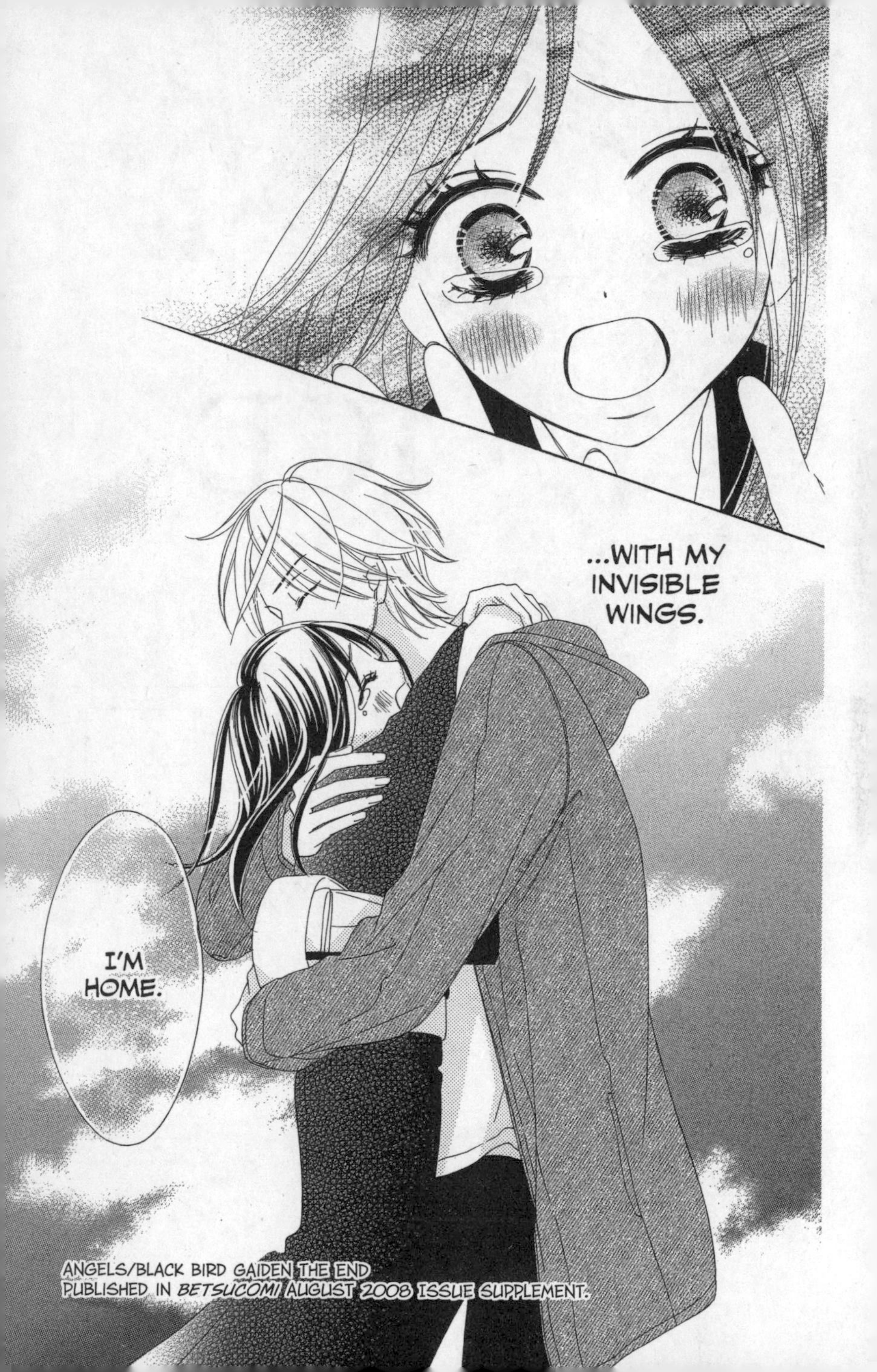
...WITH MY INVISIBLE WINGS.
I'M HOME.
ANGELS/BLACK BIRD GAIDEN THE END
PUBLISHED IN *BETSUCOMI* AUGUST 2008 ISSUE SUPPLEMENT.

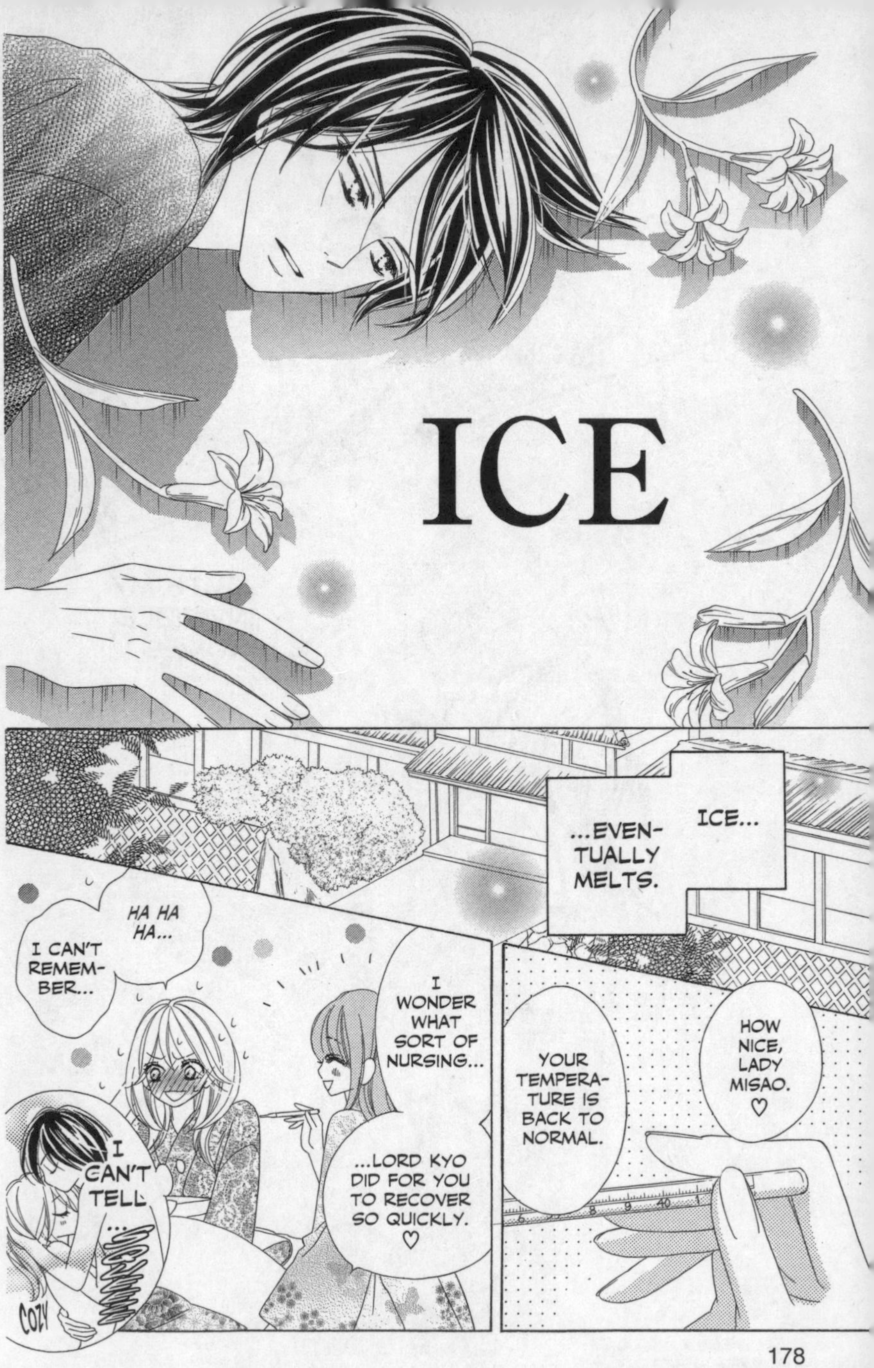
ICE
ICE...
...EVEN-TUALLY MELTS.
HOW NICE, LADY MISAO. ♡
YOUR TEMPERA-TURE IS BACK TO NORMAL.
I WONDER WHAT SORT OF NURSING...
...LORD KYO DID FOR YOU TO RECOVER SO QUICKLY. ♡
HA HA HA...
I CAN'T REMEM-BER...
I CAN'T TELL...
COZY

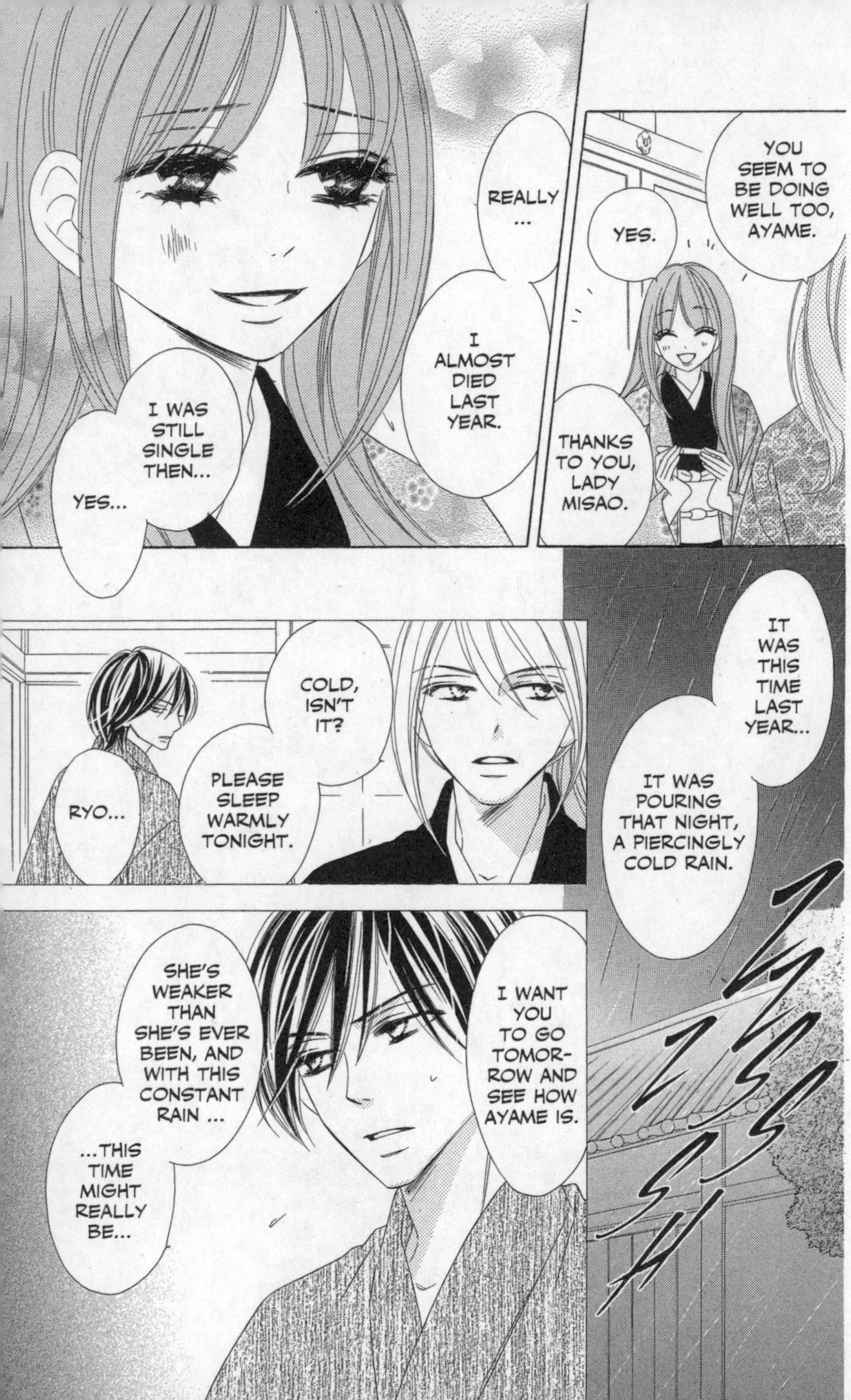
YOU SEEM TO BE DOING WELL TOO, AYAME.
YES.
THANKS TO YOU, LADY MISAO.
REALLY ...
I ALMOST DIED LAST YEAR.
I WAS STILL SINGLE THEN...
YES...
IT WAS THIS TIME LAST YEAR...
IT WAS POURING THAT NIGHT, A PIERCINGLY COLD RAIN.
COLD, ISN'T IT?
PLEASE SLEEP WARMLY TONIGHT.
RYO...
I WANT YOU TO GO TOMOR-ROW AND SEE HOW AYAME IS.
SHE'S WEAKER THAN SHE'S EVER BEEN, AND WITH THIS CONSTANT RAIN ...
...THIS TIME MIGHT REALLY BE...

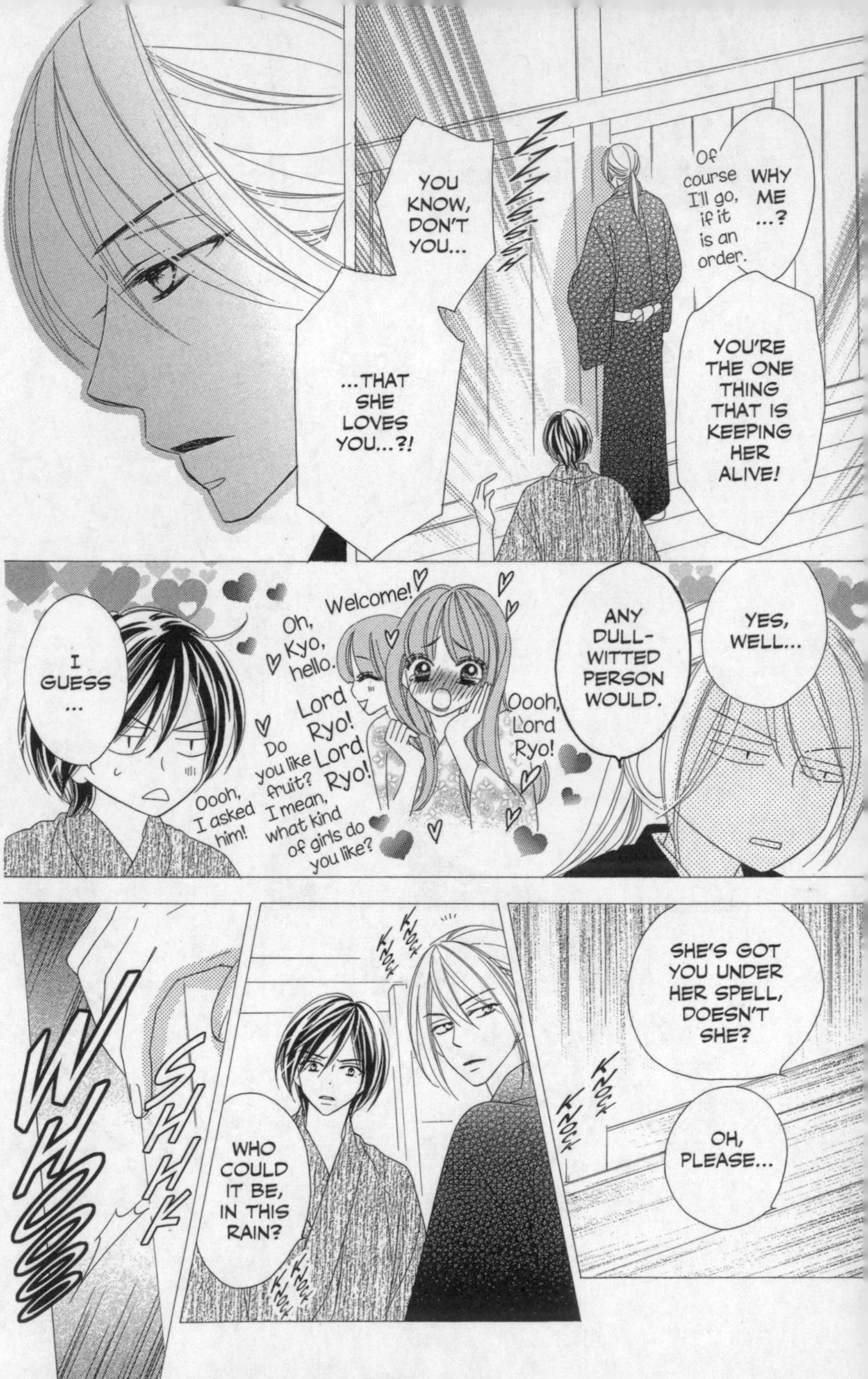
WHY ME ...?
Of course I'll go, if it is an order.
YOU'RE THE ONE THING THAT IS KEEPING HER ALIVE!
YOU KNOW, DON'T YOU...
...THAT SHE LOVES YOU...?!
YES, WELL...
ANY DULL-WITTED PERSON WOULD.
Oooh, Lord Ryo!
Welcome!
Oh, Kyo, hello.
Lord Ryo! Lord Ryo!
Do you like fruit? I mean, what kind of girls do you like?
Oooh, I asked him!
I GUESS ...
SHE'S GOT YOU UNDER HER SPELL, DOESN'T SHE?
KNOCK KNOCK
OH, PLEASE...
KNOCK KNOCK
WHO COULD IT BE, IN THIS RAIN?
KNOCK KNOCK

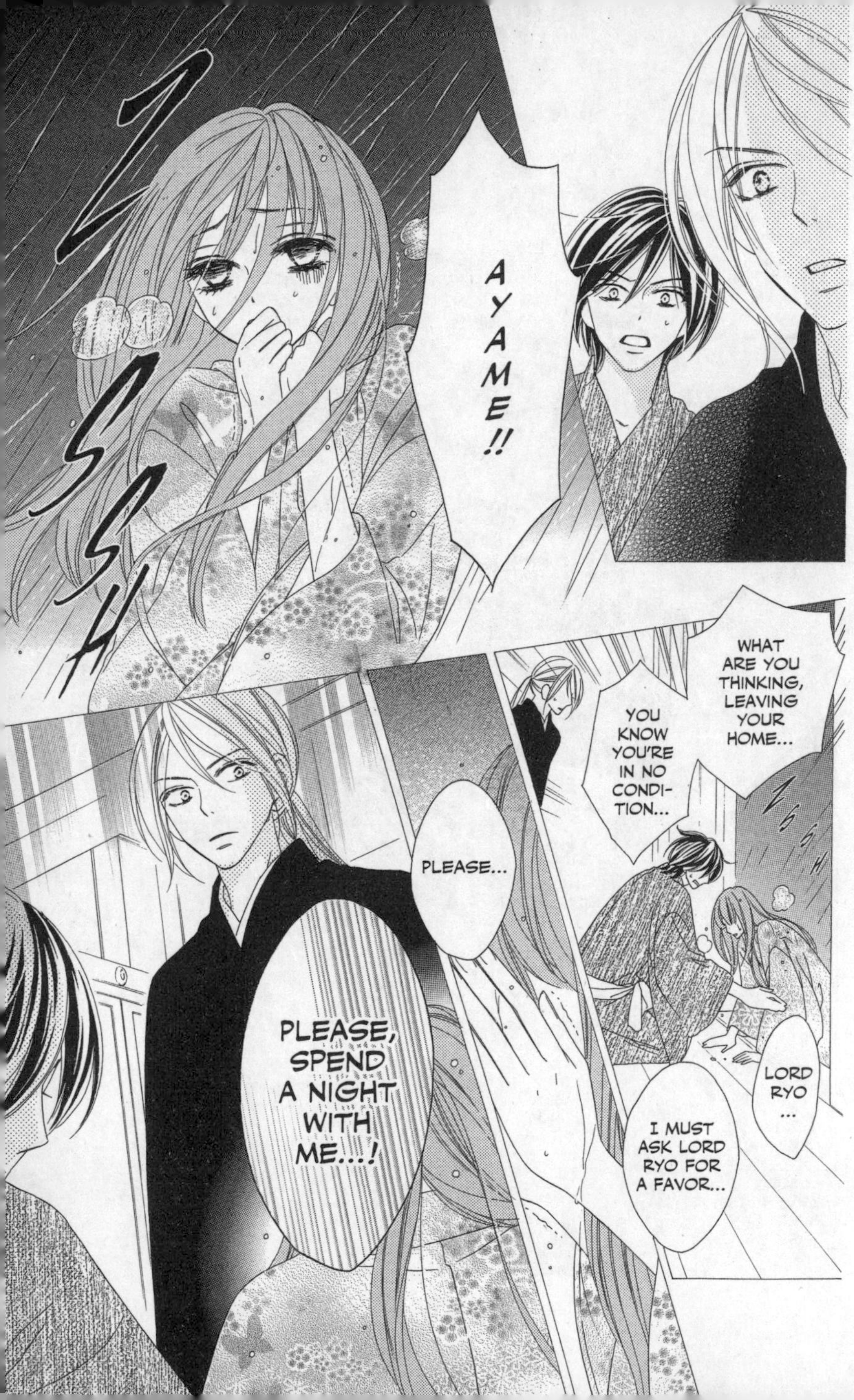
AYAME!!
WHAT ARE YOU THINKING, LEAVING YOUR HOME...
YOU KNOW YOU'RE IN NO CONDI-TION...
LORD RYO ...
I MUST ASK LORD RYO FOR A FAVOR...
PLEASE...
PLEASE, SPEND A NIGHT WITH ME...!

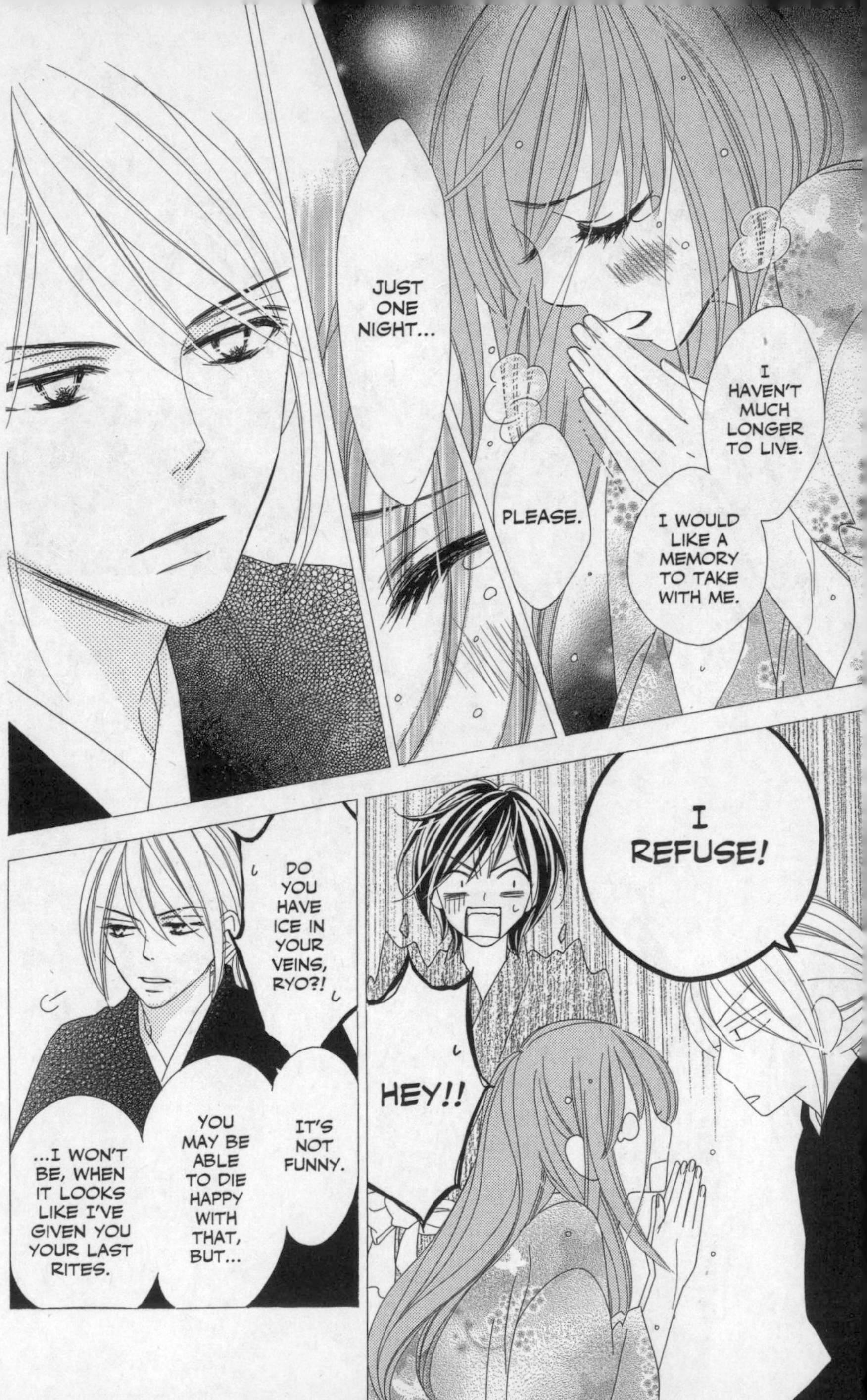
I HAVEN'T MUCH LONGER TO LIVE.
I WOULD LIKE A MEMORY TO TAKE WITH ME.
PLEASE.
JUST ONE NIGHT...
I REFUSE!
HEY!!
DO YOU HAVE ICE IN YOUR VEINS, RYO?!
IT'S NOT FUNNY.
YOU MAY BE ABLE TO DIE HAPPY WITH THAT, BUT...
...I WON'T BE, WHEN IT LOOKS LIKE I'VE GIVEN YOU YOUR LAST RITES.

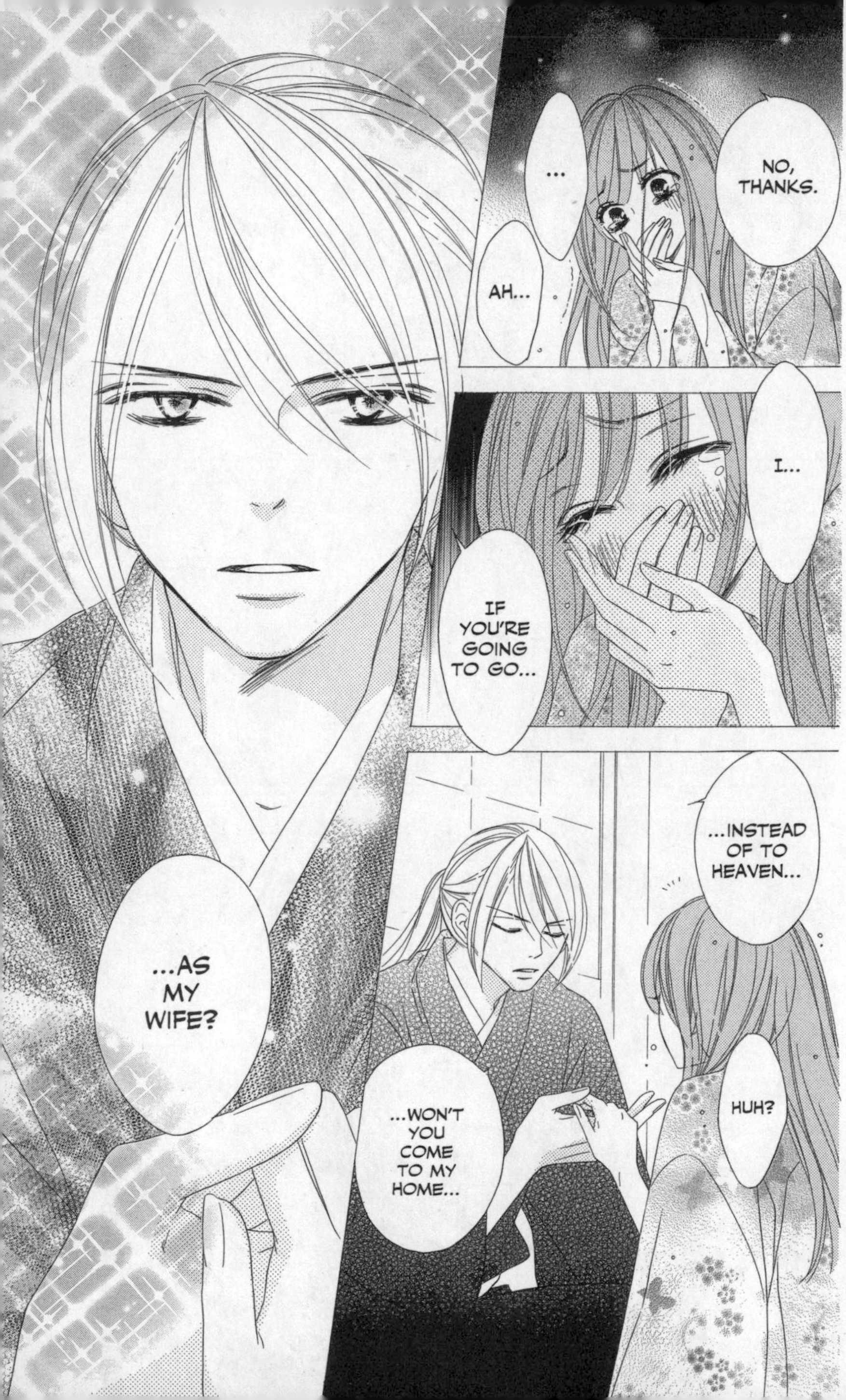
NO, THANKS.
...
AH...
I...
IF YOU'RE GOING TO GO...
...INSTEAD OF TO HEAVEN...
HUH?
...WON'T YOU COME TO MY HOME...
...AS MY WIFE?

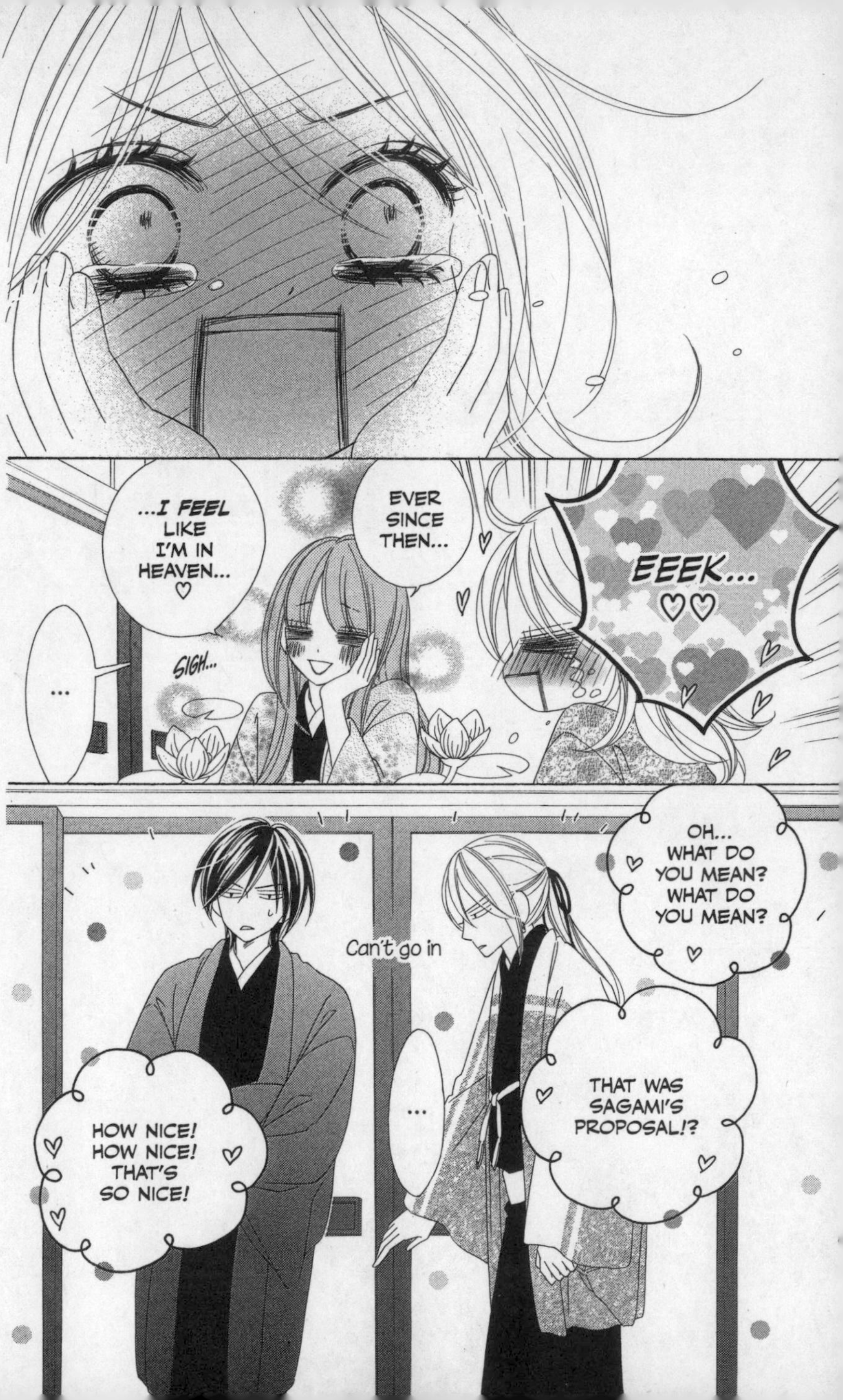
EEEK... ♡♡
EVER SINCE THEN...
...I FEEL LIKE I'M IN HEAVEN... ♡
SIGH...
...
OH... WHAT DO YOU MEAN? WHAT DO YOU MEAN?
THAT WAS SAGAMI'S PROPOSAL!?
Can't go in
...
HOW NICE! HOW NICE! THAT'S SO NICE!

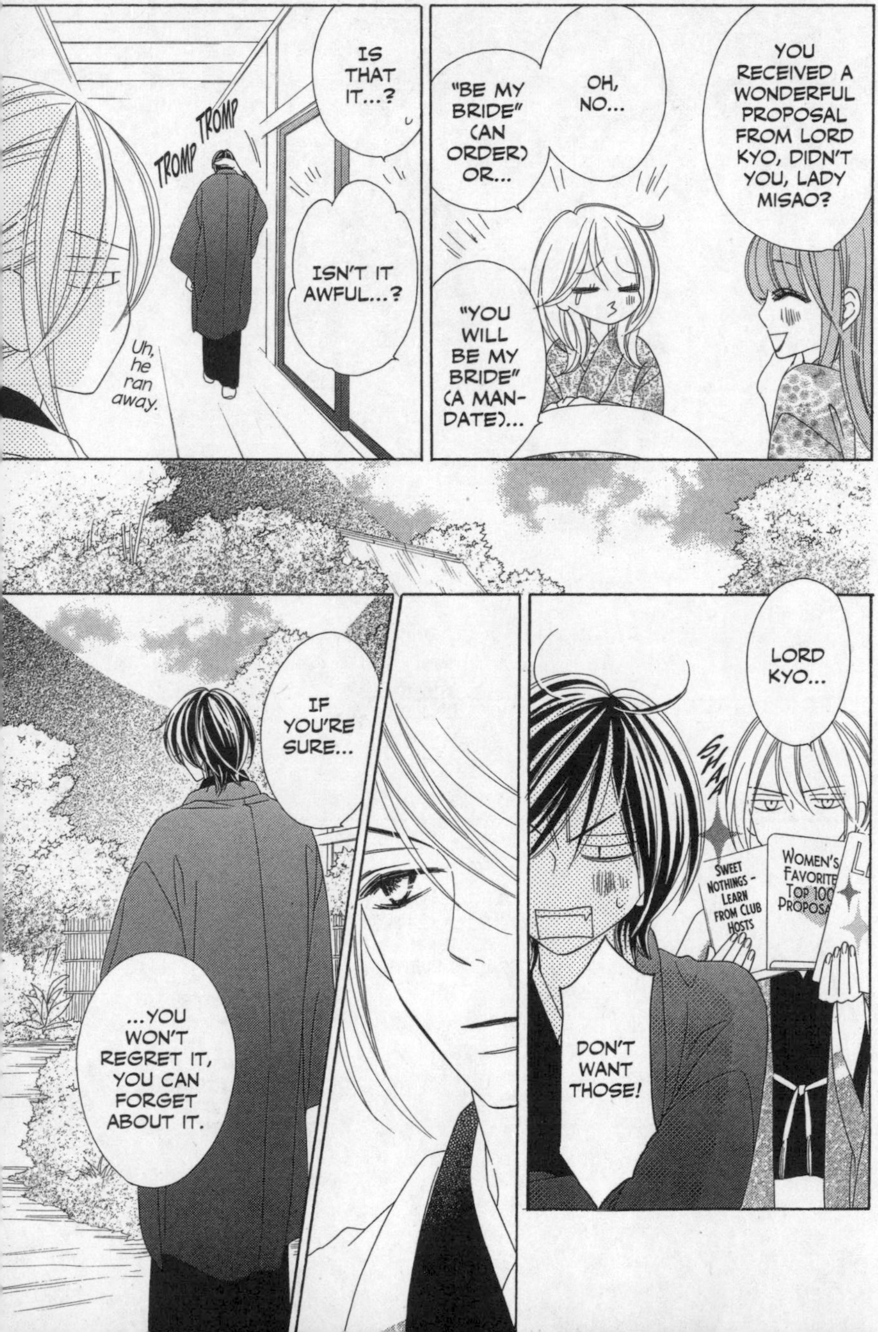

YOU RECEIVED A WONDERFUL PROPOSAL FROM LORD KYO, DIDN'T YOU, LADY MISAO?
OH, NO...
"BE MY BRIDE" (AN ORDER) OR...
"YOU WILL BE MY BRIDE" (A MAN-DATE)...
IS THAT IT...?
ISN'T IT AWFUL...?
TROMP TROMP
Uh, he ran away.
LORD KYO...
SWEET NOTHINGS - LEARN FROM CLUB HOSTS
WOMEN'S FAVORITE TOP 100 PROPOSA
DON'T WANT THOSE!
IF YOU'RE SURE...
...YOU WON'T REGRET IT, YOU CAN FORGET ABOUT IT.

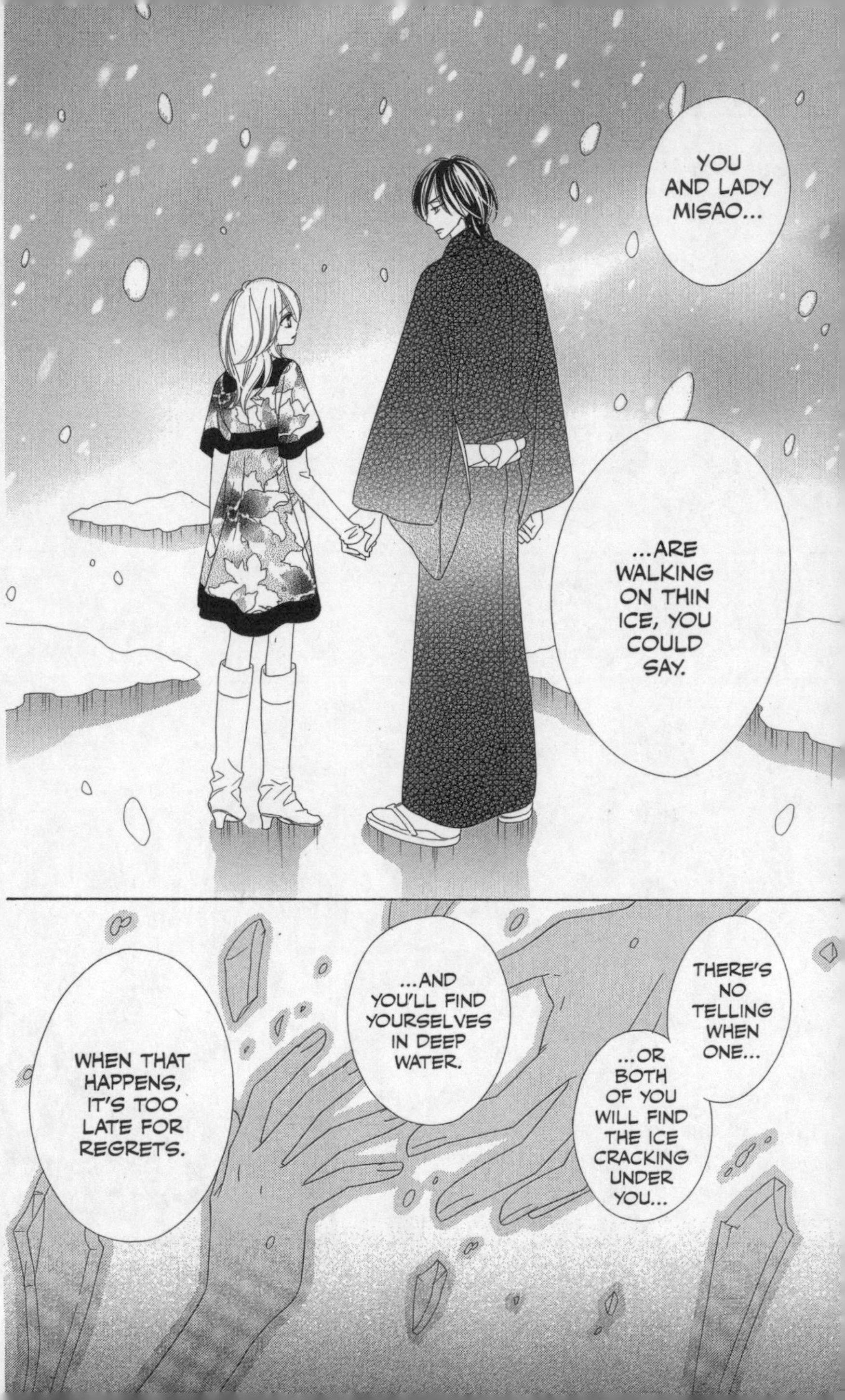
YOU AND LADY MISAO...
...ARE WALKING ON THIN ICE, YOU COULD SAY.
THERE'S NO TELLING WHEN ONE...
...OR BOTH OF YOU WILL FIND THE ICE CRACKING UNDER YOU...
...AND YOU'LL FIND YOURSELVES IN DEEP WATER.
WHEN THAT HAPPENS, IT'S TOO LATE FOR REGRETS.

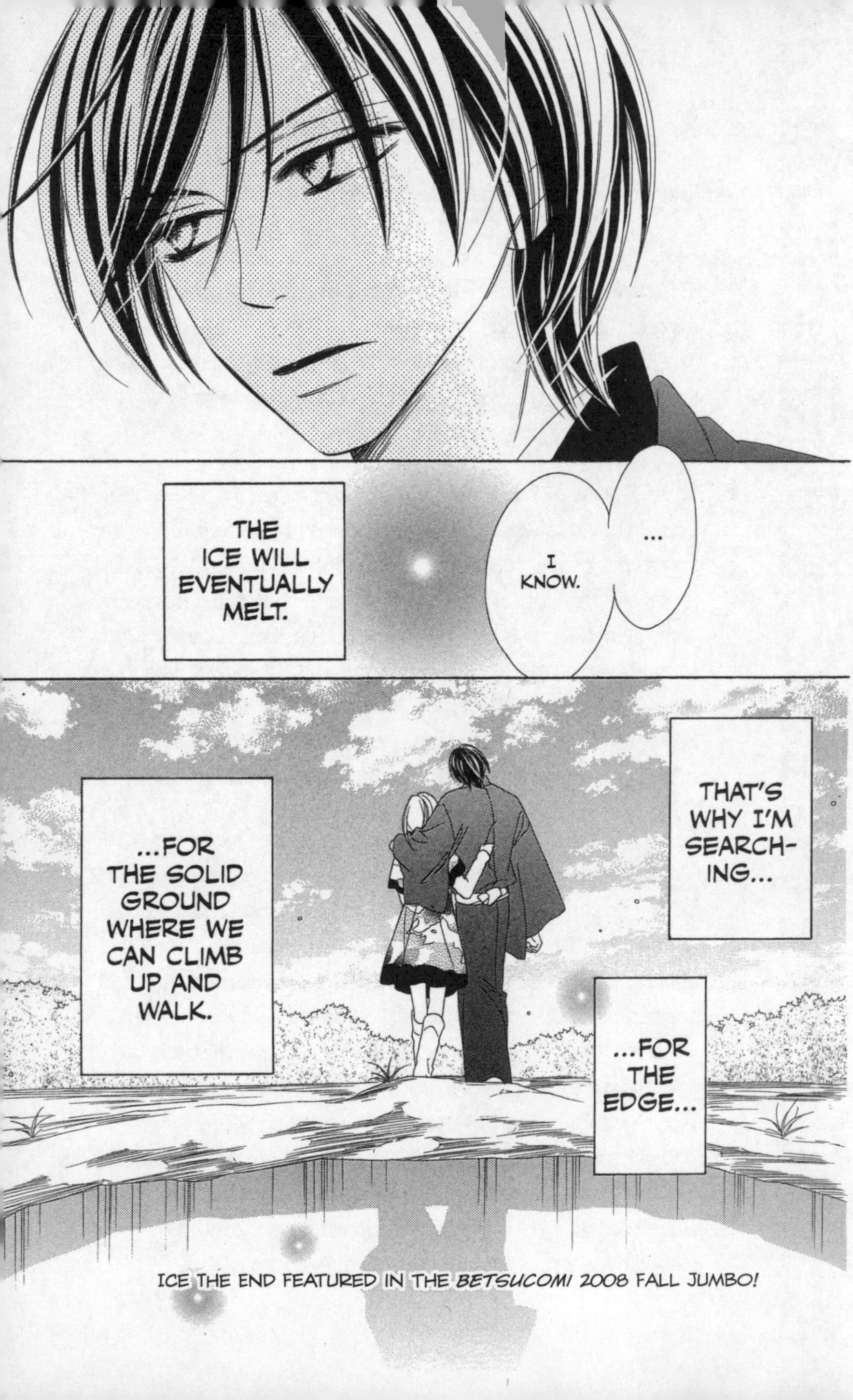
...
I KNOW.
THE ICE WILL EVENTUALLY MELT.
THAT'S WHY I'M SEARCHING...
...FOR THE EDGE...
...FOR THE SOLID GROUND WHERE WE CAN CLIMB UP AND WALK.
ICE THE END FEATURED IN THE *BETSUCOMI* 2008 FALL JUMBO!

Sorry for these wordy pages!

Thank you for reading my two strange special features!

Hello, this is Sakurakouji.
This series is on the seventh volume already. This is easily a miracle. The other day, there was another miraculous event. They made a drama CD of *Black Bird*!! I haven't seen the final product yet, but I was allowed to be there while they were recording. Here are some impressions:

When I draw a character, I don't have a certain person's voice in mind, so when I was approached to do this, I couldn't come up with any particular voice actors' names. I left it all up to the production staff, but I found that the actors who were signed for this job were a fabulous group, all very well-known, even to me. I was very nervous.♡ Takehito Koyasu, who plays Kyo, has been in the business since the days when I was in middle school and not even dreaming of becoming a manga artist yet. There is no telling what might happen in your life!

Every voice actor had a wonderful voice. They made me think, "Ah, so this is how that character sounds!" They even added to the charm of the characters, and they made me see the appeal that I had not realized was there in some of the characters.♡ 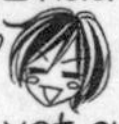 Kyo, as played by Mr. Koyasu, was cool and serious, and yet cute at times. I thought gentle and quiet Takahiro Sakurai, who played 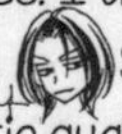 Sho, was perfect for the role. His voice has this sadistic quality to it... So sexy!! Akira Ishida, playing 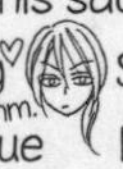
Hhm.
Sagami, sounded sexy even while delivering his brusque lines. Zenki's popularity surprised me, and I thought it was probably because he such a nice character who's kind to kids, but it wasn't so. Zenki, 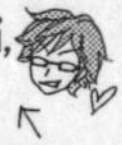 played by Hiroyuki Yoshino, was a really cool guy!

Continued

Continued

I never felt any love coming from the character named Buzen (a shocking thing to say), but I changed my mind when I heard Katsuyuki Konishi's voice. He did a wonderful job of turning Buzen into the handsome playboy I had established to begin with. Anyone would be hooked by a voice like this...!!

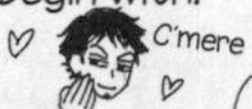
C'mere

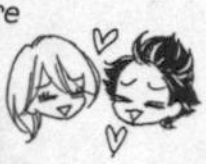

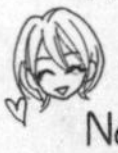

Misao, voiced by Mikako Takahashi, and Taro, voiced by Kan Nakanishi were cute—no question about it, and Hoki, voiced by Kouki Miyata, was definitely a pretty boy! And Shuhei, voiced by Kisho Taniyama, was so cool with a healthy helping of naughty in him. Kyo as a child also had a pretty-boy voice!

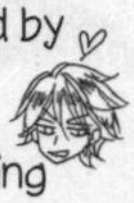

I am very grateful for this wonderful opportunity to find out just how recording is done. I would like to sincerely thank all those involved in the production, as well as everyone who has supported this series, and to those who are reading this right now. Thanks to all of you, this series, which was originally supposed to end after three chapters, has been made into a drama CD. Thank you very much! I hope you will give me your continued support! ♡

Studio Sketch

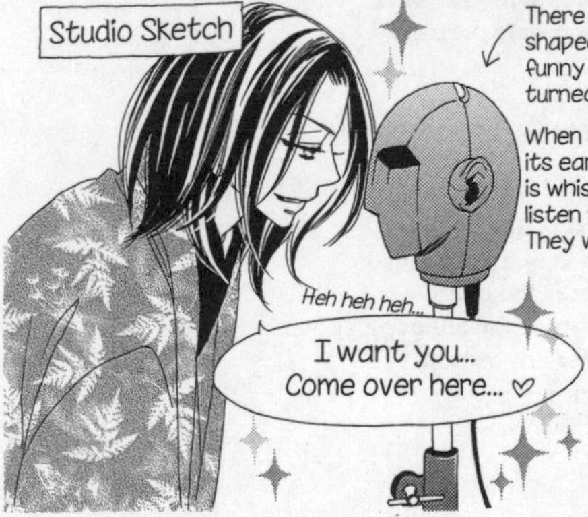
Heh heh heh...
I want you... Come over here... ♡

There were these things that were shaped like heads. I said it would be funny if they were mikes...and it turned out they really were mikes.

When a voice is recorded through its ear, it really sounds like someone is whispering in your ear when you listen to it through headphones. They were 3-D voice recording mikes!

Sojo's pick-up line.

The *Black Bird* drama CD has been released by Columbia Music Entertainment, and is on sale at stores all across Japan!

This is the end of Volume 7.... In the last volume, I said I would do my best to draw more fresh stuff, but I'm sorry there isn't much this time. I hope to see you again in the next volume...♡

An auspicious day, December 2008 Kanoko Sakurakouji

GLOSSARY

PAGE 51, PANEL 6: Onikiri, Dojigiri
Onikiri here means "ogre slayer," and *Dojigiri* means "monster slayer." They are both fairly typical names for swords.

PAGE 59, AUTHOR NOTE: *Yasha ga Ike*
The title means "Demon Pond."

PAGE 72, PANEL 2: Tsundere
The Japanese archetype of someone who is conceited, irritable, and/or violent, but can suddenly become modest and loving. This is commonly portrayed as a female trait.

PAGE 72, PANEL 6: Green gentian tea
A very bitter tea.

PAGE 150, PANEL 2: Bon season
Also called Obon, it is the Japanese celebration to honor the dead. It is celebrated in the summer, although the exact day differs by region.

Kanoko Sakurakouji was born in downtown Tokyo, and her hobbies include reading, watching plays, traveling and shopping. Her debut title, *Raibu ga Hanetara*, ran in *Bessatsu Shojo Comic* (currently called *Bestucomi*) in 2000, and her 2004 *Bestucomi* title *Backstage Prince* was serialized in VIZ Media's *Shojo Beat* magazine. She won the 54th Shogakukan **Manga Award** for *Black Bird*.

BLACK BIRD
VOL. 7
Shojo Beat Edition

Story and Art by KANOKO SAKURAKOUJI

© 2007 Kanoko SAKURAKOUJI/Shogakukan
All rights reserved.
Original Japanese edition published by SHOGAKUKAN.
English translation rights in the United States of America,
Canada, the United Kingdom, Ireland, Australia and New Zealand
arranged with SHOGAKUKAN.

TRANSLATION JN Productions
TOUCH-UP ART & LETTERING Gia Cam Luc
DESIGN Amy Martin
EDITOR Pancha Diaz

The stories, characters and incidents mentioned
in this publication are entirely fictional.

No portion of this book may be reproduced or transmitted in any form
or by any means without written permission from the copyright holders.

Printed in the U.S.A.

Published by VIZ Media, LLC
P.O. Box 77010
San Francisco, CA 94107

10 9 8 7 6 5
First printing, February 2011
Fifth printing, May 2021

www.shojobeat.com   www.viz.com

PARENTAL ADVISORY
BLACK BIRD is rated T+ for Older Teen and is
recommended for ages 16 and up. This volume
contains violence and adult situations.
ratings.viz.com